Preface

Within the last two years a number of new 16-bit microprocessors either have been announced or actually introduced by semiconductor manufacturers. Unfortunately, these microprocessors are not as easy to program or to design into microcomputer systems as their 8-bit predecessors. Because of their complexity a lot of complicated documentation must be waded through in order for the end user or design engineer to choose one of the many available microprocessors. Therefore, in this book the authors have attempted to reduce this documentation into something manageable and, at the same time, to provide a format in which the reader can easily compare the processors.

There are a number of 16-bit microprocessors that are available; some are better known than others. We have chosen to discuss the processors that we feel are, or will be, the most popular; the 8086 (Intel and Siemens), the Z8001 and Z8002 (Advanced Micro Devices and Zilog), the 9900 (Texas Instruments and AMI), the LSI-11 (DEC), the 68000 (Motorola and Rockwell International) and the 16000 (National Semiconductor).

Since one of our goals in writing this book was to compare the processors, a few simple benchmarks were included for each processor. The benchmark specifications are given in the appendix, and the actual program listings are included in Chapters 2–7. The reader should note here that the benchmarks may not be particularly valid for his or her specific application, nor is there a guarantee that every last byte or machine cycle has been tweaked out of them. The benchmarks were purposely left a little general, so that each author could show off his processor's instruction set. The same benchmark may therefore be performed in a slightly different manner from processor to processor.

Rather than try to learn all about each processor and then write about it, we chose different individuals to write about the different processor. The authors were chosen because they were working with the processor or have worked with related processors.

With so many microcomputer books available today we do not review a lot of basics. It is assumed that the reader has had some experience with microcomputers (the more the better) and already knows some of the vocabulary in the microcomputer field: RAM, ROM, EPROM, interrupt, register, address bus, data bus, etc. In the first chapter we do discuss some of these terms, but only to make sure that the authors and readers are "up to the same speed."

One point that we would like to impress upon the reader is the fact that the 16-bit microcomputers available today are complex and powerful devices. Consequently they may not be for everyone. Just because a device is "state of the art" doesn't mean that it has to be used in a product or educational course. There are many applications that can be readily solved through the careful and knowledgeable application of one of the 4-bit or 8-bit microprocessors. On the other hand, if you are one of those folks who likes "lots of horsepower," the 16-bit microprocessors are the processors for you.

Sixteen-bit processors, because they can address megabytes of memory, are very fast, have large instruction sets, and lean more towards data processing and data base management applications rather than video games, washing machine controllers, traffic light controllers, or low-cost data acquisition systems.

By writing a survey-type book, we hope to expose you to enough of the concepts and terms that you will be able to understand the very concise technical manuals that the semiconductor manufacturers often provide with their chips and systems. Without a good background in 8-bit microprocessors or microcomputers, however, one will have difficulty designing and/or programming these devices.

Because this book does involve "state of the art" devices, there are a number of people to thank for providing manuals, computers, and technical assistance, including Steve Lapham at Intel, John Springer and K. Gopinath at Advanced Micro Devices, Perry Cox and Gary Martin at National Semiconductor, and Dennis Pfleger at Motorola. We would also like to thank "a cast of thousands" at Texas Instruments for helping so much with this project. Thanks are also due the marketing and literature groups of all the manufacturers for their permission to reproduce many of their diagrams.

"The Blacksburg Group"
DAVID G. LARSEN
JONATHAN A. TITUS
CHRISTOPHER A. TITUS

16-Bit

Microprocessors

**With Contributions By
Christopher A. Titus, Johnathan A. Titus,
Alan Baldwin, W. N. Hubin, and Leo Scanlon**

Howard W. Sams & Co., Inc.
4300 WEST 62ND ST. INDIANAPOLIS, INDIANA 46268 USA

International Standard Book Number: 0-672-21805-4
Library of Congress Catalog Card Number: 81-50564

Printed in the United States of America.

Contents

CHAPTER 1

CHAPTER 2

CHAPTER 3

1

Basic Microprocessor Concepts

The six microprocessors that will be discussed in this book are extremely powerful devices that rival many of the current minicomputers in terms of the amount of memory that can be addressed, the number of instructions in the instruction set, and the number of instructions (calculations) that can be executed (performed) every second. With the exception of the LSI-11, the 8086, Z8001/2, 9900, 68000, and 16000 are relatively large integrated circuits, about ½ inch (1.3 cm) on a side and from 2 to 3 inches (5 to 7.6 cm) in length. On the other hand, the LSI-11 consists of three or four integrated circuits that are each ½ inch by 2 inches (1.3 by 5 cm). Even so, these devices contain tens of thousands of transistors, or the equivalent of over 10,000 gates. Thus they replace many hundreds of small-scale integration (SSI) and medium-scale integration (MSI) transistor-transistor-logic (TTL) parts. The microprocessor CPU chips probably require no more than 1 to 2 watts of power, whereas the equivalent TTL circuitry would require 50 watts or more.

Unfortunately, we need more than a microprocessor CPU chip(s) in order to have a microcomputer. Quite often, the CPU chip has to be used with a clock chip, buffers, latches, memories, and peripheral devices. With all of these additional integrated circuits, the user has a *microcomputer* (Fig. 1-1). The resulting microcomputer is often smaller, faster, consumes less power, and is easier to maintain than the more classical minicomputers. On the other hand, because many of these CPU chips are relatively new, they do not have much software support, no user's groups exist, and there aren't many people who are using them, compared to the 8-bit microprocessors.

Fig. 1-1. A typical, low-cost 16-bit microcomputer.

EXECUTING PROGRAMS

In order for the microprocessor to execute a program, it must receive instructions from somewhere. Instructions, along with data values, are most often stored in memory, so the microprocessor must be able to access memory in order to execute a program. Typically, the microcomputer may have thousands and thousands of memory locations that are used to store programs, along with data. In order to transfer information between itself and memory, the microprocessor communicates with only one memory location at a time. To specify which of many memory locations it is communicating with, the microprocessor generates a *memory address*. A memory address is represented by a binary number, where a logic one is a voltage greater than 2.4 V and a logic zero is a voltage less than 0.8 V.

The amount of memory that the microprocessor can address is specified by the semiconductor manufacturer, and, in doing so, *the number of binary bits that are used in a memory address are also specified*. The microprocessors that will be discussed in this book have between 16 and 24 address bits. Each address bit is assigned a significance, just as digits in a decimal number are assigned a significance. This means that A0 can have a significance of 0 or 1, since it is the least significant address bit; A1 can have a significance of 0 or 2; A2 a significance of 0 or 4; and so on.

Once the microprocessor has generated a memory address, the

electronic memory devices have to receive it, so the address pins of the microprocessor chip are wired to all the memory chips, or these pins are wired to buffers and the buffers are wired to all the memory chips. Quite often, when all the address pins or signals are being discussed as a group, they are called the *address bus*. Therefore, memory devices are wired to the microprocessor's address bus (Fig. 1-2).

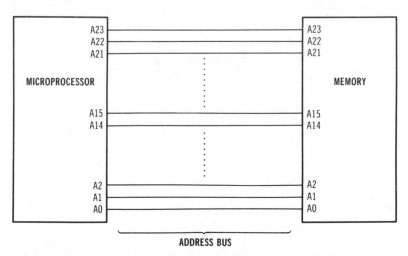

Fig. 1-2. Using address signals (the address bus) to connect memories to the microprocessor chip.

Now that the microprocessor can address, or select, one memory location among many memory locations, a means of transferring information between the microprocessor and a memory location has to be created. Since the microprocessors in this book are generally considered to be 16-bit microprocessors, there is a 16-bit data bus, which consists of 16 data signals. The data bus is wired to all memory chips, and most, if not all, peripheral devices (crt, teletypewriter, floppy disk, and the like).

Note that in Fig. 1-3 the data signals in the data bus have also been assigned a significance, just as the address bits in the address bus have been. The least significant data line or signal is D0, and it has a significance of 0 or 1. The most significant data bit is D15, and it has a significance of 0 or 32,768. Based on this information, the smallest 16-bit number is zero (0000000000000000) and the largest 16-bit number is 65,535 (1111111111111111), i.e., 32,768 + 16,384 + 8192 + · · · + 8 + 4 + 2 + 1.

Finally, since the microprocessor can both read information from memory and write information to memory, there has to be some

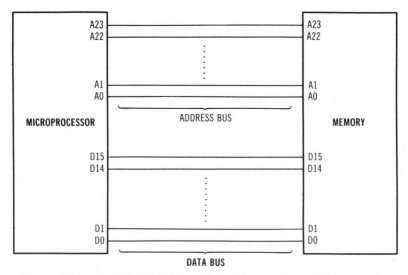

Fig. 1-3. Wiring the data bus between the microprocessor and the memories.

method that the microprocessor uses to signal memory to send information to the CPU chip or to receive information from the CPU chip. Since information can flow in both directions, but in only one direction at a time, the microprocessor has to determine when information will flow on the data bus, and in which direction. In essence, the microprocessor is the "traffic cop" for the data bus. Regardless of the

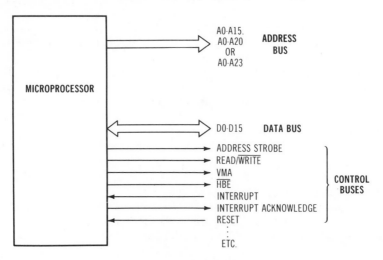

Fig. 1-4. Address, data, and control buses for a typical microcomputer system.

microprocessor being discussed, one or more signals are generated by the CPU chip that tell memory whether a *memory read, memory write,* or neither operation is taking place. The address bus, data bus, and control signals can be seen in Fig. 1-4.

REAL-WORLD MICROPROCESSORS

The microprocessor that we have been describing could be considered the "ideal" chip, because none of the microprocessors that we will be discussing is this simple. Many of the microprocessors (8086, Z8001/2, LSI-11, and 16000) have a *multiplexed address/data bus.* This means that the microprocessor uses 16 pins for both the data bus and part or all of the address bus. So that memories and peripherals know whether an address is on this bus, or that data is on this bus, the microprocessor generates a signal that indicates to all external devices that an *address* is present on this bus. Depending on the microprocessor, the bus may contain data at all other times, or a second signal may be generated that indicates that data is on the bus. In the latter case there may be times when there is neither an address *or* data on the bus.

The reason that part or all of the address bus is multiplexed with the data bus is to make the integrated circuit smaller; that is, 17 pins do the work of 32 pins. Multiplexing requires 17 pins, rather than 16 pins, with the seventeenth pin being used to indicate when an address is on the bus. The 68000 and 9900 microprocessors do not have a multiplexed address/data bus, so they have to be packaged in 64-pin packages. These 64-pin packages are large (3.2 inches, or 8.1 cm, long) and expensive. A standard 40-pin 8086 CPU chip is shown next to a 64-pin 9900 CPU chip in Fig. 1-5. If a microprocessor has

Fig. 1-5. Comparison of the sizes of the 8086 and 9900 CPU chips.

multiplexed address/data pins, the pins of the integrated circuit are usually labeled AD0 through AD15 (address/data zero through address/data fifteen).

The memory control signals that the microprocessors generate are also more complex than one might first imagine. The 8086 and Z8001/2 generate four memory control signals and the 68000, 9900, and 16000 generate three memory control signals. These devices also generate a considerable number of other control signals to control peripheral devices, other microprocessors using the same data, address and control buses, and *very* high speed peripherals.

INTERNAL MICROPROCESSOR ORGANIZATION

Before we can learn about the instructions that a microprocessor can execute, we have to find out what internal registers are available for our use, and the different ways in which the microprocessors can address memory. The registers contained within the CPU chip are usually used to store data, addresses, or instructions. In all of these microprocessors *some of the internal registers are dedicated* to a particular task, which is determined by the semiconductor manufacturer, and the programmer cannot change this task. *Other registers are general purpose,* that is, any type of information can be stored in them, and we determine, under software control, exactly how this information will be processed or altered.

As an example, all of the microprocessors have *instruction registers.* The instruction register is used to store the *operation code* or *op code* (simple binary 1s and 0s) of the instruction just read from memory. The instruction register and its related logic then decide what operations have to take place, in order for the instruction to be "executed." These operations may consist of moving a data value in the CPU chip to another register contained within the chip, or they may involve the transfer of data from one section of memory to another. The instruction register is not a general-purpose register that we can use for the temporary storage of data; its function has been "fixed" by the manufacturer.

On the other hand, most microprocessors have general-purpose registers (the 9900 is an interesting exception), which can be used to store data values, addresses, status information from peripherals, *or any other information that can be represented by a sequence of 1s and 0s.* The general-purpose registers are of more interest to the programmer than the dedicated registers, simply because the programmer can decide exactly what will be stored in these registers and when. The stack pointer, instruction register, and program counter are not general-purpose registers, and therefore the programmer does not have much flexibility when using them. Most of the time, these dedicated registers are used without the programmer worrying about what is stored in them. A typical register diagram for the 68000 is shown in Fig. 1-6. Note how some of these registers are labeled as being either address or data registers, rather than as general-purpose registers. In the 8086, Z8001/2, 9900, LSI-11, and 16000, the user has access to general-purpose registers, because they can be used to store data or addresses.

All of the microprocessors have a *flag word* or *flag register*. The flag register contains a number of flags, or logic levels, that can be tested under software control. Typically, one flag indicates whether or not the result of the last mathematical or logical operation was

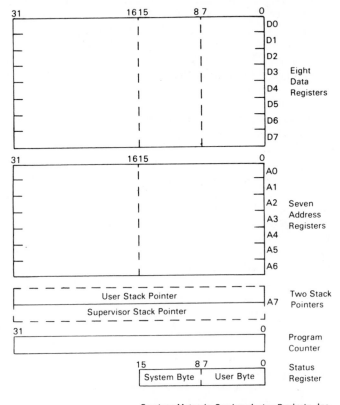

Courtesy Motorola Semiconductor Products, Inc.
Fig. 1-6. The internal registers of the 68000.

zero or nonzero. There are other flags which indicate whether a carry or overflow has occurred, what the parity of the result is, what the states of the interrupt inputs are, and whether the microprocessor is in the "user" or "supervisor" mode of operation.

INSTRUCTION SETS

Typically, one feature that distinguishes an 8-bit from a 16-bit microprocessor is its instruction set. Five of the 16-bit microprocessors that we will be discussing have multiply and divide instructions (the LSI-11 uses a special math chip for multiply and divide instructions). Even though these instructions require a large amount of time to be executed (hundreds of clock cycles), they are all faster than the equivalent subroutines that would have to be executed on most 8-bit processors. There are a number of other features that separate the 8-bit and 16-bit microprocessors. Typically, the 16-bit "machines" can address more memory, have larger instruction sets, can address more peripherals, execute programs faster, and are generally more sophisticated than the 8-bit machines. *Of course, 16-bit processors usually have 16-bit data buses, whereas the 8-bit processors have 8-bit data buses.* Exceptions to this are the 8088 and 9980, which are 16-bit processors internally though they both use 8-bit data buses.

Quite often the number of addressing modes that a microprocessor has can influence a user's choice of one microprocessor over another. However, all of the microprocessors have basically the same addressing modes, with the 16000 having the most sophisticated modes of all.

MICROCOMPUTER PROGRAMMING

Because the 16-bit microprocessors are so powerful, they also have complex instruction sets. In a single 16-bit instruction op code, there may be three or four different groups of bits that determine the addressing mode to be used, the register(s) to be used, the actual operation that is to take place (data movement, multiply, output, increment), and the number of bits involved in the operation (bit, byte, word, long word or double word, or quad word). Therefore it is not very easy to program these processors in machine language or hand-assembled assembly language.

You don't have to make a large investment in equipment, however, in order to program these microprocessors. Low-cost, single-board microcomputers are available for five of the processors (none for the 16000 as of the summer of 1981). They range in cost from $400 to $1500. Using these products the user programs the microcomputer in machine language, using either a keyboard and seven-segment displays or a teletypewriter or crt. There are also line-by-line assemblers available for the Z8001/2 and the 9900, so it is a little easier to program these processors. No such program has been announced for the 8086, LSI-11, 68000, or 16000.

If you have the money to invest in a development system, then you will have a number of editors, macro-assemblers, compilers, high-level languages, system monitors, operating systems, and debuggers to choose from. As you will see, there are a number of high-level languages available for use on these development systems, including PL/M, PL/1, FORTRAN, COBOL, Pascal, C, and PL/Z, to name just a few. All of this sophisticated software will reduce the time required to program these processors, and documentation and debugging costs should also be lower than if assembly language was used.

DEVELOPMENT SYSTEMS

Of course, each manufacturer would like to "hook you" on its development system so that you have to buy peripherals, memories, and software from it. In general, the development systems from the semiconductor manufacturers can only be used to develop software for the microprocessors that they manufacture. There are, however, a number of general-purpose development systems from companies, such as Hewlett-Packard, Tektronix, and GenRad/Futuredata, that can be used with a number of different microprocessors. Most development systems give the user the ability to simulate, with software and an additional, complex, piece of hardware, the CPU chip in a single-board microcomputer or a large system. By using the development system or host processor to simulate the action of the CPU chip in the system being tested, shorted traces on a printed-circuit board can be located, along with faulty integrated circuits. Typically, the CPU chip in the system being tested is removed, and the host processor is connected to the system being tested by means of a 40- or 64-conductor ribbon cable. The end of the ribbon cable plugs into the socket of the CPU chip.

Unfortunately, all of this hardware and software costs money, usually more than $10,000. If, however, you are doing a lot of programming or hardware development, and if time *is* money, the investment is worth it. If you are pinched for funds, the lower-cost single-board microcomputers may be the best way to get started.

The development systems for the LSI-11 and 9900 actually contain an LSI-11 or 9900 CPU, and there is considerable software available for these two processors (both development and applications software). The reason for this is that these processors are the oldest and most mature of the six processors.

For the 8086, Z8001/2, 68000, and 16000, there is some development software and almost no applications software available. The development systems that are used to prepare programs for these processors generally do not use the 8086, Z8001/2, 68000, or 16000 CPU chips, but rather their 8-bit predecessors. Therefore a development system from Intel may actually contain either an 8080 or 8085 microprocessor. This microprocessor then executes the appropriate programs so that programs for the 8086 can be edited and assembled. This process is known as *cross assembly;* programs for one processor (the 8086) are assembled on a different processor (the 8080 or 8085). The 8080 or 8085 cannot execute 8086 programs, and the 8086 cannot directly execute 8080 or 8085 programs. The development system from Zilog is based on the Z80, and is used to prepare programs for the Z8001/2.

The Motorola development system may be based on the 68000, but it is more likely that they use the 6800 or one of the other similar processors (6801, 6809, etc.). The AMD development system is based on the 8080 and is used to develop programs for the Z8001/2.

Therefore, unless you're using the 9900 or LSI-11, don't expect a large number of applications programs to be available for some time to come. As these microprocessors become more popular and there are more programmers generating programs, the number of applications programs that can be executed on these other processors will increase.

MICROCOMPUTER DESIGN

Unlike the 8-bit processors, which were fairly easy to design microcomputers with, the 16-bit processors require a handful of additional parts to make them work. Clock drivers, address/data bus demultiplexers (latches), and data bus buffers are often required. Consequently most users buy a kit or assembled 16-bit microcomputer, rather than design and build one themselves.

INTERFACING

All microprocessors must have the ability to communicate with peripheral devices. For some microcomputers these devices may be a simple multiplexed keyboard/display, and on others there may be a number of 50M- or 100M-byte fixed-head disks. The 16-bit processors that we will be discussing are no exception. They can all communicate with peripheral devices. Usually these peripherals are wired to the microcomputer's buses using the same control signals that are used to control memory. By using these signals the peripheral is interfaced to the microprocessor using *memory-mapped i/o* techniques. To communicate with a peripheral the microprocessor simply has to execute a *memory-reference instruction,* so that the memory control signals are generated. The peripheral then places information on to the data bus (memory-read) so that the microprocessor can read the data, or the peripheral gates data off of the data bus (memory-write) that the microprocessor is sending to it.

Some of the microprocessors, such as the 9900, Z8001/2, and the 8086, have other techniques that are used in interfacing. The advantage of these additional methods is that none of the microprocessor's *memory address space* is used up by peripherals. If a microprocessor can only address 65,536 memory locations (65K bytes) and peripherals use 4K or 8K bytes of address space, then the microprocessor can only have 60K or 56K bytes of memory. With the 9900, Z8001/2, and the 8086, all of the address space can be used by memory.

INTERRUPTS

All of the microprocessors can be used with interrupts. An interrupt is simply a signal that is generated by a peripheral that is used to notify the CPU that data should either be read from the peripheral or be written out to the peripheral. In general, the processors that we will be discussing can be used with a maximum of between 16 and 256 interrupting devices.

The advantage of an interrupt is the fact that the peripheral tells the microprocessor when it needs servicing. The only other way, which is much slower, is to have the microprocessor *interrogate* the peripheral, and so see if it needs servicing. The microprocessor does this many thousands of times each second, until the peripheral indicates that it either has data for the CPU or needs data from the CPU. This "polling" method is slow, and it usually prevents the processor from performing other tasks. With interrupts, the processor can be performing other tasks and is only interrupted from these tasks when the peripheral needs servicing.

SPECIAL-FUNCTION CHIPS

Quite often the semiconductor manufacturer realizes that a special chip can be designed and manufactured that can be used by a number of microcomputer system designers and end-users. As an example, the 8086 needs a special clock signal to clock the CPU chip, and rather than have engineers design this circuit with discrete transistors and resistors, Intel condensed all of the required circuitry onto one chip. There are also special peripheral chips that contain serial and parallel input/output (i/o) devices, floppy disk controllers, cathode-ray tube (crt) controllers, timers, counters, buffers, drivers, and universal peripheral controllers.

Of all of the manufacturers, Intel probably has the most special-function chips, with Zilog and Motorola being not far behind. Many of the second sources for these chips—Siemens (8086), Advanced Micro Devices (Z8001/2), Rockwell International (68000), and AMI (9900)—manufacture a number of these special-function chips.

National Semiconductor also has special-function chips that were designed for the 8080 and can be used with the 16000, and there are also some special-function chips that were designed specifically for the 16000. Digital Equipment Corporation has one special-function chip for the LSI-11: a math chip. This math chip is really just a read-only memory that contains "microcoded" instructions for the LSI-11 microprocessor. However, the end-user cannot microcode his or her own instructions for the LSI-11.

CONCLUSION

With this short introduction you should now be able to read and understand the remaining chapters in this book. However, the authors still recommend that you have some experience with 8-bit microprocessors before trying to either design with, or program, the 16-bit machines. Obviously it would be just as helpful to have some minicomputer experience.

2

The 8086

The 8086 was introduced in early 1978. It was not the first 16-bit microprocessor, being preceded by the 9900 (Texas Instruments), the LSI-11 (Digital Equipment Corp.), the microNOVA (Data General), and the 9940 (Fairchild). However, it is, and will be, a very popular microprocessor, simply because of the tremendous amount of support (both hardware and software) that Intel and its second sources will give it. Most of the 16-bit microprocessors that are now available, including the 8086, are register oriented, which means that it is often easier to manipulate data when it is stored in registers, rather than when it is stored in memory.

The 8086 CPU (Fig. 2-1) has fourteen 16-bit registers in it, eight of which can be considered to be general purpose. These registers are divided into the general register group (four registers), the pointer and index group (four registers), and the segment register group (four registers). The two remaining registers are the instruction pointer or program counter and the flag register. All of these registers and their names can be seen in Fig. 2-2.

The use of these registers and the way in which their contents are manipulated allow the 8086 to directly address 1,048,576 bytes (1 megabyte) or 524,288 sixteen-bit words of memory. Of course, this memory can be any combination of read/write (R/W) or read-only (ROM) memory. The only restrictions on the type of memory used is that, when it is reset, the 8086 begins program execution at address FFFF0 hexadecimal (FFFF0H). Also, interrupts can use up the first 1024 *words* of memory, starting at memory location zero, for interrupt service subroutine addresses.

The 8086 can also address 65K (65,536) 8-bit input/output (i/o) ports. To remain compatible with additional hardware and software

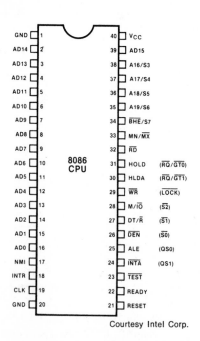

Fig. 2-1. The 8086 CPU integrated circuit.

Courtesy Intel Corp.

that Intel and its second sources may develop for the 8086, Intel has reserved the use of memory locations FFFF0H through FFFFFH (other than the reset address just mentioned) and i/o addresses between F8H and FFH. In addition, memory locations 00H through 7FH are reserved for hardware and software products that use interrupts.

The large address space of the 8086 is complemented by a powerful instruction set (135 basic instructions) that can operate on individual bits, 8-bit bytes, 16-bit words, and 32-bit double words. The greatest number of instructions, however, operate on 8- and 16-bit values. The instruction set includes data transfer, arithmetic (add, subtract, multiply and divide), bit manipulation, string, control-transfer, processor control, and multiprocessor instructions.

The basic clock speed of an 8086-based microcomputer may be between 4 MHz and 8 MHz, depending on the 8086 chip used. Assuming that a 5-MHz 8086 is being used, the shortest instructions require just 400 ns to be executed. These instructions include register-to-register move instructions, along with some of the logical and processor control instructions. The longest instruction, a signed 16-bit by 16-bit division, may require up to 42 μs to be executed.

Since the CPU chip and support circuitry can be purchased by themselves, the user has the option of *designing* and *building* a general-purpose 16-bit microcomputer with the same amount of

IBM-PC   8088 5MHz

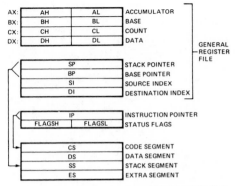

AX:	AH	AL	ACCUMULATOR
BX:	BH	BL	BASE
CX:	CH	CL	COUNT
DX:	DH	DL	DATA

GENERAL
REGISTER
FILE

	SP	STACK POINTER
	BP	BASE POINTER
	SI	SOURCE INDEX
	DI	DESTINATION INDEX

	IP	INSTRUCTION POINTER
FLAGSH	FLAGSL	STATUS FLAGS

	CS	CODE SEGMENT
	DS	DATA SEGMENT
	SS	STACK SEGMENT
	ES	EXTRA SEGMENT

Courtesy Intel Corp.

Fig. 2-2. The registers contained within the 8086 CPU chip.

"power" as many of the traditional minicomputers. For those users who want to purchase an 8086-based microcomputer, there are a number of products that range in complexity from the Intel SDK-86 (Fig. 2-3), through 8086-based CPU cards for the Multibus® (Fig. 2-4) and the popular S-100 hobbyist bus, up to "full-blown" development and business systems (Fig. 2-5). With this introduction to the 8086, let's examine its instruction set, support hardware, systems, and software.

8086 RESOURCES

Before the instruction set of the 8086 can be discussed, the "resources," the registers and memory locations, that the instructions

Courtesy Intel Corp.

Fig. 2-3. The System Design Kit for the 8086 (SDK-86).

Fig. 2-4. A single-board microcomputer based on the 8086 (SBC 86/12A).

operate on, must be examined. A summary of these registers was shown in Fig. 2-2. However, as their names imply, each register in the general register file functions in a manner in addition to that of a general-purpose register.

The General Register Group

The general register group consists of the AX (accumulator), BX (base), CX (count), and DX (data) 16-bit registers. These four registers can also be used as 8-bit registers, where the AX register contains the AH and AL registers, BX contains BH and BL, CX contains CH and CL and the DX register contains DH and DL. One rule about these registers is the fact that the L-type registers will contain D7–D0 of a 16-bit word and the H-type registers will contain D15–D8 of a 16-bit word. Thus the "H" can be thought of as representing the high byte, and the "L" can be thought of as representing the low-byte, of a 16-bit word. Not only are these 8- and 16-bit registers general-purpose, but they can also be used as an accumulator, base, count, and data register.

These registers are sometimes used by other instructions to store a *base address,* a *count,* or a *data value.* For instance, some instructions assume that there is a 16-bit base address in the BX register. Other instructions assume that a count has been loaded into either CL (8-bit) or CX (16-bit). For instance, the content of a register or memory location can be shifted or rotated to the left or to the right, by the number of bits specified by the content of the CL register. When moving strings of numeric or alphanumeric values, the CX register specifies the number of bytes or words to be moved. Finally, one of the functions of the DX register is to specify the 16-bit i/o address (port) that the 8086 is communicating with during

Table 2-1. Implied Uses for the General-Purpose Registers

Register	Operations
AX	Word multiply, word divide, word i/o
AL	Byte multiply, byte divide, byte i/o, translate, decimal arithmetic
AH	Byte multiply, byte divide
BX	Translate
CX	String operations, loops
CL	Variable shift and rotate
DX	Word multiply, word divide, indirect i/o
SP	Stack operations
SI	String operations
DI	String operations

Courtesy Intel Corp.

Courtesy Intel Corp.
Fig. 2-5. A microcomputer development system (8085-based) for the 8086.

the execution of an i/o instruction. These registers have other functions, as can be seen in Table 2-1.

The Pointer and Index Register Group

This group of four 16-bit registers consists of the SP (stack pointer), the BP (base pointer), the SI (source index), and the DI (destination index). The stack pointer is used to provide part of a 20-bit address that the 8086 uses when any information is placed on, or taken off of, the stack. The SP is used in conjunction with the stack segment (SS) register, as we shall see in the next section of this chapter. The base pointer, source index, and destination index are often used when the 8086 addresses memory. At times just the base pointer may be used, or the source or destination index may be added to the base pointer (performed by internal 8086 logic) to generate a memory address. These indexes and pointers are often used with the data segment (DS) register that will be discussed in the next section.

Of course, even though these registers are called index and pointer registers, they can still be thought of as general-purpose registers. Information can be moved between them and the other four general-purpose registers (AX, BX, CX, or DX) that were previously mentioned, just as the information in them can be shifted, added, subtracted, incremented, or decremented, to name a few possible operations.

The Segment Register Group

The segment register group consists of the code segment (CS) register, data segment (DS) register, the stack segment (SS) register, and the extra segment (ES) register. A number of instructions can be executed to alter the contents of these registers, but they are not normally considered to be general-purpose registers. *Typically, these registers are used to store a 16-bit segment address, which the 8086 uses when it addresses memory.*

ADDRESSING MEMORY

Since a number of 8086 instructions read information from, or write information to, memory, it is important to understand how the 8086 uses the index, pointer, and segment registers to address memory. As was mentioned previously, the 8086 can address 1 megabyte of memory. To do this, a 20-bit (five-digit hexadecimal) address is required. However, none of the registers that we have discussed can store a 20-bit address; they can only be used to store 16-bit values. How, then, does the 8086 *generate* 20-bit addresses?

To do this the 8086 adds an offset address or effective address

(EA) to a segment number or segment address, as shown in Fig. 2-6. Note that the segment address, which is contained in one of the four segment registers, can be thought of as being rotated or shifted to the left four times before it is added to the offset or effective address. By doing this shift or rotate, the result of the addition will always be 20 bits long. We know where the segment address comes from, but where is the offset or effective address stored?

The offset or effective address (EA) is either the content of the base pointer (BP) or base register (BX) or the content of the source index (SI) or destination index (DI), which may be added to either of these base registers. Also, it is possible to have an 8- or 16-bit displacement in an instruction. As you might guess, there are a number of different combinations of BP, BX, SI, DI, and this displacement (Chart 2-1).

Regardless of what is being added to what, the offset or effective address (the result of the addition) will always be a 16-bit value. This means that for large numbers, "wrap-around" may occur. For instance, in a particular instruction, a displacement, the source index

Chart 2-1. Different Addressing Modes and the Registers Used

BASE INDEX	BX + SI + Displacement + Segment BX + DI + Displacement + Segment BP + SI + Displacement + Segment BP + DI + Displacement + Segment
INDEX	SI + Displacement + Segment DI + Displacement + Segment
BASE	BP + Displacement + Segment BX + Displacement + Segment
BASE INDEX (NO DISPLACEMENT)	BX + SI + Segment BX + DI + Segment BP + SI + Segment BP + DI + Segment
INDIRECT	SI + Segment DI + Segment BX + Segment BP + Segment
RELATIVE	Displacement + Instruction Pointer (IP)
DIRECT	Address + Segment

Note: Displacement may be either 8 or 16 bits.

(SI), and the base register (BX) may be added together. The result of the addition may be 18 bits, *but only the 16 least significant bits of the result are added to the appropriate segment register* when the 8086 actually executes the instruction. Therefore you must use care when "base" addresses, indexes, and displacements are changed. *Also, there are a number of different base addresses, indexes, and displace-*

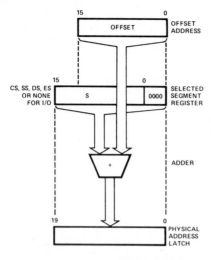

Fig. 2-6. Generating a 20-bit memory address from a segment address and a 16-bit offset or effective address.

Courtesy Intel Corp.

ments that, when added together, will produce the same 16-bit result. Note that the actual addition of all of these numbers is transparent to the user. The registers simply have to be loaded with the proper values, so that when the 8086 executes the instruction, and performs the addition (without altering any of the registers), the proper 20-bit memory address is generated.

The addresses that are generated from these indexes, pointers, and base registers are usually added to the data segment (DS) or extra segment (ES) registers. The resulting 20-bit memory address is then used when the 8086 reads or writes a byte or word to or from memory. We also have the same memory-addressing problem (segment plus effective address) when instructions are fetched from memory and executed, and also when values are placed on, or taken off of, the stack.

Therefore the 20-bit memory address used to fetch instructions from memory is generated by adding the content of the code segment (CS) register (16 bits shifted to the left by 4 bits) to the 16-bit content of the instruction pointer as in Fig. 2-6. In this case the 16-bit instruction pointer can be thought of as the offset or effective address. Wrap-around can also occur with the code segment register and the instruction pointer. Therefore, if the instruction pointer is ever incremented from FFFFH to 0000H, additional software must be executed so that the code segment register is loaded with a *new value, not simply incremented,* due to the way in which addresses are calculated (Fig. 2-6). When a stack instruction is executed by the 8086, the stack pointer (SP) is added to the stack segment (SS) register. In Fig. 2-6 the effective address would be the content of the stack pointer.

As you can see, memory addressing can be very complex. You have to ensure that the proper registers are loaded with the proper values, so that the instruction being executed generates the proper 20-bit memory address for the data value being transferred, for the instruction being read, or for the stack operation being performed. It is also important to remember that there are a number of different segment and effective addresses that, when added together, will generate the same 20-bit memory addresses.

Since the segment registers are all independent of each other, and the base, stack, and instruction pointers are all 16 bits wide, separate 65K-byte blocks of the microcomputer memory can be allocated solely for data, stack, and programs ("code"). Thus, in earlier microprocessors such as the Z80, 8080, 6800, and 8085, programs, stack and data all had to reside within one 65K-byte block of memory. Now, with separate and distinct segment registers, the amount of usable memory that can be addressed in one time is really 205K bytes, rather than 65K bytes. An additional 65K bytes of memory can also be addressed through the use of the extra segment (ES) register (Fig. 2-7).

Of course, all the segment registers can contain the same value,

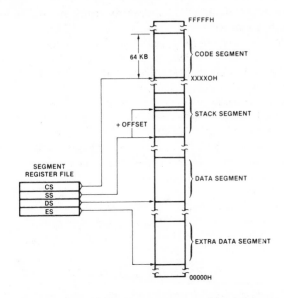

Courtesy Intel Corp.

Fig. 2-7. Segment registers addressing different portions of the 1M-byte address space.

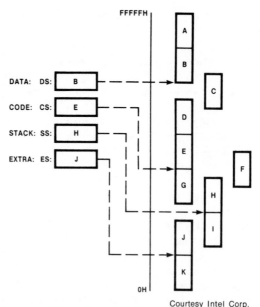

Courtesy Intel Corp.

Fig. 2-8. Using segment register values where overlap between segments can occur.

so that the stack, data, code, and extra segments are all within the same 65K bytes of memory.

Another case, which may be somewhat difficult to visualize, is where there is overlap between the segments. In Fig. 2-8 overlap between the code and data segments will occur when the code segment register is changed to "C."

One result of carefully using the segment registers is that programs can be moved to different sections of memory and still be executed, because references to data, instructions, and the stack are *relative* to the content of the segment registers. For programs to be *relocatable* they must not change the content of the segment registers, and they must have *relative transfer-of-control instructions,* such as relative jumps and calls, which the 8086 does have. In Fig. 2-9 the instructions, stack, and data values are moved, the content of the segment registers is changed, and then the program is executed, even though it resides in a completely different section of memory.

ADDRESSING I/O DEVICES

The 8086 has two different means of addressing i/o devices. Using one method an 8-bit i/o address is "embedded" in the instruction, as was the case with the 8080 and 8085. This means that this type

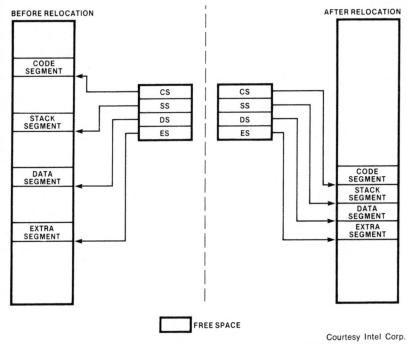

BEFORE RELOCATION

AFTER RELOCATION

FREE SPACE

Courtesy Intel Corp.

Fig. 2-9. Relocating the stack, data, instructions, and "extra data."

of instruction can only be used to address the first 256 i/o ports, out of a possible 65K. The second type of i/o instruction uses the 16-bit content of the DX register as the i/o device address. Thus any of the 65K possible i/o devices can be addressed using this method. *This address space is separate from the 1-megabyte memory address space.*

ADDRESSING SUMMARY

The different combinations of the pointers, indexes, and segment registers that the 8086 can use to address memory are shown in Chart 2-1. In all of these addressing modes, *other than relative addressing,* the 8- or 16-bit displacement is optional. Two additional and very simple addressing modes that are not shown in this chart are register and immediate addressing. They are not included in the chart because these addressing modes are used when information is already contained in a register or when information is actually contained within the instruction.

In *register addressing,* the instruction op code contains the name(s) or "addresses" of the register(s) being operated on. Thus an instruction that moves the content of one register to another register uses register addressing. If *immediate addressing* is used, the instruction actually contains a data byte or data word, along with the instruction op code. Depending on the instruction being executed, this data value (8 or 16 bits) might be moved to a register, or to a memory location, or it might be involved in a mathematical (add, subtract) or logical (AND, OR) operation. Immediate addressing means that no data value has to be read from memory using the DS register along with indexes, pointers, or a displacement. Instead, the immediate data byte or word is read from memory at the same time that the instruction op code is read from memory. In all of the remaining addressing modes the 8086 generates a memory address using various combinations of pointers, indexes, displacements, and segment addresses.

In *indirect register addressing*, the content of a register, such as BP, BX, SI, or DI, is used as the effective address (EA). No displacement is added to these pointers or indexes. The EA is then added to the content of a segment register, usually DS, to generate a 20-bit memory address. With *direct addressing*, a memory address is contained in the instruction (just as an immediate data byte is contained in an immediate instruction). This address is added to the content of a segment register to generate a 20-bit memory address.

When *indexed addressing* is used, the content of an index register (SI or DI), when added to a displacement, forms the effective address. If no displacement was used in an instruction that used this addressing mode, then it would be indirect register addressing. With *relative addressing* (which is similar to direct addressing), only a displacement is available, which is added to a segment register. Relative addressing is used with transfer-of-control instructions, such as calls and jumps, so that position-independent, or relocatable, programs are created.

In *base addressing*, the content of the BX or BP register is added to a displacement to form an effective address. Without the displacement it would be indirect register addressing. For *base indexed addressing*, the content of the base register (BX or BP) is added to an index register (SI or DI), which is added to an optional displacement. The result is the effective address, which is added to the content of a segment register.

All of these addressing modes are shown in Fig. 2-10. As you have seen, to address memory a 20-bit address must be generated by the 8086. To generate this address various pointers, indexes, displacements, and segments are added together. To fetch instructions from memory the instruction pointer is added to the code segment. For stack operations the stack pointer is added to the stack segment. When data values in memory must be accessed, the base register (BX) or base pointer (BP), an index (SI or DI), and a displacement (op-

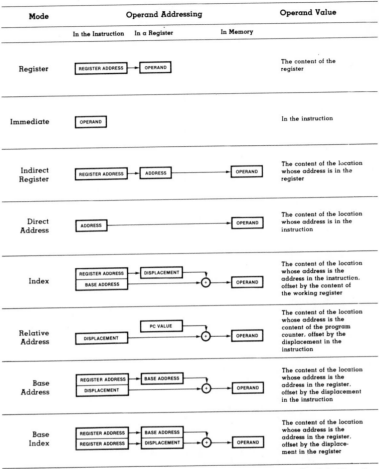

Mode	Operand Addressing			Operand Value
	In the Instruction	In a Register	In Memory	
Register	REGISTER ADDRESS → OPERAND			The content of the register
Immediate	OPERAND			In the instruction
Indirect Register	REGISTER ADDRESS → ADDRESS		→ OPERAND	The content of the location whose address is in the register
Direct Address	ADDRESS		→ OPERAND	The content of the location whose address is in the instruction
Index	REGISTER ADDRESS → DISPLACEMENT, BASE ADDRESS		→ + → OPERAND	The content of the location whose address is the address in the instruction. offset by the content of the working register
Relative Address	DISPLACEMENT	PC VALUE	→ + → OPERAND	The content of the location whose address is the content of the program counter. offset by the displacement in the instruction
Base Address	REGISTER ADDRESS → BASE ADDRESS, DISPLACEMENT		→ + → OPERAND	The content of the location whose address is the address in the register. offset by the displacement in the instruction
Base Index	REGISTER ADDRESS → BASE ADDRESS, REGISTER ADDRESS → DISPLACEMENT		→ + → OPERAND	The content of the location whose address is the address in the register. offset by the displacement in the register

Courtesy Zilog, Inc.

Fig. 2-10. A summary of 8086 addressing modes.

tional) are added to the data segment. The extra segment can also be used to address data values, along with a base, index, and displacement value. *Of course, in all but the relative and direct addressing modes, the displacement is optional.*

THE 8086 INSTRUCTION SET

Now that we know the different addressing modes that instructions can use to address memory, it would be advantageous to examine the format of the instructions of the 8086. This format is shown in Fig. 2-11.

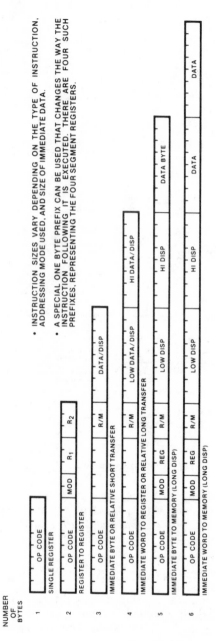

- INSTRUCTION SIZES VARY DEPENDING ON THE TYPE OF INSTRUCTION, ADDRESSING MODE USED, AND SIZE OF IMMEDIATE DATA.

- A SPECIAL ONE BYTE PREFIX CAN BE USED THAT CHANGES THE WAY THE INSTRUCTION FOLLOWING IT IS EXECUTED. THERE ARE FOUR SUCH PREFIXES, REPRESENTING THE FOUR SEGMENT REGISTERS.

NUMBER
OF
BYTES

1
| OP CODE |

SINGLE REGISTER

2
| OP CODE | MOD | R₁ | R₂ |

REGISTER TO REGISTER

3
| OP CODE | R/M | DATA/DISP |

IMMEDIATE BYTE OR RELATIVE SHORT TRANSFER

4
| OP CODE | R/M | LOW DATA/DISP | HI DATA/DISP |

IMMEDIATE WORD TO REGISTER OR RELATIVE LONG TRANSFER

5
| OP CODE | MOD | REG | R/M | LOW DISP | HI DISP | DATA BYTE |

IMMEDIATE BYTE TO MEMORY (LONG DISP)

6
| OP CODE | MOD | REG | R/M | LOW DISP | HI DISP | DATA | DATA |

IMMEDIATE WORD TO MEMORY (LONG DISP)

Fig. 2-11. The instruction format for the 8086.

Courtesy Intel Corp.

From Fig. 2-11 you can see that all of the instructions are from 1 to 6 bytes (1 to 3 words) long. Within each instruction the operation to be performed (jump, call, add, move) is specified, along with the register(s) involved, and the addressing mode to be used. If the addressing mode specifies that a displacement is to be included in the 20-bit memory address calculations, 1 or 2 bytes are used to store it in the instruction. The instruction may also specify 8 or 16 bits of immediate data, so these data bytes must also be included in the instruction. In case you are wondering how the addressing mode of the instruction is specified, the two MOD bits and three R/M bits specify it.

Even though memory for the 8086 is organized as 16-bit words, either byte in a word can be addressed. The least significant byte (D7–D0) is stored in the byte memory location with the lower address, and the most significant byte (D15–D8) is stored in the next higher byte memory location (Fig. 2-12). Therefore, because the

BYTE FORMATS

Memory Address	8086, LSI-11, 16000	9900, Z-8000, 68000
0000	LOW BYTE	HIGH BYTE
0001	HIGH BYTE	LOW BYTE
0002	LOW BYTE	HIGH BYTE
0003	HIGH BYTE	LOW BYTE
0004	LOW BYTE	HIGH BYTE
0005	HIGH BYTE	LOW BYTE

WORD FORMATS

Memory Address	8086, LSI-11, 16000	9900, Z-8000, 68000
0000	LOW | HIGH	HIGH | LOW
0002	LOW | HIGH	HIGH | LOW
0004	LOW | HIGH	HIGH | LOW

Fig. 2-12. Byte/word formats for the processors.

8086 has *single-byte* instructions, instructions of this length can be stored in either of the two byte locations within a word, as long as the next instruction is stored in the next consecutive (and available) byte memory location. Thus 8086 instructions do not have to be *word aligned*. In some processors the instructions do have to be word aligned, which simply means that all instructions must be stored on word boundaries, or in memory locations that have even-byte memory addresses.

What kinds of instructions does the 8086 have? Very simply, the 8086 can transfer data or move it around in memory or registers, and it can also perform math and logic operations and transfer program execution from one point in memory to another. The 8086 can also perform string operations, use interrupts, and control internal processor operations. The simplest instructions, and the ones that will be examined first, are the data transfer instructions.

Data Transfer Instructions

Within the category of data transfer instructions are the move, push, pop, exchange, translate, input/output, and the load and store instructions (Fig. 2-13). Of these, the move instructions are the most prevalent. Using the move instructions (which are abbreviated as MOV in their mnemonic form) the 8086 can move the content of a register (byte or word) to memory, the content of memory to a register, or the content of one register to another register. An immediate data value (byte or word) can also be moved to either a register or a memory location.

The push (PUSH) and pop (POP) instructions cause the content of a register or memory location (16 bits only) to be stored on, or retrieved from, the stack. The stack is really just a section of R/W memory that is addressed by the combination of the stack pointer (SP) and the stack segment (SS). Therefore the PUSH and POP instructions are very similar to the MOV-type instructions.

The exchange instructions (XCHG) cause either 8- or 16-bit values to be exchanged between two registers or a register and a memory location. The input (IN) and output (OUT) instructions are used to transfer data between the AX or AL register of the 8086 and peripheral (i/o) devices. The translate (XLAT) instruction is very powerful and is often used with lookup tables. Before this instruction is executed, the BX register is loaded with the base address or starting address of the lookup table. The XLAT instruction is then executed, with the AL register containing a pointer for the table (its value can only be between 0 and 255 decimal). Once the XLAT instruction has been executed, the AL register will contain the corresponding entry in the lookup table that was addressed by the combination (addition) of the pointer and the base address.

The 8086 also has four load instructions, three of which are LEA, LDS, and LES. These instructions are used to load any register (LEA), the DS register (LDS), and the ES register (LES) with 16-bit values stored in memory. The LDS and LES instructions also cause one of the general-purpose registers to be loaded with an additional 16-bit number. The final load instruction (LAHF) is used

DATA TRANSFER

MOV = Move:

	7 6 5 4 3 2 1 0	7 6 5 4 3 2 1 0	7 6 5 4 3 2 1 0	7 6 5 4 3 2 1 0
Register/memory to/from register	1 0 0 0 1 0 d w	mod reg r/m		
Immediate to register/memory	1 1 0 0 0 1 1 w	mod 0 0 0 r/m	data	data if w=1
Immediate to register	1 0 1 1 w reg	data	data if w=1	
Memory to accumulator	1 0 1 0 0 0 0 w	addr-low	addr-high	
Accumulator to memory	1 0 1 0 0 0 1 w	addr-low	addr-high	
Register/memory to segment register	1 0 0 0 1 1 1 0	mod 0 reg r/m		
Segment register to register/memory	1 0 0 0 1 1 0 0	mod 0 reg r/m		

PUSH = Push:

Register/memory	1 1 1 1 1 1 1 1	mod 1 1 0 r/m
Register	0 1 0 1 0 reg	
Segment register	0 0 0 reg 1 1 0	

POP = Pop:

Register/memory	1 0 0 0 1 1 1 1	mod 0 0 0 r/m
Register	0 1 0 1 1 reg	
Segment register	0 0 0 reg 1 1 1	

XCHG = Exchange:

Register/memory with register	1 0 0 0 0 1 1 w	mod reg r/m
Register with accumulator	1 0 0 1 0 reg	

IN=Input from:

Fixed port	1 1 1 0 0 1 0 w	port
Variable port	1 1 1 0 1 1 0 w	

OUT = Output to:

Fixed port	1 1 1 0 0 1 1 w	port
Variable port	1 1 1 0 1 1 1 w	
XLAT=Translate byte to AL	1 1 0 1 0 1 1 1	
LEA=Load EA to register	1 0 0 0 1 1 0 1	mod reg r/m
LDS=Load pointer to DS	1 1 0 0 0 1 0 1	mod reg r/m
LES=Load pointer to ES	1 1 0 0 0 1 0 0	mod reg r/m
LAHF=Load AH with flags	1 0 0 1 1 1 1 1	
SAHF=Store AH into flags	1 0 0 1 1 1 1 0	
PUSHF=Push flags	1 0 0 1 1 1 0 0	
POPF=Pop flags	1 0 0 1 1 1 0 1	

Courtesy Intel Corp.

Fig. 2-13. A summary of the 8086 data transfer instructions.

to load the AH register with 8 bits of the 16-bit flag register (see below).

The final data transfer instructions are PUSHF and POPF, which push and pop the flag word onto, and off of, the stack. What is the flag word? The flag word contains nine flags that are altered as a result of executing mathematical and logical instructions. The state of these flags can be *tested* by some of the control-transfer instructions, giving the 8086 the ability to make decisions. The organization of the flag word is shown in Fig. 2-14. The 8 least significant bits in this word are used by the LAHF instruction just mentioned.

PUSHF, POPF	U	U	U	U	O	D	I	T	S	Z	U	A	U	P	U	C
	15	14	13	12	11	10	9	8	7	6	5	4	3	2	1	0

U = UNDEFINED; VALUE IS INDETERMINATE
O = OVERFLOW FLAG
D = DIRECTION FLAG
I = INTERRUPT ENABLE FLAG
T = TRAP FLAG
S = SIGN FLAG
Z = ZERO FLAG
A = AUXILIARY CARRY FLAG
P = PARITY FLAG
C = CARRY FLAG

Courtesy Intel Corp.

Fig. 2-14. The structure of the flag word.

The Arithmetic Instructions

The 8086 can add, subtract, multiply, and divide binary numbers (signed and unsigned) and ASCII or unpacked decimal numbers (one digit per byte). The 8086 can also add and subtract packed bcd numbers (two digits per byte). In order to perform addition and subtraction the 8086 has two general-purpose addition and two general-purpose subtraction instructions. *These instructions can use all addressing modes in order to access data values in memory.* The addition instructions, add (ADD) and add-with-carry (ADC), give the 8086 the ability to add 8-bit, 16-bit, and larger numbers. For numbers larger than 16 bits the numbers are broken down into 16-bit words, and then they are added with the ADC addition instruction. The subtract (SUB) and subtract-with-borrow (SBB) instructions are used to subtract 8-bit, 16-bit, and larger numbers. The SUB instruction is used to subtract 16-bit words, and the SBB is used to subtract 16-bit "chunks" of larger numbers.

The 8086 can also multiply two 8-bit or two 16-bit numbers, with the results being 16 bits and 32 bits, respectively. The divide instructions are used to divide 16- or 32-bit numbers, by 8- and 16-bit divisors. Both the quotient and remainder would be 8 or 16 bits. Of course, both signed and unsigned numbers can be added, subtracted, multiplied, or divided.

If the 8086 is operating on numbers other than binary numbers, such as packed bcd or unpacked decimal, the adjustment instructions (AAA, DAA, AAS, DAS, AAM, or AAD) have to be executed in order to adjust the result back to the proper numeric format. The 8086 also has sign extension instructions so that signed bytes can be extended to signed words and double words. The sign of either a byte or word can also be changed by the negate (NEG) instruction.

The last "arithmetic" operations that the 8086 can perform are increment (INC), decrement (DEC), and compare (CMP). The

ARITHMETIC

ADD = Add:

Reg./memory with register to either	`0 0 0 0 0 0 d w`	`mod reg r/m`	
Immediate to register/memory	`1 0 0 0 0 0 s w`	`mod 0 0 0 r/m`	`data` `data if s:w=01`
Immediate to accumulator	`0 0 0 0 0 1 0 w`	`data`	`data if w=1`

ADC = Add with carry:

Reg./memory with register to either	`0 0 0 1 0 0 d w`	`mod reg r/m`	
Immediate to register/memory	`1 0 0 0 0 0 s w`	`mod 0 1 0 r/m`	`data` `data if s:w=01`
Immediate to accumulator	`0 0 0 1 0 1 0 w`	`data`	`data if w=1`

INC = Increment:

Register/memory	`1 1 1 1 1 1 1 w`	`mod 0 0 0 r/m`
Register	`0 1 0 0 0 reg`	
AAA=ASCII adjust for add	`0 0 1 1 0 1 1 1`	
DAA=Decimal adjust for add	`0 0 1 0 0 1 1 1`	

SUB = Subtract:

Reg./memory and register to either	`0 0 1 0 1 0 d w`	`mod reg r/m`	
Immediate from register/memory	`1 0 0 0 0 0 s w`	`mod 1 0 1 r/m`	`data` `data if s:w=01`
Immediate from accumulator	`0 0 1 0 1 1 0 w`	`data`	`data if w=1`

SBB = Subtract with borrow

Reg./memory and register to either	`0 0 0 1 1 0 d w`	`mod reg r/m`	
Immediate from register/memory	`1 0 0 0 0 0 s w`	`mod 0 1 1 r/m`	`data` `data if s:w=01`
Immediate from accumulator	`0 0 0 1 1 1 0 w`	`data`	`data if w=1`

DEC = Decrement:

7 6 5 4 3 2 1 0   7 6 5 4 3 2 1 0   7 6 5 4 3 2 1 0   7 6 5 4 3 2 1 0

Register/memory	`1 1 1 1 1 1 1 w`	`mod 0 0 1 r/m`
Register	`0 1 0 0 1 reg`	
NEG=Change sign	`1 1 1 1 0 1 1 w`	`mod 0 1 1 r/m`

CMP = Compare:

Register/memory and register	`0 0 1 1 1 0 d w`	`mod reg r/m`	
Immediate with register/memory	`1 0 0 0 0 0 s w`	`mod 1 1 1 r/m`	`data` `data if s:w=01`
Immediate with accumulator	`0 0 1 1 1 1 0 w`	`data`	`data if w=1`
AAS=ASCII adjust for subtract	`0 0 1 1 1 1 1 1`		
DAS=Decimal adjust for subtract	`0 0 1 0 1 1 1 1`		
MUL=Multiply (unsigned)	`1 1 1 1 0 1 1 w`	`mod 1 0 0 r/m`	
IMUL=Integer multiply (signed)	`1 1 1 1 0 1 1 w`	`mod 1 0 1 r/m`	
AAM=ASCII adjust for multiply	`1 1 0 1 0 1 0 0`	`0 0 0 0 1 0 1 0`	
DIV=Divide (unsigned)	`1 1 1 1 0 1 1 w`	`mod 1 1 0 r/m`	
IDIV=Integer divide (signed)	`1 1 1 1 0 1 1 w`	`mod 1 1 1 r/m`	
AAD=ASCII adjust for divide	`1 1 0 1 0 1 0 1`	`0 0 0 0 1 0 1 0`	
CBW=Convert byte to word	`1 0 0 1 1 0 0 0`		
CWD=Convert word to double word	`1 0 0 1 1 0 0 1`		

Courtesy Intel Corp.

Fig. 2-15. A summary of the 8086 arithmetic instructions.

INC and DEC instructions can be used to increment by 1 or decrement by 1 a byte or word stored in a register or memory. The compare instructions are used to compare 2 bytes or words, with one of the bytes or words being either an immediate value or register value. The other value can be in either a register or memory location.

All of the arithmetic instructions affect the flags contained within the 8086 CPU chip (Fig. 2-14). In order to find out just how these flags are set and cleared, and under what conditions, you should refer to the manufacturer's assembly language programming manual.[1] As an example, if the result of an addition is zero, the zero flag (Z) will be set to a logic one. If a carry is generated as a result of an addition, the carry flag will be set to a logic one. The sign or parity of the result will be reflected by the states of these two flags. In another section of this chapter you will see how the 8086 makes a decision, based on the states of these flags. All of the arithmetic instructions that the 8086 can execute are summarized in Fig. 2-15.

Logic Instructions

The logic instructions that the 8086 can execute are summarized in Fig. 2-16. The most interesting logic instructions are the shift, rotate, and test instructions. The AND (AND), OR (OR), and exclusive-OR (XOR) instructions are fairly common, being available on most 8- and 16-bit microprocessors. The shift and rotate instructions

LOGIC

NOT=Invert	1 1 1 1 0 1 1 w	mod 0 1 0 r/m
SHL/SAL=Shift logical/arithmetic left	1 1 0 1 0 0 v w	mod 1 0 0 r/m
SHR=Shift logical right	1 1 0 1 0 0 v w	mod 1 0 1 r/m
SAR=Shift arithmetic right	1 1 0 1 0 0 v w	mod 1 1 1 r/m
ROL=Rotate left	1 1 0 1 0 0 v w	mod 0 0 0 r/m
ROR=Rotate right	1 1 0 1 0 0 v w	mod 0 0 1 r/m
RCL=Rotate through carry flag left	1 1 0 1 0 0 v w	mod 0 1 0 r/m
RCR=Rotate through carry right	1 1 0 1 0 0 v w	mod 0 1 1 r/m

AND = And:

Reg./memory and register to either	0 0 1 0 0 0 d w	mod reg r/m		
Immediate to register/memory	1 0 0 0 0 0 0 w	mod 1 0 0 r/m	data	data if w=1
Immediate to accumulator	0 0 1 0 0 1 0 w	data	data if w=1	

TEST = And function to flags, no result:

Register/memory and register	1 0 0 0 0 1 0 w	mod reg r/m		
Immediate data and register/memory	1 1 1 1 0 1 1 w	mod 0 0 0 r/m	data	data if w=1
Immediate data and accumulator	1 0 1 0 1 0 0 w	data	data if w=1	

OR = Or:

Reg./memory and register to either	0 0 0 0 1 0 d w	mod reg r/m		
Immediate to register/memory	1 0 0 0 0 0 0 w	mod 0 0 1 r/m	data	data if w=1
Immediate to accumulator	0 0 0 0 1 1 0 w	data	data if w=1	

XOR = Exclusive or:

Reg./memory and register to either	0 0 1 1 0 0 d w	mod reg r/m		
Immediate to register/memory	1 0 0 0 0 0 0 w	mod 1 1 0 r/m	data	data if w=1
Immediate to accumulator	0 0 1 1 0 1 0 w	data	data if w=1	

Courtesy Intel Corp.

Fig. 2-16. A summary of the 8086 logic instructions.

CONTROL TRANSFER

CALL = Call:

	7 6 5 4 3 2 1 0	7 6 5 4 3 2 1 0	7 6 5 4 3 2 1 0
Direct within segment	1 1 1 0 1 0 0 0	disp-low	disp-high
Indirect within segment	1 1 1 1 1 1 1 1	mod 0 1 0 r/m	
Direct intersegment	1 0 0 1 1 0 1 0	offset-low	offset-high
		seg-low	seg-high
Indirect intersegment	1 1 1 1 1 1 1 1	mod 0 1 1 r/m	

JMP = Unconditional Jump:

Direct within segment	1 1 1 0 1 0 0 1	disp-low	disp-high
Direct within segment-short	1 1 1 0 1 0 1 1	disp	
Indirect within segment	1 1 1 1 1 1 1 1	mod 1 0 0 r/m	
Direct intersegment	1 1 1 0 1 0 1 0	offset-low	offset-high
		seg-low	seg-high
Indirect intersegment	1 1 1 1 1 1 1 1	mod 1 0 1 r/m	

RET = Return from CALL:

Within segment	1 1 0 0 0 0 1 1		
Within seg. adding immed to SP	1 1 0 0 0 0 1 0	data-low	data-high
Intersegment	1 1 0 0 1 0 1 1		
Intersegment, adding immediate to SP	1 1 0 0 1 0 1 0	data-low	data-high
JE/JZ=Jump on equal/zero	0 1 1 1 0 1 0 0	disp	
JL/JNGE=Jump on less/not greater or equal	0 1 1 1 1 1 0 0	disp	
JLE/JNG=Jump on less or equal/not greater	0 1 1 1 1 1 1 0	disp	
JB/JNAE=Jump on below/not above or equal	0 1 1 1 0 0 1 0	disp	
JBE/JNA=Jump on below or equal/not above	0 1 1 1 0 1 1 0	disp	
JP/JPE=Jump on parity/parity even	0 1 1 1 1 0 1 0	disp	
JO=Jump on overflow	0 1 1 1 0 0 0 0	disp	
JS=Jump on sign	0 1 1 1 1 0 0 0	disp	
JNE/JNZ=Jump on not equal/not zero	0 1 1 1 0 1 0 1	disp	
JNL/JGE=Jump on not less/greater or equal	0 1 1 1 1 1 0 1	disp	
JNLE/JG=Jump on not less or equal/greater	0 1 1 1 1 1 1 1	disp	
JNB/JAE=Jump on not below/above or equal	0 1 1 1 0 0 1 1	disp	
JNBE/JA=Jump on not below or equal/above	0 1 1 1 0 1 1 1	disp	
JNP/JPO=Jump on not par/par odd	0 1 1 1 1 0 1 1	disp	
JNO=Jump on not overflow	0 1 1 1 0 0 0 1	disp	
JNS=Jump on not sign	0 1 1 1 1 0 0 1	disp	
LOOP=Loop CX times	1 1 1 0 0 0 1 0	disp	
LOOPZ/LOOPE=Loop while zero/equal	1 1 1 0 0 0 0 1	disp	
LOOPNZ/LOOPNE=Loop while not zero/equal	1 1 1 0 0 0 0 0	disp	
JCXZ=Jump on CX zero	1 1 1 0 0 0 1 1	disp	

Courtesy Intel Corp.

Fig. 2-17. A summary of the 8086 control transfer instructions.

are interesting because the word or byte specified by the instruction can be shifted or rotated to the left or to the right, by the number of bits specified by the CL register. As an example, if packed bcd numbers are being operated on, any of the digits can be rotated into the 4 least significant bits of the AX register, simply by executing a 2-byte (1-word) instruction. The TEST instruction is interesting, because two 16-bit words are ANDed together by it, with the results of this logic operation reflected in the states of the flags. Neither of the 16-bit operands is altered by this instruction, however. Thus the TEST instruction simply sets or clears the flags.

Control Transfer Instructions

The control transfer instructions (Fig. 2-17) are important, because they give the 8086 the ability to make decisions. These instructions are used to test the flags, and, based on the states of the flags, the 8086 can execute one of two possible sequences of instructions. The control transfer instructions can also be used to simply jump to another section of memory and continue program execution.

The jump instructions are the simplest control transfer instructions to understand. They may either contain a displacement within the instruction, or they may address registers for memory locations that contain new values for the code segment (CS) register or the instruction pointer. Once the 8086 executes the jump instruction, it continues to execute the program stored in the specified section of memory. The 8086 also has 16 conditional jump instructions, where the jump will only be executed if the flag(s) specified in the instruction are in the proper state (logic ones or logic zeros). All conditional jumps are relative to the current content of the instructions pointer, with a range of −128 and +127 *bytes*. Thus these instructions give the 8086 decision-making capabilities.

The call (CALL) and return (RET) instructions are useful when a particular sequence of instructions must be executed a number of times in a program. Rather than repeat these instructions time and time again, they are written into memory once, and each time they must be executed the 8086 executes a call (CALL) instruction. Once the instructions in this *subroutine* are executed, the return (RET) instruction at the end of the subroutine causes the 8086 to return to the instruction stored in memory just after the call instruction. In order to do this the 8086 uses the stack (R/W memory) to save return or linking addresses. Unlike its predecessors, the 8080 and 8085, the 8086 does not have conditional call and return instructions (which were rarely used anyway).

Three of the more interesting control transfer instructions are the loop instructions (LOOP, LOOPZ or LOOPNE, and LOOPNZ or LOOPNE). These instructions all cause the content of the CX register to be decremented by 1. With the LOOP instruction, if the content of the CX register is nonzero, the 8086 loops or jumps to an instruction within the range of −128 and +127 bytes. Thus, the LOOP instruction is equivalent to a DEC CX, JNZ instruction sequence. The LOOPZ instruction (the same op code is also assigned the mnemonic LOOPE) and the LOOPNZ (LOOPNE) instruction test both the state of the zero flag *and* the content of the CX register.

Thus the 8086 can get out of a "loop" when either the CX register is zero or the condition specified in the instruction (zero or nonzero) is no longer met.

String Instructions

The string instructions that the 8086 can execute give it the ability to move, compare, and scan strings of information (Fig. 2-18). The strings that it can operate on can be numeric or alphanumeric

STRING MANIPULATION

Fig. 2-18. The 8086 string instructions.

REP=Repeat	1 1 1 1 0 0 1 z
MOVS=Move byte/word	1 0 1 0 0 1 0 w
CMPS=Compare byte/word	1 0 1 0 0 1 1 w
SCAS=Scan byte/word	1 0 1 0 1 1 1 w
LODS=Load byte/wd to AL/AX	1 0 1 0 1 1 0 w
STOS=Stor byte/wd from AL/A	1 0 1 0 1 0 1 w

Courtesy Intel Corp.

(ASCII, EBCDIC, etc.) or, in fact, any information that can be stored in memory in the form of binary information. These instructions may use just the SI and DS registers for an address, or both the SI and DS registers along with the DI and ES registers.

The move-string (MOVS) instruction is the simplest string instruction, because it can be used to move strings from one section of memory (addressed by SI and DS) to another section of memory (addressed by DI and ES). *The MOVS instruction by itself will only cause 1 byte or word to be moved.* The SI and DI registers will then be either incremented or decremented by 1 or 2, depending on the state of a single bit in the MOVS op code and a bit in the flag word. *By placing the op code for the repeat (REP) instruction in memory immediately in front of the op code for the MOVS instruction (or, for that matter, in front of the op code for any of the string instructions), the MOVS instruction will be executed the number of times specified by the content of the CX register.* Thus, if 32_{10} data values have to be moved from one section of memory to another, the CX register would be loaded with 20H. By using the repeat "prefix" and one of the string instructions, a much simpler and compact program can be written.

The CMPS and SCAS instructions are particularly interesting. The CMPS instruction is used to compare two strings on a byte-by-byte or word-by-word basis. The DI and SI indexes are automatically incremented or decremented, by 1 or 2, by these instructions. If the REP instruction is used, the 8086 will stop comparing the strings when they are no longer equal, or when the CX register has been decremented to zero. The SCAS instruction is similar to CMPS, except that one byte (word) of a string is compared to one and then successive bytes (words) of another string. If the REP instruction is used, the comparison process will continue until both bytes (words) are equal or the CX register has been decremented to zero.

Finally, the LODS instruction can be used to load the AL (AX) register with a byte (word) from a string. As such, it would not make much sense to use the REP instruction just before this instruction in a program. The STOS instruction is used to store the byte (word) contained in the AL (AX) register in memory. Again, don't use the repeat (REP) instruction just before this one unless you want to load a section of memory with the same value.

Interrupt Instructions

The 8086 has three different *types* of interrupt instructions, as shown in Fig. 2-19. The first type, INT, can be used to execute the

INT = Interrupt

Type specified	`1 1 0 0 1 1 0 1` `type`
Type 3	`1 1 0 0 1 1 0 0`
INTO=Interrupt on overflow	`1 1 0 0 1 1 1 0`
IRET=Interrupt return	`1 1 0 0 1 1 1 1`

Courtesy Intel Corp.
Fig. 2-19. The 8086 interrupt instructions.

interrupt service subroutines that are normally executed by peripherals. Therefore the INT op code and the second byte of the instruction specifies which of the 256 possible interrupt service subroutines are to be executed. This type of instruction can also be used as a 2-byte CALL instruction, as long as the proper code segment and instruction pointer values are stored within the interrupt vector table in the first 1K of memory (00H to 3FFH). This will be discussed in detail shortly.

The 8086 can also be programmed to interrupt itself if an overflow occurs. Again, this saves space in the program, rather than using one of the multibyte jump instructions. The INTO instruction is only a single byte, and its interrupt vector (four bytes) must be stored in memory starting at 010H.

Whenever one of the interrupt instructions is executed, the 8086 pushes the flags, the instruction pointer (IP), and the code segment (CS) register on the stack. It then reads a new value for the code segment and instruction pointer from the first 1K of memory, depending on which interrupt occurred. Once the interrupt service subroutine has been executed, the flags and the two "pointers" have to be popped off of the stack, so that the 8086 can return to the section

of code that was being executed when the interrupt occurred. Therefore a return-from-interrupt instruction (IRET) *must* be placed at
the end of all interrupt service subroutines, rather than just an RET
instruction. All of the interrupt instructions are summarized in Fig.
2-19. As you can see, these are 1- or 2-byte instructions.

Processor Control Instructions

The processor control instructions (Fig. 2-20) consist mostly of
flag set and clear instructions. Some of these instructions, however,
are used in multiprocessor environments (ESC and LOCK) and

PROCESSOR CONTROL

CLC=Clear carry	1 1 1 1 1 0 0 0
CMC=Complement carry	1 1 1 1 0 1 0 1
STC=Set carry	1 1 1 1 1 0 0 1
CLD=Clear direction	1 1 1 1 1 1 0 0
STD=Set direction	1 1 1 1 1 1 0 1
CLI=Clear interrupt	1 1 1 1 1 0 1 0
STI=Set interrupt	1 1 1 1 1 0 1 1
HLT=Halt	1 1 1 1 0 1 0 0
WAIT=Wait	1 0 0 1 1 0 1 1
ESC=Escape (to external device)	1 1 0 1 1 x x x | mod x x x r/m
LOCK=Bus lock prefix	1 1 1 1 0 0 0 0

Courtesy Intel Corp.

Fig. 2-20. A summary of the 8086 processor control instructions.

some are used so that an instruction uses a segment register other
than the one that is normally used. For instance, if an instruction
normally uses the data segment register as part of a memory address,
a segment override "prefix" (instruction) can cause the extra segment register to be used instead. Like the repeat (REP) instruction,
the segment override instruction (SEGMENT) is executed just before the instruction that uses the content of a segment register to
generate a 20-bit memory address. Note that not all of the segments
can be "overridden." For instance, the stack pointer will always use
the stack segment register and the instruction pointer will always use
the code segment register.

Instruction Set Conclusion

As you have seen, the 8086 has a number of powerful instructions,
ranging from the MOV instructions, through multiply and divide,
up to the string instructions. Based on the description that has been
presented, you should now see why the BX register is called the *base*
register and why the CX register is called the *count* register. Even
though these registers are general-purpose, a number of instructions
assume that data values or addresses have been loaded into them.
Therefore the accumulator or AX register and the data or DX reg-

ister will usually be the only registers that can be used to store data from mathematical, logic, or data transfer operations.

MICROPROCESSOR CHIP HARDWARE

The 8086 CPU chip (Fig. 2-1) is really available in two different configurations: the 8086 and the 8088. These two chips execute exactly the same instructions, but have slightly different internal organizations and pinouts. This can be seen in Fig. 2-21. One of the major differences is the fact that the 8086 has pins labeled AD0–AD15 (address/data 0 through address/data 15) and the 8088 simply has pins AD0–AD7. This means that the 8088 can only read and write 8 bits of information at a time, whereas the 8086 can read and write 16 bits of information at a time. For the 8088 to read a 16-bit value from memory, it must be read as two successive 8-bit bytes.

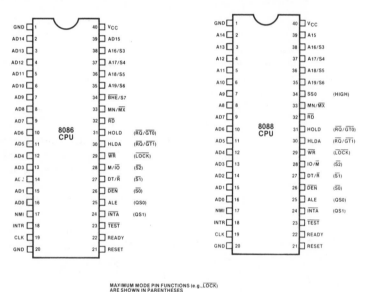

MAXIMUM MODE PIN FUNCTIONS (e.g., $\overline{LOCK}$) ARE SHOWN IN PARENTHESES

Courtesy Intel Corp.

Fig. 2-21. The pinouts for the 8086 and 8088 microprocessor chips.

Since the 8086 and 8088 are so similar, the term "8086" will be used in discussions that can be applied to both processors. When there are differences between the processors, they will be so stated. Of course, all of the information presented so far can be applied to both processors.

We should also note that Intel has decided to change the nomenclature of the 8086 and 8088 chips to iAPX86 and iAPX88, respectively. Unfortunately, this will probably create a lot of confusion, since the terms 8086 and 8088 have already been used throughout the literature.

THE 8086 AND 8088 CHIPS

The 8086 chip must generate the appropriate combination of control, data, and address signals so that it can communicate with memory and peripheral devices. To do this the 8086 has to be able to distinguish between one memory location or peripheral and another. Therefore the 8086 generates a unique 20-bit memory address or 16-bit peripheral address. As we already know, the 8086 has pins labeled AD0 through AD15, and also A16 through A19. *An address (memory or i/o) is only present on these pins when the address latch enable (ALE, pin 25, both chips) is a logic one (>2.4 V).* To distinguish between an address for memory or for a peripheral device, the 8086 also has a signal called M/$\overline{\text{IO}}$ (pronounced "memory eye oh bar"). This signal will be a logic one when the 8086 is addressing memory, and a logic zero when it is addressing peripheral or i/o devices. On the 8088 this signal is IO/$\overline{\text{M}}$, which means that it is a logic one when the 8088 is addressing peripherals, and a logic zero when it is addressing memory.

The 8086 and 8088 also have to control the flow of information on the data bus. They have to control whether information is being read from memory or peripherals, or whether information is being written to memory or peripherals. Therefore, during *any* type of *read operation,* the $\overline{\text{RD}}$ (pronounced "read bar") signal will be a logic zero. At all other times it will be a logic one. Likewise, when these processors are writing information out to memory or peripherals, the $\overline{\text{WR}}$ (pronounced "write bar") signal will be a logic zero. At all other times it will be a logic one. As a general conclusion, then, if a signal has a "bar" over it, it means that the signal is "active" in the logic zero or ground state.

As you can see by examining the pinouts for both the 8086 and 8088 (Fig. 2-21), some of the pin names are enclosed by parentheses. This means that the pins have two different functions, depending on how the CPU chip is used. In the *minimum mode* of operation, when the MN/$\overline{\text{MX}}$ signal (pin 33) is wired to +5 V, the CPU chip is being wired for use in a small, single-CPU system. The Intel SDK-86 is a good example of a minimum configuration (Fig. 2-3). When the chip is in the minimum mode of operation the signals adjacent to the pins (not in parentheses) are generated.

By wiring the MN/$\overline{\text{MX}}$ pin to ground the *maximum mode* of operation is specified, so the signals in parentheses are generated. In the maximum mode of operation, there can be a number of 8086 or

8088 CPUs that share the same memory and peripherals. There is also the possibility that there are coprocessors in the system—processors that perform operations at the same time as one of the CPU chips. There are both math and i/o coprocessors available for use with the 8086 and 8088. Since *maximum mode systems are extremely complex,* they will not be discussed in much detail.

CPU TIMING

A typical timing diagram for an 8086 read operation is shown in Fig. 2-22. In this figure the address on AD0–AD15 and on A16–A19, along with ALE, M/$\overline{\text{IO}}$ and $\overline{\text{RD}}$ and their timing relationships can be seen. The $\overline{\text{BHE}}$ (bus high enable) signal seen in this figure is often gated with A0 to select either the high byte of a word, the low byte of a word, the entire 16-bit word, or no word, in a memory location or peripheral device. Note that *data is only placed on the data bus* by memory or a peripheral *when $\overline{\text{RD}}$ is a logic zero.*

In Fig. 2-22 the address on AD0 through AD15 and on A16 through A19 is shown as being present when ALE is a logic one. Unfortunately, most memory and peripheral devices need the address to be present for up to 450 ns, before data can be either input to them or output from them. However, the ALE signal, indicating that an address is present on these pins, is only about 100 ns long. This

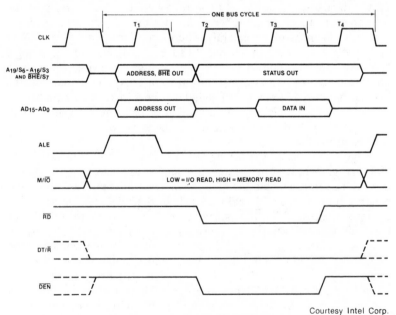

Courtesy Intel Corp.

Fig. 2-22. A read cycle for the 8086.

means that *external latches* must be wired to the bidirectional data/ address pins, so that when an address is generated by the CPU chip (ALE is a logic one), it is latched by these latches. This will cause the address to be present at the memory and peripheral devices for a period long enough for them to transfer data between themselves and the CPU properly. In fact, the address will be latched until another address and the ALE pulse are generated by the CPU. These latches are shown in Fig. 2-23 as the 8282 or 8283 devices. Note how the address/data bus is wired to the inputs (left-hand side) of these devices, but that only an address is present on their outputs (right-hand side). You can also see that ALE is used to control these latches.

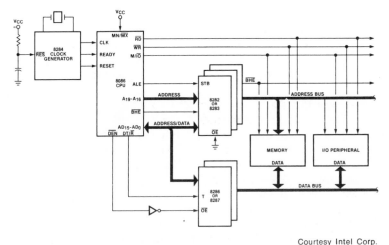

Fig. 2-23. A simple minimum-mode 8086 system with address latches, data bus buffers, memory, and peripherals.

Since the bidirectional address/data bus is also used to transmit and receive data, this bus is wired not only to these latches, but also to data bus buffers (8286 or 8287), which buffer the data bus before going to the data inputs and outputs of memory and peripheral devices. You should also observe that some of the control signals are wired to these same devices.

As you might guess, a write cycle and read cycle should look pretty much the same. The only differences would be that the $\overline{WR}$ signal is generated rather than $\overline{RD}$, and that data is placed on the data bus by the CPU rather than by a memory or peripheral device. A typical 8086 write cycle is shown in Fig. 2-24.

In the two timing diagrams that you have seen (Fig. 2-22 and 2-24), all of the signals have been referenced to a signal called CLK.

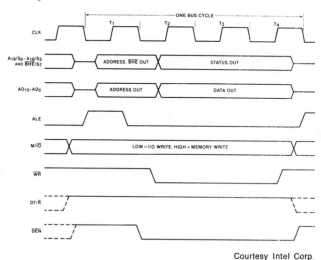

Courtesy Intel Corp.

Fig. 2-24. Typical write cycle for the 8086.

Where does this signal come from? In Fig. 2-23 you can see that the 8284 clock generator integrated circuit generates this signal, based on the frequency of the quartz crystal that is wired to it. For an 8086 the maximum crystal frequency is 15 MHz; for an 8086-2, 24 MHz; and for an 8086-4, 12 MHz. The 8284 clock chip divides these frequencies by 3, so the CLK signal has a frequency of 5 MHz, 8 MHz, or 4 MHz, respectively.

A diagram for a maximum-mode 8088-based system is shown in Fig. 2-25. Even though the 8088 only has an 8-bit bidirectional address/data bus, all 20 bits of the address still have to be latched off of the 8088 chip when ALE is a logic one. Since this is a maximum-mode system the memory and peripheral control signals are no longer generated by the 8088 chip directly (pins 24–31). Instead, an 8288 bus controller chip is required. The status signals ($\overline{S}_0$, $\overline{S}_1$, and $\overline{S}_2$) generated by the 8088 are decoded by the 8288, causing the appropriate memory and peripheral control signals ($\overline{MRDC}$, $\overline{MWTC}$, $\overline{IORC}$, $\overline{IOWC}$) to be generated by it.

MICROCOMPUTER BOARDS

Once you have decided which chip that you want to base your microcomputer on, your next decision is whether to design and build a microcomputer or to buy a kit or assembled microcomputer. Because these devices are relatively complex, many users will choose to buy a board or complete system that someone else has designed.

One of the least expensive and simplest 8086-based microcomput-

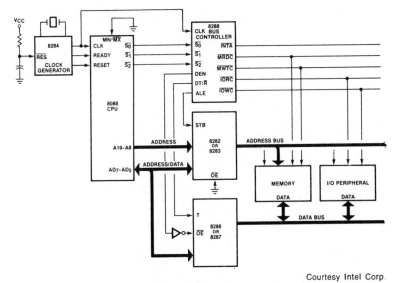

Fig. 2-25. A simple maximum-mode 8088 system.

ers to use is the Intel SDK-86 (Fig. 2-3). This microcomputer can contain up to 2K words of R/W memory and 4K words of EPROM. It also contains an asynchronous communications port, a keyboard and display, along with six 8-bit i/o ports.

The SBC 86/12A shown in Fig. 2-4 is designed to be plugged into a bus or motherboard system so that it can be easily used with additional memory and peripheral boards. The SBC 86/12A CPU board can contain up to 16K words of EPROM and 32K words of R/W memory (using piggyback expansion boards). This single-board microcomputer also contains two 16-bit interval timers that can be programmed by the user, nine vectored interrupts, power fail/interrupt circuitry, an asynchronous communications port, and three 8-bit i/o ports. We should note that the reason that this board is so complex is that a lot of logic is required to make it "bus compatible" with the other boards that can be plugged into a system. Dynamic R/W memory is also used on this board, so a dynamic R/W memory controller also had to be included on the board.

The SBC 86/12A generates Multibus-compatible signals, which means that it can be used with Multibus-compatible cards. Currently, a high-speed mathematics board, combination memory and i/o board, floppy disk interfaces (single and double density), memory boards, i/o boards, communications boards, analog converter boards along with different card cages, and power supplies are available. Floppy disks, hard disks, EPROM programmers, line printers, crt's and CPU chip emulators are also available.

Chart 2-2. Multibus-Compatible Board Manufacturers

Analog Converter Board (A/D, D/A, Mux)

Analog Devices, Inc.
Rt. 1 Industrial Park
P.O. Box 280
Norwood, MA 02062

Burr-Brown Research Corp.
International Airport Industrial Park
Tucson, AZ 85734

Data Translation, Inc.
4 Strathmore Rd.
Natick, MA 01760

Datel-Intersil
11 Cabot Blvd.
Mansfield, MA 02048

Memory Boards (R/W, EPROM)

National Semiconductor Corp.
2900 Semiconductor Dr.
Santa Clara, CA 95051

Electronic Solutions, Inc.
5780 Chesapeake Ct.
San Diego, CA 92123

Alewife Systems
26 Otis St.
Cambridge, MA 02141

Monolithic Systems Corp.
14 Inverness Dr. East
Englewood, CO 80112

Micro Memory, Inc.
9438 Irondale Ave.
Chatsworth, CA 91311

Godbout Electronics
725 Wright St.
Oakland Airport, CA 94614

Advanced Micro Devices, Inc.
901 Thompson Blvd.
Sunnyvale, CA 94086

Relational Memory Systems, Inc.
P.O. Box 6719
San Jose, CA 95150

Micro Memory, Inc.
9438 Irondale Ave.
Chatsworth, CA 91311
  (Core memory)

Central Data Corp.
P.O. Box 2530
Champaign, IL 61820
  (Disk controllers,
  Z8000 CPU boards)

Disk Controllers

NEC Microcomputers, Inc.
173 Worcester St.
Wellesley, MA 02181

Pertec Computer Corp.
12910 Culver Blvd.
Los Angeles, CA 90066

8086 CPU Cards

Systemathica Consulting Group
4732 Wallingford St.
Pittsburgh, PA 15213

TECMAR, Inc.
23414 Greenlawn
Cleveland, OH 44122

Miscellaneous

Vector Electronic Co., Inc.
12460 Gladstone Ave.
Sylmar, CA 91342
  (Prototype boards)

DOSC
OEM Products Division
175 I.U. Willets Rd.
Albertson, NY 11507
  (Video board)

Digital Pathways, Inc.
4151 Middlefield Rd.
Palo Alto, CA 94306
  (Calendar clocks)

Matrox Electronic Systems
Trimex Building
Mooers, NY 12958
  (Video, floppy disk)

Interphase Corp.
13667 Floyd Circle
Dallas, TX 75243
  (Floppy disk, hard disk, video)

A number of companies manufacture Multibus-compatible cards that can be used with the SBC 86/12A (Chart 2-2). Real-time clock, floppy disk, R/W memory, hard-wired front panel, EPROM programmer, stepper motor controller, and core memory boards, just to name a few, are available. Users should make sure that the boards are not only Multibus compatible, but also that they can be used with the SBC 86/12A. For those readers interested in the Z8001 and Z8002, there is even a CPU card that uses these CPU chips for a Multibus system. Other CPU cards based on the 8086 and 8088 will probably also be available for the S-100 and STD buses.

MICROCOMPUTER SOFTWARE

Currently, there are some programs that can be executed on an 8086-based microcomputer (Table 2-2). These include operating systems, editors, assemblers, linking loaders, and debuggers/system monitors. However, the largest amount of software for the 8086 is actually designed to be executed on an 8080- or 8085-based microcomputer. There are a number of operating systems, editors, and cross-assemblers that are used on an 8080-based microcomputer system *to prepare 8086 programs*. Once a program is prepared in this manner, either it can be down-line loaded to the 8086 microcomputer or EPROMs can be programmed.

In general, there is very little software for the 8086 compared with the amount of software available for the 8080 and 8085. This is also the case for the Z8001/2, 68000, and 16000. Most of the software for these microprocessors is actually prepared on 8-bit microcomputers. On the other hand, there is a large amount of software that can actually be executed on the 9900 and LSI-11. Of course, to use most of the development software for these microprocessors requires a lot of R/W memory and a disk or two.

BENCHMARKS

There are four tasks that were assigned to each processor: sorting numeric data, searching for ASCII strings, performing multiplication and division, and using lookup tables. The actual specifications for these benchmarks can be seen in the appendix.

Bubble Sort

The first benchmark that was executed on the SDK-86 (407-ns cycle time) can be seen in Fig. 2-26. At the start of the SORT program a number of registers have to be initialized with specific values. The AX register is loaded with 0100H, which is moved to the DS register. The BX register is then loaded with the base address of

Table 2-2. Software Sources for the 8086

Agent	Materials Available
Intel User's Library 3065 Bowers Avenue Santa Clara, CA 95051	Miscellaneous 8086 programs
Intel Corporation 3065 Bowers Avenue Santa Clara, CA 95051	Assembler, 8080/8085 to 8086/8088 converter, PL/M, linking loader
Industrial Programming, Inc. 9 Northern Blvd. Greenvale, NY 11548	Real-time operating system (MTOS-86) editor, macro-assembler, linking loader
Microsoft 10800 N.E. 8th Street Suite 819 Bellevue, WA 98004	Macro-assembler, linking loader, BASIC UNIX operating system*
The Boston Systems Office, Inc. 468 Moody Street Waltham, MA 02154	Cross assemblers
Hemenway Associates, Inc. 101 Tremont St. Boston, MA 02108	Real-time operating system, text editor
Forth, Inc. 2309 Pacific Coast Hwy. Hermosa Beach, CA 90254	PolyFORTH
MicroTec P.O. Box 60337 Sunnyvale, CA 94088	8086/8088 relocatable macro-assembler, linking loader (FORTRAN IV program that is run on minicomputers and larger)
Mark Williams Company 1430 W. Wrightwood Ave. Chicago, IL 60614	COHERENT operating system*, editor*, assembler*, cross-assembler*

*Currently not available, for future release.

some constants stored in memory, and the CX register is loaded with the content of memory addressed by BX + DS. Remember, the DS register can be thought of as being rotated to the left by 4 bits, before the addition takes place (Fig. 2-6). Therefore memory location 0170H is being addressed. The SI and DI registers are then loaded with indexes, DI eventually being 2 more than SI, since a 16-bit word uses two (1-byte) memory locations for storage. Finally, the DS register is loaded with a new segment number stored in memory, and the DL register is set to zero. This register will be tested at the end of the program to see if any exchanges took place.

Starting at NEXT, the 8086 reads a value from memory and compares it to the next value stored in memory. If the first value (SI) is less than the second value (DI), the 8086 jumps to OK, because the two numbers are in the proper order. If they are not in the

CS = 0000

```
0130   B81000     SORT:  MOV   AX,0010H    ;LOAD AX WITH 0010.
0133   8ED8              MOV   DS,AX       ;LOAD DS WITH CONTENT OF AX.
0135   BB7000            MOV   BX,0070H    ;LOAD BX WITH A BASE ADDRESS.
0138   8B0F       SORT1: MOV   CX,(BX)     ;LOAD COUNT FROM (BX+DS).
013A   8B7702            MOV   SI,(BX+02)  ;LOAD INDEX FROM (BX+DS+02).
013D   8BFE              MOV   DI,SI       ;LOAD DI WITH SAME VALUE.
013F   83C702            ADD   DI,02       ;ADD 02 TO CONTENT OF DI.
0142   8E5F04            MOV   DS,(BX+04)  ;LOAD DS FROM (BX+DS+04).
0145   B200              MOV   DL,00       ;SET EXCHANGE INDICATOR = 00.
0147   8B04       NEXT:  MOV   AX,(SI)     ;AX = (SI+DS).
0149   3B05              CMP   AX,(DI)     ;AX GREATER THAN (DI+DS) ?
014B   7606              JBE   OK          ;NO, SO JUMP TO "OK."
014D   B2FF              MOV   DL,FF       ;YES, SET EXCHANGE INDICATOR.
014F   8705              XCHG  AX,(DI)     ;EXCHANGE AX AND (DI+DS).
0151   8704              XCHG  AX,(SI)     ;EXCHANGE AX AND (SI+DS).
0153   8BF7       OK:    MOV   SI,DI       ;LOAD SI WITH DI.
0155   47                INC   DI          ;INCREMENT DI TO THE NEXT
0156   47                INC   DI          ;VALUE IN THE LIST.
0157   E2EE              LOOP  NEXT        ;"LOOP" IF CX NON-ZERO.
0159   80FAFF            CMP   DL,FF       ;DONE LIST ONCE, ANY EXCHANGES ?
015C   74DA              JZ    SORT1       ;YES, EXAMINE THE ENTIRE
015E   F4                HLT               ;LIST AGAIN.



0170   5802                                ;NUMBER OF 16-BIT WORDS (DECIMAL 600 = 0258H)
0172   0002                                ;SOURCE INDEX VALUE (0200H)
0174   1000                                ;DATA SEGMENT VALUE (0010H)



0300   .                       .           ;THE VALUES TO BE SORTED ARE
0302   .                       .           :STORED HERE IN MEMORY.
```

Fig. 2-26. An exchange (bubble sort) program for the 8086.

proper order, the exchange indicator (DL) is set to FFH, and the two values are exchanged.

If an exchange took place, the content of DI is moved to SI at OK and then the content of DI is incremented by 2, so that it can be used to address the next value in memory. The LOOP NEXT instruction decrements the content of the CX register, and, if the result is nonzero, the 8086 jumps back to NEXT. Once the CX register has been decremented to zero, the 8086 checks the content of the DL register to see if any exchanges took place. If at least one exchange did take place, the 8086 has to examine the entire list of values again. If no exchanges took place, then the list is sorted, so the 8086 executes the halt (HLT) instruction. On the SDK-86 (which uses an 8086-4), this benchmark required 13.949 s to sort 600 words of data. The time required to execute this program on a 125-ns 8086 was calculated as being 2.104 s.

One problem that all of the authors were faced with was how to initialize memory with the data values specified by the benchmark

CS=0000

```
010A  B81000            MOV   AX,0010H   ;AX = DATA SEGMENT VALUE.
010D  8ED8              MOV   DS,AX      ;LOAD DS WITH AX.
010F  B95802            MOV   CX,0258H   ;LOAD CX WITH THE COUNT.
0112  BE0002            MOV   SI,0200H   ;LOAD SI WITH THE INDEX.
0115  890C     FILLUP:  MOV   (SI),CX    ;SAVE CX IN MEMORY.
0117  46                INC   SI         ;INCREMENT THE INDEX.
0118  46                INC   SI         ;INCREMENT THE INDEX.
0119  E2FA              LOOP  FILLUP     ;"LOOP" BACK TO "FILLUP."
011B  890C              MOV   (SI),CX    ;SAVE THE LAST VALUE.
011D  F4                HLT              ;THEN HALT.
```

Fig. 2-27. Filling memory with values for the bubble sort program.

(appendix). This was easily done with a short assembly language program (Fig. 2-27). In this program the DS register was loaded with the segment value (0010H) and the SI register was loaded with the offset (0200H). The memory address generated by "adding" these two values would be 0300H. The CX register was loaded with 0258H, or 600_{10}. Starting at FILLUP, the count in CX was stored in the memory location addressed by SI and DS. The index was then incremented (INC SI, INC SI) and the 8086 looped back to FILLUP until the CX register was finally decremented to zero by this instruction. The 600th value was then saved in memory by the MOV (SI),CX instruction and then the 8086 halted.

The goal of this program was to save the worst-case arrangement of data values in memory, so that the bubble sort program would require the greatest amount of time to sort the values. For the SDK-86 (8086-4) this program required 9.530 ms. On a faster 8086, only 2.926 ms would be required (calculated).

ASCII String Search Benchmark

This benchmark tests the ability of the microprocessor to compare strings of characters that are stored in memory. The 8086 program that does this is listed in Fig. 2-28. The 8086-4 required 767 μs to find the MICRO* string at the end of the main string. On a faster 8086 system, only 235 μs would have been required.

In this program a number of pointers have to be established. The DS and ES registers are loaded with segment numbers, and DI and SI are loaded with indexes. Just after NEWT the AL register is loaded with 3FH, the value for an ASCII question mark (?). If the 8086 is addressing this character in the main string, then it has searched the entire string, without finding a match; thus it jumps to DONE. If no question mark is found, a test string character is moved to the AL register [MOV AL,(SI)], where it is compared with a main string character [CMP AL,(DI)]. If the characters are not equal, the 8086 has to find the beginning of the next string by looking for the asterisk (*) character and then incrementing an index so that it addresses the

CS = 0000

```
010A    FC                      CLD                 ;DIRECTION FLAG = INCREMENT.
010B    B82000                  MOV     AX,0020H    ;GET THE DS AND ES VALUE.
010E    8ED8                    MOV     DS,AX       ;SAVE THE VALUE IN DS.
0110    8EC0                    MOV     ES,AX       ;SAVE THE SAME VALUE IN ES.
0112    C7C30000                MOV     BX,0000     ;SET THE BASE REGISTER TO ZERO.
0116    8B3F                    MOV     DI,(BX)     ;GET DI FROM (BX+DS).
0118    8B7702      NEWT:       MOV     SI,(BX+02)  ;GET SI FROM (BX+DS+02).
011B    C7C1FFFF                MOV     CX,FFFFH    ;LOAD CX WITH FFFFH (FOR STRING OPS).
011F    B03F                    MOV     AL,3FH      ;AT END OF MAIN STRING?
0121    3A05                    CMP     AL,(DI)     ;COMPARE 3FH TO STRING VALUE.
0123    7419                    JZ      DONE        ;VALUES ARE =, WE'RE DONE.
0125    8A04                    MOV     AL,(SI)     ;GET A TEST STRING CHARACTER.
0127    3A05                    CMP     AL,(DI)     ;COMPARE IT TO A MAIN STRING CHAR.
0129    7406                    JZ      ONEOK       ;THEY MATCH, TRY THE NEXT 2
012B    B02A        END:        MOV     AL,2AH      ;NO MATCH, GET AN ASCII *.
012D    F2                      REPNE               ;REPEAT STRING "PREFIX"
012E    AE                      SCAS                ;REPEAT UNTIL THE * IS FOUND.
012F    EBE7                    JMP     NEWT        ;TRY FOR A MATCH AGAIN.
0131    46          ONEOK:      INC     SI          ;MATCH OK, INCREMENT POINTERS.
0132    47                      INC     DI
0133    B90600                  MOV     CX,0006H    ;LOAD CX WITH A COUNT.
0136    F3                      REPE                ;REPEAT AS LONG AS EQUAL.
0137    A6                      CMPS                ;COMPARE STRINGS.
0138    81F90000                CMP     CX,0000H    ;CX = 0 ?
013C    C7C1FFFF                MOV     CX,FFFFH    ;CX = FFFFH
0140    75E9                    JNZ     END         ;IF CX NOT ZERO, FIND NEXT STR.
0142                DONE:          .                ;ADDITIONAL INSTRUCTIONS
                                   .                ;ARE STORED HERE.
                                   .


0200    0003                        ;DESTINATION INDEX VALUE (0300H)
0202    0001                        ;SOURCE INDEX VALUE (0100H)


0300    4D4943524F2A                ;TEST STRING (MICRO*)


        ;MAIN STRING FOLLOWS
0500    4E414E4F2A              ;NANO*
0505    5049434F2A              ;PICO*
050A    4D4943524F434F          ;MICROCOMPUTER*
0511    4D50555445522A
0518    4D4943524F5052          ;MICROPROCESSOR*
051F    4F434553534F5F52
0526    2A
0527    4D4943524F5359          ;MICROSYSTEM*
052E    5354454D2A
0533    4D4943524F2A            ;MICRO*
0539    3F                      ;?
```

Fig. 2-28. Searching for ASCII strings with the 8086.

first character in the next string (or, possibly, the ? after the last *). The 8086 REPNE and SCAS string instructions are used to find the first character in the next string after the *.

If the first characters in the test and main strings are equal, the 8086 jumps to ONEOK, so that the remaining characters in the strings can be compared. Since there are five remaining characters to be compared (I,R,C,O, and *), the count in the CX register for the repeat string (REPE) instruction has to be set to one more (6). The strings are then compared until they are no longer equal or the count has been decremented to zero. If the count has been decremented to zero, then all of the characters in the strings matched, including the asterisk at the end of the string. If not all characters matched, the 8086 executes the CMP CX,0000 instruction as soon as the strings no longer match. Since the CX register would not be decremented to zero if this occurs, the 8086 jumps back to END so that the end of the string in the main string can be found. The 8086 can then compare the next string in the main string (if one exists) to the test string.

The memory locations that were used to store the indexes, main string and test string can also be seen in Fig. 2-28. *The only restriction on this 8086 benchmark and all of the other 8086 benchmarks is the fact that all of the "data" must be addressable using the same segment value.* Therefore they can only be used with lists or strings that require less than 65K bytes (32K words) of storage.

Square Root Determination

The square root calculation gives us the ability to judge the microprocessor's speed when it comes to multiplication and division. The 8086 program that uses the successive approximation technique for this determination is listed in Fig. 2-29.

Unlike the bubble sort and ASCII string search programs, the square root program does not have to access large amounts of data in memory. In fact, only three 16-bit memory locations are required for temporary storage. At the beginning of the SROOT program the DX register is loaded with zero, because it is one of the operands in the division (DIV) instruction. It represents the 16 msb's in a 32-bit number. The BX register is loaded with a base address and then the DS register (via the AX register) is loaded with the data segment value (0010H). Using base addressing, the AX register is then loaded with the number whose root is to be determined. The initial approximation is then calculated by dividing this number by 200_{10} (which is stored in memory location 0302H) and then adding 2 to this result.

At LOOP, this initial approximation is saved in memory. The 8086 then multiplies this number by itself [MUL AX,(BX+02)], to see if the approximation is really the square root. If it is, the 8086 will jump to DONE after comparing the result of the multiplication to the original number.

If the numbers are not equal, the 8086 gets the original number, divides it by the approximation, and adds the initial approximation to this result. This new value is then divided by 2 by shifting the result once to the right. The 8086 then jumps back to LOOP to con-

```
CS = 0000

010A  C7C20000  SROOT: MOV  DX,0000H    ;DX = 0 FOR DIVISION INSTR.
010E  BB0402          MOV  BX,0204H    ;BASE ADDRESS OF NUMBERS.
0111  B81000          MOV  AX,0010H    ;VALUE FOR THE DS REGISTER.
0114  8ED8            MOV  DS,AX       ;MOVE TO DS FROM AX.
0116  8B07            MOV  AX,(BX)     ;GET THE ORIGINIAL NUMBER.
0118  F777FE          DIV  AX,(BX-02)  ;DIVIDE BY 200 (DECIMAL).
011B  050200          ADD  AX,0002H    ;ADD 2 TO THE RESULT.
011E  894702   LOOP:  MOV  (BX+02),AX  ;SAVE APPROXIMATION IN MEMORY.
0121  F76702          MUL  AX,(BX+02)  ;MULT. APPROX. BY ITSELF.
0124  3B07            CMP  AX,(BX)     ;RESULT = ORIGINIAL NUMBER ?
0126  7410            JZ   DONE        ;YES, THEN THE 8086 IS DONE.
0128  8B07            MOV  AX,(BX)     ;NO, GET ORIGINAL NUMBER.
012A  C7C20000        MOV  DX,0000H    ;SET DX = 0 FOR DIVISION.
012E  F77702          DIV  AX,(BX+02)  ;DIVIDE ORIG. BY APPROXIMATION.
0131  034702          ADD  AX,(BX+02)  ;ADD APPROX. TO RESULT.
0134  D1E8            SHR              ;DIVIDE RESULT BY TWO.
0136  EBE6            JMP  LOOP        ;JUMP AND SAVE NEW APPROX.
0138           DONE:       .          ;ADDITIONAL INSTRUCTIONS
                            .          ;CAN BE STORED HERE.
                            .


0302  C800                             ;DECIMAL 200 OR HEX 00C8.
0304  0000                             ;NUMBER WHOSE ROOT IS TO BE DETERMINED.
0306  0000                             ;SQUARE ROOT OF NUMBER IS STORED HERE.
```

Fig. 2-29. Calculating the square root of a number using the 8086.

tinue the approximation process. Only when the approximation, when multiplied by itself, equals the original number, will the 8086 jump to DONE.

Three numbers were used in this benchmark, with one number (10,000) requiring 637 μs. The other two numbers (16,384 and 58,081) required less processing time (480 μs). On a faster 8086-based microprocessor system, only 195 μs and 147 μs would be required, respectively.

Lookup Table Benchmark

The last benchmark requires the use of a lookup table to determine the sine of an integer angle between 0 and 360 degrees, using a lookup table that contains the sines of angles between 0 and 90 degrees. This means that all angles between 0 and 360 degrees have to be reduced to angles between 0 and 90 degrees.

To perform this benchmark (Fig. 2-30) the 8086-4 required between 36 and 43 μs, depending on the angle being used. With a faster 8086, only between 11 and 13 μs would be required. The calculations involved in this "angle reduction" process have been described in the appendix. These calculations simply involve subtracting 180 or 90 degrees from the angle, or subtracting the angle from 90

```
CS = 0000

010A    8BD0      SINE:     MOV   DX,AX        ;SAVE THE ANGLE IN DX.
010C    B90000              MOV   CX,0000H     ;CX WILL HOLD THE SIGN BIT.
010F    B82000              MOV   AX,0020H     ;GET THE DS VALUE INTO AX.
0112    8ED8                MOV   DS,AX        ;MOVE AX TO DS.
0114    8BC2                MOV   AX,DX        ;GET THE ANGLE BACK IN AX
0116    81E8B400  S180:     SUB   AX,180       ;SUBTRACT 00B4 (180) FROM AX.
011A    7607                JBE   PSIGN        ;JUMP IF ANGLE ≤ 180 DEGREES.
011C    8BD0                MOV   DX,AX        ;SAVE SUBTRACTION RESULT.
011E    B90080              MOV   CX,8000H     ;SET THE SIGN BIT TO A ONE.
0121    EB02                JMP   SKIP         ;JUMP TO SKIP, ANGLE ≥ 180.
0123    8BC2      PSIGN:    MOV   AX,DX        ;GET THE ORIGINAL ANGLE.
0125    BB5A00    SKIP:     MOV   BX,005AH     ;LOAD BX WITH DECIMAL 90.
0128    2BC3                SUB   AX,BX        ;SUBTRACT 90 FROM AX.
012A    7604                JBE   OKASIS       ;JUMP IF ANGLE ≤ 90 DEGREES.
012C    2BD8                SUB   BX,AX        ;NO, SUBTRACT AX FROM BX
012E    EB02                JMP   CALCIT       ;RESULT IS IN BX.
0130    8BDA      OKASIS:   MOV   BX,DX        ;GET ANGLE INTO BX
0132    D1E3      CALCIT:   SHL   BX,1         ;SHIFT BX ONE TO THE LEFT.
0134    8B07                MOV   AX,(BX)      ;GET THE SINE FROM THE TABLE.
0136    03C1                ADD   AX,CX        ;ADD THE SIGN BIT TO THE SINE.
0138    81F80080            CMP   AX,8000H     ;RESULT = -0 ?
013C    7503                JNE   END          ;NO, RESULT IS OK.
013E    B80000              MOV   AX,0000H     ;YES, SET IT TO +0.
0141              END:        .              ;ADDITIONAL INSTRUCTIONS
                              .              ;MAY BE STORED HERE.
                              .


0200    0000      TABLE:    0000             ;SINE OF ZERO DEGREES
0202    023B                023B             ;SINE OF ONE DEGREE
0204    0477                0477             ;SINE OF TWO DEGREES
  .       .                   .              ;THE REMAINDER OF THE TABLE
  .       .                   .              ;IS STORED HERE.
```

Fig. 2-30. Calculating the sine of an angle with a lookup table.

degrees. Once these calculations have been performed, the 8086 actually "looks up" the angle just past CALCIT (Fig. 2-30). The MOV AX,(BX) instruction reads the sine value from the table, and then the ADD AX,CX instruction adds the sign bit to the sine value. If the result of this addition is a negative zero, the 8086 converts it to a positive zero (0000H). Note that this subroutine determines the sign and magnitude of the sine, not the twos complement. The 8086's performance in executing all of these benchmarks is shown below in Table 2-3.

Table 2-3. Execution Times for the 8086 Benchmarks

Benchmark	8086-4 (SDK-86)	8086 (8 MHz)
Bubble sort	13.949 s	2.104 s
Memory initialization	9.530 ms	2.926 ms
ASCII string search	767 μs	235 μs
Square Root	637/480 μs	195/147 μs
Lookup table	36/43 μs	11/13 μs

INTERFACING

In order for the 8086 to communicate with peripheral devices, the peripheral must somehow be wired to the microcomputer's data and address buses, as well as being wired to some of the microprocessor's control signals. Once this is done, the 8086 can communicate with the i/o device using either *accumulator i/o* or *memory-mapped i/o*. The hardware interfaces for these two different techniques are very similar; the real differences come about when the software for these two methods is discussed.

In accumulator i/o the 8086 can communicate with up to 65K eight-bit devices. In order to actually transfer data between one of these devices and the 8086, the CPU has to execute either an IN or OUT instruction. There are two different types of these instructions. One type has the address of the peripheral device fixed in the instruction, much like an immediate data byte. This type of instruction can only be used to address the first 256 accumulator i/o devices, starting at zero. This is the same type of i/o instruction, but different op code, that the 8080 and 8085 have. The other method uses the content of the DX register as the device address, thus gaining the ability to address 65K devices. Regardless of the type of IN or OUT instruction used, the AX register of the CPU will either transmit (output) data to the peripheral or receive data (input) from the peripheral. Thus the name: accumulator i/o.

In an accumulator i/o peripheral interface, the 16-bit device address would be present on AD0 through AD15. These address signals, along with $\overline{RD}$, $\overline{WR}$, and M/$\overline{IO}$ (IO/$\overline{M}$ in the case of the 8088), would then be gated together and the resulting logic 1 or logic 0 pulse would be used to actually gate information off of, or to gate information onto, the data bus.

As you can imagine, the AX register can become the bottleneck in i/o-intensive situations, simply because data would have to be moved from memory to it, to be output, or it would have to be moved from AX to memory, after being input. One solution to this problem is to use memory-mapped i/o. In this type of i/o the microprocessor assumes that it is communicating with a memory location, when in fact it is communicating with a peripheral device. As you might guess, this means that control signals $\overline{RD}$ and $\overline{WR}$ are used along with M/$\overline{IO}$ signal (when it is in the logic one state). Also, the complete 20-bit address bus and 16-bit data bus would have to be used in the interface design. The only advantage in using memory-mapped i/o is the fact that *any* 8086 instruction that references a memory location can now be used to communicate with a properly designed memory-mapped i/o peripheral device. Thus we no longer have a bottleneck in the AX register. Two disadvantages of memory-mapped

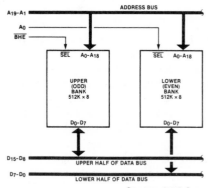

Fig. 2-31. Organizing and addressing 1M byte of memory as 512K words.

i/o are the facts that it uses up some of the address space normally reserved for memory, and it is slower than accumulator i/o, simply because of the time required to calculate 20-bit memory addresses. Of course, since the 8086 can address 1M byte of memory, it is not very likely that you will run out of memory address space.

Before the actual interfaces can be described for these interfacing techniques, the organization of the microprocessor's memory should be examined. This will demonstrate how 8- and 16-bit values are transferred between the CPU and memory.

The 8086 can address 1M byte or 512K words of memory. All memory that is wired to the microcomputer must be 16 bits wide, which means that the 8086 can selectively address either the *lower 8-bit byte* at an *even memory address* or the *upper 8-bit byte* at an *odd memory address*. The odd/even organization of memory can be seen in Fig. 2-31. As you can see, the $\overline{BHE}$ (bus high enable) signal and A0 are used to control the "bank selection." Since these signals can assume one of two possible values, there are four possible combinations of these signals that the 8086 can generate (Table 2-4).

From Table 2-4 you can see that either an 8- or 16-bit value can be transferred between memory and the CPU. If an 8-bit byte is

Table 2-4. Using $\overline{BHE}$ and A0 to Select Either Bytes or Words

$\overline{BHE}$	A0	Operation
0	0	Transfer a 16-bit word
0	1	Transfer the upper byte (odd address)
1	0	Transfer the lower byte (even address)
1	1	No transfer

transferred, it will either be the upper (odd) byte, or lower (even) byte. For a 16-bit value an even address should be used. It is possible for the 8086 to address words that start at odd bytes, but the CPU requires more time, typically 4 clock cycles, to perform this type of transfer. The 8086 also uses the same combination of signals ($\overline{\text{BHE}}$ and A0) to address peripherals, thus possessing the ability to transfer bytes or words.

A typical accumulator i/o interface that uses some 8255 programmable peripheral interface (PPI) chips is shown in Fig. 2-32. Each of the PPI chips contains four 8-bit ports, three of which are general purpose. The fourth port is a *control port* and is programmed by the user, with software, to determine which of the remaining three ports will be input or output ports. It is interesting to note how the $\overline{\text{BHE}}$, A0, and $\text{M}/\overline{\text{IO}}$ signals are used to enable the 8205 decoders. The

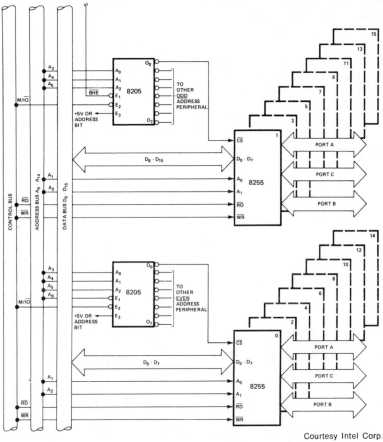

Courtesy Intel Corp.

Fig. 2-32. An accumulator i/o interface using PPI chips.

logic zero outputs of these decoders are used to enable, or select, one of the many possible 8255 chips. Based on the combination of these three signals, the outputs of the 8205 decoders are characterized as being either for even- or odd-address peripherals. In order to transfer a byte of information to the 8255 wired to the *odd decoder,* which address(es) would have to be used?

An i/o address of 0001, 0003, 0005, or 0007 could be used. Any of these addresses could be used, since the 8255s contain four ports. For the "even" PPI chip, addresses 0000, 0002, 0004, and 0006 could be used. Note that even though these i/o ports have the same addresses as some memory chips in the system, there is no conflict between the ports and memory trying to use the data bus at the same time. Remember, memory is only selected when $M/\overline{IO}$ is a logic one, and accumulator i/o devices are only selected when $M/\overline{IO}$ is a logic zero. This is why $M/\overline{IO}$ is wired to the 8205 decoder; the decoder will only function when $M/\overline{IO}$ is a logic zero.

Since the 8255 is an 8-bit (byte) device, all of its ports will have either an even or odd address. This means that only *bytes* can be transferred between a single PPI chip and the CPU. In order to transfer words two devices must be used, as shown in Fig. 2-32, rather than two ports within the same chip.

I/O SOFTWARE

Some simple i/o software examples are listed in Figs. 2-33, 2-34, and 2-35. In Fig. 2-33, the DX register is loaded with the address of

```
CS=0000


0106   BA0600       MOV DX,06H       ;LOAD DX REG. WITH 6.
0109   B88080       MOV AX,8080H     ;VAL. TO INIT. 8255s.
010C   EF           OUT DX,AX        ;OUTPUT AX USING DX AS AN
                      .              ;ADDRESS.  EXECUTE
                      .              :REMAINING INSTRUCTIONS.
                      .
020F   8B00         MOV AX,(BX+SI)   ;GET MEMORY TO AX.
0211   E704         OUT 04H,AX       ;OUTPUT TO PORT.
                      .              :EXECUTE REMAINDER OF
                      .              :PROGRAM.
                      .
```

Fig. 2-33. Writing a 16-bit word for an output port.

the two control ports in the two PPI chips. The AX register is then loaded with 8080H, which will eventually cause both PPI chips to operate in the same manner, when this value is output to the control ports. The value is output by the OUT DX,AX instruction. At some later point in the program the AX register is loaded with the

CS=0000

```
23AA   E704      LOOP:   OUT  O4H,AX      ;OUTPUT AX TO PORT 4.
23AC   40                INC  AX          ;INCREMENT 16-BIT AX.
23AD   FBFB              JMP  LOOP        ;THEN DO IT AGAIN.
```

Fig. 2-34. Incrementing register AX and writing the result to an output port.

content of memory addressed by the sum of **DS**, **BX** and **SI** (Fig. 2-6), which is then output to port 0004H.

In Fig. 2-34 the content of the AX register is output to port 0004H, the port number actually being specified as an "immediate" byte in the instruction. The content of the AX register (16 bits) is then incremented by 1, and then the 8086 jumps back, using a relative jump instruction, to the OUT instruction.

CS=0000

```
0200   B82000    IN35:   MOV  AX,0020H    ;LOAD AX WITH 0020H.
0203   8ED8              MOV  DS,AX       ;LOAD DS WITH AX VALUE.
0205   B92300            MOV  CX,0023H    ;LOAD CX WITH THE COUNT.
0208   BB0002            MOV  BX,0200H    ;LOAD BX WITH A BASE ADDRESS.
020B   E502      WAIT:   IN   AX,02H      ;LOAD AX WITH PORT 0002H.
020D   250100            AND  AX,01H      ;AND AX WITH IMMEDIATE BYTE.
0210   75F9              JNZ  LOOP        ;WAIT FOR BIT TO BE ZERO.
0212   E504              IN   AX,04H      ;LOAD AX WITH DATA FROM PORT.
0214   89C7              MOV  (BX),AX     ;SAVE AX IN (DS+BX).
0216   43                INC  BX          ;INCREMENT BX BY ONE.
0217   43                INC  BX          ;AND THEN BY ANOTHER.
0218   E2F1              LOOP WAIT        ;GO TO "LOOP" IF CX NOT ZERO.
021A   F4                HLT              ;STOP WHEN DONE.
```

Fig. 2-35. Reading data from an input port and storing it in memory.

The most complex i/o program is contained in Fig. 2-35. In this example, 35 sixteen-bit data values have to be input from a peripheral and stored in memory. Therefore a number of registers have to be initialized before data can be input and stored in memory. Since there are no immediate instructions that can be used to load the segment registers directly, the AX register is loaded with a value, which is then moved to the DS register. The CX register is loaded with 0023H, because this is the count ($023H = 35_{10}$); the number of data values to be input and stored. The BX register is loaded with 0200H, because base addressing will be used (no indexes or displacements). At WAIT the 8086 inputs a word and logically ANDs it with 0001H. If the result is nonzero, the 8086 jumps back to WAIT. If the result is zero, the 8086 loads the AX register with the content of the input port and stores this value in the memory location addressed by BX + DS (Fig. 2-6). The content of the BX register is then incremented by 2 so that the next *word* of memory can be addressed. The LOOP instruction causes the content of the CX register to be decremented by 1. If the result of this operation is nonzero, the 8086 jumps back to WAIT. Once all 35_{10} data values have been acquired and stored in memory, the 8086 will have decremented CX to zero, so the 8086 does not jump back to WAIT, but instead executes the HLT instruction, causing the processor to halt.

MEMORY-MAPPED I/O

A simple memory-mapped i/o interface that uses PPI chips is shown in Fig. 2-36. In this interface additional bits of the address bus are used by the decoders (A10 through A14). This means that the addresses shown in Fig. 2-37 have to be used to access these i/o

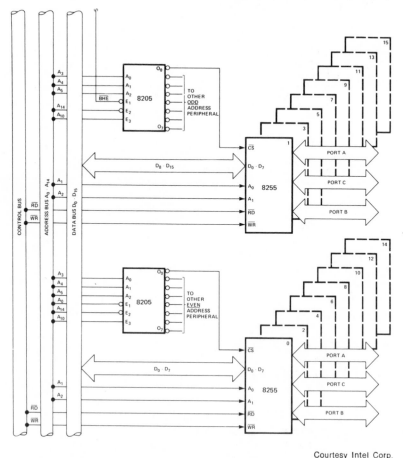

Courtesy Intel Corp.

Fig. 2-36. Using PPI chips in a memory-mapped i/o interface.

MEMORY MAP		TYPICAL PORT SELECTION			

MEMORY MAP

BOOTSTRAP	(F)FFFFH
	(F)FFF0H
USER ROM AND RAM	
	(F)C000H
	(0)043FH
MEMORY MAPPED I/O	
	(0)0400H
INTERRUPT VECTOR TABLE	
	(0)0000H

TYPICAL PORT SELECTION

PORT	DEVICE	ADDRESS (8-bit data)	
A	0	00400H	EVEN ADDRESS
B	0	00402H	
C	0	00404H	
CONTROL	0	00406H	
A	1	00401H	ODD ADDRESS
B	1	00403H	
C	1	00405H	
CONTROL	1	00407H	

Courtesy Intel Corp.

Fig. 2-37. Memory-mapped i/o addresses for the PPI chips.

ports. Of course, when data is being transferred between this interface and the CPU, the $M/\overline{IO}$ control signal will be a logic one.

Surprisingly enough, you have already seen the timing relationships of i/o transfer operations. These can be seen in Figs. 2-22 and 2-24. The only difference between a memory and i/o "cycle" is the state of the $M/\overline{IO}$ signal. NOTE: The Intel Corporation has reserved accumulator i/o locations 00F8H through 00FFH for its own use.

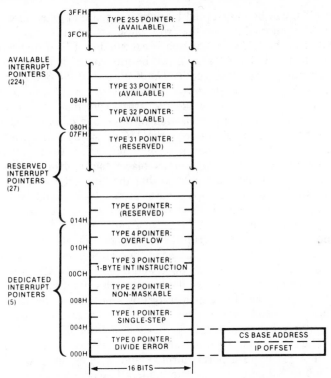

Courtesy Intel Corp.

Fig. 2-38. A typical interrupt pointer or lookup table.

Avoid using these i/o addresses (see Fig. 2-38) if you want your microcomputer to be compatible with Intel products (software and hardware).

8088 INPUT/OUTPUT

In the 8088, interface design is a little simpler than in the 8086, because the microprocessor only has an 8-bit bidirectional data bus. A 16-bit or 20-bit address still has to be decoded (accumulator i/o or memory-mapped i/o), but only one PPI chip would be needed to input or output a single 16-bit value. In fact, small, low-cost systems can be built using the 8088 and many of the specialized chips designed for the 8085, since both of these processors multiplex the data bus with the low 8 bits of the address bus. Therefore it is possible to design four- and five-chip microcomputers with the 8088.

INTERRUPTS

The 8086 can be interrupted by both internal and external events. Some of the internal events that will cause an interrupt are (1) an overflow and the INTO instruction is executed or (2) if division-by-zero is attempted. The 8086 *will not* be interrupted if it executes an illegal or unimplemented op code. *The flag word of the 8086 can also be modified so that the processor is interrupted every time a single instruction is executed. Thus the processor, with a small amount of software, can be made to single-step through a program.* The 8086 will also be "interrupted" if one of the 256 possible interrupt instructions is executed. In this case the term "interrupt" is really not being used correctly, since the programmer places the interrupt instruction in the program at specific points so that the "interrupt" service subroutines are executed. Perhaps a more proper term would be to call these instructions "vector instructions" or one-word call instructions.

For external events the INTR (interrupt), NMI (nonmaskable interrupt), and $\overline{\text{INTA}}$ (interrupt acknowledge) signals are used. The INTR and $\overline{\text{INTA}}$ pins have the same operational properties as the INT(R) and $\overline{\text{INTA}}$ pins of the 8080 and 8085. The NMI pin is often wired to devices that can signal a catastrophic failure, such as the loss of power or the failure of memory or a peripheral device. When this occurs the 8086 will always fetch a code segment and instruction pointer value from memory, starting at 00008H, and then use these values to begin executing an interrupt service subroutine. The INTR input is more general purpose and is often used with crt's, disks, and real-time clocks, just to name a few possible devices. This input is often wired to an *interrupt controller* chip so that up to 256 peripherals can use this one interrupt input.

One nice feature of the INTR input is the fact that it can be disabled by a software instruction, so that if the processor has to perform a task where it must not be interrupted by external devices, it can. The instruction that disables the INTR interrupt input is CLI. The STI instruction enables the INTR interrupt input. *These instructions do not effect the operation of the NMI interrupt input, nor do they prevent a single-step, overflow, or division-by-zero interrupt from occurring.* Of course, the overflow interrupt only occurs if the INTO instruction is executed. Likewise, one of the 256 interrupt instructions can still be executed in a program, even with the interrupt disabled. Thus the SLI and CLI instructions can only be used to enable and disable the INTR interrupt input.

If the interrupt is enabled and a peripheral takes the INTR line to a logic one, the 8086 will finish executing the current instruction and will then generate two pulses on the $\overline{\text{INTA}}$ pin. The second time that the $\overline{\text{INTA}}$ pulse is generated, external hardware places a binary number between 0 and 256 on the 8 low bits of the data bus. This number is used by the 8086 to look up a code segment and an instruction pointer value that is stored in the interrupt pointer table, contained within the first 1K of memory (Fig. 2-39).

In reality, the 8086 can be interrupted even if it has not completed executing an instruction. This, however, really doesn't matter to the user, as long as the 8086 saves enough information when the interrupt occurs so that once it has finished servicing the interrupt it can properly continue executing the task that it was executing when the interrupt occurred.

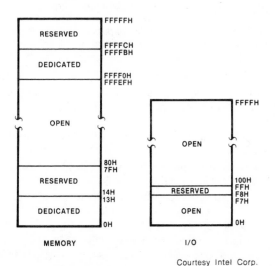

Courtesy Intel Corp.

Fig. 2-39. Reserved and dedicated i/o and memory locations.

Of course, it is not very practical to have peripherals *use* the first five pointers, since these are dedicated to internal interrupts (divide-by-zero, overflow, single-step, NMI, and a special interrupt instruction). Also, the Intel Corporation has reserved all remaining pointers up to pointer 32 for their own hardware products (Fig. 2-39).

At the same time, if you are using interrupt instructions in a program, rather than call instructions, these "interrupts" should not be assigned to peripheral hardware devices. The microprocessor would not be able to distinguish between an instruction being executed in a program and an interrupt pointer generated externally. All of the timing problems and constraints of interrupts can not be discussed in this book. Therefore, readers are referred to *8080/8085 Software Design, Book 2*.[2] Although this book deals with the 8080 and 8085, interrupts are processed in much the same manner as with the 8086.

SPECIAL-FUNCTION CHIPS

Since the 8086 and 8088 are new processors, Intel designed a number of new, special-function chips that can be used to increase the performance or flexibility of an 8086- or 8088-based microcomputer system. These chips are summarized in Table 2-5.

Table 2-5. Specialized 8086 and 8088 Support Chips

Name	Function
8282/8283	8-bit latch/buffer
8284	Clock generator and driver
8286/8287	8-bit bidirectional buffer/driver
8089	I/O processor
8289	Bus arbitrator
8288	Bus controller

Since the 8086 and 8088 have a lot in common with the 8085 and 8080, a number of the special chips that were designed for these processors can also be used with the 8086 and 8088. These chips are summarized in Table 2-6.

The 8282/8283 chips (Table 2-5) were designed to latch the address off of the address/data bus when ALE is a logic one. The outputs of these devices would normally be wired to the address inputs of memory and peripheral chips. These chips also increase the drive capability of the 8086 and 8088, with up to 32 mA of sink current and −5 mA of source current available.

The 8284 clock generator and driver chip clocks the 8086 at one-third of the quartz crystal frequency. This chip also contains some Multibus logic and also logic so that memory and peripheral devices with long access times can be used with the 8086.

The 8286/8287 eight-bit bidirectional buffer/drivers are used to increase the drive capabilities of the data bus of the microprocessor. Like the 8282/8283 these chips can sink 32 mA and source −5 mA of current.

The most complex chip of this group is the 8089 i/o processor (IOP). From the pinout of this device (Fig. 2-40) you can see that this processor is very similar to the 8086 and 8088. In fact, the 8089 is a microprocessor, having its own memory and peripheral devices. This device is designed to be used with 8086 and 8088 processors so that the 8086 and 8088 do not spend a lot of their time communicating with peripheral devices. Instead, the 8086 and 8088 spend most of their time performing calculations and only occasionally communicate with the IOP. On the other hand, the IOP spends most of its time communicating with peripherals. The IOP blocks, reduces, corrects, and alters data from peripherals, and then transfers this information to the CPU using direct memory access (DMA) techniques. Thus the 8086 or 8088 spends very little time communicating with peripherals, one of the slowest tasks possible.

The 8289 bus arbitrator chip was designed to be used in multiple-CPU environments. Since there is only one data and address bus, the bus arbitrator determines which of the CPUs can access these buses. If one of the CPUs has a "higher priority" than another CPU, it will gain access to the buses first.

Fig. 2-40. The pinout of the 8089 input/output processor (IOP).

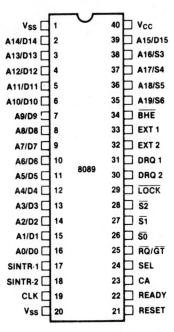

Courtesy Intel Corp.

The 8288 bus controller chip is required only in maximum-mode systems. This device uses the processor status outputs of the CPU chip (8086 or 8088; $\overline{S_0}$, $\overline{S_1}$, and $\overline{S_2}$), and generates the appropriate memory and i/o control signals.

The peripheral chips that were designed for the 8080 and 8085 can also be used with the 8086 and 8088. Specifically, the 8155/8156 and 8355/8755 memory-i/o chips can readily be adapted to small 8088-based microcomputers. On the other hand, because of their internal organization it would be difficult to use these chips with the 8086. The remaining chips in Table 2-6 can be used with either processor.

Table 2-6. Special-Function Chips for the 8080 and 8085

Name	Function
8155/8156	256-byte R/W, timer, parallel i/o (8088 only)
8355/8755	2K-byte ROM and parallel i/o (8088 only)
8041	Universal peripheral interface
8202	Dynamic R/W memory controller
8251	Communications interface (USART)
8253	Programmable interval timer (3 timers)
8237	Programmable DMA controller
8259	Programmable interrupt controller
8271	Programmable floppy disk controller
8275	Programmable crt controller
8279	Programmable keyboard/display interface

The 8041 is a single-chip microcomputer whose internal read-only memory can be programmed to do just about any low-speed peripheral task required. This single-chip microcomputer probably gave Intel the experience and insight to design the 8089 IOP. The 8202 dynamic R/W memory controller is designed to eliminate tens of chips that are normally required to refresh dynamic memory. This chip is used on the SBC 86/12A to refresh the dynamic R/W memory on the board (Fig. 2-4). The 8251 communications interface (USART) is found on both the SDK-86 and the SBC 86/12A. This device is used to transmit and receive data to and from an asynchronous peripheral, such as a crt or teletypewriter.

The 8253 programmable interval timer contains three independent 16-bit interval timers. These devices are often used for real-time and time-of-day clocks and also for period and frequency measurements. The 8237 direct memory access (DMA) controller is used with high-speed peripherals, such as hard and floppy disks, where the data transfer rate is so high that the processor cannot input or output data fast enough by executing assembly language instructions. *In DMA trans-*

fers the peripheral puts data into, or gets data out of, memory directly; the processor is not involved in the transfer at all.

The 8259 interrupt controller is the type of device that would be wired to the INTR input of the 8086 or 8088. It has a number of priority inputs so that if two or more interrupts occur simultaneously the higher priority device is serviced by the CPU first. The 8271 floppy disk controller chip does all of the formatting required to write to, or read from, a floppy disk. Because of the high transfer rates involved, this chip is often used in conjunction with the 8237 DMA controller. The 8275 crt controller is used to display information on a crt, without having to have small, display memory buffers or lots of hardwired control logic. Since this device can only store one or two lines of information that is to be displayed, it is also used with an 8237 DMA controller. The 8279 keyboard/display controller is the heart of the keyboard and display on the SDK-86. It scans a keyboard and encodes the key, and it also displays the content of a small buffer memory on seven-segment displays. The CPU loads this buffer memory with the information to be displayed, and then the information is *automatically* displayed, with no intervention required by the CPU. In fact, the CPU could halt, and the information would still be displayed.

CONCLUSION

As you have seen, the 8086 and 8088 have some very attractive features. They can address large amounts of memory and, through segmentation, can dynamically relocate programs and data. The instruction sets for these processors are powerful, because a number of different data types can be processed, from unsigned binary, signed binary, packed bcd, unpacked decimal, up to numeric and alphanumeric strings. The processors also have multiply and divide instructions, which means that they can be used in high-speed data acquisition and reduction applications.

These processors also have a large number of interrupt vectors, so that even large microcomputer systems can be designed. By using some of the special chips that have been designed for the 8086, 8088, and the common 8-bit microprocessors, powerful interfaces can be designed that relieve the CPU from a lot of simple, yet time consuming, tasks.

With the availability of a number of different boards and systems, the user is not required to design and build a system in order to get the features that he or she wants. With a system such as the SDK-86 the user can get started programming and designing interfaces fairly easily. For turn-key systems, CPU cards, such as the SBC 86/12A, can be used where expansion and flexibility are important.

One place where Intel gets very high marks is in the area of documentation. The *MCS-86 Assembly Language Reference Manual* is particularly good for assembly language programming. The *MCS-86 User's Manual*[3] and *The 8086 Family User's Manual*[4] are excellent reference books. The *MCS-86 Assembly Language Reference Manual* is especially helpful when one is programming 8086-based microcomputers on the machine/assembly language level, such as the SDK-86. The assembly manuals, user's guides, and listings provided with the SDK-86 are also well written and provide much reference material.

REFERENCES

1. Intel Corporation. *MCS-86 Assembly Language Reference Manual* (9800640-A). Santa Clara, CA, 1978.

2. Titus, C. A.; Larsen, D. G.; and Titus, J. A. *8080/8085 Software Design, Book 2,* Howard W. Sams & Co., Inc., Indianapolis, IN, 1979.

3. Intel Corporation. *The MCS-86 User's Manual, February, 1979.* Santa Clara, CA, 1979.

4. Intel Corporation. *The 8086 Family User's Manual, October, 1979.* Santa Clara, CA, 1979.

BIBLIOGRAPHY

Barlett, J., and Retter, R. "CPU Brings 16-Bit Performance to 8-Bit Systems," *Electronic Design 6,* March 15, 1979, pp. 76–80.

Davis, H. A. "Comparing Architectures of the Three 16-Bit Microprocessors," *Computer Design,* July, 1979, pp. 91–100.

Davis, S. "16-Bit Microprocessor," *EDN,* August 5, 1979, pp. 70–85.

Hemenway, J., and Teja, E. "Character-String Manipulations Power a Text Editor," *EDN,* August 20, 1979, pp. 111–116.

————. "As You Get to Know the 8086, Use Your 8-Bit Expertise," *EDN,* January 20, 1979, pp. 81–88.

Katz, B. J., *et al.* "8086 Microcomputer Bridges the Gap between 8- and 16-Bit Designs," *Electronics,* February 16, 1978, pp. 99–104.

Sugarman, R. "Computers: Our Microuniverse Expands," *IEEE Spectrum,* January, 1979, pp. 32–37.

3

The Z8001 and Z8002

Quite often in manufacturer's literature and advertisements the term "Z8000" is used when the manufacturer really means either the Z8001, the Z8002, or both the Z8001 and Z8002. Of the two CPU chips the Z8002 is the simpler, and it was commercially available in late 1979. The chip was originally designed by the Zilog Corporation and is currently second sourced by Advanced Micro Devices.

The Z8001 and Z8002 are like most of the other 16-bit microprocessor chips, because they are register oriented. The Z8002 chip (Fig. 3-1) contains 21 sixteen-bit registers, 14 of which can be considered to be general-purpose, because they can be used to store data or addresses. Sixteen of these registers can be seen in Fig. 3-2. The five additional registers in the CPU chip include a flag word, program counter, refresh counter, instruction register, and a status pointer. The Z8002 is the *nonsegmented* version of the Z8000 family of microprocessors. Therefore it does not have segment registers and cannot use segmented addresses to address memory. The result of this is that it can only address 65K bytes (32K words) of memory.

The amount of memory that the CPU chip can address is determined by the length of the program counter, which is only 16 bits long. The Z8001 is the segmented CPU chip (Fig. 3-3), and as with the 8086 a memory address is determined by both a segment value and an effective or offset address. The segmented Z8001, using a 7-bit segment value and a 16-bit offset, can address 8M bytes of memory. Unlike the operation of the 8086, the segment value and effective address are not added internally, thus external logic is required.

Like the 8086, "memory" for the Z8001 and Z8002 can be composed of both read/write memory and read-only memory. When these microprocessors are reset, the Z8001 will fetch a segment value and

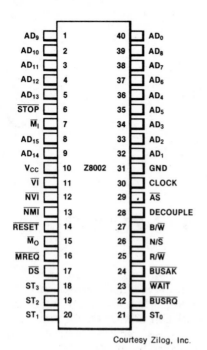

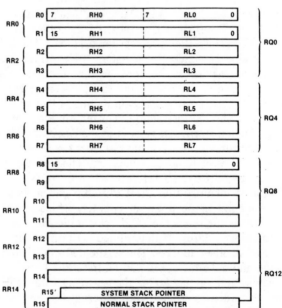

Fig. 3-1. Z8002 nonsegmented 16-bit microprocessor.

Courtesy Zilog, Inc.

Fig. 3-2. The general-purpose registers in the Z8002.

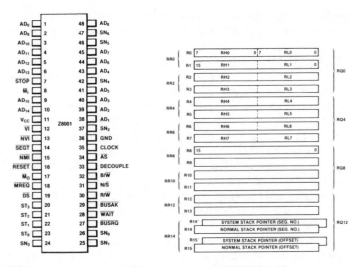

(B) Z8001 general-purpose registers.   (A) Z8001 chip.

Courtesy Zilog, Inc.

Fig. 3-3. The segmented Z8001 and its general-purpose registers.

program counter (PC) value from memory locations 4 and 6. On the other hand, the Z8002 will just fetch a program counter value from memory location 2. Thus, if memory location 2 contains 435A hexadecimal (435AH), the first instruction that will be executed by the *Z8002* must be stored in this memory location. For most practical purposes, then, the first 1K or more of memory will be ROM, and it will contain not only this address, but also the monitor, operating system, or debugger software that must be executed first. Unlike the 8086, however, interrupts do not have to use the first 1K of memory. The addresses for the interrupt service subroutines can be stored anywhere.

As was mentioned in Chapter 1, some microprocessors can communicate with peripherals using two different techniques. The Z8001 and Z8002, like the 8086, can use both *accumulator i/o* and *memory-mapped i/o*.

Two of the strong points of both the Z8001 and Z8002 (to be abbreviated Z8001/2 from now on) are the facts that they both have many general-purpose registers and that they have a very powerful instruction set. These two processors can operate on bit, byte, word, long word (32-bit), and quad-word (64-bit) values. As you might expect, though, most of the instructions operate on 8- and 16-bit values.

These two processors also have the "usual" types of instructions that can be found on most of the other 8- and 16-bit microprocessors, including data transfer, math and logic instructions, bit, processor control, and control transfer instructions. Like the other processors, the Z8001/2 also have multiplication and division instructions, including 32-bit multiplication and division. The Z8001/2 processors also have block transfer and string manipulation instructions, some of which automatically increment and decrement pointers. These instructions can also be "repeated," but unlike those of the 8086 they do not require a "repeat" instruction or "prefix." The processors also have a number of i/o and processor control instructions.

Finally, the Z8001/2 can operate in one of two possible modes: system and normal. These two different modes of operation are intended for large, multiuser, multitasking environments, where a sophisticated operating system program is present. In the normal mode, only a subset of the processor's instructions can be executed. The i/o and some of the processor control instructions (such as halt and interrupt instructions) cannot be executed. In the system mode of operation *all* instructions can be executed. In small, single-user systems, most users will execute their programs in the system mode.

The basic cycle time of these processors is 250 ns. The shortest instruction requires just 4 clock cycles, or 1 μs, and the longest instruction requires 728 clock cycles (32-bit by 32-bit division), or 182 μs, to be executed. The "average" number of clock cycles required per instruction is probably in the range of 10 to 14.

Like the other microprocessors, the Z8001 and Z8002 are available in chip form and as a single-board microcomputer. One of the most impressive low-cost Z8002-based microcomputers is the AMC 96/4016 AmZ8000 evaluation board (Fig. 3-4) because it contains a line-by-line assembler. This means that the user can enter instruction mnemonics directly into the microcomputer, rather than the user entering instruction op codes. A number of other single-board microcomputers are available, as are complete systems.

Z8000 REGISTERS

Like the 8086 and the other microprocessors, the Z8001/2 have a number of 16-bit registers (Figs. 3-2, 3-3). When these registers are used to store 16-bit values, they are labeled R0 through R15 and R15'. The R15 registers are used to store two stack pointers, one for the system mode of operation (R15') and one for the normal mode of operation (R15). Since a number of instructions assume that these two registers contain R/W memory addresses for use by a stack, these registers are not normally used for anything but stack pointers. In the segmented Z8001, two additional registers, R14 and R14', are also used to store segment values for two stack pointers.

For byte operations, each of the first eight registers is divided into two 8-bit registers. Thus, R0 is divided into RH0 and RL0. This is the same as the AX register of the 8086 being divided into AH and AL. For long-word (32-bit) operations, two of the 16-bit registers are grouped together so that the R0 and R1 registers are collectively called the RR0 register. For 64-bit operations, four registers are grouped together and are called either RQ0, RQ1, RQ2, or RQ3 (register-quadruple).

Courtesy Advanced Micro Devices, Inc.

Fig. 3-4. The AMC 94/4016 AmZ8002 evaluation board.

Of course, when using 32- and 64-bit "registers" and numbers, one must know where the most significant and least significant bits are stored. For 32-bit numbers the *most significant bits* are stored in the *even-numbered registers* and the *least significant bits* are stored in the *odd-numbered registers*. For 64-bit numbers the *most significant bits* are stored in the *lowest even-numbered register* and the *least significant bits* are stored in the *highest odd-numbered register*. As an example, for the 32-bit value 11111111111111110000000010111011, the 1111111111111111 would be stored in R0 of RR0 and the 0000000010111011 would be stored in R1 of RR0.

Unlike the 8086, the registers are not assigned specific functions, such as that of a pointer, index, or base register. Any register can be used to store a count, displacement, offset, or base address. However, this flexibility "costs us something" when the size of the instructions (number of bits for the op code) is examined.

One exception to this concerns the stack registers R15 and R15' (and R14 and R14' in the Z8001). Whenever the microprocessors do a stack operation, they assume that these registers will be used to provide an appropriate R/W memory address. Therefore, even though these registers can be used for other purposes, in most cases *they will be dedicated to providing stack addresses.*

So far the discussion of the registers has been limited to the *non-segmented* Z8002. Since the Z8001, like the 8086, has to specify a segment value, the registers in the Z8001 are used in a slightly different manner than in the Z8002. In the Z8001 two additional 16-bit registers have to be used to store the segment number for the R/W memory that is used for the stack (R14 and R14'). In fact, in many instructions two registers in the Z8001 have to be used to store a memory address, rather than the one register used in the Z8002. One register in the Z8001 would be used to store the segment number, and the other register would be used to store the 16-bit displacement, offset, or effective address. Unfortunately, the 9 bits left over in the register used to store the segment number cannot be used by the user. Therefore it would really be fairer to compare the Z8001 to the 8086 and the other processors, because the 8086 can be considered to be "segmented."

The Z8000 processors also have a flag and control word, program status area pointer, and a refresh counter (register), along with a program counter and instruction register. The flag and control word (FCW) is often grouped with the program counter (PC) and together are called the *program status registers* (Fig. 3-5). You should already know what the functions of many of these registers are, from previous discussions. The program status area pointer, or PSAP (Fig. 3-6), is primarily used when the microprocessor is interrupted, either by an internal event (trying to execute an unimplemented instruction op code, trying to execute a privileged i/o or processor control instruction in the normal mode, or a segmentation error (generated) by external hardware), or by an external event. Typical external events include interrupts, which are generated by peripherals to indicate to the CPU that they need to be "serviced" immediately.

Now that you know the nomenclature for these various registers, the authors must mention that *Advanced Micro Devices has not followed the register nomenclature that was established by Zilog.* For example, the program status area pointer is listed as the new program status area pointer (NPSAP) in AMD literature. The program status registers (Zilog) have also been called the processor status

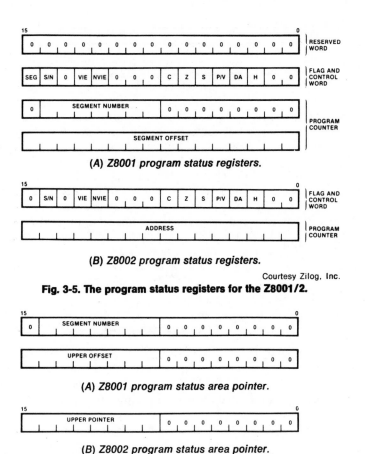

(A) Z8001 program status registers.

(B) Z8002 program status registers.

Courtesy Zilog, Inc.

Fig. 3-5. The program status registers for the Z8001/2.

(A) Z8001 program status area pointer.

(B) Z8002 program status area pointer.

Courtesy Zilog, Inc.

Fig. 3-6. The program status area pointers for the Z8001/2.

information (AMD). In general, the authors have tried to be consistent and use the Zilog nomenclature, since Zilog designed the chip.

The refresh counter is used by the Z8001/2 processors to automatically refresh dynamic memory, just as the 8-bit Z80 refreshed dynamic memory. The refresh counter can actually be loaded by the user so that the time between refresh cycles can be adjusted for different memories. The automatic refresh feature can be disabled by changing a bit (RE) in the refresh counter word (Fig. 3-7).

The flag and control word (FCW) is particularly important. A number of the flags in this word can be tested by transfer-of-control instructions. The six flags contained in the 8 least significant bits of this word are the carry (C), zero (Z), sign (S), parity/overflow (P/V), decimal adjust (DA), and half-carry (H) flags. These flags

Fig. 3-7. The internal refresh register and counter used with dynamic memories.

are usually changed by logic and mathematical instructions, so the Z8000 processors can be programmed to do a special task if an overflow occurs or if a result is equal to zero.

The most significant bits of the FCW contain control bits. The segmentation bit (SEG, Z8001 only) enables the Z8001 to operate in the nonsegmented mode so that it can execute Z8002 programs. The normal/system (N/S) bit indicates the mode of operation of the microprocessor, and determines whether or not *privileged instructions* (i/o, halt, interrupt instructions, etc.) can be executed. The vectored interrupt enable and nonvectored interrupt enable bits control whether or not the microprocessor will be interrupted by signals on pins 11 and 12 of the Z8002 or by signals on pins 12 and 13 of the Z8001.

ADDRESSING MEMORY

In order for either the Z8001 or Z8002 to perform most tasks it must be able to communicate with memory. Data values or constants may be stored in memory and the microprocessor may have to read these values, read information from a peripheral device, or store the result of an arithmetic operation in memory.

Since the Z8002 can only address 65K bytes of memory, it just has to generate a 16-bit memory address, as do many of the common 8-bit microprocessors, such as the 8080, 8085, Z80, 6800, and 6502. This 16-bit memory address may actually be contained in a *single register,* single-word memory location, or the address might even be contained in the instruction.

On the other hand, the Z8001 can address 8M bytes of memory, so it has to generate a 7-bit segment number and a 16-bit offset. The segment number is used (not added, as you might suspect) with the 16-bit offset, by the *external memory-management hardware.* This memory-management hardware actually generates the 23-bit memory address that is used to address memory. The memory-management hardware could consist of the special-function 8010 memory-management chip, or it could be built with standard TTL logic and memory integrated circuits. *The segment number and offset can be contained in either (1) two registers, (2) two-word memory locations, or (3) in the instruction itself.*

Of course, not only do 23-bit memory addresses have to be generated by the memory-management hardware when the Z8001 transfers data between itself and memory, but also when the stack is used and when instructions are fetched from memory. When a stack operation is performed, the Z8001 assumes that the stack segment number is stored in either R14 or R14′ (depending on whether it is "in" the normal or system mode of operation). The stack pointer or offset is stored in both R15 and R15′ (Fig. 3-3B). When the Z8001 fetches instructions from memory, the program counter segment value is output by the processor, along with the 16-bit program counter offset (Fig. 3-5).

As was the case with the 8086, addressing memory can become very complex. If the Z8002 is used, the user does not have to worry about segment numbers or the conversion of a segment value and offset to a 23-bit memory address. On the other hand, the addressing capabilities of the Z8001 give the user the ability to have a system with a large amount of addressable memory. As with the 8086, the Z8001 can also have separate sections of memory for programs or code (by using one segment value for the program counter segment number), data (by using a second, and different, segment number in instructions and registers), and the stack (by using a third, and different, segment number in the stack pointer). There is also the possibility that all three of these segment numbers will be the same in which case instructions, data, and the stack all reside within the same 65K bytes of memory. Finally, the external memory-management hardware can cause the same 23-bit memory address to be generated even though different segment numbers and offsets are generated by the Z8001 CPU chip.

Since the stack pointer and program counter are referenced to a segment number, it should be easy to write relocatable code for the Z8001. This is particularly important in large, multiuser systems. If your Z8001 system will eventually have all programs programmed into EPROM or ROM, the relocation capabilities of the Z8001 probably will not be used.

The only problem with relocation is the fact that many instructions actually contain a segment number and offset within themselves. However, when the Z8001 addresses memory and these segment values are output to the memory-management unit (MMU), they will be "translated" into a new segment number. This translation process can occur, because the MMU contains a small amount of R/W memory (64 memory locations). When the Z8001 outputs a segment number, this number is used to address the internal MMU R/W memory. The content of this memory location is then added to a portion of the 16-bit offset, in order to generate the 23-bit memory address (Fig. 3-8). Some additional information on the MMU will be presented in the special-function chips section of this chapter.

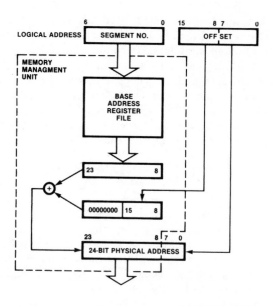

Courtesy Zilog, Inc.

Fig. 3-8. Using the 8010 memory-management unit to convert the segment number and offset to a 23-bit memory address.

ADDRESSING I/O DEVICES

The 8086, Z8001, and Z8002 use the same concepts to address peripheral devices, that is, the address space for i/o devices is separate and distinct from that of memory. To address an i/o device a *16-bit port address* is either *contained within an instruction or in a general-purpose register.* By separating i/o address space from memory address space, none of the memory address space is used up by peripherals. You could have 8M bytes of memory in a Z8001-based microcomputer system and still have up to 65K-byte i/o devices. Unfortunately, all i/o instructions are "privileged," which means that they can only be executed when the microprocessor is in the system mode. Both the Z8001 and Z8002 have special i/o instructions that are used to communicate only with the memory-management chip.

ADDRESSING SUMMARY

Unlike the 8086 the Z8000 microprocessors do not have special base and index registers. Instead, these values can be stored in the general-purpose registers of the Z8001/2. When the operation code for an assembly language instruction is generated (either by us, by hand, or by an assembler), a group of 4 bits is used to indicate which register contains the base address, index, displacement, absolute address, i/o address, or count.

The addressing modes that the Z8001/2 use are summarized in Fig. 3-9. The *register* and *immediate addressing* modes are the simplest addressing modes and really don't require an explanation. One nice feature of the immediate addressing mode is that an 8-, 16-, or 32-bit value can be loaded into a register or memory location, or be involved in a mathematical or logical operation (to name just a few possibilities).

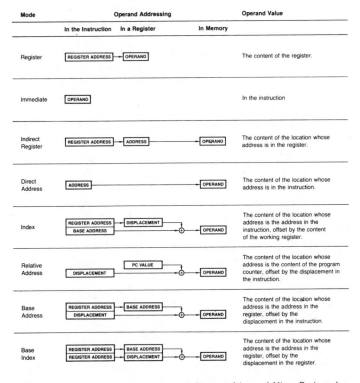

Courtesy Advanced Micro Devices, Inc.

Fig. 3-9. The addressing modes of the Z8001 and Z8002.

With *indirect addressing,* the instruction specifies a general-purpose register that contains a memory address. This address is used when the microprocessor accesses memory. For the Z8002, only a single 16-bit register is needed to store this address. On the Z8001, two registers are needed for this address: one for the 16-bit offset and another for the 7-bit segment value.

With *direct addressing,* the instruction actually contains an address, just as immediate instructions contain data values. For the Z8002, only a 16-bit address is required, while a 7-bit segment number and an 8-bit offset (segmented short offset mode) or 16-bit offset (segmented long offset mode) is required for the Z8001. When the Z8002 uses *indexed addressing* to address memory, a 16-bit address contained in the instruction is added to the index contained in a general-purpose register. The resulting 16-bit unsigned number is used as the memory address. Indexed addressing for the Z8001 is more complex. The instruction that uses indexed addressing actually contains a 16-bit offset and a 7-bit segment number. The 16-bit offset is added to the 16-bit content of a general-purpose register (index). The resulting 16-bit unsigned number is used along with the segment number specified in the instruction to address memory. With the Z8001, both segmented short (8-bit) and long (16-bit) offset modes of addressing can be used. Note that any carry from any of these 16-bit additions is ignored. Therefore it is possible for the address to wrap around, from the top of memory, back down to the bottom of memory, as was the case with the 8086.

Base addressing is very similar to indexed addressing. In base addressing, *the instruction contains a displacement, and the instruction specifies a register that contains the base address.* For the Z8002, only two unsigned 16-bit numbers are involved. For the Z8001, the 7-bit segment number and 16-bit offset are both contained in registers. Of course, the instruction contains an unsigned 16-bit displacement. With this type of addressing, the Z8001 does not have short or long offset addressing options. With *base indexed addressing,* both the index (offset or displacement) and the base address are contained in registers. For the Z8002, this simply involves the storage of two 16-bit numbers in the general-purpose registers. For the Z8001, the base address consists of the segment number and the 16-bit offset (two registers) and the index (one register).

In general, if the Z8001 is being used, an "address" will consist of both a 7-bit segment number and a 16-bit offset. Therefore these two values will either be included in the instruction's op code (for direct and indexed addressing) or will be contained in registers (for indirect, base, and base indexed addressing). In the indexed and direct addressing modes you have the option of using either an 8- or 16-bit offset, which is contained in the instruction's op code. If registers are used to store the segment number and offset, a 16-bit offset is always assumed.

The Z8000 processors are also capable of *relative addressing,* where an 8- or 12-bit signed displacement is added to the *updated* program counter (the address of the next instruction). This addressing mode is only available for the jump- and call-relative instructions.

THE Z8001/2 INSTRUCTION SET

The only difference between the Z8001 and the Z8002 is the amount of memory that they can address and, as a result of this, whether or not segment numbers are involved in address calcula-

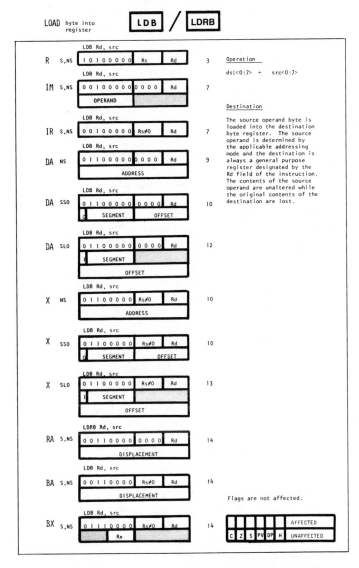

Fig. 3-10. The format for the LDB/LDRB instructions.

Table 3-1. Abbreviations Used With Instruction Descriptions

Addressing Mode	
Abbreviation	**Meaning**
R	Register
IM	Immediate
IR	Indirect register
DA	Direct addressing
X	Indexed
RA	Relative addressing
BA	Base addressing
BX	Base indexed addressing
Segmentation Information	
Abbreviation	**Meaning**
S	Segmented (Z8001)
NS	Nonsegmented (Z8002)
SS or SSO	Segmented, short offset (Z8001)
SL or SLO	Segmented, long offset (Z8001)
General Information	
Numbers to the right of instructions are the number of clock cycles required to execute it. Letters and symbols just above or to the right of each instruction op code are the format of the instruction (mnemonic) to be used when writing programs.	
Operand Information	
Abbreviation	**Meaning**
dst	Destination
src	Source
R	Register
cc	Condition code (for decision-making instructions)
n	An integer
IM	Immediate data value

tions. Therefore these processors execute exactly the same types of instructions. These instructions range from one to five words in length and must be *word aligned. This means that the most significant byte of a word must always be stored at an even byte address, and the least significant byte of a word must be stored in memory at an odd byte address.*

The format of the LDB/LDRB (load byte into register) instructions is shown in Fig. 3-10. This will give you a good idea of what the format for the Z8000 instructions looks like. Any shaded area in an instruction's op code is reserved by the manufacturer for future expansion, and should be set to zero for both the Z8001 and Z8002. As you can see, some of these instructions can only be executed on the nonsegmented Z8002 (NS: nonsegmented) and some just on the Z8001 (SSO: segmented short offset; SLO: segmented long offset). Of course, some of the instructions can be executed on both processors (S, NS: segmented and nonsegmented). A summary of the abbreviations used to characterize these instructions can be found in Table 3-1.

Load and Exchange Instructions

Like the 8086 the Z8000 microprocessors have a number of different instructions that can be used to move or transfer information between registers and memory. Therefore information can be moved to a register from a register, to a register from memory, or to memory from a register. Also, an immediate data byte (word or long word) can be moved to either a register(s) or memory location(s). The Z8000 microprocessors can also save the content of a register, immediate data word, or the content of a word memory location on the stack (pushing information), or retrieve information from the stack (popping information). Information can be "popped off" of the stack into either a register or memory, using a number of different addressing modes.

These microprocessors also have exchange instructions, which can be used to exchange the content of a register with either the content of a memory location or another register. They also have a number of novel instructions that can be used to store any group of registers in memory, such as registers R0, R1, R2, and R3, or R8, R9, and R10, or read the content of a number of consecutive memory locations into a number of consecutive registers. Finally, a group of registers can be set to zero, or a group of registers can all be loaded with the same immediate data value. The load and exchange instructions are summarized in Table 3-2. *Note that the LD-type instructions are the only Z8000 instructions that can use base or base indexed addressing.* It is very unfortunate that such a powerful addressing mode is limited to so few instructions.

The Arithmetic Instructions

The Z8001/2 can add, subtract, multiply, and divide signed and unsigned binary numbers. These microprocessors can also add and subtract bcd numbers (two digits), but a decimal adjust instruction must be executed after each bcd mathematical operation. The Z8000 processors cannot perform ASCII math (not a very big limitation).

The Z8001/2 have two different types of addition and two different types of subtraction instructions (Table 3-3). The addition instructions are used to add (ADD, ADDB, ADDL) and add with carry (ADC and ADCB). The ADD and ADC instructions are used to add words, and the instructions that end with B and L are used to process bytes and long words, respectively. The advantage of the

Table 3-2. The Z8001/2 Load and Exchange Instructions

Mnemonics	Operands	Addr. Modes	Word, Byte NS	SS	SL	Long Word NS	SS	SL	Operation
CLR CLRB	dst	R	7	-	-				Clear dst ← 0
		IR	8	-	-				
		DA	11	12	14				
		X	11	12	15				
EX EXB	R, src	R	6	-	-				Exchange R ↔ src
		IR	12	-	-				
		DA	15	16	18				
		X	16	16	19				
LD LDB LDL	R, src	R	3	-	-	5	-	-	Load into Register R ← src
		IM	7	-	-	11	-	-	
		IM	5 (byte only)						
		IR	7	-	-	11	-	-	
		DA	9	10	12	12	13	15	
		X	10	10	13	13	13	16	
		BA	14	-	-	17	-	-	
		BX	14	-	-	17	-	-	
LD LDB LDL	dst, R	IR	8	-	-	11	-	-	Load into Memory (Store) dst ← R
		DA	11	12	14	14	15	17	
		X	12	12	15	15	15	18	
		BA	14	-	-	17	-	-	
		BX	14	-	-	17	-	-	
LD LDB	dst, IM	IR	11	-	-				Load Immediate into Memory dst ← IM
		DA	14	15	17				
		X	15	15	18				
LDA	R, src	DA	12	13	15				Load Address R ← source address
		X	13	13	16				
		BA	15	-	-				
		BX	15	-	-				
LDAR	R, src	RA	15	-	-				Load Address Relative R ← source address
LDK	R, src	IM	5	-	-				Load Constant R ← n (n = 0 ... 15)
LDM	R, src, n	IR	11	-	-				Load Multiple R ← src (n consecutive words) (n = 1 ... 16)
		DA	14	15	17 } +3n				
		X	15	15	18				
LDM	dst, R, n	IR	11	-	-				Load Multiple (Store Multiple) dst ← R (n consecutive words) (n = 1 ... 16)
		DA	14	15	17 } +3n				
		X	15	15	18				
LDR LDRB LDRL	R, src	RA	14	-	-	17	-	-	Load Relative R ← src (range -32768 ... +32767)
LDR LDRB LDRL	dst, R	RA	14	-	-	17	-	-	Load Relative (Store Relative) dst ← R (range -32768 ... +32767)
POP POPL	dst, IR	R	8	-	-	12	-	-	Pop dst ← IR Autoincrement contents of R
		IR	12	-	-	19	-	-	
		DA	15	16	18	22	23	25	
		X	16	16	19	23	23	26	
PUSH PUSHL	IR, src	R	9	-	-	12	-	-	Push Autodecrement contents of R IR ← src
		IM	12	-	-	-	-	-	
		IR	13	-	-	20	-	-	
		DA	13	14	16	20	21	23	
		X	14	14	17	21	21	24	

Courtesy Zilog, Inc.

add-with-carry instructions is the fact that they can be used to add numbers that are larger than 16 bits, simply by breaking them into 16-bit "chunks" and adding them.

The subtraction instructions are very similar to the addition instructions, because subtract and subtract-with-borrow operations can be performed. The subtract-type instructions can subtract bytes, words, and long words, while the subtract-with-borrow instructions can operate on bytes and words. If bcd numbers are being added and subtracted, the programmer has to add a DAB instruction to

Table 3-3. The Arithmetic Instructions of the Z8000 Microprocessors

Mnemonics	Operands	Addr. Modes	Word, Byte NS	SS	SL	Long Word NS	SS	SL	Operation
ADC ADCB	R, src	R	5	-	-				Add with Carry $R \leftarrow R + src + carry$
ADD ADDB ADDL	R, src	R	4	-	-	8	-	-	Add $R \leftarrow R + src$
		IM	7	-	-	14	-	-	
		IR	7	-	-	14	-	-	
		DA	9	10	12	15	16	18	
		X	10	10	13	16	16	19	
CP CPB CPL	R, src	R	4	-	-	8	-	-	Compare with Register $R - src$
		IM	7	-	-	14	-	-	
		IR	7	-	-	14	-	-	
		DA	9	10	12	15	16	18	
		X	10	10	13	16	16	19	
CP CPB	dst, IM	IR	11	-	-				Compare with Immediate $dst - IM$
		DA	14	15	17				
		X	15	15	18				
DAB	dst	R	5	-	-				Decimal Adjust
DEC DECB	dst, n	R	4	-	-				Decrement by n $dst \leftarrow dst - n$ (n = 1 ... 16)
		IR	11	-	-				
		DA	13	14	16				
		X	14	14	17				
DIV DIVL	R, src	R	95	-	-	723	-	-	Divide (signed) Word: $R_{n+1} \leftarrow R_{n,n+1} \div src$ $R_n \leftarrow$ remainder Long Word: $R_{n+2,n+3} \leftarrow R_{n...n+3} \div src$ $R_{n,n+1} \leftarrow$ remainder
		IM	95	-	-	723	-	-	
		IR	95	-	-	723	-	-	
		DA	96	97	99	724	725	727	
		X	97	97	100	725	725	728	
EXTS EXTSB EXTSL	dst	R	11	-	-	11	-	-	Extend Sign Extend sign of low order half of dst through high order half of dst
INC INCB	dst, n	R	4	-	-				Increment by n $dst \leftarrow dst + n$ (n = 1 ... 16)
		IR	11	-	-				
		DA	13	14	16				
		X	14	14	17				
MULT MULTL	R, src	R	70	-	-	282*	-	-	Multiply (signed) Word: $R_{n,n+1} \leftarrow R_{n+1} \cdot src$ Long Word: $R_{n...n+3} \leftarrow R_{n+2,n+3} \cdot src$ *Plus seven cycles for each 1 in the multiplicand
		IM	70	-	-	282*	-	-	
		IR	70	-	-	282*	-	-	
		DA	71	72	74	283*	284*	286*	
		X	72	72	75	284*	284*	287*	
NEG NEGB	dst	R	7	-	-				Negate $dst \leftarrow 0 - dst$
		IR	12	-	-				
		DA	15	16	18				
		X	16	16	19				
SBC SBCB	R, src	R	5	-	-				Subtract with Carry $R \leftarrow R - src - carry$
SUB SUBB SUBL	R, src	R	4	-	-	8	-	-	Subtract $R \leftarrow R - src$
		IM	7	-	-	14	-	-	
		IR	7	-	-	14	-	-	
		DA	9	10	12	15	16	18	
		X	10	10	13	16	16	19	

Courtesy Zilog, Inc.

the program, just after the add or subtract instruction. The DAB instruction adjusts the result in bits 0 through 7 of the register that contains the result, to the proper two-digit bcd result. No four-digit (word) bcd adjustments can be performed with the DAB instruction directly (same case with the 8086). The multiplication and division instructions that these processors have are very powerful, because they can be used to multiply and divide both 16- and 32-bit numbers.

Finally, the Z8001/2 also have increment, decrement, compare, negate, and sign-extend instructions. A useful feature of the increment and decrement instructions is the fact that a register or memory location can be incremented or decremented by from 1 to 16, using a single instruction. These instructions operate exclusively on bytes and words.

A nice feature of these arithmetic instructions and the arithmetic instructions of other microprocessors is the fact that the flags are set and cleared as a result of these operations. In another section of this chapter we will discuss the transfer-of-control instructions that can test these flags. It is important that you check the manufacturer's literature[1] to determine exactly how and when these flags will be changed.

Logical Instructions

The Z8001/2 can perform a number of useful logical operations. Two words or bytes can be ANDed, ORed, exclusive-ORed or one byte or word can be complemented. A word or byte can also be "tested," that is, the byte or word can be ORed with zero, by the processor, and the flags will be set or cleared based on the result. *The zero byte or word does not have to be contained in a register, memory, or be an immediate data byte. Also, the data value being "tested" is not altered by this group of instructions.* The test instructions are not the same as the compare instructions (Table 3-4).

These two processors also have a number of shift and rotate instructions, which can shift or rotate the content of a register or memory location to the left or right, by the number of bits specified

Table 3-4. The Z8001/2 Logical Instructions

Mnemonics	Operands	Addr. Modes	Word, Byte			Long Word			Operation
			NS	SS	SL	NS	SS	SL	
AND	R, src	R	4	-	-				**AND**
ANDB		IM	7	-	-				R ← R AND src
		IR	7	-	-				
		DA	9	10	12				
		X	10	10	13				
COM	dst	R	7	-	-				**Complement**
COMB		IR	12	-	-				dst ← NOT dst
		DA	15	16	18				
		X	16	16	19				
OR	R, src	R	4	-	-				**OR**
ORB		IM	7	-	-				R ← R OR src
		IR	7	-	-				
		DA	9	10	12				
		X	10	10	13				
TEST	dst	R	7	-	-	13	-	-	**Test**
TESTB		IR	8	-	-	13	-	-	dst OR 0
TESTL		DA	11	12	14	16	17	19	
		X	12	12	15	17	17	20	
TCC	cc, dst	R	5	-	-				**Test Condition Code**
TCCB									Set LSB if cc is true
XOR	R, src	R	4	-	-				**Exclusive OR**
XORB		IM	7	-	-				R ← R XOR src
		IR	7	-	-				
		DA	9	10	12				
		X	10	10	13				

Courtesy Zilog, Inc.

Table 3-5. The Z8001/2 Shift and Rotate Instructions

Mnemonics	Operands	Addr. Modes	Clock Cycles Word, Byte NS	SS	SL	Long Word NS	SS	SL	Operation
RLDB	R, src	R	9	–	–				**Rotate Digit Left**
RRDB	R, src	R	9	–	–				**Rotate Digit Right**
RL RLB	dst, n	R R	6 for n = 1 7 for n = 2						**Rotate Left** by n bits (n = 1, 2)
RLC RLCB	dst, n	R R	6 for n = 1 7 for n = 2						**Rotate Left through Carry** by n bits (n = 1, 2)
RR RRB	dst, n	R R	6 for n = 1 7 for n = 2						**Rotate Right** by n bits (n = 1, 2)
RRC RRCB	dst, n	R R	6 for n = 1 7 for n = 2						**Rotate Right through Carry** by n bits (n = 1, 2)
SDA SDAB SDAL	dst, R	R	(15 + 3 n)			(15 + 3 n)			**Shift Dynamic Arithmetic** Shift dst left or right by contents of R
SDL SDLB SDLL	dst, R	R	(15 + 3 n)			(15 + 3 n)			**Shift Dynamic Logical** Shift dst left or right by contents of R
SLA SLAB SLAL	dst, n	R	(13 + 3 n)			(13 + 3 n)			**Shift Left Arithmetic** by n bits
SLL SLLB SLLL	dst, n	R	(13 + 3 n)			(13 + 3 n)			**Shift Left Logical** by n bits
SRA SRAB SRAL	dst, n	R	(13 + 3 n)			(13 + 3 n)			**Shift Right Arithmetic** by n bits
SRL SRLB SRLL	dst, n	R	(13 + 3 n)			(13 + 3 n)			**Shift Right Logical** by n bits

Courtesy Zilog, Inc.

in the instruction. Another bit in these same instructions also determines the direction of the shift or rotate. The Z8000 processors also have shift instructions for arithmetic values, where the sign of the value remains unaltered. The Z8001/2 shift and rotate instructions are summarized in Table 3-5.

Input/Output (I/O) Instructions

The Z8000 processors have a number of sophisticated i/o instructions, *but they can only be executed when the microprocessor is in the system mode of operation.* No i/o instructions can be executed when the microprocessor is in the normal mode.

There are basically two types of i/o instructions: one type is used to communicate with general-purpose peripherals and the other type is used *exclusively* to communicate with the 8010 memory-management unit. The i/o instructions are summarized in Table 3-6. All of the i/o instructions that begin with "S" are special i/o instructions

Table 3-6. The Input/Output Instructions of the Z8001/2

Mnemonics	Operands	Addr. Modes	Word, Byte NS	Word, Byte SS	Word, Byte SL	Long Word NS	Long Word SS	Long Word SL	Operation
IN* INB*	R, src	IR DA	10 12	– –	– –				Input R ← src
IND* INDB*	dst, src, R	IR	21	–	–				Input and Decrement dst ← src Autodecrement dst address R ← R – 1
INDR* INDRB*	dst, src, R	IR	(11 + 10 n)						Input, Decrement and Repeat dst ← src Autodecrement dst address R ← R – 1 Repeat until R = 0
INI* INIB*	dst, src, R	IR	21	–	–				Input and Increment dst ← src Autoincrement dst address R ← R – 1
INIR* INIRB*	dst, src, R	IR	(11 + 10 n)						Input, Increment and Repeat dst ← src Autoincrement dst address R ← R – 1 Repeat until R = 0
OUT* OUTB*	dst, R	IR DA	10 12	– –	– –				Output dst ← R
OUTD* OUTDB*	dst, src, R	IR	21	–	–				Output and Decrement dst ← src Autodecrement src address R ← R – 1
OTDR* OTDRB*	dst, src, R	IR	(11 + 10 n)						Output, Decrement and Repeat dst ← src Autodecrement src address R ← R – 1 Repeat until R = 0
OUTI* OUTIB*	dst, src, R	IR	21	–	–				Output and Increment dst ← src Autoincrement src address R ← R – 1
OTIR* OTIRB*	dst, src, R	IR	(11 + 10 n)						Output, Increment and Repeat dst ← src Autoincrement src address R ← R – 1 Repeat until R = 0
SIN* SINB*	R, src	DA	12	–	–				Special Input R ← src
SIND* SINDB*	dst, src, R	IR	21	–	–				Special Input and Decrement dst ← src Autodecrement dst address R ← R – 1
SINDR* SINDRB*	dst, src, R	IR	(11 + 10 n)						Special Input, Decrement and Repeat dst ← src Autodecrement dst address R ← R – 1 Repeat until R = 0
SINI* SINIB*	dst, src, R	IR	21	–	–				Special Input and Increment dst ← src Autoincrement dst address R ← R – 1

SINIR* SINIRB*	dst, src, R	IR	(11 + 10 n)			Special Input, Increment and Repeat dst ← src Autoincrement dst address R ← R - 1 Repeat until R = 0
SOUT* SOUTB*	dst, src	DA	12	-	-	Special Output dst ← src
SOUTD* SOUTDB*	dst, src, R	IR	21	-	-	Special Output and Decrement dst ← src Autodecrement src address R ← R - 1
SOTDR* SOTDRB*	dst, src, R	IR	(11 + 10 n)			Special Output, Decr. and Repeat dst ← src Autodecrement src address R ← R - 1 Repeat until R = 0
SOUTI* SOUTIB*	dst, src, R	IR	21	-	-	Special Output and Increment dst ← src Autoincrement src address R ← R - 1
SOTIR* SOTIRB*	dst, src, R	R	(11 + 10 n)			Special Output, Incr. and Repeat dst ← src Autoincrement src address R ← R - 1 Repeat until R = 0

* Privileged instructions. Executed in the system mode only.

Courtesy Zilog, Inc.

intended for use with the memory-management chip. These special instructions, however, perform the same basic operations as the other type of i/o instructions.

Basically, the i/o instructions can be used to input a byte or word into a register or memory location, and they can also be used to output a byte or word from a memory location or register. Using these instructions the Z8001/2 can address 65K-byte devices, more than enough for most applications.

The most interesting i/o instructions can actually *input or output a block of information*. Therefore the block output instructions read information from memory and output it very quickly without the traditional "loop" instructions. The input block instructions read information from peripherals and store it in memory. As an example, the INDR instruction uses three registers. One register specifies the i/o address of the peripheral that is sending data to the CPU. The second register is used to address memory where the data will be stored, and the third register contains the word count. When executed, the INDR instruction inputs a 16-bit word, stores it in memory, decrements the memory address by 2, and decrements the count by 1. If the count is nonzero, the INDR instruction is executed again. Once the specified register has been decremented to zero, the Z8001/2 executes the next instruction stored in memory after the INDR instruction.

The Z8001/2 can also input and output bytes and either increment or decrement the memory address by 1 (for bytes) or 2 (for words).

Table 3-7. The Bit Manipulation Instructions

Mnemonics	Operands	Addr. Modes	Word, Byte NS	SS	SL	Long Word NS	SS	SL	Operation
BIT BITB	dst, b	R IR DA X	4 8 10 11	- - 11 11	- - 13 14				**Test Bit Static** Z flag ← NOT dst bit specified by b
BIT BITB	dst, R	R	10	-	-				**Test Bit Dynamic** Z flag ← NOT dst bit specified by contents of R
RES RESB	dst, b	R IR DA X	4 11 13 14	- - 14 14	- - 16 17				**Reset Bit Static** Reset dst bit specified by b
RES RESB	dst, R	R	10	-	-				**Reset Bit Dynamic** Reset dst bit specified by contents R
SET SETB	dst, b	R IR DA X	4 11 13 14	- - 14 14	- - 16 17				**Set Bit Static** Set dst bit specified by b
SET SETB	dst, R	R	10	-	-				**Set Bit Dynamic** Set dst bit specified by contents of R
TSET TSETB	dst	R IR DA X	7 11 14 15	- - 15 15	- - 17 18				**Test and Set** S flag ← MSB of dst dst ← all 1s

Courtesy Zilog, Inc.

Realistically, however, some of these instructions are not particularly useful, simply because there are very few peripherals that can generate or receive information so fast. The memory-management chip is one peripheral device that does use these block transfer instructions effectively. If a peripheral cannot transfer data this fast, the CPU is usually used to coordinate the transfer of information between itself and the peripheral. Hardware flags and conditional transfer-of-control instructions (handshaking) are often used.

Bit Manipulation

The Z8000 processors have a whole class of bit manipulation instructions that most other processors do not have. These instructions are probably a result of the fact that the Z80 had the same types of instructions. These instructions are used to test the state of a bit, set it to a one, or clear it to a zero, in either a register or memory location. These different instructions are summarized in Table 3-7.

From Table 3-7 you can see that the terms "static" and "dynamic" have been used. If an instruction is "static," the bit to be changed or tested is actually specified in the instruction by 4 bits. If the instruction is "dynamic," the bit to be changed or tested is specified by the 4 least significant bits in one of the general-purpose registers.

Table 3-8. The Z8001/2 Program Control (Jump, Call, and Return) Instructions

Mnemonics	Operands	Addr. Modes	Word, Byte			Long Word			Operation
			NS	SS	SL	NS	SS	SL	
CALL	dst	IR	10	–	15				Call Subroutine
		DA	12	18	20				Autodecrement SP
		X	13	18	21				@ SP ← PC
									PC ← dst
CALR	dst	RA	10	–	15				Call Relative
									Autodecrement SP
									@ SP ← PC
									PC ← PC + dst (range -4094 to +4096)
DJNZ	R, dst	RA	11	–	–				Decrement and Jump if Non-Zero
DBJNZ									R ← R - 1
									If R ≠ 0: PC ← PC + dst (range -254 to 0)
IRET*	–	–	13	–	16				Interrupt Return
									PS ← @ SP
									Autoincrement SP
JP	cc, dst	IR	10	–	15	(taken)			Jump Conditional
		IR	7	–	7	(not taken)			If cc is true: PC ← dst
		DA	7	8	10				
		X	8	8	11				
JR	cc, dst	RA	6	–	–				Jump Conditional Relative
									If cc is true: PC ← PC + dst
									(range -256 to +254)
RET	cc	–	10	–	13	(taken)			Return Conditional
			7	–	7	(not taken)			If cc is true: PC ← @ SP
									Autoincrement SP
SC	src	IM	33	–	39				System Call
									Autodecrement SP
									@ SP ← old PS
									Push instruction
									PS ← System Call PS

Courtesy Zilog, Inc.

The instruction op code specifies which general-purpose register is to be used. Of course, the advantage of the "dynamic" instructions is the fact that as a program is executed the content of the register that specifies the bit to be operated on can be changed. In the "static" instructions this information is "fixed" much like an immediate data value.

Control Transfer Instructions

The control transfer or program control instructions are very powerful, because they give the microprocessor the ability to make decisions. These instructions are listed in Table 3-8. They can test the state of one of the flags (carry, zero, sign, parity/overflow) or a combination of these flags.

The jump instructions are the simplest of the program control instructions. They can have a displacement imbedded in the instruction, or the content of a register or memory location can provide the *address* of the next instruction to be executed. If the JR (jump rela-

Table 3-9. The Condition Codes (CC) That Can Be Tested With the Conditional Jump and Return Instructions

Code	Meaning	Flag Settings	CC Field
	Always false	–	0000
	Always true	–	1000
Z	Zero	Z = 1	0110
NZ	Not zero	Z = 0	1110
C	Carry	C = 1	0111
NC	No Carry	C = 0	1111
PL	Plus	S = 0	1101
MI	Minus	S = 1	0101
NE	Not equal	Z = 0	1110
EQ	Equal	Z = 1	0110
OV	Overflow	P/V = 1	0100
NOV	No overflow	P/V = 0	1100
PE	Parity is even	P/V = 1	0100
PO	Parity is odd	P/V = 0	1100
GE	Greater than or equal (signed)	(S XOR P/V) = 0	1001
LT	Less than (signed)	(S XOR P/V) = 1	0001
GT	Greater than (signed)	[Z OR (S XOR P/V)] = 0	1010
LE	Less than or equal (signed)	[Z OR (S XOR P/V)] = 1	0010
UGE	Unsigned greater than or equal	C = 0	1111
ULT	Unsigned less than	C = 1	0111
UGT	Unsigned greater than	[(C = 0) AND (Z = 0)] = 1	1011
ULE	Unsigned less than or equal	(C OR Z) = 1	0011

Note that some condition codes have identical flag settings and binary fields in the instruction:
Z = EQ, NZ = NE, C = ULT, NC = UGE, OV = PE, NOV = PO

Courtesy Zilog, Inc.

tive) instruction is used in a program, the signed displacement (+127 to −128) is added to the current content of the program counter. As in many other situations, wrap-around will also occur with the program counter, that is, the program counter segment number on the Z8001 will not be automatically incremented once the program counter reaches FFFFH and then goes to zero.

The Z8000 microprocessors not only have an unconditional jump instruction but also 16 conditional jump instructions that can test individual flags or combinations of flags. These instructions are summarized in Table 3-9. The conditional jump instructions are also limited to displacements of +127 and −128.

The call instructions, which are used to execute subroutines, can use the same addressing modes as the jump instructions. However, the call instructions are all unconditional. The address of the subroutine that is to be called may be contained in the CALR instruction in the form of a displacement (+2047 to −2048), or the address might be in a register or memory location (for use by the CALL instruction). Since there is always the possibility that a program is being executed in one segment while a subroutine has to be called in another segment, the call instructions can also specify a segment number. The jump instructions have the same capabilities. There is also a system call (SC) instruction which will be discussed in the section of this chapter on interrupts.

Finally, there are two different types of return (from subroutine) instructions: one for use with interrupt service subroutines (IRET) and conditional and unconditional return instructions (RET).

Table 3-10. The Z8001/2 Block Transfer Instructions

Mnemonics	Operands	Addr. Modes	Clock Cycles						Operation
			Word, Byte			Long Word			
			NS	SS	SL	NS	SS	SL	
LDD LDDB	dst, src, R	IR	20						**Load and Decrement** dst ← src Autodecrement dst and src addresses R ← R - 1
LDDR LDDRB	dst, src, R	IR	(11 + 9 n)						**Load, Decrement and Repeat** dst ← src Autodecrement dst and src addresses R ← R - 1 Repeat until R = 0
LDI LDIB	dst, src, R	IR	20	-	-				**Load and Increment** dst ← src Autoincrement dst and src addresses R ← R - 1
LDIR LDIRB	dst, src, R	IR	(11 + 9 n)						**Load, Increment and Repeat** dst ← src Autoincrement dst and src addresses R ← R - 1 Repeat until R = 0

Courtesy Zilog, Inc.

Block Transfer and String Instructions

The Z8001/2 inherited a number of instructions from their predecessor, the Z80. In particular, the Z80 and Z8001/2 all have block transfer instructions. The block transfer instructions that the Z8001/2 can execute are summarized in Table 3-10.

All of these instructions use three registers. One register contains the address where the data will be obtained from (the source), another register contains an address where the data is being moved to (the destination), and the third register contains the number of bytes or words that are to be moved. If words are being transferred, the source and destination registers are incremented or decremented by 2, and if bytes are being transferred, these registers are incremented or decremented by 1. Regardless of the type of transfer, the register that contains the count is always decremented by 1.

With these instructions you have the option of transferring one word or byte and then decrementing the count, or transferring words or bytes until the count is finally decremented to zero. This is similar to not using or using the REP instruction in front of 8086 string instructions. *The ability to either increment or decrement the addresses is very important, particularly when moving overlapping lists or other data structures.*[2]

Note that three registers (two for address, one for the count) would be required if the instruction is being executed on the Z8002. If the Z8001 is being used, five registers would be required, since each address needs two registers (one for the offset and one for the segment

Table 3-11. The String Comparison Instructions

Mnemonics	Operands	Addr. Modes	Word, Byte			Long Word			Operation
			NS	SS	SL	NS	SS	SL	
CPD CPDB	R_X, src, R_Y, cc	IR	20	-	-				**Compare and Decrement** R_X - src Autodecrement src address $R_Y \leftarrow R_Y - 1$
CPDR CPDRB	R_X, src, R_Y, cc	IR	(11 + 9 n)						**Compare, Decrement and Repeat** R_X - src Autodecrement src address $R_Y \leftarrow R_Y - 1$ Repeat until cc is true or $R_Y = 0$
CPI CPIB	R_X, src, R_Y, cc	IR	20	-	-				**Compare and Increment** R_X - src Autoincrement src address $R_Y \leftarrow R_Y - 1$
CPIR CPIRB	R_X, src, R_Y, cc	IR	(11 + 9 n)						**Compare, Increment and Repeat** R_X - src Autoincrement src address $R_Y \leftarrow R_Y - 1$ Repeat until cc is true or $R_Y = 0$
CPSD CPSDB	dst, src, R, cc	IR	25	-	-				**Compare String and Decrement** dst - src Autodecrement dst and src addresses $R \leftarrow R - 1$
CPSDR CPSDRB	dst, src, R, cc	IR	(11 + 14 n)						**Compare String, Decr. and Repeat** dst - src Autodecrement dst and src addresses $R \leftarrow R - 1$ Repeat until cc is true or $R = 0$
CPSI CPSIB	dst, src, R, cc	IR	25	-	-				**Compare String and Increment** dst - src Autoincrement dst and src addresses $R \leftarrow R - 1$
CPSIR CPSIRB	dst, src, R, cc	IR	(11 + 14 n)						**Compare String, Incr. and Repeat** dst - src Autoincrement dst and src addresses $R \leftarrow R - 1$ Repeat until cc is true or $R = 0$

Courtesy Zilog, Inc.

number). Also, it is interesting to see that it takes just as much time to transfer a word as it does a byte. Therefore the transfer-word instructions should be used to transfer bytes, as long as an even number of bytes can be transferred; it will take half as much time to transfer the bytes as words, than to transfer them as bytes. Also, the "byte count" would have to be divided by 2, in order to generate a "word count."

String Instructions

The first four types of compare instructions in Table 3-11 compare a value in a register to a value or values stored in memory. Therefore, if these string instructions are used in a program, one register is used to store a data value, one (Z8002) or two (Z8001) registers are used to store a memory address, and an additional register must be used to store a byte count or word count. When the value in the register is compared to the value in memory, the flags are set or cleared. The memory address is then either incremented or decremented, by 1 or 2, depending on whether bytes or words are being compared. The count is then decremented by 1.

One nice feature of the compare instructions is that the user can add a 4-bit condition code (Table 3-11) to the instruction. This means that strings can be compared until one is greater, equal to, or less than another string. Therefore, the user can test one of 16 possible conditions, along with whether or not the count is zero. The Z8001/2 can also repeat these operations (CPDR, CPDRB, CPIR, CPIRB) until either the count is zero or the condition specified in the instruction is met.

The remaining four types of string comparison instructions actually compare two strings that are stored in memory. Therefore two addresses are contained in the general-purpose registers, along with a byte or word count. Like the other string comparison instructions that were just mentioned, the user can specify the condition that must be met (by means of a 4-bit condition code) and whether or not the comparison process is to be repeated. The comparison will be repeated until either the count is decremented to zero or the condition specified in the instruction is met. The programmer also has the option of only performing one comparison.

In essence, the string instructions in Table 3-11 are equivalent to the 8086 SCAS and CMPS string instructions, with and without the repeat "prefix" or instruction. The 8086 instructions, however, can only test the "equal/not equal" condition. The Z8001/2 can compare until the less than or greater than condition is reached, to name just two possibilities. The Z8001/2 and the 8086 can all either increment or decrement the addresses by 1 or 2, depending on whether bytes or words are being compared. The advantage of the Z8001/2 instructions is the fact that they make it easier to *sort* alphanumeric strings (ASCII, EBCDIC, etc.), floating-point numbers, or any other values that will require more than one 16-bit word to be represented.

Translate Instructions

The Z8001/2 have a number of *lookup table* or *translate instructions,* as shown in Table 3-12. These instructions are primarily used to convert information from one data domain to another data domain. For instance, a message stored in memory in the form of ASCII characters might have to be translated into EBCDIC before it could be transmitted to a peripheral or even another computer. A message in memory might also have to be encrypted before it could be transmitted over telephone lines or *via* satellite.

The translate instructions can be used to translate a single byte

Table 3-12. The Translate (Lookup Table) Instructions

Mnemonics	Operands	Addr. Modes	Word. Byte NS	SS	SL	Long Word NS	SS	SL	Operation
TRDB	dst, src, R	IR	25	-	-				**Translate and Decrement** dst ← src (dst) Autodecrement dst address R ← R - 1
TRDRB	dst, src, R	IR	(11 + 14 n)						**Translate, Decrement and Repeat** dst ← src (dst) Autodecrement dst address R ← R - 1 Repeat until R = 0
TRIB	dst, src, R	IR	25	-	-				**Translate and Increment** dst ← src (dst) Autoincrement dst address R ← R - 1
TRIRB	dst, src, R	IR	(11 + 14 n)						**Translate, Increment and Repeat** dst ← src (dst) Autoincrement dst address R ← R - 1 Repeat until R = 0
TRTDB	src 1, src 2, R	IR	25	-	-				**Translate and Test, Decrement** RH1 ← src 2 (src 1) Autodecrement src 1 address R ← R - 1
TRTDRB	src 1, src 2, R	IR	(11 + 14 n)						**Translate and Test, Decr. and Repeat** RH1 ← src 2 (src 1) Autodecrement src 1 address R ← R - 1 Repeat until R = 0 or RH1 = 0
TRTIB	src 1, src 2, R	IR	25						**Translate and Test, Increment** RH1 ← src 2 (src 1) Autoincrement src 1 address R ← R - 1
TRTIRB	src 1, src 2, R	IR	(11 + 14 n)						**Translate and Test, Incr. and Repeat** RH1 ← src 2 (src 1) Autoincrement src 1 address R ← R - 1 Repeat until R = 0 or RH1 = 0

(character) or a complete string of characters. The memory address that addresses the string of characters stored in memory can also be either incremented or decremented. If a string of characters is to be translated, a register needs to be loaded with the "byte count." There is also another group of translate instructions (the last four in Table 3-12), which permit the user to scan a list or table until either a nonzero value is found or a count is decremented to zero. The first nonzero value will always be read into register R0.

Interrupt Instructions

The Z8001/2 do not have as many interrupt instructions as the 8086. *This means that the Z8001/2 will not be interrupted if a division-by-zero is attempted or if an overflow occurs.* The Z8001/2 can also be "single-stepped," but no interrupt is generated internally after each instruction is executed. Instead, external hardware must be used to clock the Z8001/2 CPU chip each time an instruction is to be executed. In the case of a division-by-zero or an overflow, the mathematical instructions that generate these conditions will set or clear a number of flags in the FCW (Fig. 3-5), as you would expect. These flags then have to be tested through the use of additional software instructions.

The only two interrupt instructions that the Z8001/2 can execute are enable (EI) and disable (DI) the interrupt. The Z8001/2 have three interrupt inputs: nonmaskable interrupt (NMI), vectored interrupt (VI), and nonvectored interrupt (NVI). The NMI input can never be disabled by the DI instruction. It is always enabled and is often used to indicate catastrophic problems (power failure). Both

Mnemonics	Operands	Addr. Modes	Word, Byte			Long Word			Operation
			NS	SS	SL	NS	SS	SL	
COMFLG	flags	–	7	–	–				Complement Flag (Any combination of C, Z, S, P/V)
DI*	int	–	6	–	–				Disable Interrupt (Any combination of NVI, VI)
EI*	int	–	6	–	–				Enable Interrupt (Any combination of NVI, VI)
HALT*	–	–	(8 + 3 n)						HALT
LDCTL*	CTLR, src	R	7	–	–				Load Into Control Register CTLR ← src
LDCTL*	dst, CTLR	R	7	–	–				Load from Control Register dst ← CTLR
LDCTLB	FLGR, src	R	7	–	–				Load Into Flag Byte Register FLGR ← src
LDCTLB	dst, FLGR	R	7	–	–				Load from Flag Byte Register dst ← FLGR
LDPS*	src	IR	12	–	16				Load Program Status PS ← src
		DA	16	20	22				
		X	17	20	23				
MBIT*	–	–	7	–	–				Test Multi-Micro Bit Set S if $\overline{M_I}$ is Low; reset S if $\overline{M_I}$ is High.
MREQ*	dst	R	(12 + 7 n)						Multi-Micro Request
MRES*	–	–	5	–	–				Multi-Micro Reset
MSET*	–	–	5	–	–				Multi-Micro Set
NOP	–	–	7	–	–				No Operation
RESFLG	flag	–	7	–	–				Reset Flag (Any combination of C, Z, S, P/V)
SETFLG	flag	–	7	–	–				Set Flag (Any combination of C, Z, S, P/V)

*Privileged instructions. Executed in system mode only.

Courtesy Zilog, Inc.

the VI and NVI interrupt inputs can be enabled and disabled, in any combination, by the DI and EI instructions.

The Z8001/2 also have a special return instruction, IRET, which is only used at the end of interrupt service subroutines. When an interrupt occurs, the CPU chips save the program counter (both the segment number and offset on the Z8001), the FCW, and a 16-bit interrupt identifier word. When the IRET instruction is executed at the end of an interrupt service subroutine, all of this information is popped off of the stack. When a subroutine is simply called, only the program counter is saved on the stack. Interrupts are discussed in greater detail later in this chapter.

Processor Control Instructions

The processor control instructions, along with DI and EI, are summarized in Table 3-13. These instructions are used to set, clear, and complement individual flags in the FCW, and they are also used to control the CPU chip in a multiprocessor environment (MBIT, MREQ, MSET, and MRES). The load instructions are used to read information from, and write information to, the FCW, refresh counter, program status area pointer (PSAP; both portions of the PSAP in the case of the Z8001), and both stack pointers (system and normal). As you might expect, a number of these instructions can be executed only when the CPU is in the system mode of operation.

Instruction Set Conclusion

The instruction set of the Z8001/2 is very similar to that of the 8086. Some of the differences include the ability of the Z8001/2 to divide 64-bit numbers by 32-bit numbers, and multiply 32-bit numbers by 32-bit numbers. The Z8001/2 can also execute a number of bit set, reset, and test instructions, clear and set groups of registers to a particular value, and perform block transfer and block i/o operations. These CPUs can also perform sophisticated string operations.

The Z8001 and Z8002 also have a large number of general-purpose registers, but the reader should not be misled when comparing the number of registers in the Z8001 to those in the 8086. Remember, two registers are often used to store an address in the Z8001, a segment number and a 16-bit offset, just as they were in the 8086.

MICROPROCESSOR CHIP HARDWARE

As we have already seen, two versions of the Z8000-type microprocessors are available: the segmented Z8001 and the nonsegmented Z8002. Other than the fact that these processors can address a different amount of memory, they are basically the same. The major difference is that two registers are often used to store an address in the

Table 3-14. The Status Outputs Generated by the CPU Chips

ST3	ST2	ST1	ST0	
L	L	L	L	Internal Operation
L	L	L	H	Memory Refresh
L	L	H	L	Normal I/O Transaction
L	L	H	H	Special I/O Transaction
L	H	L	L	Reserved
L	H	L	H	Non-Maskable Interrupt Acknowledge
L	H	H	L	Non-Vectored Interrupt Acknowledge
L	H	H	H	Vectored Interrupt Acknowledge
H	L	L	L	Memory Transaction for Operand
H	L	L	H	Memory Transaction for Stack
H	L	H	L	Reserved
H	L	H	H	Reserved
H	H	L	L	Memory Transaction for Instruction Fetch (Subsequent Word)
H	H	L	H	Memory Transaction for Instruction Fetch (First Word)
H	H	H	L	Reserved
H	H	H	H	Reserved

Courtesy Advanced Micro Devices, Inc.

Z8001, and only one register is used in the Z8002. However, both of these devices address memory and peripherals in the same manner, and perform the same operations when an instruction is executed or an interrupt is processed.

For the Z8001/2 to perform a useful task they must be capable of communicating with both memory and peripherals. To do this they must be able to generate data, address, and control signals to control these devices. To address memory the Z8001/2 generate a 7-bit segment number and a 16-bit offset, or a 16-bit address. To address peripherals both processors generate a 16-bit peripheral address. These processors also communicate with memory and peripherals with a 16-bit data bus, and to save pins on the integrated circuits the 16 least significant address signals are multiplexed with the 16 data signals. Therefore both the Z8001 and Z8002 have pins labeled AD0 through AD15. These signals can be seen in the pinouts for these chips in Figs. 3-1 and 3-3. The address strobe ($\overline{AS}$) signal, which is present on both of these chips, is a logic zero when an address (peripheral or memory) is present on the multiplexed address/data pins.

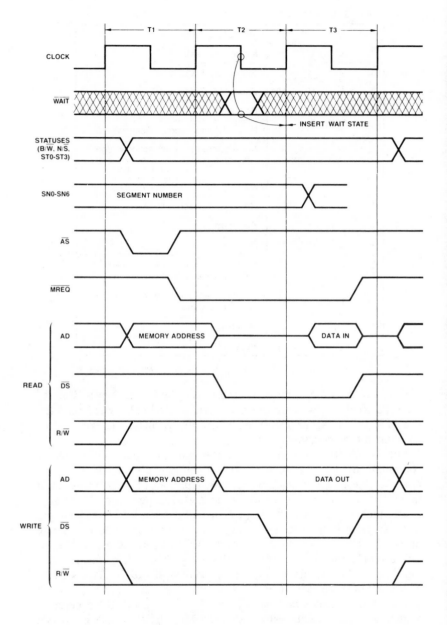

Courtesy Advanced Micro Devices, Inc.

Fig. 3-11. Z8001 memory read and memory write timing.

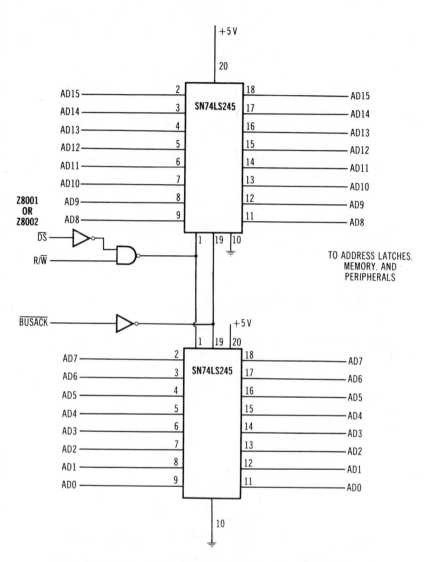

Fig. 3-12. Buffering the bidirectional data bus in a Z8001/2-based microcomputer system.

The Z8001/2 also have four outputs, ST0 through ST3, which must be externally decoded with some TTL logic, to indicate when a memory operation or peripheral operation is taking place, among other possibilities. Only five or six different states of these four signals are of any interest to the reader (Table 3-14).

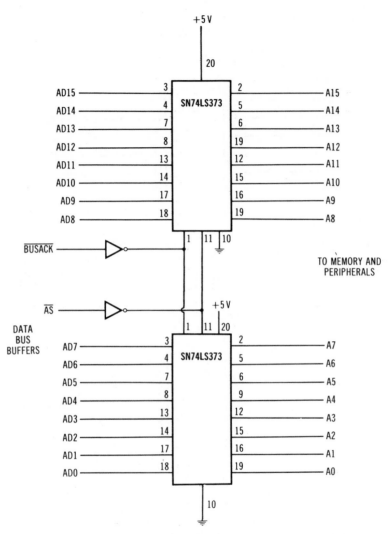

Fig. 3-13. Address latches for a Z8001/2-based microcomputer.

These processors also generate a R/$\overline{\text{W}}$ (pronounced "read write bar") signal for controlling read and write operations, a B/$\overline{\text{W}}$ ("byte word bar") signal for indicating whether a byte or word is being transferred, a data strobe ($\overline{\text{DS}}$) signal that indicates when data is on the address/data bus, and a memory request ($\overline{\text{MREQ}}$) signal to indicate when the processors are communicating with memory. The CPU chips generate and use a number of other signals for control when direct memory access peripherals and multiple processors are

Table 3-15. Independent Z8001/2 Software Vendors

Agent	Materials
Central Data Corporation P.O. Box 2530, Station M 713 Edgebrook Drive Champaign, IL 61820	Operating system, editor,* assembler,* debugger*
Hemenway Associates, Inc. 101 Tremont Street Boston, MA 02108	Operating system, editor, assembler, linking, loader, floating-point package
MicroTec P.O. Box 60337 Sunnyvale, CA 94088	Z8002 relocatable macro assembler (a FORTRAN IV program that runs on minicomputers and larger)
Microsoft 10800 N.E. 80th Street Suite 819 Bellevue, WA 98004	BASIC, UNIX*
Mark Williams Company 1430 W. Wrightwood Ave. Chicago, IL 60614	COHERENT operating system,* editor,* assembler,* cross-assembler*

*Currently not available, for future release.

used. The Z8001/2 also have an $\overline{\text{N}}$/S ("normal system bar") signal to indicate which mode of operation they are in.

CPU TIMING

Typical Z8001 memory-read and memory-write operations are shown in Fig. 3-11. As you can see, the AS signal is generated when an address is present on the address/data pins (AD0–AD15). The memory/peripheral address must be latched off of these pins, and simple (inexpensive) 4- or 8-bit latches can be used to do the job. The data strobe signal ($\overline{\text{DS}}$) is usually gated with R/W to indicate when data can be placed on the bus or can be gated off of the bus. The resulting signal is then used by both peripherals and memory.

Since the data bus is wired to all memory devices and most, if not all, peripheral devices, it must be buffered in all but the simplest systems. The data bus buffers (Fig. 3-12) and the address latches (Fig. 3-13) shown can be used with either the Z8001 or Z8002. The only difference between these two processors is that during the T1 and T2 states of operation, only the segment number is output by the Z8001.

In Fig. 3-11 you can see that a read- or write-operation requires a number of clock or "T" states. The number of nanoseconds per clock cycle is determined by external logic and must be at least 250 ns. Therefore the 8086, which has a 200-ns cycle time, is 50 ns faster than the Z8001/2. However, this does not mean that the 8086 executes any instructions faster or as fast as these two processors. That would be determined by the number of clock cycles required to execute an instruction, multiplied by the clock cycle time.

Unfortunately, *the clock input* (pin 35 of the Z8001, pin 30 of the Z8002) *is not TTL compatible.* However, a special clock chip

```
                            !Bubble sort - ascending order!
                            !Starting address of list is stored in 5400!
                            !Number of elements in list is stored in 5404!

0000 6104    5400    SORT:    LD R4,%5400      !Load address into R4!
0004 6105    5404             LD R5,%5404      !Load count into R5!
0008 AB50                     DEC R5           !Number of comparisons!
000A A2E0    INIT:            RESB RL6,#0      !Clear exchange flag!
000C 9442                     LDL RR2,RR4      !Count & address into R2 & R3!
000E 1420    COMP:            LDL RR0,@R2      !Read words into R0 & R1!
0010 8B10                     CP R0,R1         !Out of order?!
0012 E203                     JR LE,DECCNT     !No, continue!
0014 AD10                     EX R0,R1         !Yes, exchange them!
0016 1D20                     LDL @R2,RR0      !Store them in memory!
0018 A4E0                     SETB RL6,#0      !Set exchange indicator!
001A A921    DECCNT:          INC R2,#2        !Increment to next pair!
001C AB30                     DEC R3           !Decrement word count!
001E EAF7                     JR GT,COMP       !No, continue pass!
0020 A6E0                     BITB RL6,#0      !Yes, any exchanges?!
0022 EEF3                     JR NZ,INIT       !Yes, start another pass!
                                               !No, done!
```

Fig. 3-14. Bubble sort instructions for the Z8001/2.

is being designed and should be available soon. If it is not available, two integrated circuits, two transistors, and several resistors and capacitors are required to design and build a proper clock.[3] In fact, if you are interested in designing your own Z8001/2-based microcomputer, Reference 3 at the end of this chapter contains a wealth of information.

MICROCOMPUTER SOFTWARE

Currently there is very little software that can be used with the Z8001/2. Advanced Micro Computers has a nice line-by-line assembler and a debugger/monitor that can be used with their AMC 96/4016 microcomputer. Zilog also has a monitor program for their

```
                            !List starts at memory location 6000!
                            !Starting address is stored in 5400!
                            !Count is stored in 5404!

0000 7601    6000    ISORT:   LDA R1,%6000     !Load list address into R1!
0004 6F01    5400             LD %5400,R1      !and store it at %5400!
0008 2100    0257             LD R0,#599       !Load 1st word (count) into R0!
000C 4D05    5404             LD %5404,#600    !and store array size at %5404!
0010 0258
0012 2F10    LOOP:            LD @R1,R0        !Enter word into list!
0014 A911                     INC R1,#2        !Loop until R0!
0016 AB00                     DEC R0           !goes minus!
0018 EDFC                     JR PL,LOOP
```

Fig. 3-15. Initializing memory for the bubble sort instructions.

```
                  !The address of the MAIN string is stored in 5400!
                  !The address of the TEST string is stored in 5404!

0000 BD46        SEARCH:   LDK R4,#6            !Load test string length!
0002 6105   5404           LD R5,%5404          !Get test string address!
0006 6102   5400           LD R2,%5400          !Get main string address!
000A 2103   2A3F           LD R3,#'*?'          !RH3 = *, RL3 = ?!
000E 8D68                  CLR R6               !Dummy count - infinity!
0010 0A2B        MCHAR:    CPB RL3,@R2          !At end of main string?!
0012 E607                  JR EQ,FAIL           !Yes, no match!
0014 9440                  LDL RR0,RR4          !No, get length and address!
0016 BA16   002E           CPSIRB @R2,@R1,R0,NE !Compare strings!
001A EE04                  JR NZ,FOUND          !Found the test string!
001C BA24   0636           CPIRB RH3,@R2,R6,EQ  !Skip past the *!
0020 E8F7                  JR MCHAR             !Try another substring in MAIN!
0022 8D07        FAIL:     NOP                  !Didn't find the test string!
0024 8D07        FOUND:    NOP                  !Found the test string!
```

Fig. 3-16. Searching for MICRO* in the MAIN string.

```
                  !The original number is stored in 5400!
                  !The square root is returned in 5402!

0000 6101   5400  SQRT:    LD R1,%5400          !Get the original number!
0004 8D08                  CLR R0               !Clear R0, part of RR0!
0006 9404                  LDL RR4,RR0          !Save original in RR4!
0008 1B00   00C8           DIV RR0,#200         !Divide original by 200!
000C A911                  INC R1,#2            !Add 2 to the result!
000E 9442        NEXT:     LDL RR2,RR4          !Get original!
0010 9B12                  DIV RR2,R1           !Divide by last approx!
0012 A136                  LD R6,R3             !Save quotient in R6!
0014 9932                  MULT RR2,R3          !then square it!
0016 8B53                  CP R3,R5             !Equal to original?!
0018 E603                  JR EQ,DONE           !Yes, then store it!
001A 8161                  ADD R1,R6            !No, add last 2 approx!
001C B31C                  RRC R1,#1            !Divide result by 2!
001E E8F7                  JR NEXT              !and try again!
0020 6F06   5402  DONE:    LD %5402,R6          !Save the result!
```

Fig. 3-17. Approximating the square root of a number.

Z8000 development module. Perhaps the most sophisticated software is available from independent software vendors.

Central Data Corporation has an operating system/data base management system that is used with their Z8001-based CPU board, disk, multiterminals, and at least 65K words of R/W memory. They also have an editor, assembler and multiuser debugger planned for future introduction. Hemenway Associates has a Z8000-based operating system, along with an editor, assembler, and linking loader. The oper-

```
                          !Enter with the angle in R1!
                          !Exit with the signed sine in R0!


0000 8300          SINANG:   SUB R0,R0          !Clear the sign flag!
0002 0B01  00B4              CP R1,#180         !Angle in 180 - 360 range?!
0006 E103                    JR LT,SINPOS       !No, sine is positive!
0008 A50F                    SET R0,#15         !Yes, set sine bit!
000A 0301  00B4              SUB R1,#180        !Subtract 180 from angle!
000E 0B01  005A   SINPOS:   CP R1,#90          !Angle 0 - 90 ?!
0012 E203                    JR LE,GETSIN       !Yes, get angle!
0014 8D12                    NEG R1             !No, negate angle!
0016 0101  00B4              ADD R1,#180        !Add 180 to result!
001A B308          GETSIN:   RL R1,#1           !Multiply angle by 2!
001C 8510  0020'             OR R0,TABLE(R1)    !OR angle and sign bit!
                                                !DONE!
0020               TABLE:                       !Lookup table!
```

Fig. 3-18. Using a lookup table in a sine approximation.

ating system requires less than 8K words of memory and can be relocated to any starting address. Hemenway also has a floating-point
math package. Microsoft also has a BASIC interpreter for the Z8000,
for whoever is interested. All of the independent software vendors
are summarized in Table 3-15.

Of course, one method of software generation that both AMD and
Zilog promote is the cross assembly of Z8000 programs on 8080A-
and Z80-based development systems. Both AMD and Zilog have editors, assemblers, and debuggers that can be used to prepare assembly
language programs. The AMD system is based on the 8080A and
the Zilog system is based on the Z80. These are powerful development systems and they are available with BASIC, COBOL, FOR-
TRAN, and Pascal, to name just a few of the available languages.
*However, none of this software can be executed on a Z8000-based
microcomputer system.*

BENCHMARKS

The "standard" benchmarks can be seen in Figs. 3-14 through
3-18. These benchmarks were provided by Zilog, Inc., with all
benchmark times calculated by multiplying the number of clock
cycles required by each benchmark, by the cycle time (100 ns) of
a 10 MHz Z8002. Table 3-16 gives the execution times.

Bubble Sort

The bubble sort benchmark is shown in Fig. 3-14. At the start
of the BSORT instructions, register R4 is loaded with the starting

address of the list and R5 is loaded with the 16-bit count (600_{10}). This count is then decremented and at INIT, bit D0 of RL6 (the exchange indicator) is reset to zero. The LDL instruction then loads the count and list address into registers R2 and R3. At COMP a 32-bit long word (two of the 16-bit numbers) is loaded into RR0. The two 16-bit numbers are compared, and if the value in R0 is less than the value in R1, the Z8002 jumps to DECCNT. Otherwise, the two values are exchanged and are then stored back in memory. Just before DECCNT, the exchange indicator is set.

At DECCNT the memory address in R2 is incremented by 2 and the word count is decremented. If the result of this instruction is nonzero, the Z8002 jumps back to COMP. Finally, after all 600 elements in the list have been examined, the Z8002 checks the state of bit D0 in RL6. If this is nonzero, an exchange took place, so the entire list has to be examined again. Only when no exchanges have taken place during the last pass through the list will the Z8002 stop checking the list, Rough calculations indicate that 16,370,000 clock cycles or 1.637 s (10 MHz) will be required to sort the list.

Of course, a simple program was also written to initialize the list with the worst-case arrangement of the 600 data values. This program is shown in Fig. 3-15. It requires 13,242 clock cycles, or 1.32 ms, using a 10-MHz Z8002.

ASCII String Search

The ASCII string search benchmark is listed in Fig. 3-16. This program requires 945 clock cycles, or 94.5 μs (10 MHz), to be executed. At the beginning of this benchmark, R4 is loaded with the number of characters in MICRO* (6), R5 is loaded with the address of the TEST string, and R2 is loaded with the address of the MAIN string. An asterisk is then stored in RH3, a question mark is stored in RL3, and R6 is cleared. At MCHAR a MAIN string character is compared to the question mark in RL3. If the character in memory is a question mark, the Z8002 has reached the end of the list, so the microprocessor jumps to FAIL.

If the character is not a question mark, RR0 is loaded with the count in RR4 and then the strings are compared until either the count in R0 is decremented to zero or the strings are no longer equal. Only when the two MICRO* strings are compared will the microprocessor execute the JR NZ to FOUND. If the strings being compared are not equal, the Z8002 will find the beginning of the next string in the MAIN string by executing the CPIRB instruction. The content of register RH3 (an asterisk) will be compared to characters in the MAIN string until they are equal. At that point, register R2 will be addressing the next substring in the MAIN string. By jumping back to MCHAR, the Z8002 continues the string comparison process.

111

Square Root Determination

The square root approximation benchmark is listed in Fig. 3-17. The 10-MHz Z8002 requires just 51 μs to determine the square root of 58,081 and 16,384, and 71 μs to determine the square root of 10,000.

At the beginning of this benchmark, R1 is loaded with the original number and R0 is cleared to zero. This 32-bit number is then saved in RR4. The content of RR0 is then divided by 200, and the result is incremented by 2, to form the first approximation. At NEXT, RR2 is loaded with the original number, which is then divided by the first approximation in R1. The result of the division is saved in R6. The result of the division is then squared, by multiplying R3 by RR2 (R2 and R3). The result in R3 is then compared to the original number in R5 (part of RR4) and the Z8002 jumps to DONE if the numbers are equal. If the numbers are not equal, a new approximation has to be calculated, so the first approximation (R1) is added to the last approximation (R6) and the result in R1 is divided by 2 by the RRC instruction. The Z8002 then jumps back to NEXT to see if this new approximation, is, in fact, the square root of the original number.

Lookup Table Benchmark

The sine lookup table benchmark is listed in Fig. 3-18. At the beginning of this benchmark, R0 is subtracted from itself, so that the sign flag is cleared. The angle in register R1 is then compared to 180_{10}. If the angle in R1 is less than 180, the Z8002 jumps to SINPOS, since the sine of any angle between 0 and 180 degrees is positive. If the angle is greater than 180 degrees, the sine of the angle is negative, so bit 15 of R0 is set. After this bit is set, 180 is subtracted from the angle in R1 and the result is saved in R1.

At SINPOS the angle (or reduced angle) in R1 is compared to 90_{10}. If the angle is 90 degrees or less, the Z8002 jumps to GETSIN, since the sine of the angle can be looked up in the table directly. Otherwise, the angle in R1 (between 91 and 180 degrees) is negated, and then 180 is added to this value. The result is left in R1.

Table 3-16. Execution Times for the Z8002 Benchmarks

Benchmark	Execution Time
Bubble Sort	1.637 s
Memory initialization	1.32 ms
ASCII string search	94.5 μs
Square root	51/71 μs
Lookup table	4.6/7.1 μs

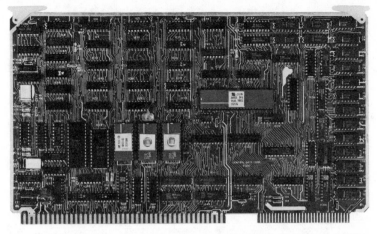

Courtesy Central Data Corporation

Fig. 3-19. The Central Data Corporation Z8001 Multibus-compatible CPU card.

Finally, at GETSIN, the "angle" in R1 is rotated to the left once, multiplying the number in R1 by 2. The content of R1 is then used as an index, and the address of TABLE is actually specified in the instruction. The content of memory at this address is ORed with the content of R0 (the sign bit) and the result is left in R0. Depending on the quadrant that the original angle is in, between 4.6 and 7.1 μs will be required to execute this benchmark on a 10-MHz Z8002.

MICROCOMPUTER BOARDS

By using the Z8001/2 you can design and build a very powerful microcomputer, or you may be interested in saving some time and actually purchase a kit or assembled Z8001/2-based microcomputer. A typical example is the AMC 96/4016 evaluation board. This relatively-low-cost microcomputer (Fig. 3-4) contains the nonsegmented Z8002 CPU chip along with up to 4K words of R/W memory and 6K words of EPROM/ROM. This board also contains two RC-232C asynchronous communications ports, three 16-bit interval timers, of which one is available to the user, and three 8-bit i/o ports. AMC also has an ASCII keyboard/20-character alphanumeric display board that can plug directly into the CPU board. There is also a line-by-line assembler and debugger/monitor that can be used with this microcomputer. This software has been reviewed.[4]

The Central Data Corporation's Z8001-based CPU card is shown in Fig. 3-19. Since this is the segmented version of the CPU chip, one would expect the CPU board to contain the 8010 memory-management chip. However, at the time that this board was designed,

113

Fig. 3-20. The Zilog Z8001/2 evaluation board.

the MMU was not available, so Central Data simulated its operation by using readily available logic and memory circuits. This board is fully Multibus compatible, so it can be used in a number of different systems. The board contains 2K words of EPROM, an interrupt controller, an arithmetic processing unit (the popular Am9511), an 8253 interval timer (which contains three 16-bit timers), along with the memory management hardware. Central Data also has a number of disk controllers, R/W memory, EPROM, and serial and parallel boards for this system.

The Zilog Z8000 development module is shown in Fig. 3-20. This Z8002-based microcomputer is very similar to the SDK-86 because neither of these microcomputers is designed for much expansion or for use with additional memory or peripheral boards. However, the Zilog microcomputer does contain 16K words of dynamic R/W memory and from 1K to 16K words of EPROM using either 2708s, 2716s, or 2732s. This single-board microcomputer also contains two serial ports and 32 bits of parallel i/o. An interesting feature of this microcomputer, which is not available on any other Z8000-based microcomputer, is the fact that either a Z8001 or Z8002 can be plugged into the board. No provision has been made for the 8010 MMU, so the Z8001 would have to be used in the nonsegmented mode of operation.

INTERFACING

Like the 8086 and the other 16-bit microprocessors, peripherals are interfaced to the Z8001/2 using the address bus, data bus, and

114

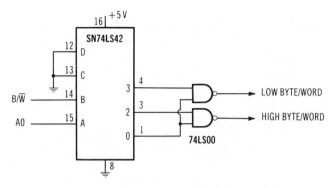

Fig. 3-21. The circuitry required to select a byte or word in memory.

some of the control signals that the CPU chip generates. *Any micro-processor that can address memory is capable of performing memory-mapped i/o.* Thus all of the microprocessors described in this book can perform memory-mapped i/o. However, some of these processors (the 8086/8088, Z8001/2, and 9900/9980) can also perform i/o without using some of the microprocessor's memory address space.

The Z8001/2, like the 8086 and 9900, have special i/o instructions. Some of these instructions are used to communicate with "standard" peripherals, while others are used solely to communicate with the 8010 MMU. Using the "standard" i/o instructions the Z8001/2 can address 65K-byte or 32K-word peripherals. Even though the Z8001 can address more memory because of segment numbers, it is still limited to 65K-byte peripheral devices. No peripheral segment numbers are ever generated. Since the Z8001/2 address i/o devices using many of the same control signals that are used when addressing memory, memory addressing will be examined first. As we know, the Z8001/2 can address a large amount of memory, using a segment number and a 16-bit offset (Z8001) or a 16-bit address (Z8002). Since the Z8002 is the simpler, it will be used in the memory addressing discussion.

The Z8002 can address either bytes or words that are stored in memory. This processor can address 65,536 bytes of memory, or 32,768 words of memory. Since memory is physically organized as 16-bit words, this means that the Z8002 can address *either* of the 2 bytes in a word. *To address the most significant byte in a word an even address is used, and to address the least significant byte in a word an odd address is used.* Words must be word aligned in memory, thus they can only be addressed with even addresses. Using the B/W ("byte word bar") signal along with A0, circuitry can be designed to select one or the other bytes, or both bytes (a word operation). This circuitry is shown in Fig. 3-21.

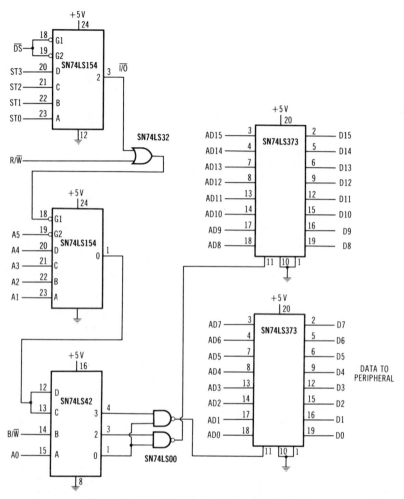

Fig. 3-22. A 16-bit output port for the Z8001/2.

Based on this, simple 8- and 16-bit input and output ports can be designed. The only difference is that i/o control signals are used, rather than memory control signals. A 16-bit output port is shown in Fig. 3-22. Only when data strobe ($\overline{DS}$) is a logic zero, indicating that the data bus may be used in a data transfer, will the upper SN74LS154 decoder be enabled. The "standard i/o" state of the Z8002 is then decoded from ST0 through ST3 (Table 3-14). Thus output 2 of this decoder (pin 3) will be a logic zero only when data is being output during a standard i/o operation. This logic zero is used to enable the second SN74LS154 decoder, which decodes A5,

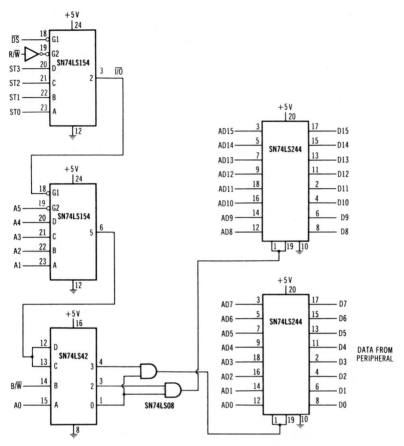

Fig. 3-23. A 16-bit input port for the Z8001/2.

A4, A3, A2, and A1 on the address bus. All of these inputs to the decoder must be logic zeros in order for output 0 (pin 1) of the decoder to go to a logic zero. *Since A6 through A15 have not been included in this interface design, this is a nonabsolute device address decoder.* This means that there are a number of different device addresses that will cause the zero output of this decoder to go to a logic zero.

The logic zero generated by this decoder is used to enable the SN74LS42 decoder that decodes the states of A0 and B/$\overline{\text{W}}$. The high-byte/word and low-byte/word signals are then used to latch either the high byte, the low byte, or both bytes (a word) off of the data bus.

With this interface a 16-bit word could be transferred out to the interface if the Z8002 outputs a word to port address XXXXXXXX-XX000000, where the Xs mean that the address bits can be either

```
TEST:       LD R0,DATA      ;Get a data word from memory.
            OUT #0,R0       ;Output the data to port 0.
            .               ;Execute the remainder.
            .               ;of the program.
            .

DATA:       045FAH          ;Data is stored here.
```

Fig. 3-24. Writing a 16-bit word stored in memory out to an output port.

```
LOOP:   OUT #0,R3       ;Output R3 to port 0.
        INC R3,1        ;Increment the content of R3 by 1.
        JR LOOP         ;Jump back and output the new value.
```

**Fig. 3-25. Writing the 16-bit contents of register R3 out to the
output port continually.**

ones or zeros. Remember, these bits are not used in the *nonabsolute
device address decoder*. To output a byte at an even address (the
most significant byte of a word), the byte would be output to port
XXXXXXXXXX000000. For the least significant byte a port address of XXXXXXXXXX000001 would be used. The important

```
TEST:   LD R2, 020H     ;Load R2 with the base address.
        LD R4, 0        ;Load R4 with the index value.
        LD R5, 024H     :Load R5 with the word count.
WAIT:   IN R0,1         ;Input port 1 into R0.
        BIT R0,1        ;Check bit D0 of R0.
        JR NZ,WAIT      ;Wait if its a 1.
        IN R0,0         ;Input the data from port 0.
        LD (R2+R4),R0   ;Store it in memory.
        INC R4,2        ;Increment R4 by 2.
        DEC R5,1        ;Decrement the word count
        JR NZ,WAIT      ;Jump if not done.
        HLT             :Then halt.
```

Fig. 3-26. Reading data from an input port and storing it in memory.

point to remember is that the $\overline{DS}$, R/$\overline{W}$, A0, and B/$\overline{W}$ signals must
be used to control the flow of information between peripherals and
the CPU chip.

A simple 16-bit input port is shown in Fig. 3-23. The important
difference here is that the logic one state of the R/$\overline{W}$ signal is used
to enable a decoder. The $\overline{DS}$, A0, and B/$\overline{W}$ signals are still used to
select either the high byte, low byte, or both bytes.

I/O SOFTWARE

Some simple i/o software examples are shown in Figs. 3-24, 3-25,
and 3-26. In Fig. 3-24 the Z8002 is used to output a 16-bit value
to an output port. To do this a data value is read from memory into
the R0 register, which is then output to port 0. Since programmable
peripheral interface (**PPI**) chips were not used in this interface, as

they were in the 8086 examples, no instructions have to be executed into order to "program" the interface to act as an output port. Due to the chips used in the design, the output port in Fig. 3-22 can *only* be used as an output port.

In Fig. 3-25 the content of register R0 is incremented and output to the output port as quickly as possible. Note that in both of these software examples (Figs. 3-24 and 3-25), OUT instructions have been used where *the 16-bit port address is specified in the instruction.*

The most complex i/o example is contained in Fig. 3-26. This example assumes that we are using the input port shown in Fig. 3-23. In this example 35_{10} data values have to be input from the input port and stored in memory. Base indexed addressing has been used in this example, so register R2 is used to store the base address, R4 contains the index, and R5 contains the word count.

At WAIT, the Z8002 inputs a value from port 1 and tests bit 0 of the value that was input. If the result is 1, the Z8002 jumps back to "WAIT" and continues executing instructions in this loop until

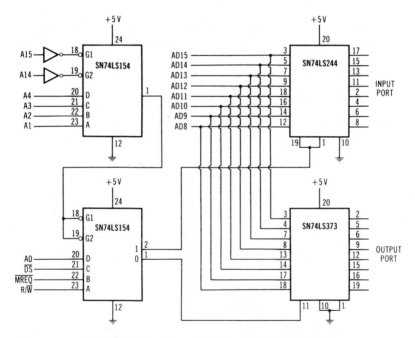

Fig. 3-27. Memory-mapped i/o ports for the Z8001/2.

bit D0 of input port 1 is a logic zero. When this occurs, the Z8002 inputs the data value from port 0, stores it in memory, and increments register R4 by 2. Register R4 is incremented by 2 so that when the next word is input from the peripheral it is stored in the next *word* memory location. The count in R5 is then decremented by 1. If the result of this instruction is nonzero, the Z8002 jumps back to WAIT. If the result is 0, the Z8002 will halt.

Note that the nice block i/o instructions that the Z8001/2 have cannot be used in this example, because there are no provisions to input information from a "slow" peripheral. Also, if the Z8001 had been used in these examples, three registers would have had to been used to store the base address and index.

MEMORY-MAPPED I/O

A memory-mapped i/o port is very similar to a standard i/o port, the only difference being that instead of decoding ST0–ST3 for the i/o request signal, the $\overline{\text{MREQ}}$ signal generated by the CPU chip is used. Since the Z8001 not only outputs a 16-bit offset, but also a 7-bit segment number, we might also consider using these 7 bits of information in the decoder design. In fact, in some systems a particular segment number might be "dedicated" to all peripherals.

A simple 8-bit input port and an 8-bit output port are shown in Fig. 3-27, using memory-mapped i/o interfacing techniques. To keep the interface simple, the high (even) byte is used for both ports.

The timing for this type of i/o transfer can be seen in Fig. 3-11. As you would expect, since the i/o device "appears" to be a memory location to the processor, the timing for a memory-mapped i/o device and a memory location is the same. Since this timing diagram is for the Z8001, a segment number is output when memory is addressed. For the Z8002 no segment number would be output. As always, the $\overline{\text{DS}}$ (data strobe) and R/W (read/write) signals must be used in the interface, along with a decoded address and the $\overline{\text{MREQ}}$ (memory request) signal.

Both methods of interfacing are relatively simple. The only advantage of standard i/o is that it does not use up any of the memory address space, and the only advantage of memory-mapped i/o is that any *memory reference* instruction can be used to communicate with the peripheral devices.

INTERRUPTS

The Z8001/2 can be interrupted by both internal and external events. If an internal event causes the Z8001/2 to be interrupted, the word "trap" is used to describe the event. For external events the word "interrupt" is used.

Both of these CPU chips have the same traps and interrupts. The processors will be "trapped" when one of the following events occurs:

(1) a system call (SC) instruction is executed, (2) an unimplemented op code is executed in a program, (3) the processor attempts to execute a privileged instruction in the normal mode of operation, and (4) a segmentation error occurs (as determined by the 8010 MMU). Regardless of the trap involved, the program counter (either 16 bits for the Z8002 or 23 bits for the Z8001), the flag and control word

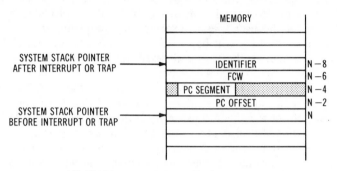

(A) Z8001 program status saving sequence.

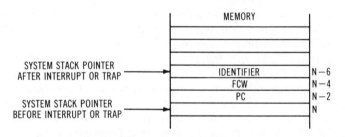

(B) Z8002 program status saving sequence.

Fig. 3-28. Information placed on the stack due to a trap or interrupt.

(FCW), and a 16-bit "identifier" (which identifies the trap that occurred) are all pushed onto the stack. The CPU then fetches from memory new program status information. To address this section of memory the program status area pointer (Fig. 3-6) is used. From this section of memory the CPU fetches a new program counter (either 16 or 23 bits) value and FCW value.

The PSAP is only 8 bits wide on the Z8002 and only 15 bits wide on the Z8001 (7-bit segment number and 8 bits of displacement).

The 8 msb's of the address (Z8002) or displacement (Z8001) must be programmed by the user. Of course, the segment number for the PSAP must also be programmed (Z8001 only). *If a trap occurs, internal CPU logic provides the 8 least significant bits, which are used along with the contents of the PSAP to address memory.*

For an interrupting peripheral device, its interface must provide the 8 least significant bits that are used with the PSAP to address memory. The state of the stack when a trap or interrupt occurs is shown in Fig. 3-28 for both the Z8001 and Z8002. The section of memory that the PSAP can address is shown in Figs. 3-29 and 3-30.

In Fig. 3-29 the user has programmed the 8 most significant bits (msb's) of the PSAP and the segment number. If a trap occurs on the Z8001 the 8 least significant bits (lsb's) will be provided by internal logic. If the user tries to execute an unimplemented op code in a program, the lsb's will be set to 00010000. If a system call instruction is executed, the lsb's will be set to 00011000, etc. For the Z8002 (Fig. 3-30), segment numbers are not used in memory addresses, so the amount of information stored in the PSAP is less. Therefore the 8 lsb's of the address that the CPU generates for a "trap" are "closer together" than the equivalent address on the Z8001.

The Z8001/2 will also access the PSAP if the user tries to execute a privileged instruction, such as an i/o instruction, when the CPU is in the normal (rather than system) mode of operation. Finally, a "segmentation trap" will occur if the memory management unit detects a "segment error." Realistically, this might be considered an interrupt since an external signal (generated by the 8010 MMU) is wired to the segment trap input of the Z8001. For additional information on the 8010 refer to the MMU data sheet.[5]

For external interrupts the user can use the $\overline{\text{NMI}}$, $\overline{\text{NVI}}$, and $\overline{\text{VI}}$ inputs to the CPU chips. If either the $\overline{\text{NMI}}$ (nonmaskable interrupt) or $\overline{\text{NVI}}$ (nonvectored interrupt) inputs are used, the Z8001/2 will always go to a specific memory location within the program status area, for the new value of the program counter (PC) and flag and control word (FCW). *If the VI (vectored interrupt) input is used to interrupt the Z8001/2, the interrupting hardware provides the 8 lsb's, that are used along with the other bits in the PSAP to address memory. This will cause the CPU to load new values into the PC and FCW.* By loading the PC with the new PC value found in the PSAP, the Z8001/2 begins to execute the interrupt service subroutine for that peripheral.

As with the 8086 it is possible for the interrupt hardware to actually access portions of the program status area that are reserved for the internal traps. Therefore, interrupt hardware should be limited to generating only "vectors" that are above 00110000 (Z8001) or 00011000 (Z8002), as seen in Fig. 3-29 and 3-30.

The system call (SC) instruction (Table 3-8) is similar to a trap. Whenever this instruction is executed, the Z8001/2 go to the program status area and read a new PC and FCW from memory. This is a 16-bit instruction, where the 8 lsb's of the instruction can have a value between 00000000 and 11111111. These 8 lsb's are used

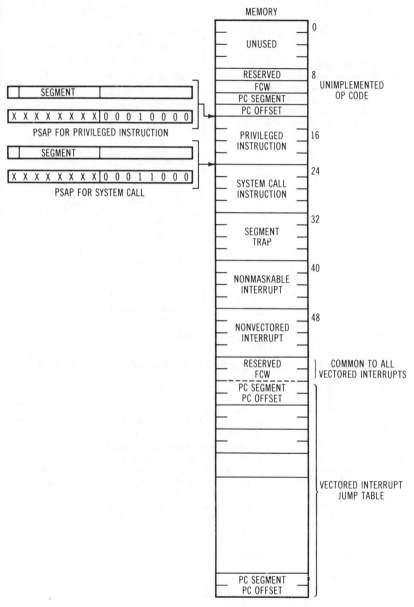

Fig. 3-29. The organization of the program status area for the Z8001.

with the PSAP to point to the proper PC and FCW in the program status area. Thus there are 256 "different 'SC' instructions."

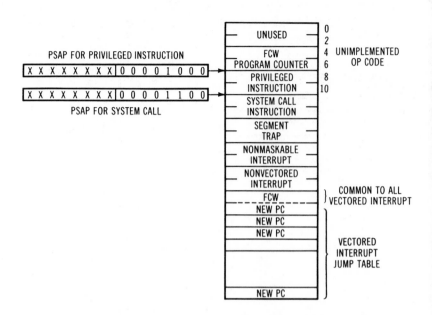

Fig. 3-30. The organization of the program status area for the Z8002.

Table 3-17. The Special-Function Chips for the Z8001 and Z8002

Name	Function
8010 MMU	Memory-management chips; uses segment numbers and offsets from the Z8001 to address 4M bytes of memory
8127 SGC	Clock generator and control logic
8036 CIO	Counter/timer with parallel i/o
8030 SCC	Serial communications controller (two ports)
8038 FIO	First-in, first-out (FIFO) input/output interface
8060 FIFO	FIFO memory and FIO expander
8016 DMA	Direct memory access (DMA) controller
8052 CRT	Cathode-ray tube (crt) controller
8068 DCP	Data encryption device
8073 STC	Counter chip

SPECIAL-FUNCTION CHIPS

There are a number of special peripheral chips that have been designed for the Z8001/2. Many of these chips are similar to those that were designed for use with the Z80. These chips are summarized in Table 3-17. In fact, Zilog uses Z80 peripheral chips on their Z8000 development module (Fig. 3-20).

The 8010 memory-management unit is an extremely complex chip that is only used with the segmented Z8001. When the Z8001 accesses memory, it outputs a 16-bit offset and a 7-bit segment number. The segment number is then used to address R/W memory within the MMU. The 16-bit value stored in this memory location (the base address register file, Fig. 3-8) is then added to a portion of the 16-bit offset.

Since the MMU only contains 64 such R/W memory locations, it can only be used to address 4M bytes of memory. Therefore two MMUs must be used with a Z8001 in order to address all 8M bytes of memory.

The MMU also permits segments of memory to be specified as either read-only, read/write, or code only. Thus the MMU will generate a segment trap if the user tries to execute data or write data into a protected (read-only) section of memory. This is a very powerful and complex chip. It must be programmed by executing software, and the special i/o instructions are used to do this.

The 8127 clock generator provides the non-TTL-compatible clock that the Z8001/2 require, along with reset, wait, and single-step inputs and additional control logic. The 8036 CIO counter/timer and parallel i/o chip contains three 16-bit counters and 20 bits of parallel i/o. The 8030 SCC serial communications controller contains two independent serial i/o ports capable of asynchronous and synchronous communications, including the ability to use SDLC, HDLC, and Bisync. This chip also generates CRC-16 error-checking information and contains modem control signals.

The 8038 FIO FIFO input/output interface unit contains 128 eight-bit FIFO (first-in, first-out) memory locations. This device is particularly useful when the Z8001/2 are used with a number of peripherals. It gives the Z8001/2 the ability to output 128 bytes or words of data, which the peripheral can then access. This reduces the amount of time that the CPU spends servicing peripherals. The block transfer i/o instructions would normally be used to communicate with a device such as this. The 8060 FIFO buffer and FIFO expander would be used with the 8038 to increase the size of the data being transferred (from 8 to 16 bits) or to increase the "depth" of the 8038 beyond 128 words.

The 8016 DMA and 8052 crt controllers are similar to the DMA and crt controllers that are available from many of the other microprocessor and semiconductor manufacturers. The 8065 burst error processor is used primarily with high-speed peripherals, such as floppy disks or hard disks, to correct errors that result during a read or write operation.

A data encryption chip is also available (8068) which implements the National Bureau of Standards (NBS) encryption algorithm. There is also a counter chip (8073) that contains five independent 16-bit counters that can count up or down in either binary or bcd. A number of standard TTL buffers, drivers, and three-state devices are also available that can be used in system, memory or interface design. Because the Z8001/2 are available from a number of manufacturers, all of these chips may not be available from a single manufacturer.

CONCLUSION

As you have seen, the Z8001 and Z8002 are powerful microprocessors. When combined with devices such as the 8010 MMU, they can be used as the heart of a very sophisticated microcomputer system, with many megabytes of memory and sophisticated operating system programs. These processors can operate on many data types, including long words (32 bits), thus making it easier to use them in "number crunching" applications. There are also a number of single-board Z8002-based microcomputers available, so the user can evaluate whether or not the Z8001/2 are the proper processors to use in an application. Of particular interest is Advanced Micro Computer's line-by-line assembler, which makes it reasonably easy to program the Z8002-based AMC 96/4016 microcomputer.

Unfortunately, there is not much software for either of these two processors at the moment. This, however, will change as soon as more users start using these processors. Most of the software that can be used with these processors is available from independent software vendors.

REFERENCES

1. Advanced Micro Devices, Inc. *AMZ8001/2 Processor Instruction Set,* 1979 (AM-PUB086).

2. Titus, C. A.; Larsen, D. G.; and Titus, J. A. *8080/8085 Software Design, Book 2,* Indianapolis: Howard W. Sams & Co., Inc., 1979.

3. Korody, P., and Alfke, R. "Learn to Apply the Power of the Z8002 by Studying a Small 16-Bit Microcomputer," *Electronic Design 22,* October 25, 1979, pp. 90–96.

4. Grappel, R. "Line-by-Line Assembler Eases Z8000 Evaluation," *EDN,* January 20, 1980, pp. 119–124.

5. Zilog, Inc. *Z8010 MMU Memory-Management Unit Product Specification,* October 1979.

4

The LSI-11

This chapter provides information on the architecture, hardware, and software of the LSI-11 series of 16-bit microprocessors. The first section surveys the minicomputer family that produced this microprocessor and suggests how this heritage has determined the LSI-11 architecture. The second section discusses the instruction set, paying particular attention to the interaction of the eight registers with the eight addressing modes. The third section offers an insight into how memory management, used to provide greater addressing capabilities, is implemented. The next two sections present an overview of the hardware and software that is available for the LSI-11 series; the interested reader will find an unusually comprehensive list of sources. The benchmark programs of the sixth section offer useful examples of programming techniques as well as suggesting typical execution speeds. Interfacing (the seventh section) with the LSI-11 is a matter of choosing appropriate boards, because the required chip set and the bus are so completely defined by the manufacturer. The last section contains some comments regarding the LSI-11's present and future place among 16-bit microprocessors.

FAMILY HISTORY: SIRED BY A MINICOMPUTER

As a direct descendant of a pioneering minicomputer, the LSI-11 has a parentage which largely determined its strengths and weaknesses. We begin, therefore, with a brief history of the PDP-11 family.

Digital Equipment Corporation (DEC) was created in 1957 when brothers Kenneth and Stanley Olsen, after an early association with the very early MIT small computers, began producing digital logic modules. In 1959 the company used its own modules to produce the

Programmed Data Processor-1 (PDP-1), an 18-bit-word $120,000 minicomputer. In 1963 the new transistor logic and magnetic core memory technology led to the PDP-5, a minicomputer with a 12-bit word, direct memory access (DMA), and real-time control capabilities. By 1968 the new integrated-circuit technology had led to an updated PDP-5 that was called the PDP-8/I. This minicomputer sold for $13,200.

In 1970 the PDP-11, sporting a 16-bit word and a sophisticated instruction set, made its appearance. The processor communicated with main memory and all peripheral devices over 72 lines (56 signal, 2 power, and 14 ground lines) called the Unibus®. No special instructions for input/output were necessary because the status and data registers for peripheral devices were treated as though they were part of the main memory. All communication over the Unibus utilized a complex, asynchronous handshaking protocol, so that emerging higher-speed peripherals were immediately compatible—they simply exchanged data and shook hands faster. With this memory-mapped input/output, data in a peripheral's data register could be tested or changed without its being brought into main memory or into the processor's registers. Newer microprocessors, such as the Motorola 6800 and 68000, have also followed this path.

That first PDP-11 has since grown into a large family of micro/mini/midicomputers that are upward compatible at the software level. Their popularity has been such that DEC computers are second only to IBM computers in *numbers*. The PDP-11/70 is currently at the top of the PDP-11 line; it uses an extra-high-speed cache memory for midicomputer performance. The PDP-11/03, using the LSI-11 or LSI-11/2 microprocessor, holds up the bottom of the line. (DEC uses the PDP-11/03 label when the LSI-11 or LSI-11/2 is boxed with a backplane and a power supply; with a similar housing the LSI-11/23 becomes the PDP-11/23. See Fig. 4-1.)

A large amount of powerful operating system, programming language, and application software has become available for the PDP-11 family. There are also many sources for supporting hardware. PDP-11s form the basis for many stand-alone, multiuser systems in educational institutions. They are also popular with oem's (original equipment manufacturers), who build laboratory equipment, such as multichannel analyzers, around them. Militarized versions of the LSI-11 and other PDP-11 members are also being used in military aircraft.

The original (1975) LSI-11 processor board was a "quad-height" (four sets of contact fingers) board 10 inches (25.4 cm) long that plugged into an 8.9-inch (20.3-cm) high backplane and contained 4K × 16 bits of RAM memory. (See Fig. 4-2.) The newer (1977) LSI-11/2 processor board is a "dual-height" board (same length,

Fig. 4-1. The PDP-11/23 with the LSI-11/23 processor.

one half the height or width) that contains the same processor chip set but no RAM (so that the size of a minimum system is reduced). The newest (1979) version, the LSI-11/23, retains the LSI-11 bus architecture but has a faster execution speed, a large instruction set, and an increased direct addressing range.

All of the LSI-11 processors utilize a reduced version of the Unibus, a bus structure that commonly goes under the name of Q-Bus. The Q-Bus consists of 72 lines (40 signal, 10 power, 8 ground, and 14 spare lines). The LSI-11 and LSI-11/2 use 16 lines for addressing and therefore can directly address only 64K bytes (or 32K sixteen-bit words); the LSI-11/23 adds two address lines from previously unused lines to furnish direct addressing for up to 256K bytes (or 128K sixteen-bit words).

A MICROPROGRAMMED PROCESSOR

Although the LSI-11 and LSI-11/2 are the lowest-cost members of the PDP-11 family, they arrived with the instruction set of the middle members (PDP-11/35/40). All of the members of the LSI-11 subgroup are *multichip* microprocessors that are *microprogrammed*

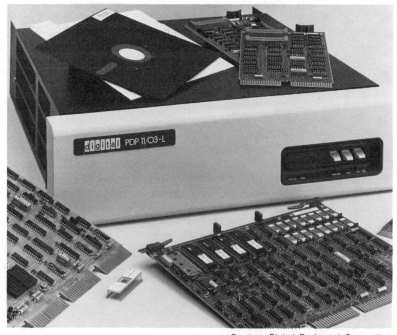

Fig. 4-2. The LSI-11 processor of the PDP-11/03 is on the quad-height board in the foreground.

so as to execute the basic PDP-11 instruction set. The LSI-11 and LSI-11/2 use four or five chips (a control chip, a data chip, two microinstruction ROM chips, and an optional microinstruction ROM chip that adds multiply/divide and floating-point instructions). The LSI-11/23 uses three or four chips (a control chip, a data chip, a memory-management chip that also includes floating-point registers and accumulator, and an optional microinstruction ROM chip that adds a full complement of floating-point instructions to the instruction set). Imbedded in the microcode are instructions that allow the user to examine and change memory and register contents and start or resume program execution directly from the system terminal (rather than having to use panel switches, for example). Also, because the instruction set is implemented by way of microcode, it is possible for a sophisticated user to *add* desired instructions to the instruction set to enhance performance for special applications. In Fig. 4-3 the pencil points to the 40-pin package containing the data and control chips (the basic processor). The microcode for the floating-point instructions resides in the optional 40-pin hybrid package next to the data and control chips.

Courtesy Digital Equipment Corporation
Fig. 4-3. The LSI-11/23 processor board.

The PDP-11 instruction set utilizes six general-purpose registers and two registers that are dedicated for use as the hardware stack pointer (SP) and the program counter (PC). Input/output is completely memory-mapped; there are no special input/output instructions.

The basic LSI-11 can directly process 16-bit word, 8-bit byte, and bit data. Most word instructions are changed to byte instructions by changing the most significant bit of the instruction from a 0 to a 1. Individual bits can be tested and changed by the use of test, logic, and shift instructions.

In addition, the LSI-11 and LSI-11/2 can directly process 32-bit double-word data when the optional extended arithmetic chip with additional microcode is plugged into a prewired socket on the processor board. These two processors utilize the system stack when executing floating-point instructions. The newest LSI-11, the LSI-11/23, using a different microcode option, adds memory management and double-precision floating-point instructions that directly process 64-bit data. Because the floating-point registers are in hardware on the memory-management chip, the LSI-11/23's effective speed in floating-point operations is enhanced by a factor of five to ten.

131

The typical microcycle time for the LSI-11 and LSI-11/2 is 380 ns; for the LSI-11/23 it is 300 ns. The processors are easily single-stepped, however, to aid in the debugging of programs. The fastest execution time is for a register-to-register transfer: 3.5 μs on the LSI-11 and 11/2; 1.72 μs on the LSI-11/23. The slowest execution time on the LSI-11 and LSI-11/2 results when the floating-point divide instructions are used: 232 μs (worst case). This same single-precision floating-point divide instruction requires a maximum of 109 μs on the LSI-11/23.

THE LSI-11 AND LSI-11/23 INSTRUCTION SETS

PDP-11/LSI-11 machine language instructions revolve around a very flexible utilization of eight 16-bit registers and a 16-bit processor status word (PS) register.

The PS register (Fig. 4-4) contains: (a) the four condition code bits (N = 1 after a negative result, Z = 1 after a zero result, V = 1 after an arithmetic overflow, and C = 1 after an arithmetic carry), (b) a trace bit for error-handling and debugging purposes, (c) 3 priority interrupt bits (only one is used on the LSI-11 and LSI-11/2, though), and 4 bits for implementing memory management (LSI-11/23 only).

The eight 16-bit registers (Fig. 4-5) include six general-purpose registers (R0 through R5) and two registers that are hardware-dedicated for use as the system stack pointer (SP) and the system

MEMORY MANAGEMENT	RESERVED FOR FUTURE USE	PRIORITY LEVEL	TRACE	CONDITION CODES			
				N	Z	V	C
BITS 15 → 12	BITS 11 → 8	BITS 7 → 5	4	3	2	1	0

Fig. 4-4. The processor status word (PS) register.

program counter (PC). Each of the general-purpose registers can be used as an accumulator (temporarily storing operands), as a pointer (pointing to the address of operands), or as an index register (pointing to the address of operands after a variable offset has been added to the register contents). The SP register is automatically invoked as an address pointer in interrupt, trap, and subroutine processing; it contains the address of the last entry on the stack. The PC register contains: (a) the address of the next instruction that is to be executed (for single-word instructions) or (b) the address of an offset or the address of a constant (for two- or three-word instructions).

Each single-operand (double operand) LSI-11 machine-language

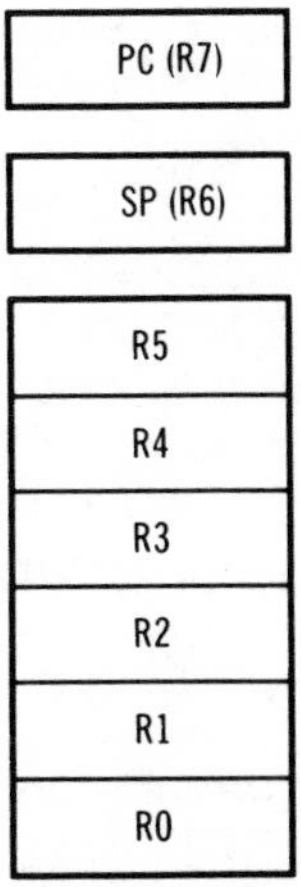

```
                                          ┌──────────────┐
                                          │   PC (R7)    │
                                          └──────────────┘

                                          ┌──────────────┐
                                          │   SP (R6)    │
                                          └──────────────┘

                                          ┌──────────────┐
                                          │     R5       │
  Fig. 4-5. The eight PDP-11/LSI-11       ├──────────────┤
          registers.                      │     R4       │
                                          ├──────────────┤
                                          │     R3       │
                                          ├──────────────┤
                                          │     R2       │
                                          ├──────────────┤
                                          │     R1       │
                                          ├──────────────┤
                                          │     R0       │
                                          └──────────────┘
```

instruction utilizes one (two) of these eight registers and each register reference must specify one of *eight* available addressing modes. Additionally, four special types of addressing result when the PC register is one of the registers specified. Therefore we present the LSI-11 instruction set in terms of (a) the eight register addressing modes with single operands, (b) the eight register addressing modes with double operands, and (c) the four special types of addressing that result when the PC register is used as one of the registers.

PDP-11s naturally utilize the base-8 number system for the recording of addresses or instruction codes because of the eight registers and the eight register addressing modes. Therefore we will use *octal notation* when specifying addresses or operation codes (op codes) in the remainder of the chapter.

Single-Operand Instructions

Single-operand instructions have the following format:

	Destination	
Op Code	*Register Mode*	*Register*
bits 15→6	bits 5→3	bits 2→0

The op code has a 0 in the most significant bit (position 15) if the instruction is a word instruction; the bit is a 1 if the instruction is a byte (or character-oriented) instruction. Thus the instruction that adds 1 to the contents of a specified *word* memory address has an assembler mnemonic of INC (for increment) and an octal op code of 0052; the instruction that adds 1 to the contents of a specified *byte* memory address has an assembler mnemonic of INCB and an octal op code of 1052. Most valid LSI-11 word instructions have byte counterparts; the add, subtract, multiply, and divide instructions are among those that do not.

Table 4-1 depicts the eight general register addressing modes for the special case of single-operand instructions; also, we have used the increment instruction to provide an example of each addressing mode. Notice how easy it is to interpret the machine instructions; the least significant octal digit indicates the destination register, and the octal digit next to it indicates the addressing mode.

Table 4-1. LSI-11/PDP-11 Single-Operand Addressing Modes

Mode	Descriptive Name	Example	
		Assembly Language*	Resulting Octal Code
0	Register	INC R1	005201
1	Register Deferred	INC (R1)	005211
2	Autoincrement	INC (R1)+	005221
3	Autoincrement Deferred	INC @(R1)+	005231
4	Autodecrement	INC −(R1)	005241
5	Autodecrement Deferred	INC @−(R1)	005251
6	Index	INC 74(R1)	005261 000074
7	Index Deferred	INC @200(R1)	005271 000200

*In general, parentheses are used to indicate a first level of indirect addressing and the "@" symbol is added to indicate a second level.

In addressing mode 0 only the specified register is affected; for example, INC R1 adds 1 to the current contents of register R1.

Addressing mode 1 is the first of the indirect (pointer) addressing modes. Thus if R1 contains 000100, the instruction INC (R1) will add 1 to the *contents* of memory location 000100.

In addressing mode 2 the specified register has its own contents automatically incremented (by 2 for a word instruction and by 1 for a byte instruction) after being used as a pointer for the operation. (However, when the SP or PC register is specified, it is *always* incremented by 2.) Thus if R1 contains 000100, the instruction INC (R1)+ will add 1 to the contents of the memory location that responds to address 000100 and then will change the contents of R1 to 000102. It can be seen that this mode allows the programmer to step through and operate on a list of bytes or words that are stored in consecutive locations, using only a single-word instruction for each operation.

Addressing mode 3 provides a *second* level of indirect addressing; the contents of the specified register contain a pointer to the *address* of the operand. Thus if R1 contains 000100 and if location 000100 contains 000300, the instruction INC @(R1)+ will increment the contents of location 000300 and will change the contents of R1 to 000102; the contents of location 000100 are not affected.

Addressing mode 4 is the same as addressing mode 2 except that the contents of the register are decremented (by 1 for a byte instruction and by 2 for a word instruction) *before* being used as the pointer to the operand location. (Again, whenever the SP or PC register is specified, it is always decremented by 2 before being used.) Modes 2 and 4 allow use of *any* of the six general-purpose registers (as well as the SP register) to be used for stack type operations (PUSH and POP), as will become clear when we discuss double-operand instructions. Therefore no special stack instructions are needed.

Mode 5 complements mode 3 by giving automatic predecrementing to the second level of indirect addressing. Thus if R1 contains 000100 and if location 000076 contains 000300, the instruction INC @−(R1) will change the contents of R1 to 000076 and then will add 1 to the contents of location 000300. Modes 3 and 5 allow the programmer to have a table of addresses of operands in contiguous locations (but the operands themselves can be randomly located) and yet use single-word instructions for each operation.

Addressing modes 6 and 7 add constant offsets to the two levels of indirect addressing. Thus if R1 contains 000100, the instruction INC 74(R1) will add 1 to the contents of location 000174. If R1 contains 000100 and if location 000300 contains 000700, the instruction INC @200(R1) will add 1 to the contents of location 000700.

Double-Operand Instructions

Double-operand instructions have the following format:

Op Code	Source Register Mode	Register	Destination Register Mode	Register
bits 15→12	bits 11→9	bits 8→6	bits 5→3	bits 2→0

Again the most significant bit of the op code is 0 for a word instruction and is 1 for a byte instruction. For example, the op code for a transfer of memory contents is 01 for a moving of words and 11 for a moving of bytes.

Table 4-2 depicts the same eight addressing modes but now shows them being used in *double*-operand instructions. Note carefully that, for clarity, we are changing the addressing mode of only the *source* registers in these examples; in each case the second (destination) register uses addressing mode 0. In practice, however, any combination is permitted, so that any two given source and destination registers have $8^2 = 64$ possible address combinations!

Mode 0 is simply a register to register transfer—the instruction with the shortest execution time. The instruction MOV R1,R2 moves the contents of R1 to R2 and leaves R1 unchanged. In mode 1, MOV (R1),R2 moves the contents of the address location pointed to by R1 into R2. In mode 2 the instruction MOV(R1)+,R2 increments R1 by 2 after executing the same operation as mode 1. In mode 3 the instruction MOV @(R1)+,R2 obtains the source operand through two levels of indirect addressing and moves it to R2; the contents of R1 are then incremented by 2. In mode 4 the instruction MOV −(R1),R2 obtains the source operand from the contents of location (R1 − 2). In mode 5 the instruction MOV @−(R1),R2 obtains the source operand using two levels of indirect addressing after first

Table 4-2. LSI-11/PDP-11 Double-Operand Addressing Modes

Mode	Descriptive Name	Example Assembly Language*	Resulting Octal Code
0	Register	MOV R1,R2	010102
1	Register Deferred	MOV (R1),R2	011102
2	Autoincrement	MOV (R1)+,R2	012102
3	Autoincrement Deferred	MOV @(R1)+,R2	013102
4	Autodecrement	MOV −(R1),R2	014102
5	Autodecrement Deferred	MOV @−(R1),R2	015102
6	Index	MOV 100(R1),R2	016102 000100
7	Index Deferred	MOV @2(R1),R2	017102 000002

*In general, parentheses are used to indicate a first level of indirect addressing and the "@" symbol is added to indicate a second level.

subtracting 2 from the contents of R1. The examples for modes 6 and 7 show how constant offsets and one or two levels of indirect addressing can be used in obtaining source operands.

Now we can see how stack-type instructions can be implemented with any of the lower seven registers (R0–R6). For example, suppose that we wish to use register R3 as a stack pointer and we wish to store and later retrieve the contents of register R0. Then the instruction MOV R0,−(R3) executes the *push operation* and the instruction MOV (R3)+,R0 executes the *pop operation*. With these instructions the stack pointer register always contains the address of the last item pushed onto the stack; any block of memory can be used for the stack.

Program Counter Mode Instructions

Now, patient reader, you should be asking questions such as, "How can I place a given constant in a given location?" and, "Is it possible to add the contents of a known location to the contents of a general register?" These are the immediate and absolute modes of addressing that are familiar to users of 8-bit microprocessors. And, happily, these addressing modes are also available on the LSI-11, because the PC register responds to *all eight* addressing modes and in addition (in its function as a program counter) it is always incremented by 2 after an instruction is fetched and before the instruction is executed. Table 4-3 shows the *four* addressing modes in which use of the PC register as a general-purpose register bestows special benefits on the user. The examples that are provided use the ADD instruction, which has an octal op code of 06.

Table 4-3. LSI-11 Program Counter (PC) Addressing Modes

		Example	
Mode	Descriptive Name	Assembly Language	Resulting Octal Code
2	Immediate	ADD #34,R1	062701 000034
3	Absolute	ADD @#34,R1	063701 000034
6	Relative	ADD A,R1	066701 (Offset)
7	Relative Deferred	ADD @A,R1	067701 (Offset)

In the instruction ADD #34,R1 note that the *immediate mode* ADD instruction is implemented by using *mode 2* and the PC register (given as register number 7) as the source operand and mode 0 and R1 as the destination operand. The processor increments the PC register by 2 immediately after fetching the 062701 instruction. The PC register now contains the address of the constant 000034 and so this is considered to be the source operand by the processor; however, *mode 2* has been specified and so the PC register will be auto-incremented to point to the next memory location (which contains the next instruction).

In the second line of Table 4-3 the *absolute mode* ADD instruction is implemented by using *mode 3* and the PC register as the source operand. This is the autoincrement *deferred* mode for the PC register and therefore the *contents* of absolute memory location 000034 are added to the contents of R1.

In the third example the *relative mode* ADD instruction is implemented by using *mode 6* and the PC register as the source operand. This is the index mode for the PC register and therefore the contents of the memory location after the instruction are used as an offset number and are *added to the current (updated) contents of the PC register to find the source operand.* (Twos complement arithmetic is used in adding the offset so that a 1 in the most significant bit of the offset is interpreted as a negative or backward offset.) If the programmer is working in machine language, he or she will know the absolute memory address of A and will also know the absolute memory address of the instruction that follows the offset; he or she can therefore calculate the proper value for the offset. Much more likely, the programmer is working in assembly language and the assembler can do this calculation for him or her. Even more important, this mode and the next one, the relative deferred mode, allow the programmer to write position-independent code (PIC) in which two or more programs are easily combined into one large program after they have been written; the offsets will not change because both A and the program code will have their addresses altered by the same amount if any addresses have to be relocated.

In the fourth example in Table 4-3 another level of indirect addressing is achieved by specifying *mode 7* and the PC register as the source operand. The instruction ADD @A,R1 will add the contents of the memory location pointed to by the contents of the address of A to the current contents of register R1.

Three-word instructions result when the PC register is used as both the source and the destination register. For example, the assembler would translate

    MOV #40,@#177566

(move the constant 40 into memory location 177566) into

    012737
    000040
    177566

in machine code.

Instruction Set Summary

The LSI-11 instruction set is summarized, with assembler mnemonics, in Tables 4-4, 4-5, and 4-6. Instructions that operate on bytes as well as on words are indicated by a (B) following the assembler mnemonic. Reference to these tables shows that: (a) all in-

Table 4-4. The LSI-11 Instruction Set: Single-Operand Instructions

Assembler Mnemonic	Operation
General	
CLR(B)	Clear
COM(B)	Ones complement
INC(B)	Increment
DEC(B)	Decrement
NEG(B)	Negate
TST(B)	Test for zero, negative, or positive
Rotate & Shift	
ROR(B)	Rotate right
ROL(B)	Rotate left
ASR(B)	Arithmetic shift right
ASL(B)	Arithmetic shift left
SWAB	Swap bytes
Multiple Precision	
ADC(B)	Add carry bit
SBC(B)	Subtract carry bit
SXT	Extend sign bit
Processor Status Operators	
MFPS	Move byte from PS register
MTPS	Move byte to PS register
Floating Point[1]	
SETF	Set FPS in SP mode
SETD	Set FPS in DP mode
SETI	Set FPS in integer mode
SETL	Set FPS in long integer mode (two-word)
NEGF(NEGD)	Negate a SP(DP) number
CLRF(CLRD)	Clear a SP(DP) number
ABSF(ABSD)	Make absolute a SP(DP) number
TSTF(TSTD)	Test a SP(DP) number
LDFPS	Load the FPS contents
STFPS	Store the FPS contents
STST	Store the FEC and FEA contents

Abbreviations
   SP = Single precision
   PS = Processor status register
   DP = Double precision (four-word numbers)
   AC = Accumulator of the floating-point processor
   FPS = Status register of the floating-point processor
   FEC = Exception (error) code register of the floating-point
          processor
   FEA = Exception (error) address register of the floating-point
          processor

[1] Optional microcode chip on the LSI-11/23 only.

Table 4-5. The LSI-11 Instruction Set: Double-Operand Instructions

Assembler Mnemonic	Operation
General	
MOV(B)	Move
CMP(B)	Compare
ADD	Add
SUB	Subtract
Logical	
BIT(B)	Bit test (logical AND)
BIC(B)	Bit clear
BIS(B)	Bit set (logical OR)
XOR	Logical exclusive OR
Extended Instruction Set (EIS)[1]	
MUL	Multiply
DIV	Divide
ASH	Arithmetic shift
ASHC	Arithmetic shift combined
Floating Instruction Set (FIS)[2]	
FADD	Floating add
FSUB	Floating subtract
FMUL	Floating multiply
FDIV	Floating divide
Floating Point[3]	
LDF(LDD)	Load SP(DP) number into accumulator (AC)
STF(STD)	Store the SP(DP) number in the AC
ADDF(ADDD)	Add, using SP(DP) arithmetic, to the contents of the AC
SUBF(SUBD)	Subtract, using SP(DP) arithmetic, from the contents of the AC
MULF(MULD)	Multiply, using SP(DP) arithmetic, the contents of the AC
DIVF(DIVD)	Divide, using SP(DP) arithmetic, the contents of the AC
CMPF(CMPD)	Compare, using SP(DP) arithmetic, the contents of the AC
MODF(MODD)	Multiply, using SP(DP) arithmetic, the contents of the AC; separate the product into integer and fractional parts; store one or both as floating-point numbers
LDCDF(LDCFD)	Load AC after conversion from DP to SP (SP to DP)
STCFD(STCDF)	Convert contents of AC from SP to DP (DP to SP) and store
LDCIF/LDCLF(LDCID/LDCLD)	Load and convert the contents of AC from integer/long integer to SP(DP)
STCFI/STCFL(STCDI/STCDL)	Convert the contents of AC from SP(DP) to integer/long integer and store
LDEXP	Load exponent into the exponent field of the AC
STEXP	Store the AC exponent
Abbreviations: Same as for Table 4-4.	

[1] Standard on the LSI-11/23; optional microcode chip on the LSI-11, LSI-11/2.
[2] Optional microcode chip on the LSI-11 and LSI-11/2 only.
[3] Optional microcode chip on the LSI-11/23 only.

put and output is memory-mapped, using the MOV, MOVB, and other instructions, (b) decimal-adjust instructions for bcd arithmetic are not available, (c) no special string-handling instructions are available, (d) there is a rich repertoire of instructions for binary arithmetic (particularly on the LSI-11/23) that can include 64-bit double-precision floating-point arithmetic and 32-bit double-precision integer arithmetic, and (e) there are many branch and jump instructions and a number of special instructions for traps, interrupts, processor and bus control, and memory management.

Unique Instructions

Several of the LSI-11 instructions are unique in their operation or are of such general utility that they will be discussed briefly.

The BIT (test bit) and BIS (set bit) instructions are common to many microprocessors. The BIC instruction, however, performs a *mask* operation rather than the more common AND operation; in other words, for each bit *set* in the source, the corresponding bit position in the destination is *cleared*. The SOB instruction (subtract one and branch back if not equal to zero) provides a natural, single-instruction loop control, as will be shown in the benchmark programs. The SXT instruction extends the sign bit through additional words for multiple-precision arithmetic and the SWAB instruction allows the swapping of the low and high bytes of any memory location or register.

Of great utility are the conditional branch instructions, of which there are 15 variations. (The mnemonics BCC and BHIS have the same op code and execute in the same manner, as do BLS and BLO.) Each branch has a range of $+128$ to -127 words relative to the branch instruction itself and is inherently position independent. The JMP instruction provides for long jumps using any of the previously described addressing modes except for mode 0; it is illegal to jump to a register.

The JSR and RTS subroutine instructions are common to almost all microprocessors. However, the LSI-11 implementation is unlike that of any other 16-bit microprocessor because it includes what is termed the "linkage register." When the JSR instruction is executed, three operations are performed: (a) the contents of the linkage register (any of the eight registers) are pushed onto the system stack, (b) the address of the first location after the JSR instruction is placed in the linkage register, and (c) the address of the subroutine is placed in the PC. It should be noted that only in the special case where the PC is the selected register does the stack contain the subroutine return address; otherwise, only the contents of the saved register are on the stack. The utility of this technique is that a subroutine called with a

JSR register, destination

Table 4-6. The LSI-11 Instruction Set: Program Control and Miscellaneous Instructions

Assembler Mnemonic	Operation
Branch	
BR	Unconditional branch
BNE	Branch if not equal to zero
BEQ	Branch if equal to zero
BPL	Branch if plus
BMI	Branch if minus
BVC	Branch if overflow clear
BVS	Branch if overflow set
BCC	Branch if carry clear
BCS	Branch if carry set
Signed Conditional Branches	
BGE	Branch if equal to or greater than zero
BLT	Branch if less than zero
BGT	Branch if greater than zero
BLE	Branch if less than or equal to zero
Unsigned Conditional Branches	
BHI	Branch if higher
BLOS	Branch if lower or the same
BHIS	Branch if higher or the same
BLO	Branch if lower
Condition Code Operators	
CLC,CLV,CLZ,CLN,CCC	Clear C,V,Z,N,all
SEC,SEV,SEZ,SEN,SCC	Set C,V,Z,N,all
Jump and Subroutine	
JMP	Jump
JSR	Jump to subroutine
RTS	Return from subroutine
MARK	Mark (aid in subroutine handling)
SOB	Subtract 1 and branch if not equal to zero
Trap and Interrupt	
EMT	Emulator trap
TRAP	Trap
BPT	Breakpoint trap
IOT	Input/output trap
RTI	Return from interrupt
RTT	Return from interrupt (trap)
Miscellaneous	
HALT	Halt
WAIT	Wait for interrupt
RESET	Reset external bus
NOP	No operation
Memory Management[1]	
MFPD	Move from previous data space
MFPI	Move from previous instruction space
MTPD	Move to previous data space
MTPI	Move to previous instruction space

[1] Optional microcode chip on the LSI-11/23 only. The 11/23 does not differentiate between the MFPD and the MFPI instructions, or between the MTPD and MTPI instructions; they are separate only to provide compatibility with other PDP-11 processors.

instruction can access a list of arguments *following* the call with either autoincrement addressing, (reg)+ (if arguments are accessed sequentially), or by indexed addressing, X(reg), (if accessed in random order). These addressing modes may also be *deferred,* @(reg)+ and @X(reg), if the parameters are operand addresses rather than the operands themselves. During the execution of the subroutine, the linkage register must be updated so that it points to the location immediately following the list of arguments. At the completion of the subroutine the

```
RTS  register
```

instruction is executed and performs two operations: (a) the contents of the linkage register are transferred into the PC and (b) the old register contents are popped from the stack back into the linkage register. The processor thus continues program execution with the first instruction *after* the subroutine's argument list.

As an example, consider the following assembly language program segment (comments follow the semicolon):

```
MAIN:     JSR    R5,SUM    ;R5←Address of ARG1
          ARG1
          ARG2
RETURN:   MOV    R0,RESULT
             .
             .
             .
```

with the following trivial subroutine:

```
SUM:   MOV  (R5)+,R0 ;R0←ARG1 & R5←Address of ARG2
       ADD  (R5)+,R0 ;R0←ARG1+ARG2 & R5←Address of RETURN
       RTS  R5         ;PC←Address of RETURN
```

When program execution jumps to the subroutine, R5 contains the address of the first parameter, ARG1. The first instruction in the subroutine moves this parameter into register R0 and also autoincrements R5 so that it points to the second parameter, ARG2. The second subroutine instruction adds ARG1 and ARG2 and stores the result in R0; it also autoincrements R5 again so that it now contains the return address. The RTS instruction moves the return address in R5 into the PC and restores the old contents of R5 by popping them off the stack.

I/O and Trap/Interrupt Instructions

The input/output and trap/interrupt procedures for the LSI-11/PDP-11 also deserve special attention.

The upper 4K words of addressable memory (octal 160000 to 177776 for the LSI-11 and LSI-11/2) is by DEC convention devoted to device (peripheral) registers, ROM loader programs, and bootstrap programs. Within this 4K block, each device or peripheral has at least one control and status register (CSR) and usually one data register (DR) associated with it. For example, DEC software assumes that a paper tape reader has a CSR at 177550 and a DR at 177552.

Data transfers can be (a) programmed, (b) interrupt driven, or (c) through direct memory access (DMA).

In programmed i/o the CSR is checked to determine if a data word or byte is available and, if so, it is read from the DR. The following assembly language program segment would do this for the paper tape reader:

```
PAPER:    TSTB   177550    ;CHECK CSR FOR DATA
          BPL    PAPER     ;LOOP BACK IF NO DATA
          MOV    177552,R0 ;TRANSFER DATA TO R0
```

(Bit 7 is the "ready" bit of a CSR. The TSTB instruction makes the processor look at this bit and, if it is a 1, set the N condition code bit in the PS register. Then the condition for branching, a positive number, is not satisfied and the MOV instruction will be executed. Note that the test does not require any transfer to an accumulator.)

Interrupt-driven i/o uses the processor more efficiently and therefore it is the most commonly used method. Bit 6 in the CSR is usually used as the interrupt enable control bit; the processor can enable the device when it is willing to service interrupts generated by it, but then the processor is free to do other tasks while waiting for data. Upon receiving the interrupt request, the processor queries the module (or board) that is the closest to it electrically. If this module did not initiate the request, it passes the query on to the next module on the bus. Thus there is a position-dependent priority structure that allows faster peripherals to be given preference. (The LSI-11/23 in addition implements a four-level hardware interrupt priority scheme using the PS register.) When the processor grants the interrupt request, it pushes its current PC and PS register contents onto the system stack (pointed to by the SP) and loads new PC and PS values starting from a location provided by the interrupting device. This interrupt address is defined by jumpers on the interface board for the peripheral and is called the *interrupt vector*. Thus, as an example, the paper tape reader has an assigned interrupt vector of 70 (octal) and, when the paper tape reader interrupts the processor, the new value for the PC register contents must be at octal location 70 and the new value for the PS register contents must be at 72. Therefore, location 70 must contain the starting address of the software handler for the paper tape reader. When the handler has completed the data or error transmission, it can execute a RTI (return from interrupt) instruction which pops the old PC and PS contents off of the system stack and into the PC and PS registers; then program execution continues from the point where it was interrupted.

High-speed peripherals, such as floppy disks or hard disks, utilize the direct-memory-access capability that is built into the LSI-11/PDP-11 architecture. Again, the processor grants a DMA request to the module electrically closest to it if more than one DMA request is active at the same time. A diagram of the DMA procedure or protocol is shown in the section on interfacing.

Next we look at the trap feature of the LSI-11. A trap can be considered to be a *software interrupt*. There are both friendly and unfriendly traps. Examples of "friendly" traps are those that result from execution of an EMT, TRAP, IOT, or BPT instruction; these allow the programmer access to system monitor capabilities or provide special subprogram capabilities. An example of an "unfriendly" trap is the hardware-generated trap caused by an attempt to use a nonexistent instruction or by the failure of a peripheral to respond to a processor-initiated request within a certain length of time (bus time-out error).

The emulator trap instruction (EMT) is used by DEC software to request services from the resident monitor of the operating system, which in turn can access device handlers. For example, the MACRO assembler will translate the program directive .TTOUTR into the instruction EMT 341, which will cause the contents of register R0 to be sent to the system terminal (assuming there is room in the monitor's buffer).

The TRAP instruction is similar to the EMT instruction except that it uses a different trap vector (34) and it has been reserved by DEC for user-generated software. Thus

```
.34 = 20000 ;PLACE 20000(8) IN LOCATION 000034(8)
TRAP    377 ;TRAP TO THIS LOCATION, WITH PARAMETERS
```

will start program execution at location 20000. The arguments after the instruction (which can be any octal number from 0 to 377) can be used to pass information to the new program. In fact, up to 400 (octal) or 256 (decimal) different subprograms could be called in this fashion.

The EMT and TRAP instructions are the two instructions whereby the assembly language programmer can utilize the services of the system monitor. Also, in any use of these instructions the resulting link to the subprogram and to the input/output handlers is inherently position independent; the monitor does not need to know where in memory the program is located and the program does not need to know where in memory the monitor is located. The TRAP instruction is also useful for inserting a patch in software. Control is always returned to the calling program with the RTI or RTT instruction.

Table 4-7. LSI-11 Reserved Trap and Interrupt Vectors

Vector (Octal)	Use
000000	Reserved by the manufacturer
000004	Bus time-out and other errors
000010	Illegal and reserved instructions
000014	BPT instruction and T bit
000020	IOT instruction
000024	Power-fail
000030	EMT instruction
000034	TRAP instruction
000060	Console terminal, input
000064	Console terminal, output
000070	Paper tape reader
000074	Paper tape punch
000100	External event line interrupt (can be used with the line clock)
000124	DMA interface
000160	Disk drive controller interface
000200	Line printer controller interface
000220	Disk drive controller interface
000244	Floating-point errors
000264	Floppy disk controller interface
000400–000414	A/D converters interface
000424–000434	IEEE instrument bus interface
000440–000450	Programmable real-time clock interface

An illegal instruction has a trap vector of 10 (octal). If the programmer stores 12 (octal) at this memory location, the PC register will be loaded with 12 and begin execution using that address when an illegal instruction is detected. If the programmer has thoughtfully placed a HALT instruction at location 12, the processor will stop immediately after the trap is executed. The programmer can then examine the stack and determine the address of the instruction that caused the error.

Unusual for a microcomputer, the LSI-11 has a power-down sequence as well as a power-up sequence. The power supply is designed to signal the processor when input power has been lost but while at least 4 milliseconds of dc power reserve remains. The processor then traps through location 24 to the power-down routine. This means that, when nonvolatile memory is used, it is possible to pull the computer's plug and then reinsert it a day later with no loss of program information or data. The LSI-11 also has four power-up jumper options on the processor board.

Programs normally start at 001000 (octal) because the operating system uses memory below that address for such things as interrupt

Chart 4-1. LSI-11 Addressing Modes and Op Codes

WORD FORMAT

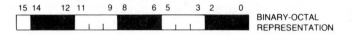

```
15 14    12 11    9 8    6 5    3 2    0
```
BINARY-OCTAL
REPRESENTATION

MODE	R

Mode	Name	Symbolic	Description
0	register	R	(R) is operated [ex. R2 = %2]
1	register deferred	(R)	(R) is address
2	auto-increment	(R)+	(R) is adrs; (R) + (1 or 2)
3	auto-incr deferred	@(R)+	(R) is adrs of adrs; (R) + 2
4	auto-decrement	−(R)	(R) − (1 or 2); is adrs
5	auto-decr deferred	@−(R)	(R) −2; (R) is adrs of adrs
6	index	X(R)	(R) + X is adrs
7	index deferred	@X(R)	(R) + X is adrs of adrs

PROGRAM COUNTER ADDRESSING

Reg = 7

MODE	7

2	immediate	#n	operand n follows instr
3	absolute	@#A	address A follows instr
6	relative	A	instr adrs + 4 + X is adrs
7	relative deferred	@A	instr adrs + 4 + X is adrs of adrs

LEGEND

Op Codes

■	= 0 for word/1 for byte
SS	= source field (6 bits)
DD	= destination field (6 bits)
R	= gen register (3 bits), 0 to 7
XXX	= offset (8 bits), +127 to −128
N	= number (3 bits)
NN	= number (6 bits)

Operations

( )	= contents of
s	= contents of source
d	= contents of destination
r	= contents of register
←	= becomes
X	= relative address
%	= register definition

Boolean

Λ	= AND
V	= inclusive OR
⩣	= exclusive OR
⌐	= NOT

Condition Codes

•	= conditionally set/cleared
−	= not affected
0	= cleared
1	= set

Chart 4-1. LSI-11 Addressing Modes and Op Codes (cont.)

SINGLE OPERAND: OPR dst

```
15                          6 5              0
┌────────────────────────────┬──────────────┐
│        OP CODE             │   SS OR DD   │
└────────────────────────────┴──────────────┘
```

Mne-monic	Op Code	Instruction	dst Result	N	Z	V	C
General							
CLR(B)	■ 050DD	clear	0	0	1	0	0
COM(B)	■ 051DD	complement (1's)	⌐ d	*	*	0	1
INC(B)	■ 052DD	increment	d + 1	*	*	*	-
DEC(B)	■ 053DD	decrement	d − 1	*	*	*	-
NEG(B)	■ 054DD	negate (2's compl)	−d	*	*	*	*
TST(B)	■ 057DD	test	d	*	*	0	0
Rotate & Shift							
ROR(B)	■ 060DD	rotate right	→ C, d	*	*	*	*
ROL(B)	■ 061DD	rotate left	C, d ←	*	*	*	*
ASR(B)	■ 062DD	arith shift right	d/2	*	*	*	*
ASL(B)	■ 063DD	arith shift left	2d	*	*	*	*
SWAB	0003DD	swap bytes		*	*	0	0
Multiple Precision							
ADC(B)	■ 055DD	add carry	d + C	*	*	*	*
SBC(B)	■ 056DD	subtract carry	d − C	*	*	*	*
SXT	0067DD	sign extend	0 or −1	-	*	0	-
Processor Status (PS) Operators							
MFPS	1067DD	move byte from PS	d ← PS	*	*	0	-
MTPS	1064SS	move byte to PS	PS ← s	*	*	*	*

DOUBLE OPERAND: OPR src, dst   OPR src, R or OPR R, dst

```
15        12 11          6 5              0
┌──────────┬──────────────┬──────────────┐
│ OP CODE  │      SS      │      DD      │
└──────────┴──────────────┴──────────────┘

15              9 8      6 5              0
┌────────────────┬────────┬──────────────┐
│    OP CODE     │   R    │  SS OR DD    │
└────────────────┴────────┴──────────────┘
```

Mne-monic	Op Code	Instruction	Operation	N	Z	V	C
General							
MOV(B)	■ 1SSDD	move	d ← s	*	*	0	-
CMP(B)	■ 2SSDD	compare	s − d	*	*	*	*
ADD	06SSDD	add	d ← s + d	*	*	*	*
SUB	16SSDD	subtract	d ← d − s	*	*	*	*

Chart 4-1. LSI-11 Addressing Modes and Op Codes (cont.)

Logical

Mnemonic	Code	Instruction	Operation	N	Z	V	C
BIT(B)	■ 3SSDD	bit test (AND)	s ∧ d	*	*	0	-
BIC(B)	■ 4SSDD	bit clear	d ← (~s) ∧ d	*	*	0	-
BIS(B)	■ 5SSDD	bit set (OR)	d ← s v d	*	*	0	-
XOR	074RDD	exclusive OR	d ← r⊕d	*	*	0	-

Optional EIS

Mnemonic	Code	Instruction	Operation	N	Z	V	C
MUL	070RSS	multiply	r ← r x s	*	*	0	*
DIV	071RSS	divide	r ← r/s	*	*	*	*
ASH	072RSS	shift arithmetically		*	*	*	*
ASHC	073RSS	arith shift combined		*	*	*	*

Optional FIS

Mnemonic	Code	Instruction	N	Z	V	C
FADD	07500R	floating add	*	*	0	0
FSUB	07501R	floating subtract	*	*	0	0
FMUL	07502R	floating multiply	*	*	0	0
FDIV	07503R	floating divide	*	*	0	0

BRANCH: B - - location

If condition is satisfied:
Branch to location,
New PC ← Update PC + (2 x offset)

$$\underbrace{}_{\text{adrs of br instr + 2}}$$

15			8	7			0
	BASE CODE				XXX		

Op Code = Base Code + XXX

Mne-monic	Base Code	Instruction	Branch Condition	
Branches				
BR	000400	branch (unconditional)	(always)	
BNE	001000	br if not equal (to 0)	≠ 0	Z = 0
BEQ	001400	br if equal (to 0)	= 0	Z = 1
BPL	100000	branch if plus	+	N = 0
BMI	100400	branch if minus	−	N = 1
BVC	102000	br if overflow is clear		V = 0
BVS	102400	br if overflow if set		V = 1
BCC	103000	br if carry is clear		C = 0
BCS	103400	br if carry is set		C = 1
Signed Conditional Branches				
BGE	002000	br if greater or equal (to 0)	≥0	N⊕V = 0
BLT	002400	br if less than (0)	<0	N⊕V = 1
BGT	003000	br if greater than (0)	>0	Z v (N⊕V) = 0
BLE	003400	br if less or equal (to 0)	≤0	Z v (N⊕V) = 1

Chart 4-1. LSI-11 Addressing Modes and Op Codes (cont.)

Unsigned Conditional Branches

BHI	101000	branch if higher	>	C v Z = 0
BLOS	101400	branch if lower or same	≤	C v Z = 1
BHIS	103000	branch if higher or same	≥	C = 0
BLO	103400	branch if lower	<	C = 1

CONDITION CODE OPERATORS:

```
      15                      5  4  3  2  1  0
     ┌────────────────────────┬──┬──┬──┬──┬──┐
     │ OP CODE BASE = 000240  │  │ N│ Z│ V│ C│
     └────────────────────────┴──┴──┴──┴──┴──┘
```
0 = CLEAR SELECTED COND. CODE BITS
1 = SET SELECTED COND. CODE BITS

Mnemonic	Op Code	Instruction	N Z V C
CLC	000241	clear C	– – – 0
CLV	000242	clear V	– – 0 –
CLZ	000244	clear Z	– 0 – –
CLN	000250	clear N	0 – – –
CCC	000257	clear all cc bits	0 0 0 0
SEC	000261	set C	– – – 1
SEV	000262	set V	– – 1 –
SEZ	000264	set Z	– 1 – –
SEN	000270	set N	1 – – –
SCC	000277	set all cc bits	1 1 1 1

JUMP & SUBROUTINE

Mne- monic	Op Code	Instruction	Notes
JMP	0001DD	jump	PC ← dst
JSR	004RDD	jump to subroutine	
RTS	00020R	return from subroutine	use same R
MARK	0064NN	mark	aid in subr return
SOB	0077RNN	subtract 1 & br (if ≠ 0)	(R) −1, then if (R) ≠ 0; PC ← Updated PC− (2 x NN)

TRAP & INTERRUPT:

EMT	104000 to 104377	emulator trap (not for general use)	PC at 30, PS at 32
TRAP	104400 to 104777	trap	PC at 34, PS at 36
BPT	000003	breakpoint trap	PC at 14, PS at 16
IOT	000004	input/output trap	PC at 20, PS at 22
RTI	000002	return from interrupt	
RTT	000006	return from interrupt	inhibit T bit trap

MISCELLANEOUS:

Mne- monic	Op Code	Instruction
HALT	000000	halt
WAIT	000001	wait for interrupt
RESET	000005	reset external bus
NOP	000240	(no operation)

Courtesy Heath Co.

Chart 4-2. LSI-11 Floating-Point Instructions and Op Codes

```
 15                          8  7  6  5              0
     ┌──────────────────────┬─────┬──────────────┐
     │ OP CODE BASE=170000  │ AC  │  SS or DD    │
     └──────────────────────┴─────┴──────────────┘
```

Mnemonic	Op Code	Instruction	Operation
CFCC	170000	copy fl cond codes	
SETF	170001	set floating mode	FD ← 0
SETI	170002	set integer mode	FL ← 0
SETD	170011	set fl dbl mode	FD ← 1
SETL	170012	set long integer mode	FL ← 1
LDFPS	1701 src	load FPP prog status	
STFPS	1702 dst	store FPP prog status	
STST	1703 dst	store (exc codes & adrs)	
CLRF,CLRD	1704 fdst	clear floating/double	fdst ← 0
TSTF,TSTD	1705 fdst	test fl/dbl	
ABSF,ABSD	1706 fdst	make absolute fl/dbl	fdst ← |fdst|
NEGF,NEGD	1707 fdst	negate fl/dbl	fdst ← -fdst
MULF,MULD	171(AC) fsrc	multiply fl/dbl	AC ← AC x fsrc
MODF,MODD	171(AC+4) fsrc	multiply & integerize	
ADDF,ADDD	172(AC) fsrc	add fl/dbl	AC ← AC + fsrc
LDF,LDD	172(AC+4) fsrc	load fl/dbl	AC ← fsrc
SUBF,SUBD	173(AC) fsrc	subtract fl/dbl	AC ← AC - fsrc
CMPF,CMPD	173(AC+4) fsrc	compare fl/dbl (to AC)	
STF,STD	174(AC) fdst	store fl/dbl	fdst ← AC
DIVF,DIVD	174(AC+4) fsrc	divide fl/dbl	AC ← AC/fsrc
STEXP	175(AC) dst	store exponent	
STCFI,STCFL } STCDI,STCDL }	175(AC+4) dst	store & convert ·fl or dbl to int or long int	
STCFD,STCDF	176(AC) fdst	store & convert (dbl-fl)	
LDEXP	176(AC+4) src	load exponent	
LDCIF,LDCID } LDCLF,LDCLC }	177(AC) src	load & convert int or long int to fl or dbl	
LDCDF,LDCFD	177(AC+4) fsrc	load & convert (dbl-fl)	

Courtesy Digital Equipment Corp.

vectors and the hardware stack. The default hardware stack begins at 000776 (octal) and has a maximum length of 256 (decimal) words. Table 4-7 lists the reserved trap and interrupt vector locations.

As a convenient reference, Charts 4-1 and 4-2 present an overview of the addressing modes and a full listing of the op codes for the instruction set. Chart 4-3 lists the op codes in numerical order; the floating-point op codes fall in the "RESERVED" range at the end of the table.

LSI-11/23 MEMORY MANAGEMENT

The 16 address lines of the basic LSI-11 processor impose a 64K-byte limitation on the memory that it can directly access. However,

Chart 4-3. LSI-11 Op Codes in Numerical Order

OP Code	Mnemonic	OP Code	Mnemonic	OP Code	Mnemonic
00 00 00	HALT	00 60 DD	ROR	10 40 00	EMT
00 00 01	WAIT	00 61 DD	ROL		
00 00 02	RTI	00 62 DD	ASR		
00 00 03	BPT	00 63 DD	ASL	10 43 77	
00 00 04	IOT	00 64 NN	MARK		
00 00 05	RESET	00 67 DD	SXT	10 44 00	
00 00 06	RTT				TRAP
00 00 07	(unused)	00 70 00			
00 00 77			(unused)	10 47 77	
00 01 DD	JMP	00 77 77		10 50 DD	CLRB
00 02 0R	RTS			10 51 DD	COMB
		01 SS DD	MOV	10 52 DD	INCB
00 02 10	(reserved)	02 SS DD	CMP	10 53 DD	DECB
		03 SS DD	BIT	10 54 DD	NEGB
		04 SS DD	BIC	10 55 DD	ADCB
00 02 27		05 SS DD	BIS	10 56 DD	SBCB
		06 SS DD	ADD	10 57 DD	TSTB
00 02 40	NOP				
		07 0R SS	MUL	10 60 DD	RORB
00 02 41		07 1R SS	DIV	10 61 DD	ROLB
	cond	07 2R SS	ASH	10 62 DD	ASRB
	codes	07 3R SS	ASHC	10 63 DD	ASLB
00 02 77		07 4R DD	XOR	10 64 SS	MTPS
				10 67 DD	MFPS
00 03 DD	SWAB	07 50 0R	FADD		
		07 50 1R	FSUB	11 SS DD	MOVB
00 04 XXX	BR	07 50 2R	FMUL	12 SS DD	CMPB
00 10 XXX	BNE	07 50 3R	FDIV	13 SS DD	BITB
00 14 XXX	BEQ			14 SS DD	BICB
00 20 XXX	BGE	07 50 40		15 SS DD	BISB
00 24 XXX	BLT		(unused)	16 SS DD	SUB
00 30 XXX	BGT				
00 34 XXX	BLE	07 67 77		17 00 00	FLOATING POINT
00 4R DD	JSR	07 7R NN	SOB		
				17 77 77	
00 50 DD	CLR	10 00 XXX	BPL		
00 51 DD	COM	10 04 XXX	BMI		
00 52 DD	INC	10 10 XXX	BHI		
00 53 DD	DEC	10 14 XXX	BLOS		
00 54 DD	NEG	10 20 XXX	BVC		
00 55 DD	ADC	10 24 XXX	BVS		
00 56 DD	SBC	10 30 XXX	BCC, BHIS		
00 57 DD	TST	10 34 XXX	BCS, BLO		

Courtesy Heath Co.

the LSI-11/23 implements a 256K-byte physical address space by using 18 address lines. The mapping, or translation, of the normal 16-bit virtual address into an 18-bit physical address is implemented by one MOS/LSI integrated circuit. The memory-management function implemented by this integrated circuit is software compatible with the larger PDP-11 processors, the PDP-11/34, -11/60, and

-11/70. A future addition to the LSI-11 family can be expected to possess the 22-bit address mapping now available on the PDP-11/70; this will require the addition of four more bus address lines and will allow access to 4M bytes of main memory.

The memory-management chip requires the processor to operate in one of two possible modes: kernel or user. In kernel mode the software has total control of the processor and may execute all instructions. In user mode (which is appropriate to a multiuser, multiprogramming operating environment) the processor is inhibited from executing certain functions that might halt the processor, access regions of memory holding the executive program, or destroy another user's data or program.

Fig. 4-6 depicts the memory-management registers and the process whereby the processor's 16-bit virtual address is translated into an 18-bit physical address for memory access. Basically, this management information is provided by two sets of eight 32-bit registers called *active page registers* (APR), one set for each of the two operating modes (kernel and user). The 32-bit APRs are physically made up of two 16-bit registers called the *page address register* (PAR) and the *page description register* (PDR). The PAR contains a 12-bit page address (all 16 bits are used on the PDP-11/70 with its 22-bit mapping) which is the base address of the page. The PDR contains information pertinent to page length, page expansion, and access control (i.e., read only, read/write, or no access).

When the management process is enabled, bits 15 and 14 of the processor status word (PS) register determine which set of APRs is to be used to describe and relocate the virtual memory addresses. Additionally, these bits select which of two hardware stack pointers (SP) is to be used during program execution. The active SP is selected by these bits even if the memory-management function is not enabled.

The virtual address is split into three sections: (a) the displacement in bytes (DIB: bits 5–0), (b) the block number (bits 12–6), and (c) the active page field (APF: bits 15–13). The three bits of the APF select one of the eight active page registers which contains the relocation information for this memory access. With the APR selected by the APF, the relocation is performed by adding the 7-bit virtual address block number to the 12-bit PAR base address to obtain the 12-bit physical block number, which is the 12 most significant bits of the physical address; the lower 6 bits (the DIB) come directly from the virtual memory address (refer again to Fig. 4-6). The maximum physical size that may be accessed by each APR is 8K bytes because only the lower 13 bits of the 16-bit virtual address can be used. The page length contained in the PDR can adjust the size that may be accessed from 1 to 128 sixty-four-byte blocks (i.e.,

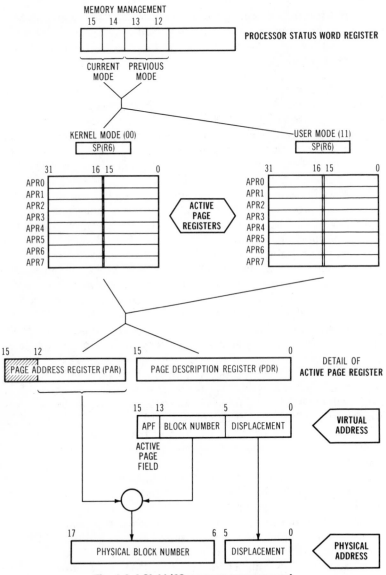

Fig. 4-6. LSI-11/23 memory management.

64 bytes to 8192 bytes); this allows the partitioning of memory into very small segments.

Simultaneously with the generation of the physical address, the page description register (PDR) contents are compared with the virtual address to ensure that the virtual address is within the specified length and that the address may be accessed (i.e., that the address is read-enabled for a read operation or write-enabled for a write operation). If the operation during this memory access is not allowed by the PDR specification, then the memory-management unit aborts

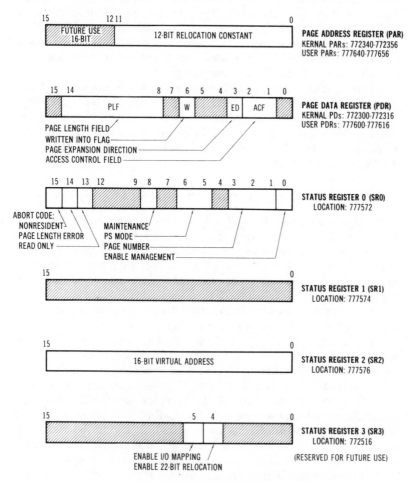

Fig. 4-7. LSI-11/23 memory management registers.

the operation and causes a trap to the vector located in kernel space at location 250. (All processor traps and interrupts always occur to vectors in kernel space.) Two of the four memory-management status registers provide information about the abort, for diagnostic purposes.

Fig. 4-7 shows the details of the APR's page address register and page description register. Also in the figure are the four memory-management status registers and the designated usage of any bits defined by the manufacturer. Status register 0 contains the management enable bit and the various error flags. If any error occurs, the appropriate error flags are set and the conditions at the time of the abort are saved in status register 0 (SR0) and in status register 2 (SR2). SR0 is used to store the mode bits from the processor status word register and the APF field of the virtual address causing the trap; SR2 is used to store the virtual address of the instruction which caused the abort. SR1 is not used but is present to maintain compatibility with other PDP-11 computers.

Status register 3 (SR3) has been reserved for future use by DEC, who has also defined bit 5 as enabling i/o mapping (only the PDP-11/70 implements this at present; it is a means of translating bus address DMA operations into 22-bit memory addresses) and bit 4 as enabling a full 22-bit (4M-byte) mapping using all 16 bits of the page address register.

LSI-11 HARDWARE IMPLEMENTATIONS

Because the LSI-11 is so closely tied to its supporting chips and to its asynchronous bus, very few users start with less than a complete processor board or with a nonstandard bus structure. The processor board is made only by DEC but is sold by a number of other distributors. A large number of other manufacturers provide supporting boards that plug into the Q-Bus.

One example of a common interface board would be a dual-height parallel interface module containing: (a) a control and status register, (b) a data register, (c) address decoding (via jumpers) for the registers, (d) an address (via jumpers) for the interrupt vector, (e) a latched 16-bit parallel-input port with one handshaking line, and (f) a latched 16-bit parallel-output port with another handshaking line. The module takes care of the complex signal exchanges and data/address demultiplexing that the Q-Bus requires and lets the user concentrate on interfacing to the data lines and to the two handshaking lines. Even a prototype board would normally be purchased with the bus handshaking logic and the bus drivers already in place.

It should be noted that Q-Bus to Unibus and Unibus to Q-Bus bus translators are readily available, so peripherals can be shared between members of the whole PDP-11 family.

The recent introduction of the LSI-11/23 showed the flexibility of an asynchronous bus structure: peripherals designed to DEC specifications for the LSI-11 and LSI-11/2 were immediately compatible with the newer, faster processor.

Chart 4-4 contains a list of manufacturers of LSI-11 and LSI-11 compatible hardware. The length and depth of this hardware support

Chart 4-4. LSI-11 Hardware Support

Manufacturers and Hardware

1. Able Computer Technology, Inc. (CF)
   1751 Langley Avenue
   Irvine, CA 92714
   (714-979-7030)

2. ACS Division (ST)
   North Atlantic Industries, Inc.
   60 Plant Avenue
   Hauppauge, NY 11787
   (516-582-6500)

3. ADAC Corporation (ABCDGJNST)
   70 Tower Office Park
   Woburn, MA 01801
   (617-935-6668)

4. Analog Devices, Inc. (AB)
   Box 280
   Norwood, MA 02062
   (617-329-4700)

5. Andromeda Systems, Inc. (ABGJKNS)
   9000 Eton Avenue
   Canoga Park, CA 91304
   (213-709-7600)

6. Burr-Brown Research Corp. (ABG)
   P.O. Box 11400
   Tucson, AZ 85734
   (602-746-1111)

7. Charles River Data Systems, Inc. (NOT)
   4 Tech Circle
   Natick, MA 01760
   (617-655-1800)

8. Chrislin Industries, Inc. (KT)
   Computer Products Division
   Westlake Village, CA 91361
   (213-991-2254)

9. Computer Technology (HNW)
   3014 Lake Shore Avenue
   Oakland, CA 94610
   (415-465-9000)

10. Dataram Corporation (KLOQSTU)
    Princeton-Highstown Road
    Cranbury, NJ 08512
    (609-799-0071)

11. Data Systems (NV)
    3130 Coronado Drive
    Santa Clara, CA 95051
    (408-249-9353)

12. Data Systems Corporation (V)
    8716 Production Avenue
    San Diego, CA 92121
    (714-566-5500)

13. Data Translation (ABJ)
    4 Strathmore Road
    Natick, MA 01760
    (617-655-5300)

14. Datel Systems, Inc. (AB)
    1020 Turnpike St.
    Canton, MA 02021
    (617-828-8000)

15. Datrex, Incorporated (O)
    3101 W. Thomas Road
    Suite 109
    Phoenix, AZ 85017

16. Dicom Industries, Inc. (NO)
    715 N. Pastoria Avenue
    Sunnyvale, CA 94086

17. Digital Equipment Corporation
    (ABCDEFGHIJKLMNOPRSTUV)
    Direct Sales Catalog
    Merrimack, NH 03054
    (800-258-1710)

18. Digital Pathways, Inc. (JK)
    4151 Middlefield Road
    Palo Alto, CA 94306
    (415-493-5544)

19. Distributed Logic Corporation (NO)
    12800G Garden Grove Blvd.
    Garden Grove, CA 92643
    (714-534-8950)

20. Ex-Cell-O Corporation (N)
    Remex Division
    1733 Alton Street
    P.O. Box 19533
    Irvine, CA 92713
    (714-557-6860)

Key to Products

A = A/D converters
B = D/A converters
C = Bus terminators/Diagnostic cards/Bus
    buffers/Bus translators
D = Serial interface (asynchronous)
E = Serial interface (synchronous)
F = Multiterminal serial interface

G = Parallel input/output interface
H = DMA interface
I = General-purpose bus interface
    (wire-wrappable)
J = Clocks/timers
K = Semiconductor or memory boards
L = Core and wire memory boards

157

Chart 4-4. LSI-11 Hardware Support (cont.)

Manufacturers and Hardware

21. Fabri-Tek Inc. (K)
    5901 South County Road 18
    Minneapolis, MN 55436
    (612-935-8811)

22. First Computer Corporation (T)
    825 North Cass Avenue
    Westmont, IL 60559
    (312-920-1050)

23. Heath Company (DGKNST)
    Benton Harbor, MI 49022
    (616-982-3309)

24. Matrox Electronic Systems, Ltd. (W)
    2795 Bates Road
    Montreal, Quebec H3S 1B5 Canada
    (514-481-6838)

25. MDB Systems Inc.
    (ABCDEGHIJMRSTVXY)
    1995 N. Batavia St.
    Orange, CA 92665
    (714-998-6900)

26. Micro Memory, Inc. (L)
    9434 Irondale Avenue
    Chatsworth, CA 91311
    (213-998-0070)

27. Mostek Corporation (K)
    1215 West Crosby Road
    Carrollton, TX 75006
    (214-323-8802)

28. National Instrument (Z)
    8900 Shoal Creek
    Building A117
    Austin, TX 78758
    (512-454-3526)

29. National Semiconductor Corp. (K)
    2900 Semiconductor Drive
    Santa Clara, CA 95051
    (408-737-5000)

30. Norden Systems (T)
    United Technologies Corporation
    Norden Place
    Norwalk, CT 06856
    (203-852-5000)

31. Nortek, Inc. (DEGW)
    2432 N.W. Johnson Street
    Portland, OR 97210
    (503-226-3515)

32. Peritek Corporation (HW)
    3014 Lakeshore Avenue
    Oakland, CA 94610
    (415-465-9000)

33. Plessey Peripheral Systems (DKNST)
    17466 Daimler Avenue
    Irvine, CA 92714
    (714-540-9945)

34. Scanoptik, Inc. (C)
    P.O. Box 1745
    Rockville, MD 20850
    (301-762-0612)

35. Siemens Electric Limited (CMW)
    9829-45 Avenue
    Edmonton, Alberta, T6E 5C8 Canada
    (403-436-6640)

36. Terak Corporation (T)
    14405 North Scottsdale Road
    Scottsdale, AZ 85260

37. Toko America, Inc. (LM)
    5520 West Touhy Avenue
    Skokie, IL 60077
    (312-677-3640)

38. Vector Electronic Co., Inc. (R)
    12460 Gladstone Avenue
    Sylmar, CA 91342
    (213-365-9661)

39. Wesperline (QS)
    Division of Western Peripherals
    1100 Claudina Place
    Anaheim, CA 92805
    (714-991-8700)

40. Xylogics, Inc. (O)
    42 Third Avenue
    Burlington, MA 01803
    (617-272-8140)

Key to Products

M = ROM/PROM memory boards
N = Floppy disks/controllers
O = Hard disks/controllers
P = Cassettes
Q = Nine-track magnetic tape drives/controllers
R = Wire-wrap boards
S = Backplanes/power supplies/enclosures

T = Systems
U = LSI-11 processors
V = Line printer controllers
W = Graphics displays/controllers
X = Paper tape/card readers and controllers
Y = Plotters/controllers
Z = IEEE 488 interfaces

suggests one of the primary reasons for the popularity of this microprocessor.

LSI-11 SOFTWARE

Software support is another primary reason for the popularity of the LSI-11. Among the minicomputer manufacturers, many users consider DEC software to be the best. Also, many specialty programs (including cross assemblers, video editors, math packages, and word processing editors) are available for a nominal copying and handling fee from DECUS, the Digital Equipment Corporation Users Society. Other manufacturers supply alternate operating systems and additional languages.

The LSI-11 and LSI-11/2 are supported by DEC with the RT-11 (Real Time-11) Operating System, which includes single job and foreground/background monitors, a file handler, line editor, macro assembler, librarian, and other utilities. Higher-level languages available with this operating system include FORTRAN IV (1966 Standard), BASIC, MULTIUSER BASIC, and FOCAL. The current RT-11 BASIC is below modern microcomputer standards. FOCAL is a DEC language that is similar to BASIC but has distinct advantages in a real-time application.

The LSI-11/23 is additionally supported with the RSX-11M or RSX-11S operating system which features multiuser and multitasking capabilities. With this operating system, enhanced versions of BASIC, FORTRAN, and ANSI 74 COBOL are available, as well as software for data management and intersystem communications.

The University of Southern California at San Diego developed the up-and-coming Pascal language on the PDP-11 (UCSD Pascal®) for educational purposes, and this language, along with a complete operating system, is available from source No. 4 in Chart 4-5. Another software house (source No. 9) provides a Pascal that executes more efficiently (because it doesn't utilize an intermediate pseudocode) and includes extensions such as double precision. Source No. 15 supplies the Idris® operating system, which is a subset of Bell Laboratories UNIX® system, along with a compiler for the C language and Pascal.

The personal computer market is well served by the Heath Company (source No. 5), which provides the DEC processor board along with kits for a cabinet, power supply, interface cards, and floppy disk drives. Heath also provides a modified earlier version of the RT-11 operating system, BASIC, and FORTRAN (1966). Heath's BASIC and FORTRAN are earlier releases by DEC, but Heath does provide a "business" version of BASIC that supports versatile string handling, formatting, and long-integer precision.

Chart 4-5. LSI-11 Software Support

1. Andromeda Systems, Inc.
   (peripheral software)
   9000 Eton Avenue
   Canoga Park, CA 91304
   (213-709-7600)

2. Digital Equipment Corporation
   (see text)
   Direct Sales Catalog
   Merrimack, NH 03054
   (800-258-1710)

3. First Computer Corporation
   (word processing)
   Corporate Square
   825 N. Cass Avenue
   Westmont, IL 60559
   (312-920-1050)

4. Forth, Inc. (polyForth)
   Manhattan Beach, CA 90266

5. Heath Company (operating
   system, BASIC, FORTRAN)
   Benton Harbor, MI 49022
   (616-982-3309)

6. Micro Focus, Inc. (COBOL)
   1601 Civic Center Drive
   Suite 203
   Santa Clara, CA 95050
   (408-984-6961)

7. Micropi (Pilot)
   Lummi Island, WA 98262

8. National Instrument
   (peripheral software)
   8900 Shoal Creek
   Building A117
   Austin, TX 78758
   (512-454-3526)

9. Oregon Software (Pascal)
   2340 S.W. Canyon Road
   Portland, OR 97201
   (503-226-7760)

10. Plessey Peripheral Systems
    (peripheral software)
    17466 Daimler Avenue
    Irvine, CA 92714
    (714-540-9945)

11. SoftTech Microsystems (operating
    system, Pascal, FORTRAN,
    cross-assemblers)
    9494 Black Mountain Road
    San Diego, CA 92126
    (714-578-6105)

12. Sorrento Valley Associates
    (Pascal)
    San Diego, CA

13. Unique Automation Products
    (word processing, filers, editors)
    17922 Sky Park Circle, Suite L
    Irvine, CA 92714
    (714-549-4832)

14. Virtual Systems (cross assemblers)
    1500 Newell Avenue, Suite 406
    Walnut Creek, CA 94596
    (415-935-4944)

15. Whitesmiths, Ltd. (Idris operating
    system, C language, Pascal)
    Systems Division
    127 W. 80th Street
    New York, NY 10024
    (212-799-1200)

BENCHMARKS

In the listings of the benchmark programs in this section, note that: (a) the number in the first column (LINE) counts the lines appearing in the *source* assembly language program, (b) the second column (ADDRESS) contains the unlinked octal address of the following instruction, (c) the third column (OBJECT CODE) gives the octal machine language code that is to be placed at that address, (d) the fourth column (LABEL) begins the source assembly language program with any symbolic address labels that the programmer used, (e) the fifth column (INSTRUCTION MNEMONIC) contains assembly language instructions or directives to the assembler, (f) the sixth column (OPERANDS) contains the source and destination operands, and (g) the last column (COMMENTARY) is reserved for the programmer's enlightening comments and is begun with a semicolon.

All of the benchmark programs were run on the computer system shown in Fig. 4-19, which uses the LSI-11/2 processor. This particular processor includes the optional microcode chip that adds floating-point and multiply/divide instructions. However, only the third benchmark program (square root) utilized any of these instructions.

All of these programs would have been executed significantly faster if an LSI-11/23 had been used. The actual speed advantage of the LSI-11/23 depends on the number of floating-point and double-precision operations that are involved. DEC suggests that the LSI-11/23 is 2.5 times faster than the LSI-11 or LSI-11/2.

Bubble Sort

Fig. 4-8 is a listing of the first benchmark program, the worst-case bubble sort of 600 (decimal) sixteen-bit numbers into ascending order. The section with a subtitle of BENCHMARK INITIALIZATION creates the worst case by: (a) storing the largest number (decimal 599) at the beginning of the list (which has an address label of LSTADD), (b) decrementing this number and storing it at the next higher address, and (c) continuing this process until the smallest number (0) has been stored at the highest address. Note how transparently each assembly language instruction is translated into octal machine code, with the mode of addressing and the source and destination operands clearly delineated. Note, too, how the SOB R0, LSET1 instruction (subtract one from the contents of register R0 and branch to LSET1 if not equal to zero), along with the autoincrement addressing mode with register R1, produces a *two-word* loop that initializes all of the table contents except the very last one!

The actual sorting takes place in the second section of the benchmark. The assembler directive .BLKW (line 5) reserves a block of 600 locations for the list. (The decimal point after the number tells the assembler that 600 is a decimal number.) On the next line the assembler directive .WORD stores the address of the beginning of the list at the current program address; the apostrophe after this address signifies that the octal code for this address will have to be changed when the program addresses are given new, absolute values by the linker (relocation). Execution efficiency is enhanced by using the fastest instructions (register-to-register transfers) within the inner loop. Try to follow the interplay of direct and indirect addressing and autoincrement, indexed, and autodecrement addressing modes. The

LINE	ADDRESS	OBJECT CODE	LABEL	INSTRUCTION MNEMONIC	OPERANDS	COMMENTS
1				.SBTTL	BENCHMARK INITIALIZATION
2					;
3	000002	016700	SETUP:	MOV	LENGTH,R0	;R0 IS LENGTH OF TABLE
		002334				
4	000006	016701		MOV	LSTADD,R1	;ADDRESS OF TABLE
		002326				
5	000012	010021	LSET1:	MOV	R0,(R1)+	;SAVE VALUE IN TABLE
6	000014	077002		SOB	R0,LSET1	;LOOP UNTIL R0=0
7	000016	010021		MOV	R0,(R1)+	;LAST ELEMENT
8						;

LINE	ADDRESS	OBJECT CODE	LABEL	INSTRUCTION MNEMONIC	OPERANDS	COMMENTS
1				.SBTTL	BENCHMARK
2				;	BUBBLE SORT
3						;
4		001130		LEN=600.		;600. ELEMENT LIST
5	000060		LIST:	.BLKW	600.	
6	002340	000060'	LSTADD:	.WORD	LIST	
7	002342	001127	LENGTH:	.WORD	LEN-1	
8						;
9						;
10	002344	012703	BENCH:	MOV	#-1,R3	;EXCHANGE VALUE IS ALL 1'S
		177777				
11	002350	016700	LP1:	MOV	LENGTH,R0	;SET UP LENGTH OF LIST
		177766				
12	002354	016701		MOV	LSTADD,R1	;GET POINTER TO LIST
		177760				
13	002360	005002		CLR	R2	;CLEAR EXCHANGE FLAG
14	002362	022111	LP2:	CMP	(R1)+,(R1)	;COMPARE A AND B
15	002364	002405		BLT	SKIP	;IF A<B THEN MAY BE THRU
16	002366	014104		MOV	-(R1),R4	;ELSE SAVE A IN REG R4
17	002370	016121		MOV	2(R1),(R1)+	;MOVE B INTO A
		000002				
18	002374	010411		MOV	R4,(R1)	;MOVE A INTO B
19	002376	010302		MOV	R3,R2	;SET EXCHANGE INDICATOR IN R2
20	002400	077010	SKIP:	SOB	R0,LP2	;LOOP TIL LAST ELEMENT CHECKED
21	002402	020203		CMP	R2,R3	;EXCHANGE FLAG SET?
22	002404	001761		BEQ	LP1	;IF SO - LOOP BACK
23						; & START THRU LIST AGAIN
24	002406	000000		HALT		;FINISHED
25						;

Fig. 4-8. Benchmark program: bubble sort.

execution time for this program was 10.5 seconds, as determined by use of the system line clock. (The timekeeping sections of the programs are not listed.)

ASCII String Search

Fig. 4-9 is a listing of the second benchmark program, a string search. The assembler directive .NLIST inhibits the printing of the octal code for the 39 bytes that contain the string; .LIST reenables it. The .EVEN directive ensures that the next instruction has an even address, as all instructions must have. Line 16 uses the byte version of the compare instruction to see if R0 is now pointing to an address containing the ASCII value (signified by the apostrophe) of the asterisk (*) character, which is being used to flag the end of each inner string. With no special string instructions available, the test string and the current inner string must be checked character by character (lines 21 through 27). This program was executed 1000 (decimal) times and the line clock then showed that each program execution required 979 μs.

Square Root Determination

The multiplication/division benchmark is presented in Fig. 4-10. On line 5, N is the label for the address of the number whose square root is to be found; this listing is for the run in which the chosen number was the second one: 10,000 (decimal). The @ symbol before N on line 12 signifies that the *contents* of address N, and not

LINE	ADDRESS	OBJECT CODE	LABEL	INSTRUCTION MNEMONIC	OPERANDS	COMMENTS
1				.SBTTL	BENCHMARK	
2				;	STRING SEARCH	
3				;		;
4				.NLIST	BIN	
5	000050		MAIN:	.ASCII	/NANO*PICO*MICROCOMPUTER*MICROPROCESSOR*/	
6	000117			.ASCII	/MICROSYSTEM*MICRO*?/	
7	000142		TEST:	.ASCII	/MICRO*/	
8				.EVEN		
9				.LIST	BIN	
10						;
11	000150	000050'	MAINA:	.WORD	MAIN	;ADDRESS OF MAIN STRING
12	000152	000142'	TESTA:	.WORD	TEST	;ADDRESS OF TEST STRING
13						;
14	000154	016700 177770	BENCH:	MOV	MAINA,R0	;GET MAIN ADDRESS
15	000160	000403		BR	LP2	;SET UP START
16	000162	122027 000052	LP1:	CMPB	(R0)+,#'*	;END OF STRING?
17	000166	001375		BNE	LP1	;LOOP UNTIL FOUND
18	000170	016701 177756	LP2:	MOV	TESTA,R1	;GET TEST ADDRESS
19	000174	121027 000077		CMPB	(R0),#'?	;END OF MAIN?
20	000200	001411		BEQ	NOTFND	;STRING NOT FOUND
21	000202	122011		CMPB	(R0)+,(R1)	;COMPARE FIRST BYTES
22	000204	001366		BNE	LP1	;IF NOT - GET TO NEXT STRING
23	000206	005201		INC	R1	;UPDATE TEST STRING ADDRESS
24	000210	121021	LP3:	CMPB	(R0),(R1)+	;COMPARE NEXT CHARACTER
25	000212	001363		BNE	LP1	;NO MATCH - RESTART
26	000214	122027 000052		CMPB	(R0)+,#'*	;END OF STRING CHARACTER?
27	000220	001373		BNE	LP3	;IF NOT - TRY NEXT CHARACTER
28	000222	000000	FOUND:	HALT		;FOUND STRING
29	000224	000000	NOTFND:	HALT		;STRING NOT FOUND
30						;
31						;

Fig. 4-9. Benchmark program: string search.

N itself, are to be moved to register R2. The divide instruction in line 16 (DIV #200.,R0) uses the source operand (the decimal number 200) as the divisor and the contents of the register immediately above the destination register (R1 in this case) as the dividend; the quotient is stored in the destination register (R0) and any remainder is stored in the next higher register (R1). Actual execution times were 458 μs (square root of 58,081), 628 μs (square root of 10,000), and 457 μs (square root of 16,384).

```
              OBJECT              INSTRUCTION
LINE  ADDRESS CODE   LABEL        MNEMONIC  OPERANDS    COMMENTS

 1                                .SBTTL    BENCHMARK
 2                                ;         MULTIPLICATION/DIVISION
 3                                ;         SQUARE ROOT CALCULATION
 4                                                      ;
 5    000050  000056' N:          .WORD     NUMBER+2    ;NEED ROOT OF NO.,THIS ADDRES
 6    000052  000000  SQRTN:      .WORD     0           ;RESULT STORED AT THIS LOCATION
 7                                                      ;
 8    000054  161341  NUMBER:     .WORD     58081.
 9    000056  023420              .WORD     10000.
10    000060  040000              .WORD     16384.
11                                                      ;
12    000062  017702  BENCH:      MOV       @N,R2       ;GET NUMBER
              177762
13    000066  005000              CLR       R0          ;FIRST APPROXIMATION
14    000070  010201              MOV       R2,R1       ;R1 IS NOW THE DIVIDEND
15                                                      ;  FOR THE DIVIDE INSTRUCTION
16    000072  071027              DIV       #200.,R0    ;DIVIDE N BY 200
              000310
17                                                      ;QUOTIENT LEFT IN R0
18    000076  062700              ADD       #2.,R0      ;2 + N/200.
              000002
19    000102  010067              MOV       R0,SQRTN    ;SAVE RESULT AS THE
              177744
20                                                      ;    FIRST APPROXIMATION
21    000106  005000  LP1:        CLR       R0          ;COMPUTE N DIVIDED BY
22    000110  010201              MOV       R2,R1       ;   THE LAST APPROXIMATION
23    000112  071067              DIV       SQRTN,R0    ;EACH TIME THROUGH THIS LOOP
              177734
24    000116  066700              ADD       SQRTN,R0    ;ADD THE LAST APPROXIMATION
              177730
25                                                      ;    TO THIS VALUE
26    000122  006200              ASR       R0          ;DIVIDE THE RESULT BY 2
27    000124  010067              MOV       R0,SQRTN    ;SAVE THIS NEW APPROXIMATION
              177722
28                                                      ;    AT SQRTN
29    000130  070067              MUL       SQRTN,R0    ;COMPUTE APPROXIMATION**2
              177716
30    000134  020201              CMP       R2,R1       ;IS IT EQUAL TO N?
31    000136  001363              BNE       LP1         ;LOOP UNTIL EXACT RESULT
32                                                      ;    IS OBTAINED
33    000140  000000  DONE:       HALT                  ;FINISHED
34                                                      ;
35                                                      ;
```

Fig. 4-10. Benchmark program: multiplication/division (square root).

Lookup Table

Our fourth benchmark program (Fig. 4-11) uses a lookup table to determine the sine of any specified angle in the range of 0 to 360 degrees, assuming an angular resolution of 1 degree.

There are 91 possible (absolute) values for the sine of an angle with this kind of resolution, and these values (multiplied by 10,000 to make them all integers, for economy of storage and speed of retrieval) are stored in successive locations in lines 4 through 22. Line 25 specifies the address of the angle; in this particular listing the chosen angle was 315 (decimal) degrees, which is stored at relocatable address 000360 (octal). (The 315 degrees is located 14 decimal or 16 octal bytes above the address of the beginning of the list of angles.)

Lines 35 through 37 adjust the angle to make it less than 180 degrees. (In this particular program, this would change 315 degrees to 135 degrees.) The angles in quadrants 3 and 4 all have negative sines;

```
                 OBJECT              INSTRUCTION
LINE  ADDRESS    CODE     LABEL      MNEMONIC   OPERANDS      COMMENTS

 1                                   .SBTTL     BENCHMARK
 2                                   ;          SINE LOOKUP
 3                                   .NLIST     BIN           ;INHIBIT BINARY LISTING
 4    000050              SINE:      .WORD      0000.,0175.,0349.,0523.,0698.
 5    000062                         .WORD      0872.,1045.,1219.,1392.,1564.
 .
 .
 .
21    000322                         .WORD      9962.,9976.,9986.,9994.,9998.
22    000334                         .WORD      10000.
23                                   .LIST      BIN           ;ENABLE BINARY LISTING
24                                   ;
25    000336    000360'   ANGLA:     .WORD      ANGLES+16     ;ADDRESS OF ANGLE DATA
26    000340    000000    SINANG:    .WORD      0
27                                   ;
28                                   .NLIST     BIN
29    000342              ANGLES:    .WORD      0.,45.,90.,135.,180.,225.,270.,315.,360.
30                                   .LIST      BIN
31                                   ;
32    000364    005002    BENCH:     CLR        R2            ;INITIALIZE RESULT (+)
33    000366    017701               MOV        @ANGLA,R1     ;GET ANGLE IN R1
                177744
34    000372    020127               CMP        R1,#180.      ;IS ANGLE < 180 DEGREES?
                000264
35    000376    100404               BMI        SKIP1         ;IF SO - SKIP AHEAD
36    000400    162701               SUB        #180.,R1      ;SUBTRACT 180 FROM
                000264
37                                   ;              ANGLES IN QUADRANT 3 & 4
38    000404    012702               MOV        #100000,R2    ;SET MSB (SIGN BIT)
                100000
39                                   ;              TO 1 (NEGATIVE SIGN)
40    000410    020127    SKIP1:     CMP        R1,#91.       ;IS ADJUSTED ANGLE
                000133
41                                   ;              LESS THAN 91. DEGREES?
42    000414    100403               BMI        SKIP2         ;IF SO - SKIP AHEAD
43    000416    162701               SUB        #180.,R1      ;ELSE COMPUTE (180. - ANGLE)
                000264
44    000422    005401               NEG        R1            ;ALL ANGLES ARE NOW
45                                   ;               IN THE FIRST QUADRANT
46    000424    006301    SKIP2:     ASL        R1            ;MAKE WORD ADDRESS
47    000426    066102               ADD        SINE(R1),R2   ;ADD VALUE FROM TABLE
                000050
48    000432    022702               CMP        #100000,R2    ;IS THE SINE EQUAL TO -0?
                100000
49    000436    001001               BNE        SKIP3         ;IF NOT - SKIP AHEAD
50    000440    005002               CLR        R2            ;ELSE 0
51    000442    010267    SKIP3:     MOV        R2,SINANG     ;SAVE AS SIGN MAGNITUDE RESULT
                177672
52    000446    000000               HALT
53
```

Fig. 4-11. Benchmark program: lookup table (sine of an angle).

a 1 is placed in the most significant bit of the result to retain this information.

In lines 40 through 45 the angle is adjusted once more to place it in the first quadrant. (In this particular program, our 135 degrees now becomes $-\{135-180\} = 45$ degrees.) Line 46, ASL R1, multiplies the angle by 2 so that it will point to the proper location in the sine table (because the values are stored in successive words, not in successive bytes).

Line 47 *adds* the value from the sine table (using mode 6 indexed addressing for register R1) to the contents of R2 (so that any sign bit will be retained). Finally, the sine of the specified angle (multiplied by decimal 10,000) is stored at address SINANG with the msb signifying the sign of the sine.

Execution times for this program were (a) first quadrant: 64 μs, (b) second quadrant: 74 μs, (c) third quadrant: 75 μs, and (d) fourth quadrant: 85 μs.

Block Transfer

The last benchmark is presented in Fig. 4-12. Here we have a program that moves 256 (decimal) sixteen-bit numbers from one block of memory (the source block) to a second block of memory

```
            OBJECT                INSTRUCTION
LINE ADDRESS CODE    LABEL         MNEMONIC  OPERANDS    COMMENTS

 1                                 .SBTTL    BENCHMARK
 2                                 ;         BLOCK MOVE
 3                                                       ;
 4   000050            FROM:       .BLKW     256.        ;SOURCE BLOCK
 5   001050            TO:         .BLKW     256.        ;DESTINATION BLOCK
 6   002050   000400   LEN:        .WORD     256.        ;BLOCK LENGTH
 7                                                       ;
 8   002052   000050'  FADD:       .WORD     FROM        ;ADDRESS OF SOURCE BLOCK
 9   002054   001050'  TADD:       .WORD     TO          ;ADDRESS OF DESTINATION BLOCK
10   002056   002050'  BLEN:       .WORD     LEN         ;ADDRESS OF LENGTH OF BLK MOVE
11                                                       ;
12   002060   016700   BENCH:      MOV       FADD,R0     ;SOURCE ADDRESS
              177766
13   002064   016701               MOV       TADD,R1     ;DESTINATION ADDRESS
              177764
14   002070   017702               MOV       @BLEN,R2    ;BLOCK LENGTH
              177762
15   002074   012021   LP:         MOV       (R0)+,(R1)+ ;MOVE WORD
16   002076   077202               SOB       R2,LP       ;LOOP UNTIL FINISHED
17   002100   000000   DONE:       HALT
18                                                       ;
19                                                       ;
```

Fig. 4-12. Benchmark program: block move.

(the destination block). Once the block parameters are moved into registers R0, R1, and R2, the transfer is accomplished with only two words of instructions (using that fine SOB instruction once again). Execution time for this benchmark was 3265 μs.

Table 4-8 summarizes the execution times for these five benchmark programs.

LSI-11 INTERFACING: THE Q-BUS

The LSI-11 is available only as a board-level microcomputer; as such, the interfacing protocol has been completely defined by Digital Equipment Corporation. The LSI-11 bus, the Q-Bus, is composed of two 36-contact connector blocks. Each connector block is double sided and has 18 contacts per side. The Q-Bus contains the address, data, and control signals as well as the power and ground connections for each module that is attached to the bus. Table 4-9 lists the DEC mnemonics as well as the dedicated use for each of the 72 lines on the Q-Bus. The "B" that begins each mnemonic does indeed stand for "Bus."

Table 4-8. Execution Times for the Benchmark Programs

Benchmark Program	LSI-1 1/2 Execution Time
1. Bubble sort (600 16-bit numbers, worst case)	10.5 s
2. String search	979 μs
3. Multiplication/division (square root)	458 μs ($\sqrt{58,081}$) 628 μs ($\sqrt{10,000}$) 457 μs ($\sqrt{16,384}$)
4. Lookup table (sine of an angle)	64 μs (1st quadrant) 74 μs (2nd quadrant) 75 μs (3rd quadrant) 85 μs (4th quadrant)
5. Transfer of a block of 256 words to a different area in memory	3265 μs

LSI-11 bus signals are bidirectional and the lines use resistive terminations to produce a passive high level; the true or asserted state is produced when the line is pulled to a low level by the processor or other device. Devices are connected to the Q-Bus via high-impedance bus receivers and open-collector drivers.

Data Transfer Bus Cycles

In Fig. 4-13 we present the handshaking and timing relationships for the DATI data transfer bus cycle. This bus cycle is used by the processor, as bus master, when it is fetching an instruction or when it is executing an instruction requiring only the reading of a data word from a memory location. An example of this type of instruction is MOV (R1),R2 (obtain the data word at the location pointed to by the contents of register R1 and move it into register R2).

The cycle is identified as an input cycle by a high (unasserted) level on the BWTBT line during the time that the BDAL lines are being used as address lines. The addressed location must respond to the BDIN strobe within 10 μs or a bus time-out error and the appropriate trap will occur. On the final handshake, though, the bus master has no alternative but to wait for the negation of BRPLY before concluding the cycle.

A second type of data transfer bus cycle is DATO or DATOB (Fig. 4-14) in which data is written out to memory or to a peripheral device. An example of an instruction requiring the DATO bus cycle is MOV R1,(R2) (transfer the contents of register R1 to the address pointed to by the contents of register R2). If only a byte

Table 4-9. The Q-Bus

Label	Description	Number of Lines
Data/Address Lines		
BDAL0–BDAL17	Multiplexed data/address lines	18
BBS7	This line is asserted when an address is in the normal input/output page (in the upper 4K of addressing range)	1
Data Control		
BSYNC	Address strobe signal	1
BDIN	Data-in strobe	1
BDOUT	Data-out strobe	1
BWTBT	Write a byte of data	1
BRPLY	Device response	1
Interrupt		
BIRQ7–BIRQ4	Interrupt priority levels	4
BIAKO	Interrupt acknowledge output	1
BIAKI	Interrupt acknowledge input	1
DMA Control		
BDMR	DMA request	1
BDMGO	DMA grant output	1
BDMGI	DMA grant input	1
BSACK	Bus grant acknowledge	1
System Control		
BHALT	Processor halt	1
BREF	Memory refresh cycle	1
BDCK	DC power OK	1
BPOK	AC power OK	1
BEVENT	Bus interrupt (vectored at address 100)	1
BINIT	Bus initialization	1
Power, Ground, and Spares		
+5 Vdc		3
+12 Vdc		2
−12 Vdc		2
+12 Vdc battery		2
+5 Vdc battery		1
Grounds		8
Spares		14

and not a full word is being transferred, the bus master will assert BWTBT when putting the data on the bus data/address lines. You can see that, except for the use of the BDOUT strobe, the handshaking protocol is very similar to that used for the DATI bus cycle.

The third and last type of data transfer bus cycle, DATIO or DATIOB, combines the two previous bus cycles (Fig. 4-15). This

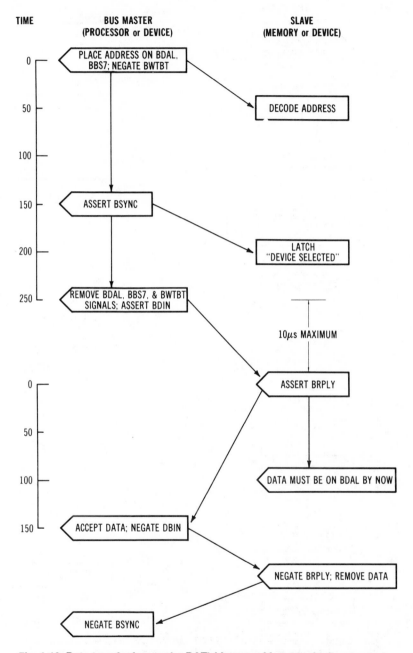

Fig. 4-13. Data transfer bus cycle: DATI (data word input to the bus master).

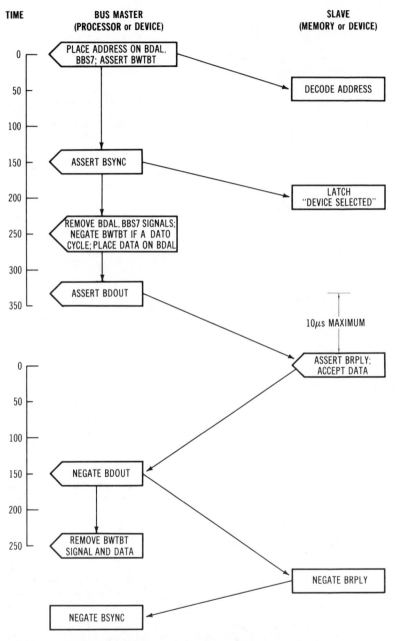

Fig. 4-14. Data transfer bus cycle: DATO and DATOB (data word output and data byte output, respectively, from the bus master).

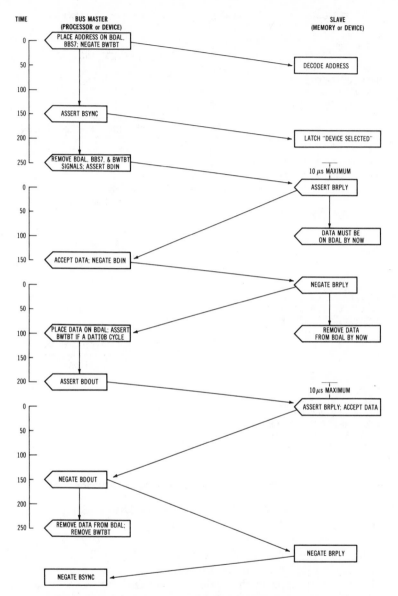

Fig. 4-15. Data transfer bus cycle: DATIO and DATIOB (data word input/output and data byte input/output, respectively, by the bus master).

cycle is used when an instruction requires both input from, and output to, a given memory location. An example of such an instruction is **INCB** (R1) (increment the byte at the location pointed to by the

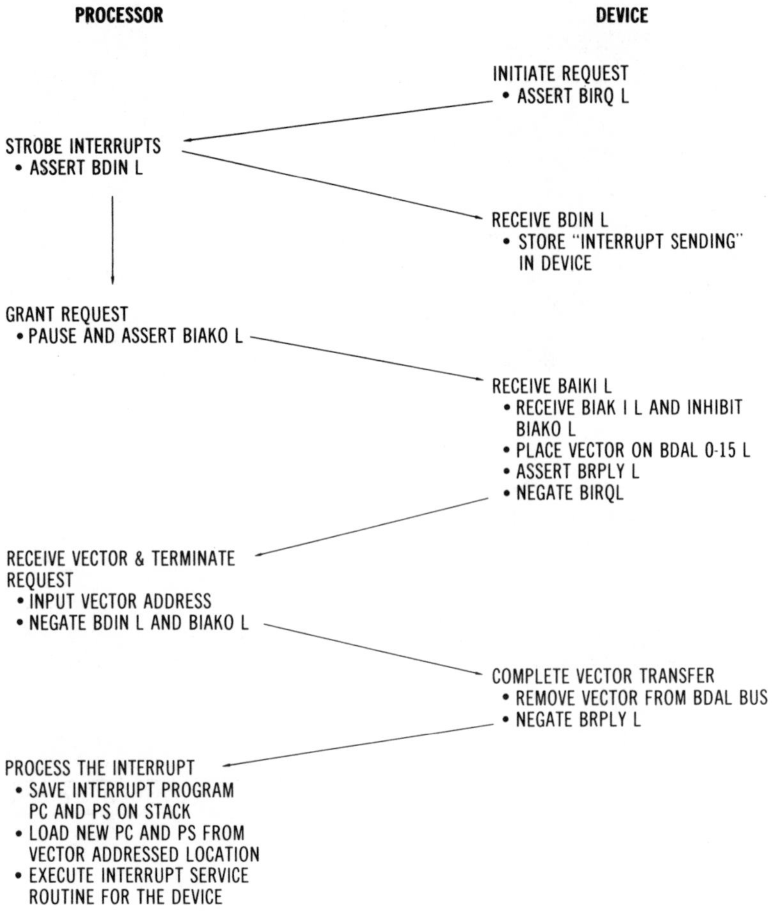
PROCESSOR
DEVICE
INITIATE REQUEST
• ASSERT BIRQ L
STROBE INTERRUPTS
• ASSERT BDIN L
RECEIVE BDIN L
• STORE "INTERRUPT SENDING" IN DEVICE
GRANT REQUEST
• PAUSE AND ASSERT BIAKO L
RECEIVE BAIKI L
• RECEIVE BIAK I L AND INHIBIT BIAKO L
• PLACE VECTOR ON BDAL 0-15 L
• ASSERT BRPLY L
• NEGATE BIRQL
RECEIVE VECTOR & TERMINATE REQUEST
• INPUT VECTOR ADDRESS
• NEGATE BDIN L AND BIAKO L
COMPLETE VECTOR TRANSFER
• REMOVE VECTOR FROM BDAL BUS
• NEGATE BRPLY L
PROCESS THE INTERRUPT
• SAVE INTERRUPT PROGRAM PC AND PS ON STACK
• LOAD NEW PC AND PS FROM VECTOR ADDRESSED LOCATION
• EXECUTE INTERRUPT SERVICE ROUTINE FOR THE DEVICE

Courtesy Digital Equipment Corporation

Fig. 4-16. Interrupt request acknowledge sequence.

contents of register R1), which would use the DATIOB form (asserting BWTBT with the data output). The processor would read the data, increment it, and then write it back into memory.

The times given on the left side on each of Figs. 4-13 through 4-15 are *minimum* times in general. For example, the processor could require additional time in the middle of the DATIO cycle to execute a particular instruction.

Interrupt and DMA Bus Cycles

An interrupt requires a somewhat similar interplay of signals on the asynchronous Q-Bus; Fig. 4-16 depicts this interrupt bus cycle. Finally, Fig. 4-17 presents the direct memory access bus cycle.

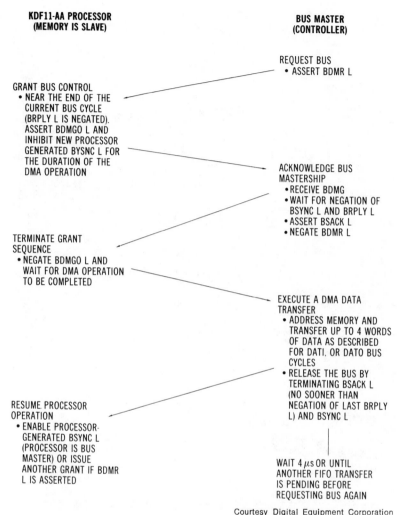

KDF11-AA PROCESSOR
(MEMORY IS SLAVE)

BUS MASTER
(CONTROLLER)

REQUEST BUS
• ASSERT BDMR L

GRANT BUS CONTROL
• NEAR THE END OF THE
CURRENT BUS CYCLE
(BRPLY L IS NEGATED).
ASSERT BDMGO L AND
INHIBIT NEW PROCESSOR
GENERATED BYSNC L FOR
THE DURATION OF THE
DMA OPERATION

ACKNOWLEDGE BUS
MASTERSHIP
• RECEIVE BDMG
• WAIT FOR NEGATION OF
BSYNC L AND BRPLY L
• ASSERT BSACK L
• NEGATE BDMR L

TERMINATE GRANT
SEQUENCE
• NEGATE BDMGO L AND
WAIT FOR DMA OPERATION
TO BE COMPLETED

EXECUTE A DMA DATA
TRANSFER
• ADDRESS MEMORY AND
TRANSFER UP TO 4 WORDS
OF DATA AS DESCRIBED
FOR DATI. OR DATO BUS
CYCLES
• RELEASE THE BUS BY
TERMINATING BSACK L
(NO SOONER THAN
NEGATION OF LAST BRPLY
L) AND BSYNC L

RESUME PROCESSOR
OPERATION
• ENABLE PROCESSOR-
GENERATED BSYNC L
(PROCESSOR IS BUS
MASTER) OR ISSUE
ANOTHER GRANT IF BDMR
L IS ASSERTED

WAIT 4 μs OR UNTIL
ANOTHER FIFO TRANSFER
IS PENDING BEFORE
REQUESTING BUS AGAIN

Courtesy Digital Equipment Corporation

Fig. 4-17. Direct memory access (DMA) sequence.

This discussion of bus cycles should make it clear why users of the LSI-11/PDP-11 normally interface to the processor using plug-in boards that already contain the hardware that can satisfy the specified protocol for data transfer, interrupt handling, and DMA operations.

TWO LSI-11 SYSTEMS

The LSI-11 is well suited to dedicated applications in science laboratories. Fig. 4-18 shows an example of a sophisticated laboratory

Fig. 4-18. Instructional hands-on LSI-11 laboratory microcomputer system; with a single-user operating system the computer supports FORTRAN, BASIC, and the MACRO assembler.

computer system (designed, built, and being used by A. Baldwin) that is based on the LSI-11. The system as shown performs a dual function: (a) the training of students in the software and hardware aspects of the modern computer-based laboratory and (b) actual data acquisition and processing. The processor and peripheral boards are plugged into the backplane from the open front panel (lower half of the rack on the left in the picture). This allows students to configure the system with just the peripherals they need. The system includes the following components: an LSI-11/2 processor, two serial interfaces, a high-speed (180 characters per second) matrix printer, a dual-drive floppy disk system, a ½-inch (1.27 cm) IBM-compatible nine-track magnetic tape transport and controller, and a 16-bit parallel input/output module. The system also contains a 512- × 512-point graphics display, a 24-line by 80-character video output which overlays the graphics display, a 16-channel analog-to-digital converter, a 4-channel digital-to-analog converter with additional digital outputs, an X-Y/point plotter, and a programmable timer module for real-time control.

The LSI-11 is a somewhat expensive processor for use in a home computer, even in the kit form supplied by the Heath Company. It can, however, be justified (a) for its minicomputer software and, particularly, (b) if it permits a scientist or engineer to retain software compatibility with his or her professional equipment. The per-

Fig. 4-19. A home computer system based on the LSI-11 processor.

sonal computer system shown in Fig. 4-19 is based on the Heath kit; this LSI-11 is being supported by six other microprocessors: one for the floppy disk drive controller, one for the digitizing pad, two for the plotter, and two for the plotter/digitizer interface. The interface programs were developed on the LSI-11 and then committed to ROM in the laboratory, taking advantage of software compatibility.

CONCLUSION

The strengths of the LSI-11 family lie in: (a) the elegance of its instruction set, which leads to programming efficiency at the assembly language level, (b) the minicomputer-level software support which it has inherited, (c) the wealth of its hardware support, from many sources, and (d) the flexibility of its asynchronous bus structure. The weaknesses of the family lie in (a) its limited memory addressing capabilities (particularly noticeable as operating systems grow larger and larger), and (b) its moderate execution speed.

Presently the LSI-11 is the most widely used 16-bit microprocessor. The newer 16-bit microprocessors are clearly challenging it, as the weaknesses listed above suggest. However, its strengths will not quickly be surpassed by the competition and it can be expected to remain very popular. Many PDP-11 users will continue to take advantage of the family software compatibility, particularly as new versions of the LSI-11 emulate the upper members of the family. The present limitations on the amount of memory that the LSI-11 can address are partially solved by the LSI-11/23, and certainly the next version of the LSI-11 will match the capabilities of its newer competitors. It will not be as easy to increase the speed of the LSI-11; the multiplexing of data and address information on the LSI-11 bus and the asynchronous nature of this bus necessarily impose speed constraints. The LSI-11 will, however, be able to achieve effective speed improvements for many applications (as it has already with the LSI-11/23) by utilizing higher-speed processing of "bottleneck" tasks, such as double-precision floating-point multiply/divide.

BIBLIOGRAPHY

Bell, C. Gordon; McNamara, John E.; and Mudge, J. Craig. *Computer Engineering (A DEC View of Hardware Systems Design)*. Digital Press, 1978. Discussion of Digital Equipment Corporation and each of its computer families. Nine chapters are devoted to the architecture of the PDP-11/LSI-11 computer family.

Cooper, James W. *The Minicomputer in the Laboratory, With Examples Using the PDP-11*. New York: John Wiley & Sons, Inc., 1977. Basic minicomputer architecture, PDP-11 assembly language programming, and laboratory applications.

Digital Equipment Corp. *Memories and Peripherals* (Microcomputer Handbook Series). Maynard, MA: Digital Equipment Corp., 1978-79. General and detailed specifications of the backplanes, power supplies, cabinets, integrated circuits, and interface boards available from DEC.

————. *Microcomputer Processor Handbook.* Maynard, MA: Digital Equipment Corp., 1979. Detailed description of the LSI-11 instruction set, timing, and Q-Bus structure. (The handbooks for the upper members of the PDP-11 family provide additional information on the implementation of memory management.)

————. *Technical Documentation Catalog.* Maynard, MA: Digital Equipment Corp. Software documentation, hardware manuals, and engineering drawings are included in this catalog.

Dickhut, Duane; Hashizume, Burt; and Johnson, William N. "LSI Trio Calls the Tunes in Microcomputer's CPU," *Electronics,* July 17, 1980, pp. 130-135. This article describes the components, operating modes, and expandable microinstruction set of the LSI-11/23.

Eckhouse, Richard H., Jr., and Morris, L. Robert. *Minicomputer Systems—Organization, Programming and Applications (PDP-1)*, 2nd ed. Englewood Cliffs: Prentice-Hall, Inc., 1979. The text provides details on the instruction set, on hardware, and on programming with MACRO assembler.

Gill, Arthur. *Machine and Assembly Language Programming of the PDP-11.* Englewood Cliffs: Prentice-Hall, Inc., 1978. PDP-11 architecture, instruction set, assembler, and linker are discussed in this textbook.

Kraft, George D., and Toy, Wing N. *Mini/Microcomputer Hardware Design.* Englewood Cliffs: Prentice-Hall, Inc., 1979. Processor architecture design and instruction set design, with examples from the PDP-11, are discussed.

Singer, Michael. *PDP-11 Assembler Language Programming and Machine Organization.* New York: John Wiley & Sons, Inc., 1980. New LSI-11 owners will appreciate this new text. It covers assembly language programming along with some relevant aspects of the operating system, such as the monitor calls and the on-line debugging technique.

5

The 9900

The Texas Instruments family of 9900-series microprocessor integrated circuits was developed in the mid-1970s and was based on the central processor unit (CPU) architecture of the 990 minicomputer family. Although the 9900 family has been available for some time, it is still quite competitive with other, newer, 16-bit microprocessor systems, as well as being fairly simple and easy to use. It is particularly recommended for people who are being exposed to minicomputers or 16-bit microcomputers for the first time. The first of the 9900-series of microprocessor integrated circuits, or chips, is the TMS9900, a 64-pin package which is about ¾ inch by 3⅛ inches (2 cm by 8 cm). Later versions of the 9900 include the TMS9980A, TMS9981, TMS9985, and TMS9940. Each of these four devices has special functions and features that will be discussed in later sections of this chapter. In the following discussions, examples, and programs the TMS9900 will be used as the model.

GENERAL DESCRIPTION

The 9900 is a memory-based computer having only three accessible registers within the central processing unit. These registers are the program counter (PC), the workspace pointer (WP), and the status register (ST). There are no other readily accessible registers, all other temporary information being stored in external read/write (R/W) memory. The 9900 can directly address up to 65,536 *bytes* of memory, or 32,768 *words* of memory. It is important to remember that a byte consists of 8 bits, while a word consists of 16 bits. The memory capacities of the 9900 are generally abbreviated as 64K bytes and 32K words, respectively. It is understood that the notation "K" means

1024 memory locations. Although the 9900 is a 16-bit computer, only 15 address bus lines have been provided to address the various types of memory circuits that will be used to store program steps or other information. These bits have been implemented as the 15 most significant bits, leaving the least significant 16th bit unavailable. Thus, when words are addresses, each address will be an even number, for example 0AF8 would be followed by 0AFA, and 1234 would be followed by 1236. All of the addresses are specified in base 16, or hexadecimal, notation. To avoid confusion with decimal numbers, all of the hexadecimal (or hex) numbers will have a suffix of H, for example, 0FF8H.

The least significant bit in the 16-bit address is actually implemented within the 9900 CPU, but it is used internally to distinguish between byte and word operations, the only two types of operations that the 9900 can perform. There are some individual bit manipulations that can be performed by the input/output (i/o) operations, but they will be discussed later. Unfortunately, Texas Instruments has used a "backwards" notation for the data bus and address bus signals, with A0 being the *most significant bit,* or msb, and A14 being the *least significant bit,* or lsb. (Remember that there are only 15 address bits.) This notation is somewhat confusing to people who have become accustomed to the more normal notation, where the bit notation number increases from right to left. Rather than mix notations, the Texas Instruments' notation has been used throughout this chapter, so keep this in mind when you read other chapters and compare computers.

The 9900 has a cycle time that may vary from 500 nanoseconds (ns) to 300 ns, providing cycle frequencies of 2 MHz and 3.3 MHz, respectively. The 9900 is a *dynamic* device, so the clocks may not be interrupted or stopped without the loss of information, addresses, etc., within the CPU. Enhanced versions of the 9900 are available such that clock rates of up to 4 MHz are possible. A typical example is the TMS9900-40. Each of the instructions that the 9900 can execute can be broken into a number of consecutive machine cycles, either for a memory transfer or for an arithmetic-logic unit (alu) operation. Each cycle is 2 clock cycles long. Thus the fastest instruction is a workspace register transfer, taking 1 cycle, while the slowest instruction is a division operation, taking up to 62 cycles. If a 2-MHz clock frequency is used to control the 9900, the time required for the workspace register transfer would be 1 microsecond (μs), while the division operation would require up to 31 μs. The actual time required by the division operation ranges from 46 cycles to 62 cycles, depending on the data values that are used for the division operation.

The TMS9900 chip requires a complex series of four timing signals: ϕ1 through ϕ4. These signals are best generated by using a

Fig. 5-1. A TM990/100M computer module.

Fig. 5-2. A TM990/189 University Board computer.

TIM9904 clock generator/driver chip, made specifically for this purpose. The other 9900-family microprocessor chips do not require the use of such complex timing signals.

Typical of available 9900-based computer systems are the TM990/100M, as shown in Fig. 5-1, and the TM990/189, shown in Fig. 5-2. The TM990/100M is a fully assembled computer with on-board read/write memory, read-only memory, serial i/o, parallel i/o, and a bus connector for further expansion. The serial i/o port on this board may be used to communicate with a teletypewriter or terminal, and read-only memory chips are available that are preprogrammed with a monitor program, so that simple programs may be loaded and tested on the computer system. A small hand-held terminallike device has been developed for the TM990/100 board, as shown in Fig. 5-3. This terminal allows the user to enter short programs rather quickly in hexadecimal format, although the lack of a "hard copy" output device will be felt by some users who like a permanent record of their results and program tests.

Fig. 5-3. A TM990/301 terminal, used with TM990/100M boards.

Courtesy Texas Instruments, Inc.

The TM990/189 is also a stand-alone computer, with on-board read/write memory, read-only memory, parallel i/o, and serial i/o. This board also contains a calculatorlike terminal that is used with a read-only memory-based monitor program so that information may be entered into the computer. A simple line-by-line assembler is also provided so that short programs may be entered in mnemonic form, being translated into hexadecimal (really binary) form by the assembler program. This greatly simplifies the preparation of short programs, and the TM990/189 should appeal to many people for this reason. This computer cannot be expanded very easily, since no bus connector is provided.

Texas Instruments, as well as other suppliers, provides a wide variety of add-on boards, so that large computer systems can be built up from CPU cards, such as the TM990/100. Two examples are the TM990/210 memory expansion board and the TM990/310 i/o expansion board. Among the other manufacturers, Analog Devices, Inc., (Norwood, MA 02062), has a series of analog signal processing boards that are compatible with the TM990 bus configuration.

THE 9900 INSTRUCTION SET

The 9900 central processing unit contains only three registers: the program counter (PC), the workspace pointer register (WP), and the status register (ST). None of these registers is available for general-purpose use. Instead, the 9900 uses read/write memory for its register space. Up to 16 general-purpose registers may be in use at any time. These registers are located in read/write memory by the 16-bit address in the workspace pointer register. There are no restrictions on the addresses that can be used by the WP, but there are some practical limits, as will be shown later. The address in the WP points to the first register in the workspace, with subsequent 16-bit registers occupying locations at the next 15 even addresses. (Remember, the 9900 uses only even addresses, since the lsb in the 16-bit address is not used.) Thus, if the WP has been loaded with address 1020H, register 0 will be found at address 1020H, register 1 at 1022H, register 2 at 1024H, and so on, up to register 15 at 103EH. A diagram of the register arrangement is shown in Fig. 5-4. You

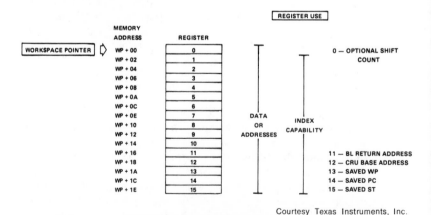

Courtesy Texas Instruments, Inc.

Fig. 5-4. Representation of the 16 workspace registers located in R/W memory.

should note that any of the 16 registers may be used to hold information (data) or addresses, while only registers 1 through 15 may be used for indexing operations. The last five registers may be used for general-purpose storage, but they have special functions as well. Register 11 is used to contain a 16-bit return address when subroutines are used. Likewise, registers 13, 14, and 15 are used to temporarily store the contents of the computer's WP, PC, and ST registers. Keep in mind that these 16 registers are in read/write memory and not in the CPU chip itself. Register 12 is used for i/o addressing, as will be explained later. The 4 least significant bits (D12–D15) in register 0 are used for shifting operations. If the special functions described above are not going to be used, then the registers may be used for general-purpose storage of information that may be required by a program.

The 9900 contains a status register (ST) that is used by various software instructions, so that the results of various operations can be monitored or tested. While the ST contains 16 bits, only 11 have been provided with specific functions, the remaining 5 having been reserved by Texas Instruments for use in large computer systems. A diagram showing the arrangement of the various flag bits in the ST is provided in Fig. 5-5. The use of the various flag bits is detailed

0	1	2	3	4	5	6	7	8	9	10	11	12	13	14	15
ST0	ST1	ST2	ST3	ST4	ST5	ST6		not used (=0)				ST12	ST13	ST14	ST15
L>	A>	=	C	O	P	X							Interrupt Mask		

Courtesy Texas Instruments, Inc.
Fig. 5-5. Status register flag.

in Chart 5-1. There are a number of software instructions that will affect the various bits, and there are other instructions that may be used to test these bits.

9900 Addressing Schemes

The 9900 has several types of addressing schemes available for use by the programmer. Although some microprocessors of recent origin use many different types of addressing, the 9900 has only five basic addressing modes which are detailed below:

1. *Workspace Register Addressing*—In this mode of addressing the information to be used in the operation is located in one of the workspace registers. The number of that workspace register is contained in the instruction, or operation code (op code). For example, if information is to be moved from register 1 to register 5, the following instruction would be used: MOV R1,R5. This operation is shown in Fig. 5-6. Note that the contents of the program counter (PC) located the instruc-

Chart 5-1. Flag Bit Positions, Abbreviations, and Definitions

0	1	2	3	4	5	6	7	8	9	10	11	12	13	14	15
LGT	AGT	EQ	C	OV	OP	X						Interrupt Mask			

Status Register Bit		
0	LGT	— *Logical Greater Than* — set in a comparison of an unsigned number with a smaller unsigned number.
1	AGT	— *Arithmetic Greater Than* — set when one signed number is compared with another that is less positive (nearer to $-32,768$).
2	EQ	— *Equal* — set when the two words or two bytes being compared are equal.
3	C	— *Carry* — set by carry out of most significant bit of a word or byte in a shift or arithmetic operation.
4	OV	— *Overflow* — set when the result of an arithmetic operation is too large or too small to be correctly represented in 2's complement form. OV is set in addition if the most significant bit of the two operands are equal and the most significant bit of the sum is different from the destination operand most significant bit. OV is set in subtraction if the most significant bits of the operands are not equal and the most significant bit of the result is different from the most significant bit of the destination operand. In single operand instructions affecting OV, the OV is set if the most significant bit of the operand is changed by the instruction.
5	OP	— *Odd Parity* — set when there is an odd number of bits set to one in the result.
6	X	— *Extended Operation* — set when the PC and WP registers have been to set to values of the transfer vector words during the execution of an extended operation.
7-11		— Reserved for special Model 990/10 computer applications.
12-15		— *Interrupt Mask* — All interrupts of level equal to or less than mask value are enabled.

Courtesy Texas Instruments, Inc.

tion, and the instruction specifies that the sum of the WP register and *two times the register number* be used to locate the contents of register 1. The register number is multiplied by two to specify the new *even* address, since odd addresses are not used, as far as we are concerned. Two of these operations are required: one specifying register 1 and another specifying register 5.

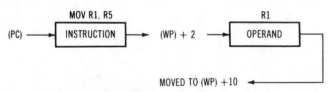

Fig. 5-6. Use of workspace register addressing to move register contents R1→R5.

2. *Workspace Register Indirect Addressing*—In this addressing
mode a register is pointed to, but the contents of the register
are used as a 16-bit address that actually locates the information that is to be operated on by the instruction. An example
of this operation is DEC *7. This operation will decrement
the contents of a memory location by 1. The address of that
location is contained in register 7. The asterisk indicates that
the workspace register indirect addressing mode is to be used.
This type of addressing is shown in Fig. 5-7.

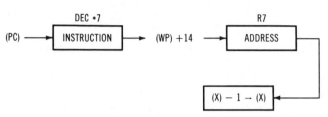

**Fig. 5-7. Use of workspace register indirect addressing to get the address
of an operand.**

3. *Workspace Register Indirect Addressing with Autoincrement*—
This addressing mode is useful when a number of consecutive
memory locations must be addressed and their contents used in
an operation. The addressing mode is very similar to that used
in workspace register indirect addressing in that the contents
of a register are again used as a 16-bit address, to locate information that is to be used by the instruction. However, once the
information has been located, the address contained in the
workspace register is altered. The contents of the register may
be incremented by 2, if a word-type operation is taking place,
or it may be incremented by only 1, if a byte-type operation
is taking place. For example, if you needed to add the contents
of several memory locations, to yield a single sum, the following instruction could be used in a loop: A *3+,2. In this case
the contents of register 3 is used as an address to point to information that is added to the contents of register 2. The result
is stored in register 2. Once the address in register 3 has been
used by the instruction, it is automatically *incremented by 2,*
to point to the next successive word to be used in the addition
operation the next time that the A *3+,2 instruction is encountered in the loop. The workspace register indirect addressing with autoincrement mode is quite useful when there are a
number of contiguous memory locations that contain information that will be used. Examples include generating sums, comparing a set of values with an unknown, searching a table for a

matching value, and so on. The generalized operation of this addressing mode is shown in Fig. 5-8.

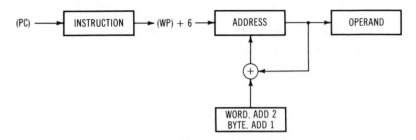

Fig. 5-8. Use of workspace register indirect addressing with autoincrement.

4. *Direct Addressing*—In the direct addressing mode the address information is actually contained within the instruction, so no registers are involved in the addressing. Of course, this means that a second word is required to hold the 16-bit address of the information that is to be used in the operation. For example, if you needed to increment a count in memory location 368AH, the address could be specified in the instruction: INC @>368A. The greater-than notation (>) is a Texas Instruments notation for hexadecimal numbers. The operation of this addressing mode is shown in Fig. 5-9.

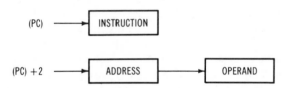

Fig. 5-9. The direct addressing mode uses an address word that is part of the instruction.

5. *Indexed Addressing*—In the 9900 the indexed addressing mode generates an address that is used to point to the information to be used by the instruction. The address is generated by adding the value contained in one of the workspace registers (not register 0) to the value of the second word of the instruction. The contents of the workspace register are called the *indexed value,* and the second byte of the instruction is called the *base address*. This mode is shown in Fig. 5-10. An example is useful to illustrate the operation of this addressing mode. Suppose that it is necessary to compare two words, one located in register 8 and one located in memory, but not in a workspace

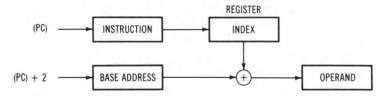

Fig. 5-10. Using indexed addressing to generate a new address of
an operand.

register. In this case another register could be used temporarily
to store the required memory address, and the workspace register indexed addressing could be used; for example, C R8,*R9.
In this case register 9 contains the address of the word that
is to be compared with the contents of register 8. Suppose,
however, that a number of pieces of information are to be
compared to the contents of register 8. You might suggest the
use of the workspace register indirect addressing with autoincrement, but this allows the addresses to be increased by only
1 or 2 at a time. The indexed addressing mode provides more
flexibility.

Let us again consider the comparison problems, but let's see
how the indexed addressing mode can be used to solve it. Now,
register 8 still contains one of the values, but the base address
of the series of locations that are to be used is placed in the
instruction as the second word. Register 6 is now specified as
containing the indexed value, so that when its contents are
added to the base address, 0200H, the resulting 16-bit sum
points to the location that contains the other value that is to
be compared to register 8: C R8,@>0200(6) or C R8,@>
0200(R6). This is shown in Fig. 5-11. Why is this addressing

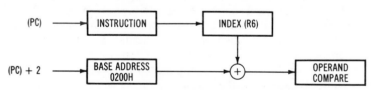

Fig. 5-11. Using the indexed addressing mode for a compare operation,
C R8,@>200(R6).

mode useful? It allows the contents of a register to be added
to a base address to form a new address. The contents of the
register are unchanged, so *new addresses may be calculated,*
pointing to entries in various memory locations, and so on.

This is particularly useful when accessing tables and arrays of information and when calculating the location of specific pieces of information in these data structures.

The 9900 has three other addressing modes that are important to consider. These are described below:

1. *Program Counter Relative Addressing*—In this addressing mode the contents of the program counter are used in calculating a new address. This means that a *displacement* may be used to generate a new address, centered on the present address of the program counter (PC). The displacement is a signed value, represented as an 8-bit twos complement number having values between −128 and +127. The program counter relative addressing mode is only useful for the control transfer operations, since it allows the computer to be routed back to a point at a lower PC value or to jump ahead to a point at a higher PC value.

2. *Immediate Addressing*—This is a rather simplistic type of addressing, since it simply means that the value to be used by the instruction is contained in the next consecutive word in memory. Thus the instruction LWPI >0200 would mean: load the WP with the value 0200H. In memory the instruction would occupy two consecutive memory locations, x and x+2:

   x   02E0H   Op code for LWPI
   x+2   0200H   Value to be put in WP

3. *CRU Addressing*—This mode of addressing deals with the use of register 12 to address special i/o devices. Simply stated, some i/o device addresses are generated by using a 12-bit portion of register 12. Bits D3–D14 are used, and we will leave a more complete discussion for later in the chapter.

The instructions for the 9900 are either one word or two words in length. For the most part the two-word instructions contain a second word that is either an immediate data word that is to be used in an operation, such as being loaded into a register or added to a register, or an address word that is used to specify a particular memory location. Most of the instructions have only one word, since extensive use is made of the 16 workspace registers, as will be shown in the next section.

Instruction Formats

The 9900 has nine instruction formats that can be used to describe all of its instructions. The formats are shown in Fig. 5-12, along with some explanatory information. For the most part, the instructions

Instruction Format	*Instruction Coding Fields**					
1 (Arithmetic)	CODE	B	T_d	D	T_s	S
2 (Jump/CRU)	CODE	DISPLACEMENT				
3 (Logical)	CODE	D	T_s	S		
4 (CRU)	CODE	C	T_s	S		
5 (Shift)	CODE	C	W			
6 (Program)	CODE	T_s	S			
7 (Control)	CODE	0000				
8 (Immediate)	CODE	00	W			
9 (Multiply, Divide, & Extended Operation)	CODE	D	T_s	S		

*The Fields are defined as follows:

CODE — Indicates the bits defining the operation code
B — Byte/Word Indicator (Single bit)
D — Workspace Register of the destination code (4 bits)
T_d — Addressing mode of the destination operand (2 bits)
S — Workspace Register of the source operand (4 bits)
T_s — Addressing mode of the source operand (2 bits)
C — Shift or Bit count (4 bits)
W — Indicates Workspace Register to be used (4 bits)

Courtesy Texas Instruments, Inc.

Fig. 5-12. The 9900 instruction and op-code formats.

are easy to break apart. For example, the D and S information in an instruction simply refers to the 4-bit binary code for the register involved in the operation. The D stands for the destination register, while the S stands for the source register. The T_d and T_s information tells the 9900 what type of addressing mode is to be used. The information for these bits is provided in Table 5-1. Based upon the past discussion of the addressing modes, you should be able to fill in the various "blanks" for the type of addressing that is required, as each of the instructions is discussed.

Data Transfer Instructions

The 9900 has a number of instructions that are used to move information from one place to another. Examples include the *load* instructions that are used to load information into various registers as a program is executed. Such loading operations use two-word instructions, with the information that is to be loaded contained in the second word. An example is LI 5,0, which loads register 5 with zero. Information can also be moved from register to register, from memory to register, and so on. Likewise, the ST and WP contents can be moved into one of the workspace registers. Remember, many of the data transfer and other instructions can be used in a number of different addressing modes, for example, the instruction MOV *9+,*5 transfers the contents of the memory location addressed by register 9 to the memory location that is addressed by the contents of register 5. After the transfer has been completed, the address in register 9 is incremented by 2. There are eight data transfer instructions.

Mathematical Instructions

The 9900 has a variety of useful mathematical instructions. These include instructions that can be used for addition, subtraction, multiplication, and division. There are instructions that allow bytes and words to be added and subtracted. When byte-type operations are performed, either the most significant byte or the least significant byte may be specified. Even addresses are used to select the most significant bytes, while odd addresses are used to specify the least significant bytes. You can also perform an add immediate operation. The multiply and divide operations are particularly useful when performing complex and not-so-complex mathematical operations. These two operations use straight 16-bit binary operations without signs. The 16-bit by 16-bit multiplication involves a multiplier that may be addressed in any way. The multiplicand must be contained in one of the workspace registers, R, with the result of the multiplication, the product, being placed in registers R and R+1. Register R will contain the most significant 16 bits, with register R+1 containing the least significant 16 bits.

Table 5-1. Summary of Addressing Modes for the 9900

Type of Addressing	Operand Format	Memory Location Specified	MOV Instruction Example Coding	Result	T_d or T_s Field Code
Workspace Register	n	Workspace Register n Rn	MOV 3,5	R3 ⟶ R5	00
Workspace Register Indirect	*n	Address given by the contents of workspace register n M(Rn)	MOV *3,*5	M(R3) ⟶ M(R5)	01
Workspace Register Indirect, Autoincrement	*n +	As in register Indirect; address register Rn is incremented after the operation (by one for byte operations, by two for word operations)	MOV *3 +,*5 +	M(R3) ⟶ M(R5), R3 + 2 ⟶ R3, R5 + 2 ⟶ R5	11
Symbolic Memory	@exp	Address is given by value of exp. M(exp)	MOV @ONE, @10	M(ONE) ⟶ M(10)	10
Indexed Memory	@exp(n)	Address is the sum of the contents of Rn and the value of exp M(Rn + exp)	MOV @2(3), @DP(5)	M(R3 + 2) ⟶ M(R5 + DP)	10

Notes:

n is the number of the workspace register: $0 \leq n \leq 15$; n may not be 0 for indexed addressing.

exp is a symbol, number, or expression

The T_d and T_s fields are two bit portions of the instruction machine code. There are also S and D four bit fields, which are filled in with the four bit code for n. n is 0 for symbolic or direct addressing.

The division operation uses the registers in a similar manner. However, this operation divides a 32-bit dividend by a 16-bit divisor. The divisor may be addressed in any way, with the dividend being located in any two consecutive registers: R and R+1. After the division operation the 16-bit quotient is left in register R, with the remainder in register R+1.

The remaining mathematical operations are straightforward, providing means for incrementing and decrementing numbers by either 1 or 2. These are useful instructions for keeping track of counts, loops, etc., and for addressing values in tables and arrays. Another useful instruction, negate, can be used to generate the twos complement of 16-bit numbers. The 9900 can also generate the absolute value of a 16-bit number.

Unlike other 16-bit microcomputers, the 9900 does not have any special instructions that will allow it to perform mathematical manipulations using the binary coded decimal (bcd) numbering system. The TMS9940, however, does have special instructions, so that bcd addition and subtraction operations may be performed. There are 13 mathematical instructions.

Logical Instructions

The 9900 has a number of logical instructions that are best broken into three subgroups: compare instructions, logic instructions, and shift instructions. The compare instructions allow individual words or bytes to be compared to one another, with the results of these operations being reflected in the various bits of the status register (ST). Besides comparing values that are contained in memory and in the workspace registers, a compare immediate instruction may be used to compare words to a constant 16-bit value that is part of the two-word compare instruction. The 9900 has two other comparison operations that are quite useful. These two operations, compare ones corresponding and compare zeros corresponding, allow individual logic ones and logic zeros to be tested in an entire 16-bit word in a single operation.

The compare zeros corresponding operation compares the bits that have been set (logic one) in the mask word (MASK) with the logic zeros in the word being tested (TEST). This is shown in Fig. 5-13. Note that the logic ones in the MASK determine which bit positions are being checked for logic zeros. In Fig. 5-13 each of the

MASK	0000	1100	1100	1111
TEST	0111	0001	0001	0000
BITS TESTED		XX	XX	XXXX	EQ = 1

Fig. 5-13. Using the compare zeros corresponding instruction.

192

set bits in the MASK word had a corresponding logic zero bit in the TEST word. Thus each logic one in the MASK compared with a logic zero in the TEST, yielding an equal condition that set the equal (EQ) flag in the status register.

In Fig. 5-14 the compare logic ones corresponding operation is illustrated. Note that whenever a compare-corresponding operation is used, the mask bits of interest are logic ones. In Fig. 5-14 the MASK has been set up to test for positions that contain logic ones. Since the TEST word contains logic ones in all of the positions that were set to logic ones in the MASK word, the equal condition is indicated by the EQ flag.

The two bit-comparison operations are quite useful when it is necessary to test and compare *patterns* of logic ones and zeros in various

MASK	0 1 0 0	1 1 0 0	0 0 0 1	0 0 0 0	
TEST	0 1 1 0	1 1 1 0	0 0 0 1	1 0 1 1	
BITS TESTED	X	X X	X		EQ = 1

Fig. 5-14. Using the compare ones corresponding instruction.

words. You should be able to see that the bits that were not tested were not important, and they could be logic ones or logic zeros. Likewise, none of the information that is used in the comparison operations, MASK or TEST, is altered by the testing process.

The logical operations include the standard AND, OR, exclusive-OR, and invert operations. The AND and OR operations are limited to the immediate addressing mode, so they will find use only when one of the words to be used in the AND or OR operation can be included in the program. This is not a serious limitation, however, since with some additional software steps there are other operations that can perform similar logical operations. There are also several operations that are used to set and clear bits. The simplest of these are set to ones, which sets the addressed location to all ones, or FFFFH, and clear, which clears the addressed location to all zeros, or 0000H.

The remaining clear and set operations are a bit more complex, using a mask word to determine which of the bits in the location (register) to be operated upon are to be set or to be cleared. These set and clear operations may be used with either words or bytes. The set ones corresponding instruction sets to a logic one those bits for which a logic one bit is found in the mask. Likewise, the set zeros corresponding instruction clears those bits for which a logic one is found in the mask. It does not matter what state the bits are in prior to the set or clear operation. These two operations provide a convenient means of setting and clearing individual bits.

The set ones corresponding operation is simply a logical OR operation but with the added feature that all of the addressing modes may be used. This means that by using the set ones corresponding instruction with inversion instructions, almost any logical operation may be performed, including AND, NAND, and NOR.

There are four shift operations that may be used for bit testing and for arithmetic operations. These are the shift right arithmetic (SRA), shift left arithmetic (SLA), shift right logical (SRL) and shift right circular (SRC). The actual operations of these four instructions are diagrammed in Fig. 5-15. In the SRA operation the

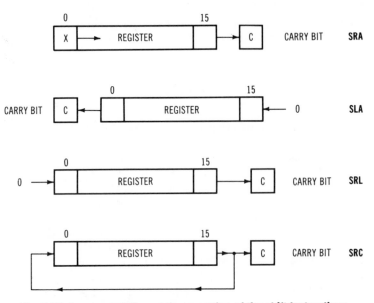

Fig. 5-15. A representation of the operation of the shift instructions.

value of the most significant bit is shifted into the vacant bit positions that remain after the word has been shifted. In the SLA and SRL operations, zeros are shifted into the vacated bit positions. In all cases, when a "new" bit is shifted into the carry, the bit that was there previously is "lost." In the SRC operation, however, the bit shifted into the carry is recirculated back into the word that is being shifted. The shift operations can operate on the contents of the workspace registers, and the number of positions to be shifted is incorporated in the op code for the instruction; for example, in SRL 5,3 the contents of register 5 are shifted three positions to the right, with the 3 most significant bits being filled with zeros. If the shift count is set to zero, a 16-bit shift operation takes place. There are 19 logical instructions.

Control Transfer Instructions

There are many useful instructions in this classification, providing means for implementing loops and decision-making operations in programs. The first group of control transfer instructions is called "unconditional," since there are no conditions attached to their execution. The unconditional jump instruction allows the programmer to transfer control to any instruction that is within the range of −128 to +127 words from the value of the program counter. When using relative addressing, be sure to count the "distance" in the number of words and not as the difference in memory addresses. You must also remember that the PC will be one word ahead of the jump op code. Thus, to jump relative from the jump command at address 0116H back to address 0100H, the displacement would be decimal −12, or F4H, in twos complement hexadecimal notation. An unconditional branch operation may be used if the location that is to be jumped to is outside of the range of the displacement range for the jump instruction. The address to be used by the branching operation may be specified in any manner; for example, the address could be located in a workspace register or in a memory location. If the location that is to be branched to is within the −128 to +127 range of the PC, the unconditional jump operation is recommended, since it takes a shorter time to perform the control transfer operation.

The 9900 implements an interesting instruction, execute, which allows a single instruction to be addressed and executed. Unlike an unconditional jump, or branch, operation, only the addressed instruction is executed, after which the program continues its normal operation. This instruction is particularly useful if you are writing a debugger to trace the flow of your programs.

The conditional control transfer instructions perform relative jumps, based upon the conditions of the various flags in the status register.

Table 5-2. Conditional Jump Instructions and Their Corresponding Flags

Mnemonic	L>	A>	EQ	C	OV	OP	Jump if:	CODE*
JH	X	—	X	—	—	—	$L> \bullet \overline{EQ} = 1$	B
JL	X	—	X	—	—	—	$\overline{L>} + EQ = 0$	A
JHE	X	—	X	—	—	—	$L> + EQ = 1$	4
JLE	X	—	X	—	—	—	$\overline{L>} + EQ = 1$	2
JGT	—	X	—	—	—	—	$A> = 1$	5
JLT	—	X	X	—	—	—	$\overline{A>} + EQ = 0$	1
JEQ	—	—	X	—	—	—	$EQ = 1$	3
JNE	—	—	X	—	—	—	$EQ = 0$	6
JOC	—	—	—	X	—	—	$C = 1$	8
JNC	—	—	—	X	—	—	$C = 0$	7
JNO	—	—	—	—	X	—	$OV = 0$	9
JOP	—	—	—	—	—	X	$OP = 1$	C

Note: In the Jump if column, a logical equation is shown in which $\bullet$ means the AND operation, + means the OR operation, and a line over a term means negation or inversion.

*CODE is entered in the CODE field of the OPCODE to generate the machine code for the instruction.

Courtesy Texas Instruments, Inc.

Each of the 6 most significant flag bits (logical greater than, arithmetic greater than, equal, carry, overflow, and odd parity) may be used in a conditional jump instruction. The remaining flags cannot be tested or used by the conditional jump instructions. The instruction mnemonics and their corresponding flag conditions are shown in Table 5-2. Note that some of the conditional jump instructions actually test two flags. Some of the flags may be tested as being either logic one or logic zero (for example, the carry flag), while overflow and odd parity flags may only be tested for one logic state. Many of the instructions alter the various flags, so that the results of those operations may be used as the basis for having the program decide whether or not to branch.

Since the 9900 does not have any general-purpose internal registers, it handles the access of subroutines in an unusual fashion. Therefore we will discuss the use of subroutines in some detail.

Unlike many of the 8-bit microprocessors, the 16-bit 9900 does not use an external stack area in read/write memory for storing return addresses and register information when subroutines are used in a program. A special set of subroutine control instructions is used, and it is important that you understand these if you wish to use subroutines, something that few programmers can do without.

The simplest subroutine calling command is the branch and link (BL) instruction, *which can use any addressing mode to point to any memory location.* Thus it is not limited to a fixed range of displacements. Unlike a simple branch operation, the branch and link operation actually stores the contents of the PC prior to performing the branch to the new address. The PC is stored in register 11 in the workspace. Consequently, this register contains a linking address that "marks" the next instruction that follows the branch and link instruction in the main program. After the branch operation has taken place, the 9900 starts to operate on a new series of instructions in the subroutine that was pointed to by the branch and link instruction. Once the subroutine has been completed, it is necessary to use the linking address stored in register 11 to point back to the main program. The address can be used quite easily by performing a workspace register indirect branch to register 11: B *11. This causes the computer to branch to the address contained in register 11, returning control back to the main program. Thus the branch and link operation is used as a simple subroutine call in which the contents of the PC are stored in register 11 prior to the actual branch. The branch is unconditional. An example of this operation is shown in Fig. 5-16. Unfortunately, the subroutine must use the same set of 16 workspace registers.

It is possible to perform programming tricks so that a new set of workspace registers may be set up for the subroutine, but the 9900 has a simple instruction that serves the same purpose. This is branch

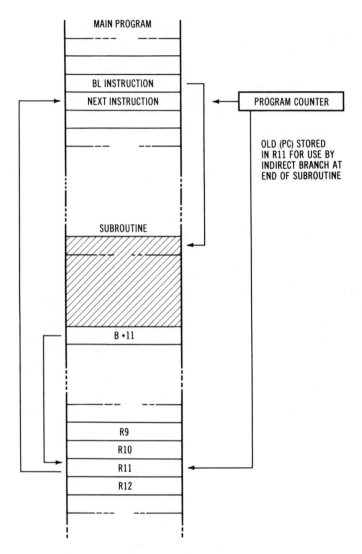

Fig. 5-16. Using the branch and link (BL) instruction to call subroutines.

and load workspace pointer (BLWP). This operation allows a new set of workspace registers to be set up for the subroutine, since a new workspace pointer may be established during the branching operation. Again, *this branch and load workspace pointer operation may use any addressing mode to specify a memory address.* When the BLWP instruction is used, the location pointed to by the instruction contains the address for the new workspace pointer, and the next consecutive location contains the new information for the PC. Since the entire workspace area is going to be reassigned, prior to the actual branch and load operation, the 9900 stores the old workspace pointer in the new register 13, the old PC in the new register 14, and the status register information in the new register 15. Thus the subroutine that is called by the BLWP instruction cannot use these registers, since they contain information that will be used to link the subroutine back to the main program. An example of this operation is shown in Fig. 5-17.

Returning from the subroutine to the main program is fairly simple, since a special instruction has been provided just for this purpose. The return with workspace pointer (RTWP) instruction provides the necessary link by loading the WP from new register 13, the PC from new register 14, and the status register from new register 15, when it is executed at the end of a subroutine. Note that the RTWP instruction should be used to end subroutines that are accessed with BLWP instructions, and it must not be used to end subroutines that are accessed by branch and link instructions.

There is one other control transfer operation that is implemented in the 9900: the extended operation. This instruction (XOP) allows the programmer to define special operations that may be called with simple instructions. It is not recommended for people who are just starting to use the 9900. There are several XOP instructions implemented in some of Texas Instruments' software monitor packages, so that useful subroutines are available to the user. The XOP operation works in a way that is similar to the BLWP.

You have probably noted that the branch and link operation did not allow for subroutines to be nested, that is, for one subroutine to call another one, which would in turn call one more. This results from the shared use of the same set of registers. When saving a return address in register 11, it proves difficult to call a second, unrelated subroutine, since its return address must be placed in register 11, too. Using various software techniques an external stack could be set up in read/write memory, so that the addresses in register 11 could be temporarily stored outside of the workspace registers, but this takes additional programming time and it is easy to become confused by the many transfers to and from the registers and the stack area. The alternative is to use the branch and load workspace pointer. The only disadvantage to this is that a new set of 16 workspace registers must be set up for each subroutine. Although this may seem to be wasteful of read/write memory, most programs will not nest subroutines too deeply, having one subroutine call another, which will call another, and so on, so we doubt that this will be much of a problem. Keep in mind that even though a new workspace has been established you can still access the information in the old workspace, simply by

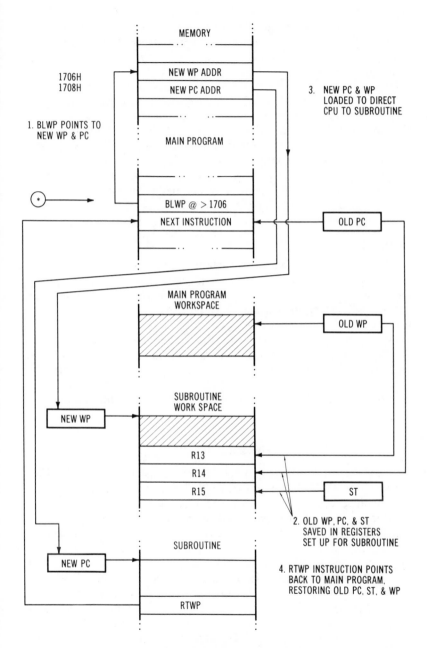

Fig. 5-17. Use of the BLWP subroutine call and the RTWP return instructions. Start at *.

using the old workspace pointer, in register 13, with indirect addressing. For additional useful techniques, we suggest that you obtain a copy of *9900 Family System Design,* 1978, from Texas Instruments, Inc., Houston, TX 77001.

Input/Output Instructions

The 9900 has five instructions that are used to control the input/ output functions. These include instructions that transfer information to and from the computer, and instructions that allow individual bits to be set, cleared, and tested. Since the 9900 uses its own special type of input/output transfer technique, we will leave a complete description of the i/o control instructions for the section on interfacing. Of course, if memory-mapped i/o techniques are to be used, in which i/o devices appear to be memory locations, any of the memory data transfer instructions may be used.

Instruction Summary

The 9900 has 72 basic instructions, which is quite small when compared with the instruction sets of other 16-bit microcomputers and even some 8-bit microcomputers. This figure does not count the various addressing modes that may be used to modify the instructions, but the addressing modes do not create any new operations. While the instruction set is fairly small, this does not reflect poorly on the capability of the chip, since the 9900 architecture is really an outgrowth of the 9900 minicomputer family. For the old timers, the Digital Equipment Corporation PDP-8 family had only eight basic instructions, but disk operating systems, BASIC, and other languages were readily available.

THE 9900 FAMILY

The 9900 family of microcomputer chips consists of the TMS9900, TMS9980A, TMS9981, and TMS9940. The latter three are enhanced and modified versions of the basic 9900 chip. In each case the basic 9900 instruction set has been used, along with the same internal architecture, sets of registers, and so on.

The TMS9900 is a large 64-pin dual in-line integrated-circuit package. A pin configuration for the chip is shown in Fig. 5-18. You should be able to readily identify the 16 data bus lines, and the 15 address lines. The 9900 requires three voltages: −5 volts (pin 1) at about 1 milliampere (1 mA), +5 volts (pins 2 and 59) at about 75 mA, and +12 volts (pins 26 and 40) at about 45 mA. Several of the pins on the 9900 chip are unused (NC) and should not be connected to anything.

The 9900, as noted previously, requires a special four-phase clock

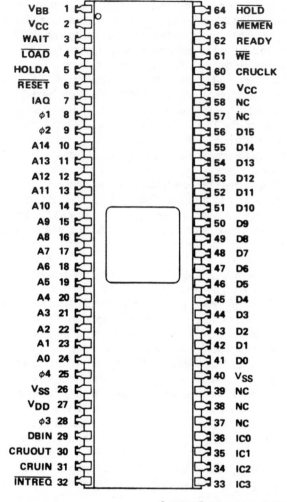

V_{BB}	1		64	$\overline{HOLD}$
V_{CC}	2		63	$\overline{MEMEN}$
WAIT	3		62	READY
$\overline{LOAD}$	4		61	$\overline{WE}$
HOLDA	5		60	CRUCLK
$\overline{RESET}$	6		59	V_{CC}
IAQ	7		58	NC
$\phi1$	8		57	NC
$\phi2$	9		56	D15
A14	10		55	D14
A13	11		54	D13
A12	12		53	D12
A11	13		52	D11
A10	14		51	D10
A9	15		50	D9
A8	16		49	D8
A7	17		48	D7
A6	18		47	D6
A5	19		46	D5
A4	20		45	D4
A3	21		44	D3
A2	22		43	D2
A1	23		42	D1
A0	24		41	D0
$\phi4$	25		40	V_{SS}
V_{SS}	26		39	NC
V_{DD}	27		38	NC
$\phi3$	28		37	NC
DBIN	29		36	IC0
CRUOUT	30		35	IC1
CRUIN	31		34	IC2
$\overline{INTREQ}$	32		33	IC3

Courtesy Texas Instruments, Inc.
Fig. 5-18. Pin configuration for the TMS9900 chip.

signal that is not compatible with standard transistor-transistor logic (TTL) levels. Thus a clock generator chip, the TIM9904 is available to generate the necessary clock signals. This is probably the most complex part of using a 9900 chip in a small computer system, since the remaining control lines are compatible with TTL logic levels and can directly drive low-power Schottky (LS) TTL chips.

The main signals that are of interest are the memory and data bus control signals and the input/output (i/o) control signals. The memory control signals are memory enable, $\overline{MEMEN}$, a logic-zero signal that indicates that the address bus contains valid address information, data bus input, DBIN, a logic one signal that indicates that the data bus is being used for input operations, and write enable, $\overline{WE}$, a logic zero signal that is used to indicate a write operation. The use of these signals is shown in the memory bus timing diagram, Fig. 5-19. In this figure a read cycle and a write cycle are illustrated. To allow for the use of "slow" memory devices the 9900 may be forced into a wait state, by asserting the READY input. The wait states are indicated by a logic one on the WAIT output. One wait state has been inserted into the memory write cycle, just to illustrate its use.

The three important i/o control signals are control register input, CRUIN, control register out, CRUOUT, and control register clock, CRUCLK. These will be described in more detail in the section discussing various i/o techniques. The 9900 frequently communicates with i/o devices through a serial, bit-by-bit communication technique. This uses the control register. The timing of the CRU control signals with respect to the four-phase clock and the address bus is shown in Fig. 5-20.

The TMS9980A and TMS9981 are two very similar variations of the basic 9900, so it is wise to discuss both of these devices at the same time. The difference that is immediately obvious is that these two microprocessor chips are housed in standard 40-pin dual in-line packages, so they are very easy to breadboard and build into small computer systems. There are a number of other technical differences that actually make the 9980A/9981 easier to use than the 9900. These newer chips use an 8-bit bidirectional data bus, so that standard memory and i/o chips, developed for 8-bit microcomputers, are easily used in 9980A and 9981 systems. Internally the chip is still a 16-bit microprocessor, and the 9900 instruction set is preserved. The addressing capability is somewhat smaller than it is for the 9900, being only 16K *bytes* of memory. This can be expanded by using some external logic, but most applications that use either the 9980A or the 9981 probably will not need a great deal of memory beyond the 16K limit.

The 9980A and 9981 have some other interesting features. Both are limited to four levels of priority interrupt, plus the reset and load functions. These interrupts are levels 0 through 4. Neither of the chips requires the complex four-phase clock signal that is used by the 9900. The 9980A has an external clock input, with an on-chip clock generator circuit. The 9981 goes even further, having a crystal used with the chip to generate the timing. The 9980A requires the same voltage supplies as the 9900, while the 9981 uses only the +5- and +12-volt power supplies. The pin configurations for the TMS-9980A and TMS9981 are *not* compatible, so you cannot simply switch between one or the other.

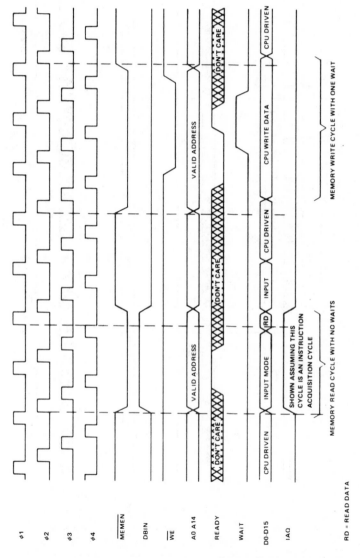

φ1

φ2

φ3

φ4

$\overline{\text{MEMEN}}$

DBIN

$\overline{\text{WE}}$

A0 A14   VALID ADDRESS   VALID ADDRESS

READY   DON'T CARE   DON'T CARE   DON'T CARE   DON'T CARE

WAIT

D0-D15   CPU DRIVEN   INPUT MODE $\overline{\text{RD}}$ INPUT   CPU DRIVEN   CPU WRITE DATA   CPU DRIVEN

IAQ   SHOWN ASSUMING THIS CYCLE IS AN INSTRUCTION ACQUISITION CYCLE

RD = READ DATA

MEMORY READ CYCLE WITH NO WAITS

MEMORY WRITE CYCLE WITH ONE WAIT

Fig. 5-19. Memory bus timing relationships of the 9900.

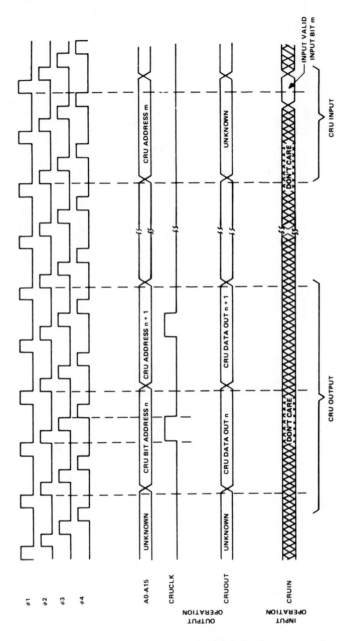

Courtesy Texas Instruments, Inc.

Fig. 5-20. CRU control timing relationships of the 9900.

The TMS9940 microprocessor chip is actually a stand-alone micro-computer, since it includes on-chip read-only memory (2K bytes) and read/write memory (128 bytes). Since the 9940 will find use in many control applications that will not be general purpose, some of the special features of the device will be listed, instead of a detailed discussion:

- four priority interrupts
- on-chip counter/timer
- 32 general-purpose i/o bits
- on-chip erasable ROM (EPROM)
- i/o expansion for 256 bits
- various clock speeds available

9900 BOARD-LEVEL HARDWARE

There are quite a few microcomputer boards available for the 9900 series of microcomputers, providing various configurations of the CPU chip, memory, i/o devices, and other useful functions. Examples of these boards and functions include the TM990/100M and TM990/101M 9900-based CPU boards, and the TM990/180M 9980A-based CPU board, all from Texas Instruments. There are also several expansion boards available from Texas Instruments:

- TM990/201 16K-word ROM/EPROM and 8K-word R/W memory board
- TM990/206 8K-words R/W memory board (space available for PROMs)
- TM990/310 i/o expansion for 48 lines, plus interrupts, clocks, etc.
- TM990/302 combination PROM programmer, R/W memory, PROM memory, and serial/cassette i/o board

Most of the boards from sources other than Texas Instruments are used for interfacing standard TM990 module-based computer systems with analog signals, either to measure them or to control them. A representative example is:

- RTI-1240 series of i/o modules—Analog Devices, Inc., Norwood, MA 02062

The authors are not aware of any other manufacturers who now have TM990-compatible expansion boards. However, the 9900-series of microprocessor and peripheral chips is available from a second source: American Microsystems, Inc., 3800 Homestead Road, Santa Clara, CA 95051.

9900 SOFTWARE

There is considerable software for the 9900 family of microprocessors, being mainly available from Texas Instruments. This software includes editors, assemblers, disk operating systems, BASIC language interpreters, debuggers, monitors, and special software development packages that can be run on 9900-based computers. Other, more complex programs, which include linking loaders, system emulators, logic tracers, and PROM programming programs, are available. Since the requirements for the systems on which these programs can be run vary from program to program, the authors suggest that you carefully evaluate your program development and computational needs before purchasing any software packages.

BENCHMARK PROGRAMS

Several test programs, or benchmarks, have been assigned to the 9900 so that its performance can be compared with that of some of the other 16-bit processors described in this book. Since a large 9900-based development system was not available, all of the benchmarks in this section were run on a TM990/189 system, which is based on the TMS9980 processor. Because the 9980 uses an 8-bit data bus instead of a 16-bit data bus, the data transfer operations take longer, causing the programs to be executed more slowly than they would if they were run on a 9900-based computer. However, the benchmarks are realistic, as most new applications will use the TMS9980 chip in place of the larger TMS9900. The clock frequency of the 9980 on the TM990/189 is 2 MHz.

Bubble Sort

The first benchmark program is listed in Fig. 5-21, and it is a bubble sort program that will sort 600 entries in a table that is stored in R/W memory. To provide a standard set of data values in the table, a short program has been included at the start of the benchmark to perform this operation. The actual benchmark program specifications are provided in the Appendix and you are referred to this section for additional information. The "loader" program is halted with a dummy jump, or dummy loop, at address 0244H. The sorting program starts at ST, or address 024CH. The load immediate instructions have been used to load the registers with the starting address of the table and also the count, or number of entries in the table. For additional flexibility these values may be stored in predetermined locations in R/W memory and loaded into the appropriate registers with commands such as MOV @ADDR,R1 and MOV @COUNT, R2. These are also 2-word instructions, so changes to the main sorting program are fairly simply made.

```
                            AORG >0240
      0230    02E0          LWPI >0200            SET WORKSPACE POINTER
      0232    0200
      0234    0201          LI R1,>0350           SET STARTING ADDRESS
      0236    0350
      0238    0202          LI R2,>0257           SET FIRST VALUE
      023A    0257
      023C    CC42    A     MOV R2,*R1+           STORE VALUE IN MEMORY (AUTO INC)
      023E    0602          DEC R2                DECREMENT COUNTER
      0240    16FD          JNE A                 IF NOT ZERO, JUMP
      0242    CC42          MOV R2,*R1+           STORE LAST VALUE
      0244    10FF    X     JMP X                 DUMMY LOOP (STOP)
      0246    020C          LI R12, 0020          SET UP I/O REGISTER ADDRESS
      0248    0020
      024A    1D00          SBO 0                 TURN ON ONE BIT
      024C    0201    ST    LI R1,>0350           SET UP ADDRESS POINTER
      024E    0350
      0250    0202          LI R2,>0257           SET UP COUNT
      0252    0257
      0254    0203          LI R3,>0000           SET UP EXCHANGE INDICATOR
      0256    0000
      0258    C131    LP    MOV *R1+,R4           GET FIRST VALUE
      025A    8444          C R4,*R1              COMPARE IT TO NEXT VALUE
      025C    1607          JH SW                 IF FIRST GT SECOND, GO SWITCH THEM
      025E    0602    P     DEC R2                DECREMENT THE COUNT
      0260    16FB          JNE LP                IF NOT ZERO, GO ON TO NEXT VALUES
      0262    0283          CI R3,>FFFF           IF ZERO, CHECK EXCHG INDICATOR
      0264    FFFF
      0266    13F2          JEQ ST                IF EQUAL GO TO ST, AND CHECK LIST
      0268    1E00          SBZ 0                 IF NOT EQUAL, NOT FFFFH, CLEAR BIT
      026A    10FF    Z     JMP Z                 DUMMY LOOP (STOP)
      026C    C151    SW    MOV *R1,R5            SWITCH ROUTINE
      026E    0641          DECT R1
      0270    C191          MOV *R1,R6
      0272    C445          MOV R5,*R1
      0274    05C1          INCT R1
      0276    C446          MOV R6,*R1
      0278    0203          LI R3,>FFFF
      027A    FFFF
      027C    10E0          JMP P
```

Fig. 5-21. A bubble sort benchmark program for the 9980.

The sorting program operates by comparing two values in consecutive locations within the table. If the data at location x is greater than the data at location $x+1$, the two values are switched, to put them in ascending order. Whenever a switch takes place, the exchange indicator is set to be nonzero, indicating that the table should be checked again. Only after there are no switches during a pass through the table does the program complete its operation. In this program extensive use has been made of register indirect and register indirect autoincrement instructions.

In order to time the period required by the program to sort the information in the list, two i/o control instructions have been included in the program so that an output bit will be turned on (logic one) for the time required by the program. This technique worked quite well, and it was also used in the other benchmark programs for the same purpose. The sorting routine took about 33 seconds to sort the 600 entries in the table. Remember that in the 9980 this table requires 1200 *bytes* of R/W memory.

ASCII String Search

The second benchmark program involved searching through a list of information that has been coded in ASCII format. The object was to attempt to match a test string of ASCII values with a main string of ASCII values, until a match was found. Each set of ASCII values is separated by an asterisk, and the complete list is terminated, or delimited, with a "?" In the string search program listed in Fig. 5-22 the initial constants and addresses are stored in R/W memory and are brought into the registers with MOV commands. Thus it is relatively easy to change the starting addresses of the test string, the main string, and also the values to be used for the delimiters in the strings.

The string search program first checks to be sure that it hasn't reached the end of the main string, by checking for the delimiter, "?" After this test it starts to compare the characters in the test string with the characters in the main string. If a match takes place, the string length counter is decremented, and the next character is tested. If the string length counter is decremented to zero, the test string has matched a portion of the main string. If, however, there is a mismatch during the search, the main string address pointer is advanced to the start of the next complete section, after the asterisk, and the test string pointer is reinitialized along with the string length counter. Thus, if the test string, MICRO*, is matched against MICROCOMPUTER*, there is a mismatch between the * in the test string and the C in the main string word, MICROCOMPUTER. This mismatch causes the matching process to start again, with the next complete word in the main string: MICROPROCESSOR*. Once a mismatch takes place, there is little sense in continuing the search with the present main string word.

This benchmark program contains the i/o control commands so that the program can be timed. With the standard main string and test string, it took about 2.25 ms to perform the match between MICRO* in both strings. In this program the register indirect autoindex address mode was used to compare the values in the two strings. The values were never actually brought into any of the workspace registers. The POINT routine is used to advance the address pointer to the start of the next complete word in the main string, whenever a mismatch takes place. The 9900 does not have any instructions that operate on ASCII values as such. Since each ASCII value requires only 8 bits, two characters are stored in each 16-bit word. The compare bytes (CB) instruction is used, with even addresses specifying the most significant byte, and odd addresses specifying the

```
                        AORG >0240
0240 02E0             LWPI >0200              LOAD WORKSPACE POINTER
0242 0200
0244 020C             LI R12,>0020            SET UP I/O REGISTER ADDRESS
0246 0020
0248 1D00             SBO 0                   SET I/O BIT TO A ONE
024A C060             MOV @ST,R1              SET UP STRING POINTER
024C 0520
024E C0A0             MOV @QU,R2              SET UP ASCII "?"
0250 0522
0252 C0E0             MOV @AK,R3              SET UP ASCII "*"
0254 0524
0256 C120      AGN    MOV @UN,R4              SET UP TEST STRING POINTER
0258 0526
025A C160             MOV @CT,R5              SET UP TEST STRING LENGTH
025C 0528
025E 9442             CB R2,*R1               COMPARE  CHARACTER TO "?"
0260 1304             JEQ DONE                IF EQUAL, END OF STRING TEST
0262 9D31      LP     CB *R1+,*R4+            COMPARE STRING CHARACTERS
0264 1604             JNE POINT               IF NOT EQUAL, GO TO POINT
0266 0605             DEC R5                  IF EQUAL, DECREMENT COUNT
0268 16FC             JNE LP                  IF COUNT NOT ZERO, TEST NEXT CHAR
026A 1E00      DONE   SBZ 0                   DONE, TURN OFF I/O BIT
026C 10FF      X      JMP X                   DUMMY JUMP (STOP)
026E 0601      POINT  DEC R1                  SEARCH FOR NEXT "*" IN MAIN STRING
0270 90F1             CB *R1+,R3
0272 13F1             JEQ AGN
0274 10FD             JMP $-3                 JUMP BACK # FROM CURRENT (PC)

                        AORG >0500            TEST STRING STORED HERE IN ASCII
0500 4D49             DATA 'MI'
0502 4352             DATA 'CR'
0504 4F2A             DATA 'O*'

                        AORG >0520            ADDRESS & CONSTANTS STORED HERE
0520 0600      ST     DATA  0600              ADDRESS OF MAIN STRING
0522 3F00      QU     DATA  3F00              ASCII "?"
0524 2A00      AK     DATA  2A00              ASCII "*"
0526 0500      UN     DATA  0500              ADDRESS OF TEST STRING
0528 0006      CT     DATA  0006              CHAR IN TEST STRING, +1 FOR "*"

                        AORG >0600
0600 4E41             DATA  'NA'              NANO
0602 4E4F             DATA  'NO'
0604 2A50             DATA  '*P'              PICO
0606 4943             DATA  'IC'
0608 4F2A             DATA  'O*'
060A 4D49             DATA  'MI'              MICROCOMPUTER
060C 4352             DATA  'CR'
060E 4F43             DATA  'OC'
0610 4F4D             DATA  'OM'
0612 5055             DATA  'PU'
0614 5445             DATA  'TE'
0616 522A             DATA  'R*'
0618 4D49             DATA  'MI'              MICROPROCESSOR
061A 4352             DATA  'CR'
061C 4F50             DATA  'OP'
061E 524F             DATA  'RO'
0620 4345             DATA  'CE'
0622 5353             DATA  'SS'
0624 4F52             DATA  'OR'
```

Fig. 5-22. Searching for a matching ASCII string.

```
0626   2A4D        DATA   '*M'        MICROSYSTEM
0628   4943        DATA   'IC'
062A   524F        DATA   'RO'
062C · 5359        DATA   'SY'
062E   5354        DATA   'ST'
0630   454D        DATA   'EM'
0632   2A4D        DATA   '*M'        MICRO
0634   4943        DATA   'IC'
0636   524F        DATA   'RO'
0638   2A3F        DATA   '*?'        ?=MAIN STRING DELIMITED (END)
```

Fig. 5-22. Searching for a matching ASCII string — cont.

least significant byte. Whenever a register is used to store a value that is to be used in a byte comparison, the addressed byte will be compared with the most significant byte in the register. You can see that this type of comparison is used to check for the "?" and "*" in the strings.

Calculation of Square Roots

The third benchmark involves the calculation of the square root of an unknown number (Fig. 5-23). Actually, only three numbers are tested using the benchmark: 10,000, 16,384, and 58,081. The algorithm, or procedure used in the calculations, is described in the Appendix and it will not be repeated in detail here. Simply stated, the square root operation uses a series of approximations to home in on the square root. A first approximation is used and is divided into the unknown number. Even though various mathematical operations can be used in this program, it was easier to use an increment-by-2 operation to add 2, rather than an addition command, and also a logical shift operation was used to perform a divide-by-2 operation. Registers 5 and 6 are used in this program to hold the two latest approximations. This routine is completed when the square of the latest approximation is equal to the unknown number. For this reason, only numbers with integer roots are tested.

In this benchmark the unknown number is stored in R/W memory, and the result is also placed in R/W memory, once the routine has computed the root. The times required were 860 μs for the root of 10,000, and 680 μs for the roots of 16,384 and 58,081.

Lookup Table

The last benchmark (Fig. 5-24) involves generating the trigonometric sine of any integral angle, between 0 and 360 degrees. Rather than develop a program that would actually calculate the sine, a lookup table is used, with the various sine values being located in sequential memory addresses. To save space, only the sine values for angles between 0 and 90 degrees will be placed in the table. Thus all of the other angles must be reduced to their equivalent angles, be-

```
                    AORG  >0240
0240   02E0         LWPI  >0200              LOAD WORKSPACE POINTER
0242   0200
0244   020C         LI  R12,>0020            LOAD I/O ADDRESS REGISTER
0246   0020
0248   1D00         SBO  0                   SET I/O BIT
024A   0204         LI  R4,>00C8             CONSTANT DECIMAL 200
024C   00C8
024E   0201         LI  R1,>0000             CLEAR MSBY OF DIVIDEND
0250   0000
0252   C0A0         MOV  @>0350,R2           GET UNKNOWN VALUE
0254   0350
0256   3C44         DIV  R4,R1               DIVIDE IT BY DECIMAL 200
0258   05C1         INCT  R1                 ADD 2
025A   C141         MOV  R1,R5               STORE IT IN REGISTER 5
025C   0201   LOOP  LI  R1,>0000             CLEAR MSBY OF DIVIDEND
025E   0000
0260   C0A0         MOV  @>0350,R2           GET UNKNOWN VALUE
0262   0350
0264   3C45         DIV  R5,R1               DIVIDE BY APPROXIMATION
0266   C185         MOV  R5,R6               PUT OLD APPROX IN REGISTER 6
0268   C141         MOV  R1,R5               PUT NEW APPROX IN REGISTER 5
026A   3845         MPY  R5,R1               SQUARE THE NEW APPROX
026C   8802         C  R2,@>0350             COMPARE IT TO THE UNKNOWN
026E   0350
0270   1307         JEQ  DONE                IF SQUARE OF APPROX = UNKNOWN
0272   A146         A  R6,R5                 ADD APPROXIMATIONS AND DIVIDE BY
0274   0915         SRL  R5,1                2 TO GET NEXT TRY AT THE ROOT
0276   10F2         JMP  LOOP                GO BACK AND TRY AGAIN

                    AORG  >0280
0280   C805   DONE  MOV  R5,@>0360           OK, STORE THE ROOT AT 0360
0282   0360         SBZ  0                   CLEAR THE I/O BIT
0284   1E00   X     JMP  X                   DUMMY JUMP (STOP)
0286   10FF

                    AORG  >0350
0350   0000         DATA  >0000             UNKNOWN VALUE GOES HERE

                    AORG  >0360
0360   0000         DATA  >0000             ANSWER FOUND HERE
```

Fig. 5-23. A square root calculation benchmark program.

tween these limits. For example, the sine of 110 degrees is the same
as that for 70 degrees. Likewise, the sine of 315 degrees is the same
as that for 45 degrees, except that it is negative. This means that not
only must the equivalent angle be determined, but also the sign of
the sine.

Once the angle has been determined, the computer can be pointed
to a memory location that contains the proper value. This benchmark
program generates numbers that are between 0 and 90, or 0H and
5AH. These are used as the address pointers. The angle calculations
are not difficult, and you may refer to the flowchart in the appendix
for a complete description of the process.

The program cannot use the addresses of the angles directly as
they are generated, since they are (a) located in a section of memory
that is reserved for use by the TM990/189, and (b) both even and

```
                        AORG  >0240
0240  02E0            LWPI  >0200              LOAD WORKSPACE POINTER
0242  0200
0244  020C            LI  R12,>0020            LOAD I/O ADDRESS REGISTER
0246  0020
0248  1D00            SBO  0                   SET I/O BIT
024A  0209            LI  R9,>005A            CONSTANT DECIMAL 90
024C  005A
024E  0208            LI  R8,>00B4            CONSTANT DECIMAL 180
0250  00B4
0252  C160            MOV·@>0350,R5           GET UNKNOWN ANGLE
0254  0350
0256  C106            MOV  R5,R4              COPY IT TO REG 4
0258  6108            S  R8,R4                SUBTRACT 180 FROM UNKNOWN
025A  1503            JGT  NEG                IF RESULT IS >0, THEN SIGN IS NEG
025C  C105            MOV  R5,R4              COPY ANGLE TO REG 4 AGAIN
025E  04C6            CLR  R6                 CLEAR SIGN REGISTER, MUST BE POS
0260  1002            JMP  OVER               JUMP OVER NEXT OPERATION
0262  0206      NEG   LI  R6,>8000            SET SIGN BIT IN REG 6 FOR NEG SIGN
0264  8000
0266  6109      OVER  S  R9,R4                SUBTRACT 90 FROM UNKNOWN ANGLE
0268  1502            JGT  AHD                IF ANGLE IS >90, THEN GO AHEAD
026A  A109            A  R9,R4                OTHERWISE, ADD 90 BACK TO IT
026C  1002            JMP  DONE               AND YOU ARE DONE
026E  6244      AHD   S  R4,R9                IF ANGLE IS <90, REGENERATE IT
0270  C109            MOV  R9,R4              STORE IT IN REG 4
0272  0A14      DONE  SLA  R4,1               YOU GOT THE ANGLE, NOW GET THE SINE
0274  A1A4            A  @TABLE(R4),R6         INDEX THE ANGLE WITH THE FIRST TABLE
0276  0370                                    ADDRESS ADD THE SIGN BIT AND STORE IT
0278  C806            MOV  R6,@>0360          AT 0360.
027A  0360
027C  1E00            SBZ  0                  CLEAR I/O BIT
027E  10FF      X     JMP  X                  DUMMY JUMP (STOP)


                        AORG  >0350
0350  0000            DATA  >0000             ANGLE VALUE GOES HERE (DEGREES)

                        AORG  >0360
0360  0000            DATA  >0000             SINE VALUE IS PUT HERE

                        AORG  >0370             SINE VALUE TABLE
0370  0000            DATA  >0000             SINE OF 0 DEGREES
0372  0000            DATA  >0000             SINE OF 1 DEGREE
0374  0000            DATA  >0000             SINE OF 2 DEGREES
                                              ETC...
```

Fig. 5-24. A sine function lookup table benchmark program.

odd, while the 9900 family only addresses even words. To overcome these problems, the angle address is multiplied by 2 with a shift-left arithmetic operation, so that it becomes even. The address is then added to a base address for the sine lookup table, which may be located anywhere in memory. In this case the even address information is contained in register 4, which is used to address the location through indirect addressing: @TABLE(R4). The indexed addressing is used to not only locate the table entry, but to add it to the sign information, leaving the result in register 6. This is then stored in R/W memory, at address 0360H. The unknown angle is specified by the contents of location 0350H, and the table of sine values starts at address 0370H. These addresses can be easily changed to accommodate other arrangements of R/W memory, read-only memory, and i/o devices. The time required for an angle-to-sine conversion using this lookup table program was about 160 μs.

INTERFACING THE 9900

The 9900 is not difficult to interface to external, digital signals that are compatible with standard transistor-transistor logic (TTL) voltage and current levels. There are two basic methods of interfacing: memory-mapped i/o interfacing, which is a parallel technique, and control register unit (CRU) i/o interfacing, which is a high-speed serial technique. Since the memory-mapped i/o technique is fairly straightforward, we will start our discussion with this technique.

Memory-Mapped I/O

When memory-mapped i/o techniques are used to interface external devices to the 9900, the external devices are interfaced through simple logic circuits that appear to the computer to be read/write memory locations. Simple latch integrated circuits are used for output ports, and three-state integrated circuits are used for input ports. Since memory addressing techniques will be used to identify each memory-mapped i/o port, the complete memory address bus must be decoded to identify a single port. Address lines A0–A14 may be decoded in various ways, with decoders, gates, and digital comparators to generate a memory address. The address is gated with the control signals from the 9900, write enable ($\overline{WE}$), and data bus input (DBIN), to generate the proper device select signals. The memory-mapped input port and output port shown in Fig. 5-25 illustrates how this may be accomplished for memory address FF0AH. Memory read and memory write instructions may be used to access these ports. For example, MOV *R3,R5 could be used to transfer the information from the input port into register 5, assuming that register 3 had been loaded with address FF0AH first.

Assuming that the memory address is still in register 3, the information in register 7, for example, could be transferred to the output port by using the instruction MOV R7,*R3. The byte move instruction (MOVB) may also be used, if 8-bit transfers are required. The memory-mapped i/o interfacing technique is well established, and it is easy to implement. However, it does have the disadvantage that th 16-bit data bus must be connected to each i/o port, and if read/

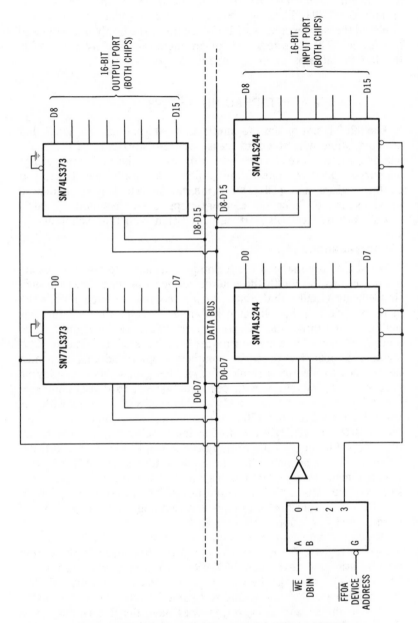

Fig. 5-25. Memory-mapped i/o ports for address FF0AH.

write memory is at a premium, some valuable address space is taken up by the memory-mapped i/o devices.

CRU I/O

The second interfacing method involved the transfer of information to and from the 9900 in a serial, bit-by-bit, format. This technique is not unique to the 9900, being used by the Data General microNova computer, too. In 9900-based computer systems the control register unit i/o technique addresses individual bits, rather than bytes or words. In this way the CRU technique allows individual bits to be input and output, as well as bytes, words, and portions thereof. The technique is very flexible, but it does require explanation. In the first place, there are special CRU instructions that are used in programs to control the flow of information to and from CRU-controlled i/o devices. Second, Texas Instruments has developed a number of special-purpose interface chips that are supported by the CRU interfacing technique.

Instead of addressing bytes or words for i/o transfers, individual bits must be addressed, so the CRU i/o ports must be set up so that the individual input bits and the individual output bits may be accessed. Bit-addressable input ports are easily constructed from eight-line-to-one-line and sixteen-line-to-one-line multiplexers, while addressable latches provide output port functions. Examples of input port multiplexers are the SN74150, SN74151, and SN74LS251 integrated circuits. The SN74LS259 is a typical addressable latch. Addressable latches for high-current sinking and sourcing are available, too, represented by the Signetics NE590 and NE591. A typical CRU input port and output port is shown in Fig. 5-26. Note that there are no connections to the 16-bit data bus. The input data is fed to the CRUIN input, and the output data is obtained from the CRUOUT output. The CRU clock output, CRUCLK, controls the synchronization of the CRUOUT signal line. No synchronization is required for the CRUIN function. The address bus is used to address the individual bits, with the least significant 4 bits, A11–A14, directly addressing the bits, and the remaining address bits providing the device select signal to the i/o ports.

The address bus is used to address the individual bits, with the least significant 3 bits, A12–A14 directly addressing groups of 8 bits for the SN74LS251 input multiplexers and for the SN74LS259 addressable latches. Address bits A3 through A8 are gated together to enable the two SN74LS138 decoder chips. In the upper decoder the CRUCLK signal is combined with address bits A9 through A11 so that the output data bits will be accessed with addresses 1111 1100 0000 through 1111 1100 1111. The input multiplexers are addressed in a similar manner, except that the CRUCLK signal is not used for input operations. Since the lower decoder is set up in a similar manner, it will respond to the same series of addresses as the output port.

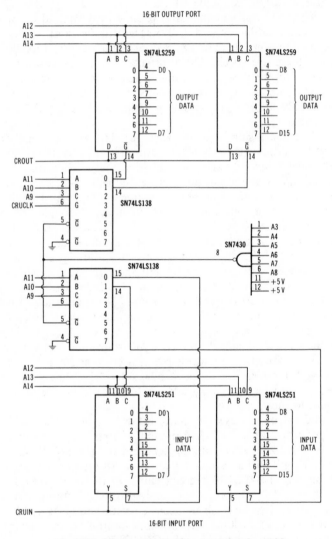

Fig. 5-26. CRU-controlled i/o ports for the 9900.

While the same address may be used, the ports are distinguished by the use of the CRUOUT and CRUCLK signal for the output port, and the use of the CRUIN signal for the input port.

When the CRU i/o technique is used, register 12 is used to store a *CRU base* address. For a group of 16 i/o bit addresses, this base address is the lowest bit address. Since address lines A3 through A14 are the only ones used in the CRU i/o technique, up to *4096 bits* may be addressed. This provides for 256 16-bit i/o ports. The CRU base address used in register 12 must be placed so that the address bits are placed corresponding to bits D3 through D14. The remaining bits should be zeros. It is important to keep in mind that when you are accessing a bit with a 12-bit address of 0110 0000 1010, or 60AH, the bits in register 12 will be 0000 1100 0001 0100, or 0C14H, since the bits have been "justified" one position to the left so that they line up with bits D3 through D14.

In most cases when the CRU i/o technique is used, the bits are addressed in groups, or blocks, of 16 bits each. This keep things simple, and it is easy to keep track of the various bits. Information in the various CRU control instructions allows you to select individual bits or groups of bits within each block of 16. In the example just noted, the address of the bit was 0110 0000 1010. In most cases this would correspond to the twelfth bit (bit AH) within the block starting at address 0110 0000 0000. The twelfth bit is readily described by information in the CRU instructions.

It should be fairly simple to see how the multiplexers and addressable latches can serve as parallel-to-serial and serial-to-parallel converters, respectively, so that the serial transfers can take place without a great deal of difficulty. The main advantages of this method of controlling i/o devices in 9900-based systems are that no memory addresses are required for i/o device addressing and only a few signal connections are required. While addresses are used to control the CRU i/o devices, they do not use the memory control signals and are not active at the same time that memory would be.

Now that the simple CRU i/o interface has been described, you should be ready to examine the five CRU control instructions. The simplest of these are the load CRU (LDCR) and store CRU (STCR). The LDCR instruction specifies the source of the information, using any of the addressing modes, and it also specifies how many of the bits are to be loaded, starting with the lsb. An example of the LDCR instruction is LDCR R2,8. This instruction transfers the 8 least significant bits from register 2 to the CRU output device starting with the bit addressed by bits D3 through D14 (A3–A14) in register 12. If register 12 contains the address 0000 0010 0000 0000, or 0200H, the bits would be loaded to CRU output bit addresses 0001 0000 0000 through 0001 0000 0100. If you specify a transfer of zero bits,

LDCR R2,0, all 16 bits will be transferred. The store CRU instruction works in a similar manner, except that the information is transferred into the 9900. Again, the number of bits to be transferred to the 9900 must be specified in the instruction, as must the destination for the information. For example, the command STCR *5+,0 would transfer 16 bits of information to the memory location addressed by the contents of register 5. After the transfer the address in register 5 would be autoincremented (by 2) to point to a new location. This also illustrates the use of "zero" bits to cause the transfer of all 16 bits. Again, the address contained in register 12 would specify the first CRU i/o bit for the transfer, which would be the lsb of the 16-bit word transferred to the 9900. Since the address is stored in a general-purpose register, it can be modified or changed at will to suit particular needs or changing i/o base addresses. The base address does not have to start at 16-bit address boundaries, that is, at addresses 000H, 010H, 020H, and so on. You can specify any base address you wish, so that you could even transfer the middle 8 bits from an input port, simply by setting the address at four higher that the base address (remember to offset the address to the left when loading it into register 12). In this case the middle 8 bits would be transferred to the 8 least significant bits in the destination location or register, since the CRU instructions start to load and store with the least significant bit. The 9900 does not know that you have "fooled" with the CRU base address to start a transfer in the middle of an i/o port.

The remaining CRU control instructions deal with setting, clearing, and testing individual bits—useful functions in situations where individual bits are used to control and sense different conditions. The set bit to logic one (SBO), set bit to logic zero (SBZ), and test bit (TB) should be self explanatory as far as their individual functions are concerned. Each of these instructions uses the base address in register 12 to locate individual bits. An offset, however, is contained in the instruction for each operation, so individual bits may be readily located without modifying the address that is actually stored in register 12. The displacement is a signed displacement between −128 and +127, so a wide range of bit locations may be addressed in all of the CRU i/o ports have addresses that are within a 256-address block.

An example of the SBO operation is SBO 3, with address 0420H, located in register 12. Since the address in register 12 has been shifted to the left one position to line up the address bits, the actual base address for the CRU is 0210H. Thus the SBO 3 operation sets the bit at CRU i/o address 0213H.

The bit testing operation works with a displacement in a similar way. It does not change an addressed bit, but simply transfers its state into the EQ flag bit, so that it may be tested by conditional jump instructions. The TB operation does not actually test the bit, it simply inputs its state so that it may be tested later.

While the CRU i/o interfacing technique may seem to be a bit confusing at first, it is a powerful and flexible technique, particularly when used with the compatible i/o chips that are available from Texas Instruments.

Interfacing Examples

In this section some simple examples will be provided so that you can clearly see how the CRU interfacing technique may be used. The i/o ports presented in Fig. 5-26 will be used as the basic i/o ports for these examples. You have already seen how information may be transferred to and from various memory locations and workspace registers and i/o devices. Now some short programs will be used to actually perform some function using the i/o port. In the first example a 16-bit count will be decremented by 1, and the resulting count will be output to the 16-bit output port. The process will be repeated, so that a constantly decreasing binary count will appear at the 16 output lines. The program to do this is shown in Fig. 5-27.

```
        LWPI >0200      LOAD WORKSPACE REGISTER
        LI R12,>1F80    LOAD CRU I/O ADDRESS
        LI R2,>0000     INITIALIZE COUNT
OUT     LDCR R2,0       OUTPUT IT (ALL 16 BITS)
        DEC R2          DECREMENT THE COUNT
        JMP OUT         GO BACK & OUTPUT IT AGAIN
```

Fig. 5-27. A simple 16-bit decrement program.

Note that register 12 must be loaded with the base address for the output bits, FC0H, but that it must be shifted one place to the left to properly align the address bits with bits D3 through D14. Thus the actual address placed in register 12 is 1F80H.

In the next example the input port will be used to transfer information into the 9900 from a standard 8-bit keyboard. The keyboard will provide a flag pulse that may be tested by the 9900 to determine that a valid 8-bit key code is available. The 8 data bits will be connected to the 8 lsb's, with the keyboard flag being connected to input bit D4. The keyboard flag arrangement is shown in Fig. 5-28. Note that a flip-flop has been used to "catch" the positive edge of the flag signal. Since the flag output by the keyboard is present for only a microsecond or so, the 9900 might miss it if the flip-flop were not used to catch it. Once the flag has been tested and the data acquired from the input port, the flag must be cleared so that the flip-flop can detect the next key code. In this case one of the output port data bits is used for the flag-clearing operation. The program that is used

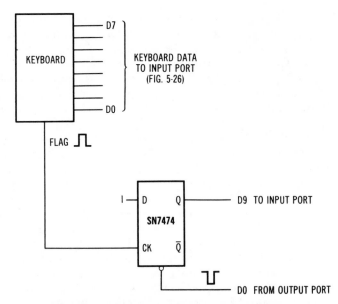

Fig. 5-28. Keyboard flag arrangement for CRU.

to acquire 35_{10} eight-bit values from the keyboard is shown in Fig. 5-29. As you look through this program example, note the type of addressing that is used to access the i/o ports, and the file of values that have been input from the keyboard.

INTERRUPTS

The 9900 microprocessor chip provides for 15 levels of priority interrupt, along with a reset ($\overline{\text{RESET}}$) and load ($\overline{\text{LOAD}}$) function.

```
        LWPI >0200              LOAD WORKSPACE REGISTER
        LI R5,@>0400            GET STARTING ADDR OF STORAGE AREA
        LI R2,>0023             SET UP COUNT
MORE    SBO 0                   SET FLAG CLEAR BIT TO LOGIC 1
TEST    TB 9                    TEST FLAG BIT
        JNE TEST                NO FLAG, CHECK AGAIN TILL FOUND
        STCR *R5+,8             STORE DATA USING AUTO INCREMENT,
        SBZ 0                   8 BITS & CLEAR THE FLAG BIT
        DEC R2                  DECREMENT THE COUNT
        JNE MORE                MORE? IF SO, GO BACK FOR THEM
DONE    Program Continues Here


        AORG >0400
        DATA>0000               STARTING ADDRESS OF DATA FILE
                                GOES HERE
```

Fig. 5-29. A simple keyboard control program.

The priority interrupts are maskable, so that interrupts with a priority below a certain level may be disabled while higher priority interrupts are enabled. There are no provisions within the 9900 itself for selectively masking individual interrupts. An interrupt request input line ($\overline{\text{INTREQ}}$) is used to signal the 9900 that an interrupt sequence is to be initiated. The actual interrupt operation is very similar to that of the branch and link workspace pointer (BLWP) operation, in which a new set of workspace registers is designated, and the WP, PC, and ST saved in the new workspace registers 13, 14, and 15. However, there are some important differences.

Now let's examine a typical interrupt sequence. We will assume that all of the priority interrupts have been enabled and that the 9900 is ready to accept a request for an interrupt. When the $\overline{\text{INTREQ}}$ line is placed in the logic zero state by an external interrupting device, the device must also furnish some other information for the 9900 to use in determining the priority level of the device. Four inputs are provided for this purpose: IC0 (msb) through IC3 (lsb). Thus the interrupting device must not only request an interrupt but it must provide its priority code as well. Interrupt level 0 is the reset interrupt and it has the highest priority, while interrupt level 15 is an external device interrupt and it has the lowest priority.

The 9900 sets aside some memory locations that contain the new WP and PC values that are to be used by the interrupt service subroutine. Thus the interrupt has the same effect as a BLWP instruction. However, the memory locations that are used to store the WP and PC values for each of the interrupts are fixed and you cannot change them. The various interrupts and their corresponding vector location and interrupt code information are listed in Table 5-3. For example, if interrupt level 5 is to be used, the new WP and PC values

Table 5-3. Interrupt Code Information

Interrupt Level	Vector Location (Memory Address In Hex)	Device Assignment	Interrupt Mask Values To Enable Respective Interrupts (ST12 thru ST15)	Interrupt Codes IC0 thru IC3
(Highest priority) 0	00	Reset	0 through F*	0000
1	04	External device	1 through F	0001
2	08		2 through F	0010
3	0C		3 through F	0011
4	10		4 through F	0100
5	14		5 through F	0101
6	18		6 through F	0110
7	1C		7 through F	0111
8	20		8 through F	1000
9	24		9 through F	1001
10	28		A through F	1010
11	2C		B through F	1011
12	30		C through F	1100
13	34		D through F	1101
14	38		E and F	1110
(Lowest priority) 15	3C	External device	F only	1111

*Level 0 can not be disabled.

Courtesy Texas Instruments, Inc.

for the level 5 interrupt service subroutine must be loaded into memory locations 0014H and 0016H, respectively.

When an interrupt is detected by the 9900, it gets the new WP and PC information from the vector locations and sets up a new workspace area. The old WP, PC, and ST information is stored in registers 13, 14 and 15, respectively, in the new workspace area. This provides the link back to the program that was interrupted by the external device, and an interrupt service subroutine can be ended with a return with workspace pointer (RTWP) instruction, which will restore the old WP, PC, and ST information.

Since the interrupts can be masked, a mask must be loaded into the status register before there is any attempt to use the interrupts. The load interrupt mask immediate (LIMI) instruction is used to load the 4-bit interrupt mask, without affecting any of the other flag bits. Only the 4 least significant bits in the immediate data word have any affect on the status word bits. In the previous example, in which an interrupt level of 5 was used, the interrupt mask would have to be set to be 5 or greater, up to 15, or FH. The 9900 does something interesting with the interrupt mask when it is interrupted. After the WP, PC, and ST information has been transferred to the new set of workspace registers, the interrupt mask in the status register is decremented by 1, in this case, to 4. This means that while the 9900 is servicing the level 5 interrupt, only interrupts with a higher priority may interrupt it. Not even another level 5 interrupt can interrupt the 9900. When the RTWP instruction is executed at the end of the level 5 interrupt service subroutine, the old, preinterrupt status word is restored, changing the interrupt mask back to 5. Of course, you can defeat this with various software tricks, so that lower priority interrupts or no interrupts are allowed, simply by reloading the interrupt mask at the start of the interrupt service subroutine. It is interesting to note that the LIMI instruction is the only interrupt control instruction that the 9900 has.

9900 PERIPHERAL AND INTERFACE CHIPS

The 9900 family contains some very useful peripheral controller and interface chips that make the task of connecting 9900-based computers to external electronic devices fairly easy. For complete descriptions of these devices, you should refer to the individual data sheets and descriptive literature. The information in this section should be used as an introduction, since it does not contain all of the necessary information to allow you to actually use the devices described.

The *TMS9901 programmable systems interface* is a 40-pin package that allows you to interface up to 15 interrupt lines, 16 output lines, or 22 input lines to 9900 systems. Individual interrupt bits may be masked on or masked off. A 14-bit timer function is also provided on the chip. Many 9901 chips may be used in a computer system to expand the i/o lines. The CRU i/o mode is used.

The *TMS9902 asynchronous communications controller* is used in 9900 computer systems so that communications with other asynchronous-serial i/o devices are possible. The chip acts like a standard universal asynchronous receiver transmitter (UART) chip, providing for from 5 to 8 data bits, and 1, 1½, or 2 stop bits in the serial data stream. An on-chip interval timer is also provided in this 18-pin package. The CRU i/o mode is used.

The *TMS9903 synchronous communications controller* can be used for either synchronous- or asynchronous-serial data transfers. All of the important serial i/o protocols are supported: bisync, SDLC, HDLC, ADCCP, etc. The CRU i/o mode is used.

Some of the other 9900 family peripheral devices include the following:

- TMS9909 floppy disk controller (FDC)
- TMS9911 direct memory access controller (DMAC)
- TMS9914 general-purpose interface bus adapter (GPIBA)
- TMS9918 video display processor
- TMS9927 video timer/controller

There are also some 9900 family i/o and control chips that are listed with both SN7400-series and 9900-series part numbers. These are:

- TIM99600 or SN74LS600   memory refresh controller
- TIM99610 or SN74LS610   memory mapper
- TIM99630 or SN74LS630   error detection and correction circuit

CONCLUSION

In this chapter you have been introduced to the Texas Instruments 9900 series of microprocessor chips and related devices. While the 9900 was an early entry in the 16-bit microprocessor field, it continues to be a processor that deserves attention from people who are considering the use of a 16-bit processor. Its instruction set may not be as "rich" as some but, with fewer complex instructions to be misused, it can easily solve almost all problems that can be solved on other 16-bit computers.

Although some people may not be used to the CRU interfacing method, this mode is quite flexible, and it is used when interfacing with many of the 9900 family chips. The availability of software from Texas Instruments is a big plus in favor of using the 9900. Unfortunately, the lack of supporting hardware from a number of competitive manufacturers not only limits the number of things that you can do with a 9900-based computer, it also means that users are locked in to single-supplier or single-source products. The TMS9900 and other products are offered by a second source, American Microsystems, Inc.

The programs for the benchmarks and for the short examples provided in the text were written on a TMS990/189 university board with the standard on-board line-by-line assembler. The assembler proved to be extremely useful and easy to use, converting mnemonic instructions into their hexadecimal form and actually loading them into read/write memory. For students and users who are just starting to use the 9900, the availability of the assembler on a small system means that the tedious and error-prone hand assembly process is eliminated. Of course, the program is not a full-blown editor/assembler software support package, but it is very worthwhile, saving time and energy. One note of caution, though: it is quite difficult to teach the use of the system interrupts, timers, keyboard, etc., because they are implemented in some nonstandard and poorly documented ways. Likewise, there are several extended operations (XOPs) implemented in the monitor/assembler program, but these, too, are not always well documented.

BIBLIOGRAPHY

1. Texas Instruments, Inc. *TMS9980A/TMS9981 Microprocessor Data Book.* November, 1977.

2. Texas Instruments, Inc. *9900 Family Systems Design and Data Book.* 1978.

3. Texas Instruments, Inc. *Introduction to Microprocessors Hardware & Software, Learning with the TM990/189 University Board.* 1979.

4. Dollhoff, T. "μP Software: How to Optimize Timing & Memory Usage," *Digital Design,* December, 1976, pp. 48–58.

5. Davis, S. "Microprocessors," *EDN,* August 5, 1979, pp. 71–85.

6. Davis, H. A. "Comparing Architectures of Three 16-Bit Microprocessors" *Computer Design,* July, 1979, pp. 91–100.

6

The 68000

The 68000 is the first advanced 16-bit microprocessor with a 32-bit internal architecture, and the first with 16-megabyte nonsegmented direct memory addressing. Developed by Motorola, it has 17 general-purpose 32-bit registers, plus a 32-bit program counter and a 16-bit status register. Eight of the general-purpose registers are data registers, seven are address registers, and two are stack pointers (one for user programs, the other for supervisory programs).

GENERAL DESCRIPTION

The eight data registers can be used to perform 8-bit byte, 16-bit word, and 32-bit "long word" operations. The address registers can function as base address registers and software stack pointers, and can be used to address bytes, words, and long words. Any of the 17 general-purpose registers may be used as an index register.

Although the program counter is 32 bits long, only the low-order 24 bits are currently used. The address bus is 24 bits wide, which gives the 68000 the ability to directly address up to 16 megabytes (16,777,216 bytes) of memory—the same addressing range as the IBM 370s! Very few of these memory locations are dedicated to a specific task by the 68000. The lowest 8 bytes of memory hold the reset vector and therefore must reside in ROM. Additional locations in the low 1024 bytes are allocated to interrupt vectors, error vectors, and vectors for other types of "exceptions," but these locations can reside either in ROM or in read/write memory. The remainder of the 68000's 16-megabyte memory map can be used any way that the user wants to.

The 68000 has a 16-bit data bus, asynchronous control lines for 68000 peripheral devicess, and synchronous control lines for slower, Motorola MC-6800 (and other) 8-bit peripheral devices. Since the

68000 peripheral devices, and synchronous control lines for slower, *plexed with the address bus,* as is the case with a number of the other microprocessors. The 68000 also provides both hardware- and software-interrupt capabilities, as well as a trace mode for software debugging.

Designed with operating systems support in mind, the 68000 operates in two different states: a *user state* for normal functions and a *supervisor state* for executing certain privileged instructions. All instructions can be executed if the 68000 is in the supervisor state; most of these instructions are available if the 68000 is in the user state.

The software capabilities of the 68000 are impressive by any standard, and they reflect the fact that this microprocessor has been designed by programmers, for programmers. As you will discover in this chapter, many of the instructions, when combined with the 68000's versatile addressing modes, more closely resemble high level language statements than the assembly language instructions of traditional 4-bit and 8-bit microprocessors. The 68000 can operate on five different types of data: bits, 4-bit binary coded decimal (bcd) digits, 8-bit bytes, 16-bit words, and 32-bit long words. The instruction set contains 56 basic instruction types but by combining these instructions with the 14 addressing modes and five data types, there are more than *1000 instructions* that the 68000 can execute.

The 68000 is being offered in 4-, 6-, 8-, and 10-MHz versions, which have clock periods 250, 167, 125, and 100 ns, respectively. The fastest instruction—for example, an instruction that copies the contents of one register into another—executes in four clock cycles, or 50 ns at 8 MHz. The slowest instruction—a 32-bit by 16-bit signed divide—can take up to 170 clock cycles, or 21.25 μs at 8 MHz, to execute.

With the 68000, *input/output is memory-mapped;* that is, the 68000 has no separate i/o instructions, but "sees" peripheral devices as memory locations in its 16-megabyte memory map. In programming i/o operations the instructions used to transfer data to and from peripheral devices are the same instructions that are used to move data in and out of memory locations or registers.

Introduced in late 1979, the 68000 is now in full production. In addition to Motorola, it is available, through alternate-source agreements, from Rockwell International Corporation, Signetics/Phillips, Mostek, and Hitachi. In Europe the 68000 is also available from EFCIS (Thomson-CSF).

As of this writing, Motorola is offering two 68000-based system support products. Motorola Microsystems (2200 W. Broadway, Mesa, AZ 85201) is offering the *MEX68KDM Design Module,* which is designed to interface to the company's EXORciser®/micromodule

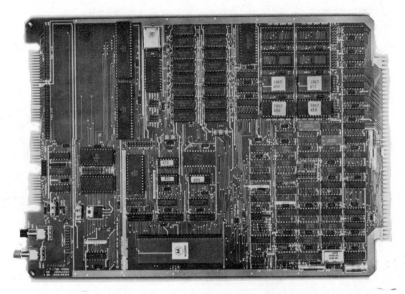

Fig. 6-1. The Motorola MEX68KDM microcomputer.

bus. The MEX68KDM, shown in Fig. 6-1, includes an 8K-byte system monitor (called MACSbug®), 32K bytes of dynamic read/write memory, two serial RS-232C ports, two 16-bit parallel i/o ports, three 16-bit counter/timers, sockets for up to 48K bytes of ROM/EPROM user memory, and a breadboard area for user-designed i/o. A bus adapter module permits 16-bit memory extensions on the 8-bit EXORciser data bus. The MACSbug monitor provides extensive debug routines, so the user can examine and change memory locations or registers, set breakpoints, trace and display instructions, and control many other processor operations.

Motorola Semiconductor Products (P.O. Box 20912, Phoenix, AZ 85036) is offering *EXORmacs®,* a complete microcomputer development system for the 68000 microprocessor. The system, shown in Fig. 6-2, includes a microcomputer chassis with the system modules, an intelligent crt terminal, a 132-column printer, and a 1-megabyte, dual-drive floppy disk. An internal debug module includes MACSbug firmware, map switching, and bus arbitration logic and ports.

Scientific Enterprises, Inc., (9375 S.W. Commerce Circle, OR 97223) also offers a microcomputer development system for the 68000. Their system, the Software Synthesizer®, centers around two elements: the Software Synthesis Language (SSL) and a 16-bit Perkin-Elmer minicomputer with 256K bytes of memory, a 38M-byte Winchester disk system, four video terminal work stations, and

Fig. 6-2. The Motorola EXORmacs Development System.

a 13-byte cartridge tape drive for disk backup and archiving. SSL is a high-level language that allows a program to be developed as a set of software components, in much the same way as hardware is constructed from individual components.

Telesoft (10639 Roselle St., San Diego, CA 92121) is offering a computer system called the Workstation, which incorporates its 68000 MPU in a DEC Q-bus backplane. It has a 4M-byte address space and comes with 256K bytes of read/write memory, an intelligent terminal, and dual floppy disks. A 10M-byte hard disk is available as an option. Telesoft also offers an optional Ada compiler for the system.

MicroDaSys (P.O. Box 36215, Los Angeles, CA 90036) is offering two 68000-based systems: a two-board set and a Miniframe® system. The two-board set is comprised of a CPU board and a RAM board. The CPU board has two microprocessors (a 6809, to take care of i/o operations, and a 68000), memory management circuitry, eight RS-232C serial i/o ports and eight parallel ports, and a floppy disk interface. The RAM board has 128K bytes of read/write memory and space for an additional 512K (using 4116s) or 2M (using 6664s) bytes. The Miniframe system, which comes in a rack-mountable enclosure, includes the CPU/RAM two-board set (but with 256K bytes of read/write memory) plus power supplies, a fan, RS-232 connectors and two Shugart single/double-density 8-inch floppy disk drives.

Manufacturers of "universal" microprocessor development systems are also offering 68000 emulation options. These include The Boston

Systems Office, Emulogic, GenRad/Futuredata, Tektronix, Phillips Industries, and Hewlett-Packard.

INTERNAL REGISTERS

In this section we will discuss the internal registers of the 68000. As mentioned in the introduction to this chapter, the 68000 has many of the characteristics of both a 16-bit and 32-bit microprocessor. All eight of its data registers are 32 bits wide, as are its seven address registers and two stack pointers. The program counter is also a 32-bit register, but only the low-order 24 bits are routed out of the chip. (The fact that the program counter is 32 bits wide leads one to conclude that perhaps Motorola's next major offering will be a 32-bit version of the 68000!) The organization of the seventeen 32-bit reg-

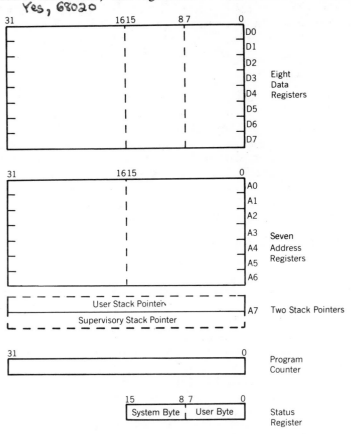

Courtesy Motorola Semiconductor Products, Inc.

Fig. 6-3. 68000 programming model.

isters and 16-bit status register in the 68000 is shown in Fig. 6-3.

The Data and Address Registers

In Fig. 6-3 the eight *data registers* (D0 through D7) are drawn with dashed-line divisions between bit positions 7 and 8, and 15 and 16. These divisions are intended to show that the contents of these registers may be accessed as 8-bit bytes, 16-bit words, or 32-bit long words. Similarly, the seven *address registers* (A0 through A6) have only one dashed-line division because their contents can be accessed only as 16-bit words or 32-bit long words; individual bytes within the address registers cannot be addressed.

Although all registers are general-purpose, the instruction set tends to recognize that the data registers will primarily be employed to hold data, and the address registers will primarily be used to hold memory addresses. For this reason, byte or word information loaded into a data register will rarely be sign-extended to 32 bits (there are a few exceptions), whereas word information loaded into an address register will always be sign extended, automatically.

Stack Pointers

Note that the two stack pointers (user stack pointer and supervisory stack pointer) are represented as address register A7 in the programming model. The stack pointers "share" this address assignment because the 68000 always operates in one of two states; it operates in the user state when user programs are being executed, and in the supervisory state when a supervisor program is being executed. Therefore the A7 address register acts as the user stack pointer when the 68000 is in the user state, and as the supervisory stack pointer when the 68000 is in the supervisory state.

The Program Counter

Since 24 bits of the program counter are used for external addressing, the 68000 can generate addresses from $000000 to $FFFFFF ("$" denotes hexadecimal). Word and long-word operands in memory are always accessed with even-numbered addresses—$000000, $000002, . . . , $FFFFFE—whereas bytes can be accessed with either odd- or even-numbered addresses. Bits 1 through 23 of the program counter are routed out of the chip to form address bus lines A1 through A23, respectively. Bit 0 of the program counter is internally encoded with the operand length in the instruction being executed to form two "data strobe" signals, called upper data strobe ($\overline{\text{UDS}}$) and lower data strobe ($\overline{\text{LDS}}$). For word transfers, both data strobes are asserted. For byte transfers, only one of the data strobes is asserted; $\overline{\text{UDS}}$ is asserted if an even-numbered byte is being transferred, and $\overline{\text{LDS}}$ is asserted if an odd-numbered byte is being transferred.

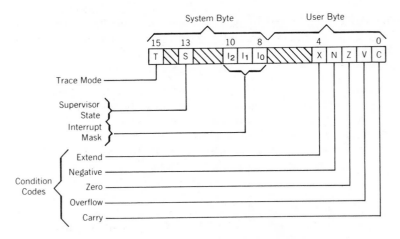

Fig. 6-4. 68000 status register.

The Status Register

The 68000 status register is divided into a system byte and a user byte, as shown in Fig. 6-4. The user byte holds five *condition code flags:*

- *Bit 0, carry* (*C*) is used to record any carry produced by an add operation, any borrow produced by a subtract operation, or the value of a bit after a shift operation. Carry also reflects the result of a compare operation. A carry sets this bit to logic one; otherwise it is cleared to logic zero.
- *Bit 1, overflow* (*V*) is meaningful only during operations on signed numbers. This bit is set to logic one if an add or subtract operation has produced a result that exceeds the twos complement range of numbers; otherwise it is cleared to logic zero. Overflow is also set to logic one if the most significant bit of the operand is changed at any time during an arithmetic shift operation.
- *Bit 2, zero* (*Z*) is set to logic one if the result of an operation is zero; otherwise it is cleared to logic zero.
- *Bit 3, negative* (*N*) is set to logic one if a signed arithmetic operation or an arithmetic shift operation produces a negative result; otherwise it is cleared to logic zero. In other words, the N flag follows the most significant bit of an operand, regardless of whether the operand is 8, 16, or 32 bits long.
- *Bit 4, extend* (*X*) functions as a carry bit for multiprecision operations. It is affected by add, subtract, negate, and shift operations, during which it receives the state of the carry (C) bit.

The 68000 contains conditional branch instructions that test the state of the C, V, Z, and N bits, and cause program execution to continue either in-line or at some other location, based on the result of this test.

The system byte of the status register (Fig. 6-4) has three fields:

- *Bits 8–10* hold an *interrupt mask* (I0, I1, and I2), which allows interrupt requests below a specified priority level to be masked out, or ignored, by the 68000 microprocessor.
- *Bit 13, supervisory* (*S*), indicates whether the 68000 is operating in the supervisor state (S = 1) or the user state (S = 0).
- *Bit 15, trace mode* (*T*), enables the built-in debug circuitry of the 68000. When T is set to logic 1, the 68000 will "single step" through a program. That is, after each instruction is executed, the 68000 will enter the supervisor state and vector to a special, user-written trace service routine. The service routine can be used to examine the current contents of selected memory locations and registers, look at status, or perform a variety of other debugging operations.

If the contents of the status register are ever read, all of the unused bits will be read as logic zeros.

ADDRESSING MODES

The 68000 has 14 operand addressing modes, giving it perhaps the most flexible addressing capability of any of the microprocessors described in this book. As Table 6-1 shows, these 14 modes fall into six basic addressing groups: register direct, address register indirect, absolute, program counter relative, immediate, and implied. Table 6-1 also presents a symbolic definition of how the effective address (the actual address of an operand in memory) is calculated for each mode, along with the generalized form of the assembler syntax for each instruction operand that employs that particular mode.

Most of the addressing mode descriptions to follow will include an example of the mode's usage with the 68000's move instruction. The move instruction has the general format

MOVE.X (EA$_{source}$),(EA$_{destination}$)

where the suffix .X specifies the length of the data being transferred, and may be .B (for byte), .W (for word), or .L (for long word). If the .X suffix is omitted, the 68000 assembler assumes that a word-length operand is being transferred. Note that the move instruction has two operands; one addresses the memory location or register that contains the data to be moved (the *source*), and the other addresses the memory location or register that the data is to be moved to (the *destination*).

Table 6-1. The 68000 Addressing Modes

Mode	Generation	Assembler Syntax
Register Direct Addressing		
Data register direct	$EA = Dn$	Dn
Address register direct	$EA = An$	An
Address Register Indirect Addressing		
Register indirect	$EA = (An)$	(An)
Postincrement register indirect	$EA = (An)$, $An \leftarrow An + N$	$(An)+$
Predecrement register indirect	$An \leftarrow An - N$, $EA = (An)$	$-(An)$
Register indirect with offset	$EA = (An) + d_{16}$	$d(An)$
Indexed register indirect with offset	$EA = (An) + (Ri) + d_8$	$d(An,Ri)$
Absolute Data Addressing		
Absolute short	$EA = $ (Next word)	$xxxx$
Absolute long	$EA = $ (Next two words)	$xxxxxxxx$
Program Counter Relative Addressing		
Relative with offset	$EA = (PC) + d_{16}$	d
Relative with index and offset	$EA = (PC) + (Ri) + d_8$	$d(Ri)$
Immediate Data Addressing		
Immediate	$DATA = $ Next word(s)	$\#xxxx$
Quick immediate	Inherent data	$\#xx$
Implied Addressing		
Implied register	$EA = SR, USP, SP, PC$	

Notes:
EA = effective address
An = address register
Dn = data register
Ri = address or data register used as index register
SR = status register
PC = program counter
SP = active system stack pointer

USP = user stack pointer
d_8 = 8-bit offset (displacement)
d_{16} = 16-bit offset (displacement)
N = 1 for byte, 2 for words, and 4 for long words
( ) = contents of
← = replaces

The move instruction is one of the most impressive in the instruction set. It can move anything, from anywhere to anywhere! The move instruction allows data to be moved between registers, from register to memory, from memory to register, or directly from one memory location to another (without affecting any register).

In *register direct addressing,* the data operand is in one of the eight data registers or address registers. (With these modes you are, in effect, using the 68000 as you would a 16-register hand-held calculator!) For example, the instruction

MOVE.L   A0,D1

copies the 32-bit contents of address register A0 into data register D1.

In *address register indirect addressing,* the contents of an address register "points to" the operand. That is, the specified address register holds a base address which the 68000 will use to calculate the effective address of the data operand. The relationship between the address register contents and the effective address depends on which of the five addressing modes is being employed.

For the simplest of these five modes, called "address register indirect addressing," the address register holds the effective address itself. For example, the instruction

MOVE.W   (A0),D1

will load the low-order 16 bits of data register D1 with the word whose memory address is in address register A0. Fig. 6-5 shows how this instruction operates if A0 points to location $53F00, and location $53F00 contains the value $1C9A.

The 68000 also provides postincrement and predecrement modes with address register indirect addressing. These modes update an address register automatically, so that the programmer does not have

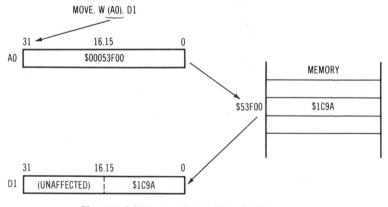

Fig. 6-5. Address register indirect addressing.

to increment or decrement a pointer with a separate instruction. The first of these modes, postincrement address register indirect, *adds* 1, 2, or 4 to an address register *after* the register has been used. The increment value (1, 2, or 4) depends on whether a byte, word, or long word operation is specified in the instruction mnemonic. This mode is extremely useful for moving blocks of data from one portion of memory to another, with increasing addresses. For example, if the source block is being pointed to by A0, and the destination block is being pointed to by A1, the instruction

MOVE.W   (A0)+,(A1)+

will move one data word from the source block to the destination block, then automatically update the pointers by 2, to point to the next higher source and destination locations. Of course, the preceding MOVE instruction can be used in a loop to transfer any number of data words from one portion of memory to any other portion of memory!

The predecrement address register indirect mode is similar to the postincrement mode, except that it *subtracts* 1, 2, or 4 from an address register *before* the register is used. Again, the decrement value depends on whether a byte, word, or long word operation is specified in the instruction mnemonic. This mode is useful for moving blocks of data from one portion of memory to another, with decreasing addresses. For example, the instruction

MOVE.W   D1,-(A1)

will decrement address register A1 by 2, and then store the low word of D1 in the memory location addressed by this value. Observe that in this application A1 is serving as a stack pointer. This instruction could be one of several instructions which build a user stack (separate from the system user stack of the 68000) in memory. In fact, the predecrement mode allows any address register to readily serve as a stack pointer, so *the 68000 can be used to maintain eight separate user stacks in memory!* These stacks, however, are not as easy to use (access) as the two system stacks.

The remaining two address register indirect addressing modes support data tables by permitting offsets and indexes to be applied to an indirect address pointer. The first of these modes, the *address register indirect with offset mode*, adds a 16-bit signed integer to the contents of an address register, and then uses the result to address an operand.

The address register indirect with offset mode is especially useful for assessing a particular element in a list or lookup table. For these applications an address register is initialized with the starting address of the table, and the element's relative position (its "offset") is specified in the instruction. The offset is always a byte value, so if a table holds byte data values, the offset is simply the element number (0, 1, 2, and so on). For tables holding word or long word data values, the offset must be the element number multiplied by 2 or 4, respectively.

For example, if address register A0 holds the starting address of a word-based data table in memory, the instruction

    MOVE.W   14(A0),D1

will load data register D1 with the 16-bit value of the eighth element (element 7) in the table. Fig. 6-6 shows how this instruction operates if the table starts at $53F00. Adding the offset, decimal 14 (hexadecimal E), to the starting address yields an effective address of $53F0E, which is assumed to contain the value $1C9A.

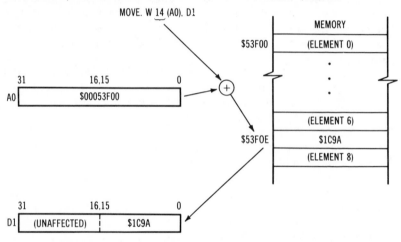

Fig. 6-6. Address register indirect with offset addressing.

Note that because the offset is a 16-bit signed integer, the address register indirect with offset mode can span up to 32,767 bytes higher in memory, and up to 32,768 bytes lower in memory, than the address in the address register. If you are operating on word or long word data, these offset limits translate to 16,383 words or 8191 long words forward, and 16,384 words or 8192 long words backward.

The final addressing mode in this group, *indexed address register indirect with offset,* adds an 8-bit signed integer and the contents of an index register (a data register or address register) to the contents of an address register, and then uses the result to address an operand. Being 32 bits long, the signed value in the index register can be used to access data anywhere in the 68000's addressing range.

With its two separate offsets this addressing mode is useful for accessing two-dimensional arrays. During such applications an address register typically holds the starting address of the array, and the offset and index register provide row and column displacements. An an example, assume that the starting address of a word-based array is in address register A0 and that a 32-bit index is in address register A1. With these values in the registers, the instruction

```
MOVE.W   14(A0,A1.L),D1
```

will load the low word of data register D1 with the contents of the eighth element (element 7) in the indexed column of the array. Note that this same instruction can be used to access the eighth element of *any* column in the array by simply altering the contents of index register A1 between accesses. Observe that the notation A1.L in the instruction causes the full 32-bit contents of A1 to be used as the index.

In *absolute addressing,* the effective address is contained in the instruction, rather than in a register. The 68000 has two absolute addressing modes: absolute short addressing, in which the instruction contains a 16-bit address (sign extended to 32 bits), and absolute long addressing, in which the instruction contains a full 32-bit address. The absolute short addressing mode allows you to access only the lowest 32K bytes in memory (addresses 0 through $7FFF), or the highest 32K bytes in memory (addresses $FF8000 through $FFFFFF), whereas the absolute long addressing mode allows you to access any location in the 16-megabyte address space of the 68000.

Of these two absolute addressing modes, absolute short-addressed instructions occupy one word less in memory and are executed in four fewer cycles. The designers of the 68000 intend absolute short addressing to be employed to access frequently used data and temporary data stored in the extreme 32K bytes of memory. For example, to load the word in location $3F00 into the low-order half of data register D1, we can use the instruction

```
MOVE.W   $3F00,D1
```

which is the absolute short-addressed (two-word, 12-cycle) equivalent of the absolute long-addressed (three-word, 16-cycle) instruction

```
MOVE.W   $03F00,D1
```

Note that the .W suffix refers to the length of the data to be moved, rather than the length of the absolute address.

The *program counter relative addressing* modes are useful for developing position-independent or "relocatable" programs. These are programs that, once written and assembled, may be executed *anywhere* in memory. Programs sold in ROM, for instance, are often relocatable. In this form of addressing, the effective address is calculated by adding a specified value to the address contained in the program counter. Which address is contained in the program counter? The PC contains the address of a portion of the instruction being executed that holds a signed displacement, or "offset." Therefore program counter relative addressing allows access to operands that are located some number of bytes higher in memory, or lower in memory, than the current instruction.

The 68000 has two program counter relative addressing modes: relative with offset and relative with index and offset. In the simpler mode, relative with offset, the effective address is the sum of the address in the program counter and a sign-extended 16-bit displacement integer in the extension word. With an assembler, you need not specify the displacement directly; the assembler will calculate it for you. For example, the instruction

MOVE.W   LABEL,D1

will cause the assembler to calculate the displacement between the move instruction's extension word and the location that has the label LABEL, and use this displacement to form the extension word. At execution time the 68000 microprocessor will load the contents of location LABEL into the low-order 16 bits of data register D1. You will note that because the displacement is a 16-bit signed integer, LABEL must be no more than 16,383 words higher in memory, or no more than 16,384 words lower in memory, than the instruction's extension word.

Let's now move on to the other program counter relative addressing mode: relative with index and offset. Here, the effective address is the sum of the extension word address in the program counter, a sign-extended 8-bit displacement integer in the extension word, and the contents of an index register (data register or address register). This mode is particularly useful for reading values from a list or table, For such applications the sum of the program counter and 8-bit displacement addresses the beginning of the table, and the index register provides the displacement to the desired data location; this is illustrated in Fig. 6-7.

If the data table starts at the memory location labeled TABL, the instruction

MOVE.W   TABL(A0.L)#,D1

will cause the assembler to calculate the displacement between the instruction's extension word and the location having the label TABL, and use this displacement to form the extension word. At execution time the 68000 microprocessor will add the 32-bit contents of address register A0 to the calculated table starting address and then load the contents of the resulting address into the low-order 16 bits of data register D1. Because the offset is an 8-bit signed integer, TABL must be no more than 63 words higher in memory or no more than 64 words lower in memory than the instruction's extension word.

Immediate data addressing is used to specify a constant data operand, as opposed to the contents of a register or memory location. With this addressing mode the constant is contained in the instruction. If the constant is a word or long word value, it will reside in one

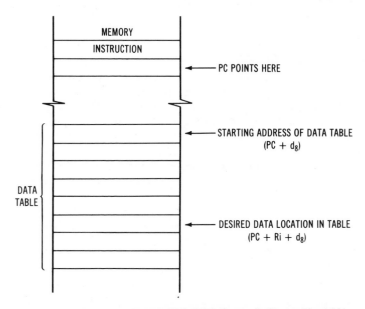

Fig. 6-7. Program counter relative with index and offset addressing.

or two extension words that follow the operation code or "op code" of the instruction; in the manufacturers' literature, this is called the "immediate mode." If the constant is a byte value, the value is imbedded in the low-order 8 bits of the operation word; the manufacturers' literature refers to this as the "quick immediate mode." In either case an immediate data operand is identified to the assembler by prefixing it with a # character.

For example, the instruction

```
MOVE.W  #$8342,D1
```

loads the immediate word value $8342 into the low-order 16 bits of data register D1. The immediate value $8342 will not be sign extended here because D1 is a data register. If the destination is an address register, however, the immediate word value will always be sign extended. Therefore, the instruction

```
MOVEA.W  #$8342,A0
```

will load the value $FFFF8342 into address register A0. The "A" in the MOVEA instruction indicates that an address register is involved in the data transfer.

The quick immediate mode can only be used with three instruction types: add, move, and subtract. These instructions have "quick" variations; add quick (ADDQ), move quick (MOVEQ), and subtract quick (SUBQ). The quick immediate value is always sign-extended to a long word, so the instruction

```
MOVEQ  #$57,D1
```

causes the value $00000057 to be loaded into data register D1.

Some instructions make implicit reference (that is, they use *implied addressing*) to the program counter (PC), the system stack pointer (SP), the supervisor stack pointer (SSP), the user stack pointer (USP), or the status register (SR). For example, the jump instruction (JMP) always loads a jump address into the program counter, although the program counter is not explicitly identified as a destination register in the instruction. Table 6-2 provides a list of the instructions that use implied addressing, and the registers implied.

Table 6-2. Implicit Instructions

Instruction	Implied Register(s)
Branch Conditional (B_{cc}), Branch Always (BRA)	PC
Branch to Subroutine (BSR)	PC, SP
Check Register against Bounds (CHK)	SSP, SR
Test Condition , Decrement and Branch (DB_{cc})	PC
Signed Divide (DIVS)	SSP, SR
Unsigned Divide (DIVU)	SSP, SR
Jump (JMP)	PC
Jump to Subroutine (JSR)	PC, SP
Link and Allocate (LINK)	SP
Move Condition Codes (MOVE CCR)	SR
Move Status Register (MOVE SR)	SR
Move User Stack Pointer (MOVE USP)	USP
Push Effective Address (PEA)	SP
Return from Exception (RTE)	PC, SP, SR
Return and Restore Condition Codes (RTR)	PC, SP, SR
Return from Subroutine (RTS)	PC, SP
Trap (TRAP)	SSP, SR
Trap on Overflow (TRAPV)	SSP, SR
Unlink (UNLK)	SP

Courtesy Motorola Semiconductor Products, Inc.

THE 68000 INSTRUCTION SET

Now we are prepared to discuss the instruction set of the 68000 and how these instructions are used.

15	14	13	12	11	10	9	8	7	6	5	4	3	2	1	0
Operation Word (first word specifies operation and modes)															
Immediate operand (if any, one or two words)															
Source effective address extension (if any, one or two words)															
Destination effective address extension (if any, one or two words)															

Courtesy Motorola Semiconductor Products, Inc.
Fig. 6-8. Instruction format.

Instruction Format

Instructions can occupy from one to five words in memory, as shown in Fig. 6-8. The longest instruction would consist of an operation word, along with two two-word address extensions. All instructions have an operation word, or *op word,* which contains the binary bits that the 68000 decodes to determine the instruction type, operand addressing mode(s), and the length of the instruction. Additional "extension words" are required for addressing modes that use constants (immediate values), absolute addresses, or displacement offsets. Two-word data values are always stored in high-word/low-word order in memory, as are addresses (except when they are pushed onto the system stack).

Instruction Types

As mentioned previously, the 68000 has 56 basic instruction types. The assembler mnemonics and the descriptions of these instructions are summarized in Table 6-3. Further, eight of these instructions have variations, or subsets, to perform special operations; these variations are summarized in Table 6-4.

Essentially, the 68000 instruction set gives the microprocessor the ability to move information between memory locations, i/o devices, and general-purpose registers (in any combination), to perform single-precision and multiprecision arithmetic operations on binary and binary coded decimal numbers, to perform logical operations, to shift and rotate the contents of memory locations and registers, to manipulate individual bits, to control the sequence of program execution, and to control overall system operation.

Many of these instructions can operate on byte-, word- or long word-length data, depending on whether the programmer applies a ".B," ".W," or ".L" suffix to the instruction mnemonic. These suffixes have already been demonstrated in the preceding discussion of addressing modes, in which they were applied to the MOVE instruction. Let us now proceed to the instruction group descriptions, start-

Table 6-3. The 68000 Instruction Set

Mnemonic	Description
ABCD	Add Decimal with Extend
ADD	Add
AND	Logical And
ASL	Arithmetic Shift Left
ASR	Arithmetic Shift Right
B$_{cc}$	Branch Conditionally
BCHG	Bit Test and Change
BCLR	Bit Test and Clear
BRA	Branch Always
BSET	Bit Test and Set
BSR	Branch to Subroutine
BTST	Bit Test
CHK	Check Register Against Bounds
CLR	Clear Operand
CMP	Compare
DB$_{cc}$	Test Cond., Decrement and Branch
DIVS	Signed Divide
DIVU	Unsigned Divide
EOR	Exclusive Or
EXG	Exchange Registers
EXT	Sign Extend
JMP	Jump
JSR	Jump to Subroutine
LEA	Load Effective Address
LINK	Link Stack
LSL	Logical Shift Left
LSR	Logical Shift Right
MOVE	Move
MOVEM	Move Multiple Registers
MOVEP	Move Peripheral Data
MULS	Signed Multiply
MULU	Unsigned Multiply
NBCD	Negate Decimal with Extend
NEG	Negate
NOP	No Operation
NOT	One's Complement
OR	Logical Or
PEA	Push Effective Address
RESET	Reset External Devices
ROL	Rotate Left without Extend
ROR	Rotate Right without Extend
ROXL	Rotate Left with Extend
ROXR	Rotate Right with Extend
RTE	Return from Exception
RTR	Return and Restore
RTS	Return from Subroutine

Mnemonic	Description
SBCD	Subtract Decimal with Extend
S_{cc}	Set Conditional
STOP	Stop
SUB	Subtract
SWAP	Swap Data Register Halves
TAS	Test and Set Operand
TRAP	Trap
TRAPV	Trap on Overflow
TST	Test
UNLK	Unlink

Courtesy Motorola Semiconductor Products, Inc.

ing with the data movement group, which includes the MOVE instruction.

Data Movement Instructions

The data movement instructions (Table 6-5) are used to transfer information between memory and the 68000 general-purpose registers. The fundamental instruction in this group is the familiar move (MOVE) instruction, which can be used to transfer byte, word, or long word data between memory locations, between a memory location and a data register, or between data registers.

This group also includes several instructions that perform more specific types of move operations. The move-address (MOVEA) instruction can transfer word or long word addresses between a memory location and an address register, or between address registers. The move multiple-registers (MOVEM) instruction can transfer word or long word data between selected registers (up to 16) and consecutive memory locations, and it is often used to construct reentrant subroutines. The move peripheral data (MOVEP) instruction can transfer data between a data register and alternate bytes of memory to facilitate interfacing to 8-bit peripheral support chips. The move quick (MOVEQ) instruction loads an 8-bit immediate value into a data register, as a 32-bit sign-extended long operand. The contents of any two general-purpose registers can be exchanged (EXG) and register halves can be swapped (SWAP), which exchanges the high-order and low-order 16 bits of a 32-bit data register.

Two other instructions transfer a computed effective address, rather than the *contents* of memory at that address. The load effective address (LEA) instruction loads the effective address into an address register, whereas the push effective address (PEA) instruction pushes the effective address onto the active system stack (user stack or supervisory stack). The PEA instruction is especially useful for passing

Table 6-4. Variations of Instruction Types

Instruction Type	Variation	Description
ADD	**ADD**	Add
	ADDA	Add Address
	ADDQ	Add Quick
	ADDI	Add Immediate
	ADDX	Add with Extend
AND	**AND**	Logical And
	ANDI	And Immediate
CMP	**CMP**	Compare
	CMPA	Compare Address
	CMPM	Compare Memory
	CMPI	Compare Immediate
EOR	**EOR**	Exclusive Or
	EORI	Exclusive Or Immediate
MOVE	**MOVE**	Move
	MOVEA	Move Address
	MOVEQ	Move Quick
	MOVE from SR	Move from Status Register
	MOVE to SR	Move to Status Register
	MOVE to CCR	Move to Condition Codes
	MOVE to USP	Move to User Stack Pointer
NEG	**NEG**	Negate
	NEGX	Negate with Extend
OR	**OR**	Logical Or
	ORI	Or Immediate
SUB	**SUB**	Subtract
	SUBA	Subtract Address
	SUBI	Subtract Immediate
	SUBQ	Subtract Quick
	SUBX	Subtract with Extend

Courtesy Motorola Semiconductor Products, Inc.

parameters to a subroutine, by pushing the address of the parameter —or the starting address of several consecutively stored parameters— onto the stack.

The final two instructions in this group, link (LINK) and unlink (UNLK), are primarily used with subroutines, so they will be discussed separately, following the description of the program control instructions.

Integer Arithmetic Instructions

The 68000 can add, subtract, multiply, divide, and compare two operands. It can also clear, test, sign extend, and negate (twos com-

Table 6-5. Data Movement Instructions

Instruction	Operand Size	Operation
EXG	32	Rx → Ry
LEA	32	EA → An
LINK	—	An → SP@- SP → An SP + d → SP
MOVE	8, 16, 32	(EA)s → EAd
MOVEM	16, 32	(EA) → An, Dn An, Dn → EA
MOVEP	16, 32	(EA) → Dn Dn → EA
MOVEQ	8	#Imm → Dn
PEA	32	EA → SP@-
SWAP	32	Dn [31:16] ↔ Dn [15:0]
UNLK	—	An → SP SP @+ → An

Notes: s = source, d = destination, [ ] = bit numbers.

plement) a single, specified operand. The instructions that perform these tasks are summarized in Table 6-6.

The add (ADD) instruction operates on byte, word, and long word data operands, with one operand in a memory location and the other in a data register. The 68000 also provides several special-purpose variations on the add instruction. Add address (ADDA) adds a word or long word address in memory to the contents of an address register, *without affecting any condition codes* (all other add instructions do). Another variation, add immediate (ADDI), permits a constant to be added to a memory location or data register; this instruction occupies two or four words in memory. A shorter and faster version of ADDI, called add quick (ADDQ), adds a value between 1 and 8 to the destination and occupies only one word in memory. ADDQ replaces the increment instruction found in most 8-bit microprocessors.

The 68000 also has subtract versions of the four add instructions just described. They are called subtract (SUB), subtract address (SUBA), subtract immediate (SUBI), and subtract quick (SUBQ). Like ADDA the SUBA instruction does not affect the condition codes. Another subtractlike instruction, negate (NEG), generates the twos complement of an addressed byte, word, or long word operand by subtracting the operand from zero.

Table 6-6. The Integer Arithmetic Instructions

Instruction	Operand Size	Operation
ADD	8, 16, 32	Dn + (EA) → Dn
		(EA) + Dn → EA
		(EA) + #xxx → EA
	16, 32	An + (EA) → An
ADDX	8, 16, 32	Dx + D6 + X → Dx
	16, 32	Ax@- Ay@- + X → Ax@
CLR	8, 16, 32	0 → EA
CMP	8, 16, 32	Dn – (EA)
		(EA) – #xxx
		Ax@+ – Ay@+
	16, 32	An – (EA)
DIVS	32 ÷ 16	Dn/(EA) → Dn
DIVU	32 ÷ 16	Dn/(EA) → Dn
EXT	8 → 16	$(Dn)_8$ → Dn_{16}
	16 → 32	$(Dn)_{16}$ → Dn_{32}
MULS	16 * 16 → 32	Dn * (EA) → Dn
MULU	16 * 16 → 32	Dn * (EA) → Dn
NEG	8, 16, 32	0 – (EA) → EA
NEGX	8, 16, 32	0 – (EA) – X → EA
SUB	8, 16, 32	Dn – (EA) → Dn
		(EA) – Dn → EA
		(EA) – #xxx → EA
	16, 32	An – (EA) → An
SUBX	8, 16, 32	Dx – Dy – X → Dx
		Ax@- - Ay@- - X → Ax@
TAS	8	(EA) – 0, 1 → EA[7]
TST	8, 16, 32	(EA) – 0

Note:
[ ] = bit number

Courtesy Motorola Semiconductor Products, Inc.

The instructions we've just described can add or subtract operands that are up to 32 bits long. However, many applications require numbers longer than 32 bits to be added or subtracted. The 68000 has special instructions to suit those applications, too.

If you are all familiar with arithmetic operations on "multiprecision" numbers, you know that you must first add the least significant parts (bytes, words, or long words) of the operands, and then add the next more significant parts, *including any carry from the first addition.* Except for **ADDA**, all of the add instructions just discussed set the extend (X) bit of the status register if the addition produces a carry, and reset the extend bit if no carry occurs. The 68000 has a special instruction that adds two data registers or two memory locations, with the X bit included in the addition. This instruction is called add extended (ADDX).

Similarly, to subtract two multiprecision numbers, you must first subtract the least significant parts (bytes, words, or long words) of the operands, and then subtract the next more significant parts, *including any borrow from the first subtraction.* Except for SUBA, all of the previously discussed subtract instructions set the extend (X) bit of the status register if the subtraction produces a borrow, and clear the extend bit if no borrow occurs. The 68000 has a special instruction that subtracts two data registers or two memory locations, with the X bit included in the subtraction. This instruction is called subtract extended (SUBX). The NEG instruction also has a negate-with-X variation, called negate with extend (NEGX).

The 68000 has multiplication instructions for signed and unsigned numbers, using the mnemonics MULS and MULU. These instructions multiply two word operands and place the 32-bit product in a data register. Division operations are also available for signed and unsigned numbers, using the mnemonics DIVS and DIVU. These instructions divide a long word dividend (32 bits) by a word divisor (16 bits) and place the 16-bit quotient and 16-bit remainder in the lower half and upper half of a data register, respectively.

It is possible to operate on mixed-size data, too, by applying an instruction called sign extend (EXT). This instruction extends the sign bit (the most significant bit) of a number in a data register from a byte to a word, or from a word to a long word. Thus a byte can be added to a word, or a word can be multiplied by a byte.

Most programs do not execute all instructions consecutively, as they are stored in memory, but rather execute the instructions in a sequence that depends on various status conditions. That is, programs usually contain loops, jumps, and branches that cause the microprocessor to transfer program execution from one place to another in a program. The instructions that cause program execution to be transferred will be described when we discuss the program control instructions of the 68000. At this point we will discuss a few instructions that are commonly used to configure the condition codes on which program control instructions make their transfer/no-transfer "decisions."

One of the most widely used instruction types on which decisions are based is the compare instruction. The compare instruction subtracts a source operand from a destination operand, but does not save the result. Instead, *the condition code flags in the status register are set or cleared, based on the "result" of this subtraction.* Once the flags have been set or cleared, they can be tested with the program control instructions.

The compare (CMP) instruction compares a source operand with the byte, word, or long word contents of a data register. Word or long word operands can be compared to an address register with a variation of the CMP instruction, called compare address (CMPA). The compare immediate (CMPI) instruction compares a byte, word, or long word immediate value with a destination operand. The compare memory (CMPM) instruction compares two memory locations.

There are also two special "test" instructions, which compare an operand with zero and record the result in the N and Z condition code flags. These two instructions are similar, but test and set (TAS) sets the high-order bit of the operand after the compare, whereas test (TST) does not affect the operand. The TAS instruction is useful for allocating resources in a multitasking or multiprocessor system.

The final instruction in this group, clear (CLR), simply resets the specified byte, word, or long word to zero.

The Logical Instructions

The basic instructions in this group are logical AND (AND), logical OR (OR), logical exclusive-OR (EOR), and logical complement (NOT). These instructions (Table 6-7) can operate on byte, word,

Table 6-7. The Logical Instructions

Instruction	Operand Size	Operation
AND	8, 16, 32	Dn ∧ (EA) → Dn (EA) ∧ Dn → EA (EA) ∧ #xxx → EA
OR	8, 16, 32	Dn ∨ (EA) → Dn (EA) ∨ Dn → EA (EA) ∨ #xxx → EA
EOR	8, 16, 32	(EA) ⊕ Dy → EA (EA) ⊕ #xxx → EA
NOT	8, 16, 32	~(EA) → EA

Note:
~ = invert

Courtesy Motorola Semiconductor Products, Inc.

and long word operands. Variations of the AND, OR, and EOR instructions permit a constant to be applied as source data. These variation instructions are AND immediate (ANDI), OR immediate (ORI), and exclusive-OR immediate (EORI). They, too, operate on an operand of any length.

Shift and Rotate Instructions

Certain programming situations require shifting or rotating the contents of a register or memory location. Such situations include aligning operands for floating-point operations and aligning data masks. The 68000 has a group of shift and rotate instructions (Table 6-8) that can shift or rotate an operand to the right or to the left. If the operand is contained in a data register, it can be displaced by the bit count contained in another data register (0 to 64 shifts) or in the instruction (1 to 8 shifts). If the operand is contained in a memory location, it can be displaced only one bit position.

Unsigned numbers can be shifted using the logical shift instructions, LSL and LSR. Signed numbers can be shifted using the arithmetic shift instructions, ASL and ASR. In both cases, bits shifted out of the operand are entered into the carry (C) and extend (X) condition code flags.

There are four rotate instructions. In all four instructions, bits shifted out of the operand are entered into carry (C). However, for the two rotate without extend instructions, ROL and ROR, the bit shifted out of one end of the operand is entered into the opposite end of the operand. When the two rotate with extend instructions, ROXL and ROXR, are executed, the bit shifted out of one end of

Table 6-8. The Shift and Rotate Instructions

Instruction	Operand Size	Operation
ASL	8, 16, 32	$\boxed{X/C} \leftarrow \boxed{\longleftarrow} \leftarrow 0$
ASR	8, 16, 32	$\boxed{\longrightarrow} \rightarrow \boxed{X/C}$
LSL	8, 16, 32	$\boxed{X/C} \leftarrow \boxed{\longleftarrow} \leftarrow 0$
LSR	8, 16, 32	$0 \rightarrow \boxed{\longrightarrow} \rightarrow \boxed{X/C}$
ROL	8, 16, 32	$\boxed{C} \leftarrow \boxed{\longleftarrow}$
ROR	8, 16, 32	$\boxed{\longrightarrow} \rightarrow \boxed{C}$
ROXL	8, 16, 32	$\boxed{C} \leftarrow \boxed{\longleftarrow} \leftarrow \boxed{X}$
ROXR	8, 16, 32	$\boxed{X} \rightarrow \boxed{\longrightarrow} \rightarrow \boxed{C}$

Courtesy Motorola Semiconductor Products, Inc.

the operand is entered into extend flag (X) and the previous value of this flag is shifted into the opposite end of the operand.

Since shifting a number to the left doubles its value and shifting a number to the right halves its value, the shift instructions provide quick-executing alternatives to the 68000's slow multiply and divide instructions, if you are multiplying or dividing by some power of 2.

Bit Manipulation Instructions

The 68000 has four special instructions that test the state of a specified bit in a memory location or register, record the state of that bit in the zero (Z) condition code flag, and perform some operation based on the test result. These instructions are called bit test (BTST), bit test and set (BSET), bit test and clear (BCLR), and bit test and change (BCHG); they are summarized in Table 6-9.

Table 6-9. The Bit Manipulation Instructions

Instruction	Operand Size	Operation
BTST	8, 32	$\sim$ bit of (EA) $\rightarrow$ Z
BSET	8, 32	$\sim$ bit of (EA) $\rightarrow$ Z 1 $\rightarrow$ bit of EA
BCLR	8, 32	$\sim$ bit of (EA) $\rightarrow$ Z 0 $\rightarrow$ bit of EA
BCHG	8, 32	$\sim$ bit of (EA) $\rightarrow$ Z $\sim$ bit of (EA) $\rightarrow$ bit of EA

Courtesy Motorola Semiconductor Products, Inc.

Binary Coded Decimal Instructions

The binary arithmetic instruction ADDX, SUBX, and NEGX discussed previously each have a counterpart that operates on multi-precision binary coded decimal (bcd) bytes. These instructions are add decimal with extend (ABCD), subtract decimal with extend (SBCD), and negate decimal with extend (NBCD); they are summarized in Table 6-10. Because these three instructions always include the extend (X) condition code flag in the operation, the X bit

Table 6-10. The Binary Coded Decimal Instructions

Instruction	Operand Size	Operation
ABCD	8	$Dx_{10} + Dy_{10} + X \rightarrow Dx$ $Ax@_{-10} + Ay@_{-10} + X \rightarrow Ax@$
SBCD	8	$Dx_{10} - Dy_{10} - X \rightarrow Dx$ $Ax@_{-10} - Ay@_{-10} - X \rightarrow Ax@$
NBCD	8	$0 - (EA)_{10} - X \rightarrow EA$

Courtesy Motorola Semiconductor Products, Inc.

Table 6-11. The Program Control Instructions

Instruction	Operation
Conditional	
Bcc	Branch conditionally (14 conditions)
	8- and 16-bit displacement
DBcc	Test condition, decrement counter, and branch.
	16-bit displacement
Scc	Set byte conditionally (16 conditions)
Unconditional	
BRA	Branch always
	8- and 16-bit displacement
BSR	Branch to subroutine
	8- and 16-bit displacement
JMP	Jump
JSR	Jump to subroutine
Returns	
RTR	Return and restore condition codes
RTS	Return from subroutine

Courtesy Motorola Semiconductor Products, Inc.

must be cleared (usually with an ANDI.B #$EF,SR instruction) before you operate on the least significant bcd bytes. Most programmers prefer this minor inconvenience to the "decimal adjust" instructions required with some other 8- and 16-bit microprocessors.

Program Control Instructions

Although program instructions are stored consecutively in memory, programs rarely execute exactly in this order. All but the simplest programs contain branches, jumps, and subroutine calls that alter the sequence in which the microprocessor executes the program. The program control instructions (Table 6-11) are the 68000 instructions that transfer program control from one portion of a program to another.

The first three instructions in Table 6-11, branch conditionally (Bcc), test condition, decrement and branch (DBcc), and set byte conditionally (Scc), are *conditional instructions*. Their mode of operation differs, depending on the state of one or more condition code flags. The "cc" suffix on each of these instruction mnemonics represents the condition tested. The condition codes are summarized in Table 6-12. The Bcc instructions will not accept the always true (T) and always false (F) conditions, but all 16 of the conditions are testable by the DBcc and Scc instructions.

With the Bcc instruction, if the test condition specified in the instruction is met, program control is transferred to the location specified in the instruction, otherwise execution continues with the next instruction. These instructions can be one or two words long. If you use the form Bcc.S, the assembler will produce a one-word instruction with an 8-bit signed relative displacement imbedded in the op word. With an 8-bit displacement the branch target can be up to 63 words higher in memory, or 64 words lower in memory, than the Bcc op word plus 2. If you omit the .S suffix, the assembler will produce a two-word instruction with a 16-bit signed relative displacement in the second word. With a 16-bit displacement the branch target can be up to 16,383 words higher in memory or 16,384 words lower in memory, than the Bcc.

The DBcc variants are unique, high-levellike instructions that are designed to act as terminators for repetitive loops. When a DBcc instruction is executed, the 68000 interrogates the condition codes to find out whether the specified condition has been met. If the condi-

Table 6-12. Conditional Tests

Mnemonic	Condition	Encoding	Test
T	true	0000	1
F	false	0001	0
HI	high	0010	$\overline{C} \cdot \overline{Z}$
LS	low or same	0011	$C + Z$
CC	carry clear	0100	$\overline{C}$
CS	carry set	0101	C
NE	not equal	0110	$\overline{Z}$
EQ	equal	0111	Z
VC	overflow clear	1000	$\overline{V}$
VS	overflow set	1001	V
PL	plus	1010	$\overline{N}$
MI	minus	1011	N
GE	greater or equal	1100	$N \cdot V + \overline{N} \cdot \overline{V}$
LT	less than	1101	$N \cdot \overline{V} + \overline{N} \cdot V$
GT	greater than	1110	$N \cdot V \cdot \overline{Z} + \overline{N} \cdot \overline{V} \cdot \overline{Z}$
LE	less or equal	1111	$Z + N \cdot \overline{V} + \overline{N} \cdot V$

Courtesy Motorola Semiconductor Products, Inc.

tion is met, program execution "falls through" to the next instruction. If the condition is not met, the 68000 decrements the specified data register by 1; if the data register has been decremented to −1, program execution "falls through" to the next instruction; otherwise the 68000 branches to the specified label. As you can see, it's easiest to remember how the DBcc variants operate if you think of them as "Don't Branch" instructions! Finally, the Scc instructions test the specified condition and set the addressed byte to all ones if the condition is met and to all zeros if it is not met.

The *unconditional instructions* in Table 6-11 consist of two relative-addressed branch instructions, branch always (BRA) and branch to subroutine (BSR). This table also contains two absolute-addressed jump instructions, jump (JMP) and jump to subroutine (JSR). A jump instruction can be used to transfer program control *anywhere* in memory, whereas a branch instruction is limited to a 16-bit offset from the instruction, as described in the preceding paragraph. The *return instructions,* return and restore condition codes (RTR) and return from subroutine (RTS), read the program counter and condition codes, or just the program counter, from the stack, respectively.

The Link and Unlink Instructions

The 68000's link (LINK) and unlink (UNLK) instructions are used to allocate and deallocate data areas on the system stack for nested subroutines, linked lists, and other procedures. Basically, following a procedure call (e.g., a call to a nested subroutine), LINK sets up an address register pointer to the data area and moves the stack pointer down in memory, just past the data area. Upon completion of the subroutine, UNLK reverses this sequence, thereby restoring the stack pointer and address registers to their original, pre-LINK values.

The LINK instruction has two operands: an address register and a displacement value. While the nested subroutine is being executed, the specified address register will hold the starting address of that subroutine's stack data area; this address register is called the *frame pointer (FP)*. The displacement value specifies the length of the data area, in bytes, to be allocated. When LINK is executed, the 68000 pushes the current contents of the FP onto the stack, decrements the stack pointer (SP) by 4, loads that stack pointer value into the FP register, and then decrements the stack pointer by the specified displacement. After LINK has been executed the address register holds the starting address of the data area and the stack pointer points to the location that follows the data area. At this point the subroutine can easily use the data area by accessing it with the address register indirect with offset addressing mode (either indexed or unindexed). Figs. 6-9A and 6-9B show the system stack after a subroutine call and after LINK, respectively.

Fig. 6-9C shows the stack pointer addressing memory at even lower addresses, due to some subroutine stack operations. This figure is included to emphasize that the UNLK instruction will affect an orderly return (Fig. 6-9D), regardless of how the stack pointer has been altered since LINK. The UNLK instruction, which is normally executed just before returning from the subroutine, simply loads the stack pointer from the FP register, and then reinitializes the FP register by pulling its original value from the top of the stack.

Following UNLK, both the FP and the SP contain the values they held prior to LINK.

System Control Instructions

System control is accomplished by using privileged instructions, trap generating instructions, and instructions that use or modify the status register. These instructions are summarized in Table 6-13.

Privileged instructions can only be executed when the 68000 microprocessor is operating in the supervisor state. The reset external devices (RESET) instruction asserts the $\overline{RESET}$ line of the 68000, which is wired to all external devices in the system but does not

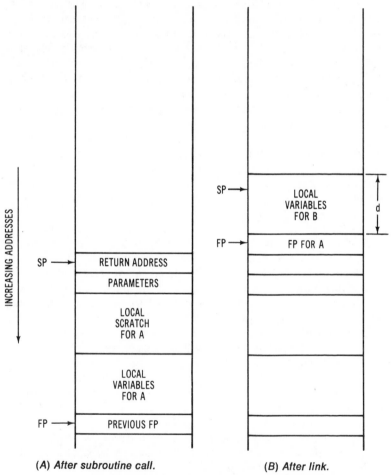

(A) After subroutine call.   (B) After link.

Fig. 6-9. Link and unlink instructions allocate and deallocate

affect the microprocessor. Return from exception (RTE) reads the contents of the status register (both system and user byte) and program counter from the stack. (A discussion of exceptions is forthcoming in this chapter.) Stop program execution (STOP) loads an immediate value into the status register, and then the 68000 microprocessor stops fetching and executing instructions. Execution will not resume until the 68000 receives a sufficiently high priority interrupt request or an external reset. The remaining privileged instructions include three logical operations that operate on the status register (ORI to SR, ANDI to SR, and EORI to SR) and two MOVE instructions. Move user stack pointer (MOVE USP) loads the cur-

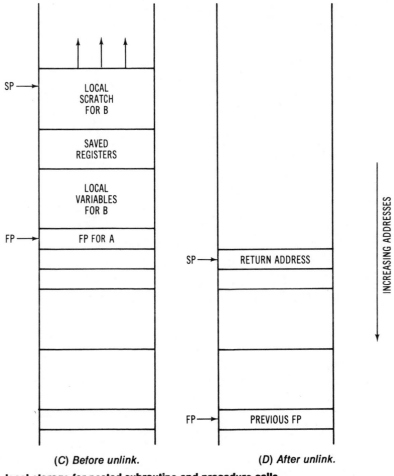

(C) *Before unlink.*   (D) *After unlink.*

local storage for nested subroutine and procedure calls.

rent contents of the user stack pointer into an address register, or vice versa, while load new status register (MOVE EA to SR) initializes the status register with the content of a memory location.

Traps and other exceptions are described in detail in a subsequent part of this chapter. For now, it is sufficient to mention that the three *trap generating instructions* in Table 6-13 include an instruction that initiates a trap operation unconditionally, trap (TRAP), and two

Table 6-13. The System Control Instructions

Instruction	Operation
Privileged	
RESET	Reset external devices
RTE	Return from exception
STOP	Stop program execution
ORI to SR	Logical OR to status register
MOVE USP	Move user stack pointer
ANDI to SR	Logical AND to status register
EORI to SR	Logical EOR to status register
MOVE EA to SR	Load new status register
Trap Generating	
TRAP	Trap
TRAPV	Trap on overflow
CHK	Check register against bounds
Status Register	
ANDI to CCR	Logical AND to condition codes
EORI to CCR	Logical EOR to condition codes
MOVE EA to CCR	Load new condition codes
ORI to CCR	Logical OR to condition codes
MOVE SR to EA	Store status register

Courtesy Motorola Semiconductor Products, Inc.

instructions that initiate trap operations based on some conditions, trap on overflow (TRAPV) and check register against bounds (CHK). The CHK instruction compares the low-order word in a data register with both zero and an addressed twos complement integer. If the register contents are less than zero or greater than the specified integer, the 68000 initiates trap processing. The program control instruction return and restore condition codes (RTR) are used to effect a return from a trap.

The *status register instructions* are used to initialize (MOVE EA to CCR) and perform logical operations on the condition code register (ANDI to CCR, EORI to CCR, and ORI to CCR), and to save the status register in memory (MOVE SR to EA).

MICROPROCESSOR CHIP HARDWARE

The 68000 microprocessor is packaged in a 64-pin dual in-line package (DIP), with the pinouts shown in Fig. 6-10. Note that each pin on the integrated circuit has been assigned a symbolic name and that some of these symbolic names have a "bar" drawn over them, for example, $\overline{AS}$, $\overline{UDS}$, $\overline{LDS}$, and $\overline{DTACK}$, while most symbolic names have no bar over them. This convention is intended to distinguish between signals that are active in the low or logic zero state (with a bar) and signals that are active in the high or logic one state (without a bar). To eliminate the logic zero/logic one and high/low confusion, we will hereafter refer to signals as being *asserted* if they are true and *negated* if they are false.

The Data Bus and Address Bus

Like the other microprocessors in this book, the 68000 is a 16-bit microprocessor, which means that the basic unit of information, the word, is 16 bits wide. No more than 16 bits of information can be transferred to and from memory and the input/output (i/o) devices at one time. To transfer more than 16 bits requires additional transfer operations. All information transfers between the 68000 and external devices are conducted on the 16-line data bus (D0–D15).

Which device in the system is to receive the information from, or transmit the information to, the 68000 microprocessor? The microprocessor identifies the appropriate device in a transfer operation by transmitting its address throughout the system over 23 lines (A1–A23) that are collectively known as the *address bus*. Being 23 bits wide, the address bus can select any of 8,388,608 word locations, or 8 megawords. The 68000 microprocessor notifies all system devices that a valid address is on the address bus by asserting the address strobe line ($\overline{AS}$).

Conventional 8-bit microprocessors, like the 8080, 6800, and 6502, have control lines to communicate only with synchronous devices. That is, these microprocessors are designed to interface with external devices which must accept output data, or supply input data, within a specified amount of time. Communicating with slower, asynchronous devices requires special interface hardware and software. The 68000, however, can be interfaced to either synchronous or asynchronous devices, and it has a set of control lines for each type. Let's begin by discussing the *asynchronous control* lines.

68008 Pinout (subset)

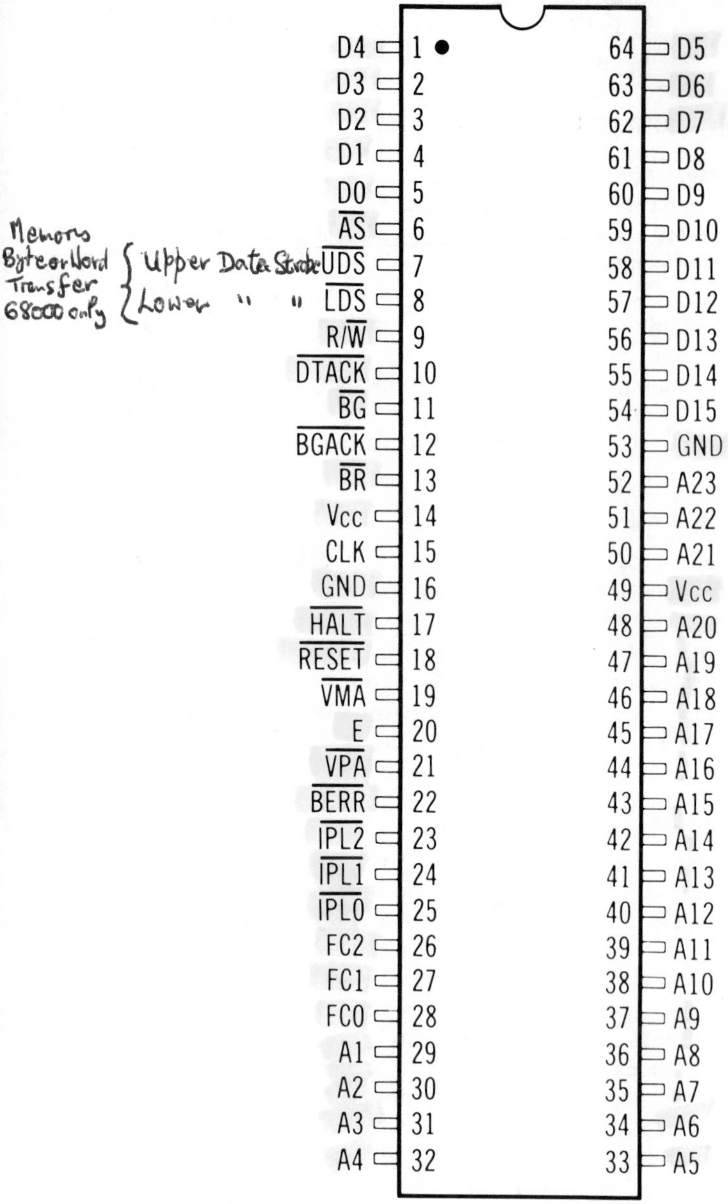

Memors
Byte or Word   { Upper Data Strobe UDS
Transfer   { Lower   "   "   LDS
68000 only

D4	1 ●	64	D5
D3	2	63	D6
D2	3	62	D7
D1	4	61	D8
D0	5	60	D9
$\overline{AS}$	6	59	D10
$\overline{UDS}$	7	58	D11
$\overline{LDS}$	8	57	D12
R/$\overline{W}$	9	56	D13
$\overline{DTACK}$	10	55	D14
$\overline{BG}$	11	54	D15
$\overline{BGACK}$	12	53	GND
$\overline{BR}$	13	52	A23
Vcc	14	51	A22
CLK	15	50	A21
GND	16	49	Vcc
$\overline{HALT}$	17	48	A20
$\overline{RESET}$	18	47	A19
$\overline{VMA}$	19	46	A18
E	20	45	A17
$\overline{VPA}$	21	44	A16
$\overline{BERR}$	22	43	A15
$\overline{IPL2}$	23	42	A14
$\overline{IPL1}$	24	41	A13
$\overline{IPL0}$	25	40	A12
FC2	26	39	A11
FC1	27	38	A10
FC0	28	37	A9
A1	29	36	A8
A2	30	35	A7
A3	31	34	A6
A4	32	33	A5

Courtesy Motorola Semiconductor Products, Inc.
Fig. 6-10. Pinouts of the 68000 microprocessor.

Asynchronous Control Lines

As you will recall, the 68000 can access individual bytes within a word, so we normally refer to this microprocessor's 16-megabyte addressing capability, rather than its 8-megaword addressing capability. How are individual bytes addressed? They are addressed by the state of two control lines: upper data strobe ($\overline{\text{UDS}}$) and lower data strobe ($\overline{\text{LDS}}$). When $\overline{\text{UDS}}$ is asserted (i.e., low) information is transferred on the high-order eight lines of the data bus, D8 through D15. When $\overline{\text{LDS}}$ is asserted, information is transferred on the low-order eight lines of the data bus, D0 through D7. During word length transfer operations, both strobe lines, $\overline{\text{UDS}}$ and $\overline{\text{LDS}}$, are asserted, and information is transferred on all 16 data bus lines, D0 through D15.

How can an addressed external device know whether the 68000 wants to input (read) information from it or output (write) information to it? The external device knows this by sensing the state of a read/write control line (R/W), which is high (logic one) during a read cycle and low (logic zero) during a write cycle. Once an external device either has placed data on the data bus, for a read operation, or has gated data off the data bus during a write operation, the device notifies the 68000 by asserting the data transfer acknowledge ($\overline{\text{DTACK}}$) line. When the processor senses $\overline{\text{DTACK}}$ during a read cycle, it latches the data and then terminates the bus cycle. When the processor senses $\overline{\text{DTACK}}$ during a write cycle, it simply terminates the bus cycle. Because bus termination hinges on reception of $\overline{\text{DTACK}}$, the speed of the 68000 depends on the speed of the

Table 6-14. Function Code Lines Inform External Devices of the Operating State of the 68000

Function Code Output			
FC2	FC1	FC0	Reference Class
0	0	0	(Unassigned)
0	0	1	User Data
0	1	0	User Program
0	1	1	(Unassigned)
1	0	0	(Unassigned)
1	0	1	Supervisor Data
1	1	0	Supervisor Program
1	1	1	Interrupt Acknowledge

Courtesy Motorola Semiconductor Products, Inc.

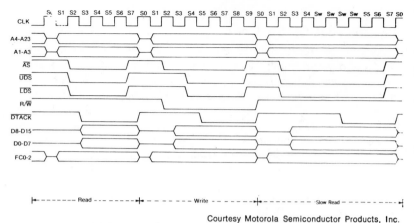

Courtesy Motorola Semiconductor Products, Inc.
Fig. 6-11. Timing for a word read and write cycle.

device being accessed. That is, *the 68000 slows down for devices having longer access times, and speeds up for devices having shorter access times!*

Function Code Lines

For both synchronous and asynchronous transfer operations, the 68000 accompanies the address bus information with "qualitative" information on three function code lines (FC0, FC1, and FC2). The function code lines tell external devices whether user data, a user program, supervisor data, or a supervisor program is being addressed. The function code lines (Table 6-14) can be externally decoded and used to extend the address space of the 68000 to four 16-megabyte segments, for a total of *64 megabytes*. The function code lines may also be used by an external device (such as a memory-management unit) to ensure that certain operations are conducted in the correct microprocessor state.

Timing for Asynchronous Data Transfers

Before moving on to a discussion of the synchronous bus control lines, we should look at how the asynchronous bus control signals interact during data transfer operations. Fig. 6-11 shows the timing of these signals during normal word-length read and write cycles, and during a "slow" (delayed $\overline{DTACK}$) read cycle. These waveforms are referenced to the 68000 input clock signal, CLK. With an 8-MHz input, CLK has a period of 125 nanoseconds and changes state every 62.5 nanoseconds. A normal (undelayed) read cycle lasts four CLK cycles, or 500 ns, at 8 MHz. Due to internal propagation delays and the need for driving R/$\overline{W}$ low, a normal (undelayed) write cycle takes one additional CLK cycle, for a total of 625 ns at

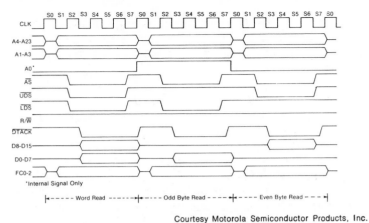

Fig. 6-12. Timing for a word and byte read cycle.

8 MHz. The 68000 expects to receive $\overline{\text{DTACK}}$ after AS, but before state 5 (read) or state 7 (write). If $\overline{\text{DTACK}}$ is not received before this machine state, the 68000 will automatically insert "wait" states into the read or write cycle. The righthand portion of Fig. 6-11 shows how wait states are induced in a read cycle.

Fig. 6-12 shows the timing waveforms for word, odd-byte, and even-byte read cycles, with one additional signal that was not included in Fig. 6-11. This signal, A0, is an internal signal that is derived from the least significant bit of the address bus. For a byte transfer, if A0 is a logic one, only the lower data strobe ($\overline{\text{LDS}}$) signal will be asserted, and the data byte will be gated onto data bus lines D0 through D7. Conversely, if A0 is a logic zero, only the up-

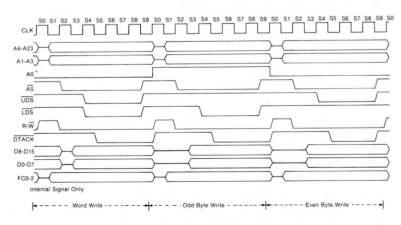

Fig. 6-13. Timing for a word and byte write cycle.

per data strobe (UDS) signal will be asserted, and the data byte will be gated onto data bus lines D8 through D15. Fig. 6-13 shows the comparable timing waveforms for word, odd-byte, and even-byte write cycles.

Synchronous Control Lines

The 68000 has three control lines that can be used to interface the microprocessor with synchronous peripheral devices, such as the devices that Motorola offers in its MC6800 family. The synchronous bus control lines that the 68000 generates are: enable (E), valid peripheral address ($\overline{\text{VPA}}$), and valid memory address ($\overline{\text{VMA}}$).

The enable (E) line carries the bus clock with which 6800 peripherals synchronize data transfers. This free-running clock corresponds to E or $\phi 2$ in existing 6800 systems. The E clock is output with a frequency that is one-tenth of the 68000 input clock, CLK, so in an 8-MHz 68000 system, E has a frequency of 800 KHz. Further, E has a 40/60 duty cycle; it is high for four CLK cycles, then is low for six CLK cycles.

Valid peripheral address ($\overline{\text{VPA}}$) is an input line which notifies the 68000 that a 6800 device is being addressed, and therefore data transfer should be synchronized with the enable (E) clock. As you can see, $\overline{\text{VPA}}$ is the synchronous bus' equivalent of $\overline{\text{DTACK}}$. The 68000 responds to $\overline{\text{VPA}}$ by asserting valid memory address ($\overline{\text{VMA}}$), which is used by attached 6800 peripherals to generate the proper chip select. Fig. 6-14 shows the timing relationships between the 68000 microprocessor and attached 6800 peripherals.

Bus Arbitration and System Control Lines

The bus arbitration lines, $\overline{\text{BR}}$, $\overline{\text{BG}}$ and $\overline{\text{BGACK}}$, are used by direct memory access (DMA) and microprocessor systems to gain control of the microprocessor's buses. The system control lines, $\overline{\text{RESET}}$, $\overline{\text{BERR}}$ and $\overline{\text{HALT}}$, are used to control the 68000 or indicate its state. The $\overline{\text{RESET}}$ and $\overline{\text{HALT}}$ lines are bidirectional, so they can either be used to reset or halt the microprocessor or be used to indicate that the microprocessor is being reset or has halted.

Interrupt Control Lines

The three interrupt control lines, $\overline{\text{IPL0}}$, $\overline{\text{IPL1}}$, and $\overline{\text{IPL2}}$, input the encoded priority level of an active interrupt request to the 68000 microprocessor. If the level reflected in these bits is higher than the interrupt mask value in the status register (Fig. 6-4 and accompanying text), the 68000 will call an associated interrupt service routine through a special vector in memory. Vectoring will be discussed in the "Exception Processing" portion of this chapter.

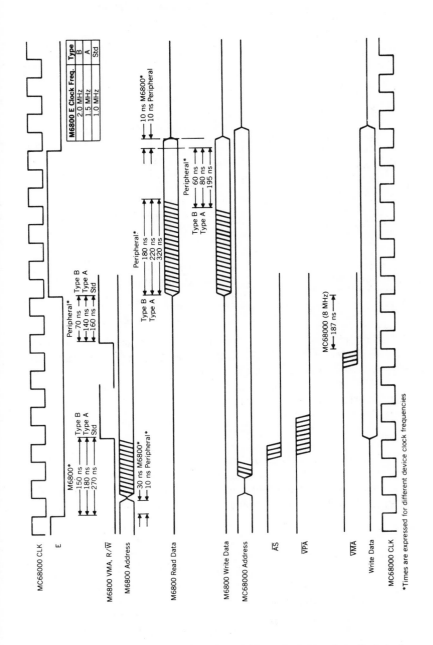

Fig. 6-14. 68000 to 6800 peripheral timing diagram.

263

Table 6-15. Software Sources for the 68000

Supplier	Products
Boston Systems Office 469 Moody Street Waltham, MA 02154	Cross librarian, cross linkage editor and simulator/debugger to run on PDP-11
Creative Solutions, Inc. 4801 Randolph Road Rockville, MD 20852	Forth language package to run on Motorola MEX68KDM design module
Hemenway Associates, Inc. 101 Tremont St., Suite 208 Boston, MA 02108	Floating-point math package, Pascal/I compiler
Telesoft 10639 Roselle St. San Diego, CA 92121	Pascal and Ada compilers, translators
System-Kontakt, Inc. 6 Preston Court Bedford, MA 01730	Cross-assembler, Pascal compiler to run on PDP-11
Whitesmith's Ltd. P.O. Box 1132 Ansonia Station New York, NY 10023	C and Pascal compilers to run under UNIX/V32, VERSAdos and other operating systems

MICROCOMPUTER SOFTWARE

Table 6-15 lists some suppliers who have announced software support products for the 68000. Note that most of these products are designed around Pascal, which perhaps indicates not only the ever-growing popularity of this language, but the adaptability of the 68000 to structured languages in general.

BENCHMARKS

This section presents some "real" programs for the 68000 microprocessor—the four benchmarks that are defined in the appendix and applied to the other microprocessors in this book. The benchmarks perform these tasks: (1) bubble sorting a list of values in memory,

```
*    THIS ROUTINE STORES A 600-WORD LIST IN MEMORY, STARTING AT
*    LOCATION $500.  THE 600 WORDS HAVE THE VALUES 599 THROUGH
*    0, RESPECTIVELY.  THE ROUTINE ALSO STORES THE LIST'S STARTING
*    ADDRESS IN LOCATIONS $400 (HIGH ADDRESS) AND $402 (LOW ADDRESS)
*    AND THE WORD COUNT MINUS ONE IN LOCATION $404.
*
ISORT   LEA      $500,A0       LOAD LIST ADDR INTO A0
        MOVE.L   A0,$400       AND STORE IT AT $400
        MOVE     #599,D0       LOAD FIRST WORD INTO D0
        MOVE     D0,$404       AND STORE IT AT $404
LOOP    MOVE     D0,(A0)+      ENTER WORD IN LIST
        DBEQ     D0,LOOP       AND LOOP UNTIL DONE
```

Fig. 6-15. Initialization routine for 68000 bubble sort benchmark.

```
*   THIS PROGRAM ARRANGES THE 16-BIT ELEMENTS OF A LIST IN
*   ASCENDING ORDER, USING BUBBLE SORT.  THE STARTING ADDRESS
*   OF THE LIST IS IN LOCATIONS $400 (HIGH ADDRESS) AND $402
*   (LOW ADDRESS).  THE WORD COUNT MINUS ONE IS IN LOCATION $404.
*   REGISTERS USED:  A0, A1, D0, D1, D2 AND D3.
*
SORT      MOVEA.L   $400,A1        LOAD START ADDR INTO A1
          MOVE      $404,D3        AND WORD COUNT INTO D3
          CLR.B     D1             EXCHANGE FLAG = $00
INIT      MOVEA.L   A1,A0          COPY START ADDR INTO A0
          MOVE      D3,D0          AND WORD COUNT INTO D0
COMP      MOVE      (A0)+,D2       FETCH WORD INTO D2
          CMP       (A0),D2        NEXT WORD GT. THIS ONE?
          BLS.S     DECCNT         YES. CONTINUE
          MOVE      (A0),-2(A0)    NO. EXCHANGE THESE
          MOVE      D2,(A0)         TWO WORDS
          TAS       D1             TURN EXCHANGE FLAG ON
DECCNT    DBF       D0,COMP        DEC. WORD COUNT.  DONE?
          NOT.B     D1             YES. IS EXCHANGE FLAG ON?
          BPL.S     INIT           IF SO, START OVER
DONE      .                        OTHERWISE, EXIT
          .
```

Fig. 6-16. 68000 bubble sort benchmark.

(2) searching an ASCII string, (3) finding the square root of a number, and (4) deriving the sine of an angle using a lookup table.

Bubble Sort

The bubble sort benchmark arranges a 600-word list in memory in increasing order. To provide a "worst case" the words in the list are initially in decreasing order, with the value 599_{10} at the beginning of the list and the value 0 at the end of the list. Fig. 6-15 contains a 68000 program that can be used to enter the unsorted list into memory and to store the starting address and word count at locations $400/$402 and $404, respectively. This initialization sequence employs a two-instruction LOOP to store the list values in memory. The loop is terminated with the instruction DBEQ D0, LOOP, which causes LOOP to be executed repeatedly, until word counter D0 has been decremented to zero. The ISORT routine occupies 11 words in memory and takes 12,655 cycles, or 1581.8 μs, to execute.

Fig. 6-16 presents the bubble sort benchmark as a program labeled SORT. This program loads the list's starting address and word count into A1 and D3, respectively, and then clears the low-order byte of data register D1 to zero. This byte functions as an *exchange flag,* which will indicate whether or not any elements in the list have been exchanged during a sorting pass through the list; $00 indicates no exchange, and $80 indicates that an exchange occurred.

The remainder of the SORT program is comprised of two programming loops: an outer loop and an inner loop. The outer loop extends from the INIT label to the final instruction, BPL.S INIT. This loop will be executed once for each value in the list and will cause one value to "bubble up" to its final location. The outer loop begins with two **MOVE** instructions, which copy the list's starting address and word count into registers A0 and D0, respectively. The outer loop ends with two instructions that check whether the exchange flag has been set during the sort operation, with a branch back to INIT if it has been set.

The inner loop extends from the COMP label to the DECCNT label. This loop will also be executed once for each value in the list and will actually perform the required exchange operations. The inner loop begins by loading a word from the list into D2. Address register indirect with postincrement addressing is used to perform the fetch, so that A0 will automatically point to the next word in the list. The word in D2 is then compared with the next word in the list. If these words are not already in increasing order, two **MOVE** instructions exchange their positions in memory, and the instruction TAS D1 sets bit 7 of D1 to 1. The final instruction in the loop (DBF D0, COMP) decrements the word count and branches back to the beginning of the loop (at COMP) if the word count is not yet −1. The SORT program occupies 18 words in memory, and takes 16,134,684 cycles, or 2.0168 s, to execute for our "worst case" list.

Incidentally, you will note that on completion of each sorting pass in which an exchange occurred, the instruction BPL.S INIT causes program execution to branch back to INIT, to reinitialize the starting address and word count. Because D0 receives the original word count (599, for our example), each sorting pass will include compare operations on the *entire* list. Since previously sorted (or "bubbled up") values at the end of the list need not be included in the compare operations, the algorithm could be made more efficient by loading a decremented word count into D0 following each sorting pass. This improvement could be made quite easily by decrementing data register D3 before returning to begin a new pass.

ASCII String Search

This benchmark involves determining whether or not a short ASCII string (the "test" string) is included in a longer ASCII string (the "main" string) in memory. For benchmark purposes, we will be

```
ISERCH  MOVE.L    #$500,$400    STORE MAIN ADDR AT $400
        MOVE.L    #$600,$404    AND TEST ADDR AT $404
*   THE STRING TABLES FOLLOW
        ORG       $500
MSTRNG  DC.B      'NANO*'
        DC.B      'PICO*'
        DC.B      'MICROCOMPUTER*'
        DC.B      'MICROPROCESSOR*'
        DC.B      'MICROSYSTEM*'
        DC.B      'MICRO*?'
        ORG       $600
TSTRNG  DC.B      'MICRO*'
```

Fig. 6-17. Initialization routine for 68000 ASCII string search benchmark.

searching for the test string MICRO* in the main string

NANO*PICO*MICROCOMPUTER*MICROPROCESSOR*
MICROSYSTEM*MICRO*?

Fig. 6-17 contains the initialization instructions for this benchmark. It consists of just two LEA instructions and a series of assembler byte-length Define Constant (DC.B) directives.

Fig. 6-18 is the ASCII string search benchmark, a program labeled SEARCH. After initializing address registers A0 and A1 with the starting addresses of the main string and test string, the 68000 loads the first character in the main string into data register D0. The load

```
*   THIS PROGRAM SEARCHES AN ASCII STRING IN MEMORY, CALLED THE
*   "MAIN STRING," FOR THE PRESENCE OF ANOTHER ASCII STRING,
*   CALLED THE "TEST STRING."  WORDS IN THE MAIN STRING ARE
*   TERMINATED BY ASCII ASTERISK (*) CHARACTERS, AS IS THE
*   TEST STRING, AND THE MAIN STRING IS TERMINATED BY AN ASCII
*   QUESTION MARK (?) CHARACTER.
*   THE STARTING ADDRESS OF THE MAIN STRING IS IN LOCATIONS
*   $400 AND $402.  THE STARTING ADDRESS OF THE TEST STRING IS
*   IN LOCATIONS $404 AND $406.  THE LOWER-ADDRESSED LOCATION
*   CONTAINS THE HIGH-ORDER HALF OF THE ADDRESS IN BOTH CASES.
*   ADDRESS REGISTER A0 WILL REFLECT THE RESULT.  IF THE SEARCH
*   WAS SUCCESSFUL, A0 WILL HOLD THE ADDRESS OF MATCHING WORD'S
*   ASTERISK TERMINATOR.  IF THE SEARCH WAS UNSUCCESSFUL, A0
*   WILL HOLD THE ADDRESS OF THE MAIN STRING'S QUESTION MARK
*   TERMINATOR.
*   REGISTERS USED:  A0, A1 AND D0.
*
SEARCH  MOVEA.L   $400,A0        LOAD MAIN STRING ADDR INTO A0
MADDR   MOVEA.L   $404,A1        LOAD TEST STRING ADDR INTO A1
MCHAR   MOVE.B    (A0)+,D0        AND MAIN STRING CHAR INTO D0
        CMPI.B    #'?',D0        LAST CHARACTER?
        BEQ.S     DONE           YES.  EXIT
        CMP.B     (A1),D0        NO.  TEST CHAR = MAIN CHAR?
        BEQ.S     MAYBE          YES.  GO DO NEXT COMPARE
NOCMP   CMPI.B    #'*',(A0)+     END OF WORD IN MAIN STRING?
        BEQ.S     MCHAR          YES.  GO GET NEXT MAIN CHAR
        BRA.S     NOCMP          NO.  WAIT FOR * CHAR
MAYBE   ADDQ.L    #1,A1          INC.  TEST STRING ADDR
        CMPI.B    #'*',(A1)      END OF TEST STRING?
        BNE.S     MCHAR          NO.  GO GET NEXT MAIN CHAR
        CMPI.B    #'*',(A0)      YES.  ARE THE CHARS EQUAL?
        BNE.S     MADDR          NO.  GO RESTART SEARCH
DONE    .                        YES.  EXIT
        .
```

Fig. 6-18. 68000 ASCII string search benchmark.

operation is performed with address register indirect with postincrement addressing, so that A0 will subsequently point to the next character in the main string. If the character in D0 is not the main string terminator (ASCII ?), the first characters in the two strings are compared. If they match, program execution branches to label MAYBE, where the comparison process continues for subsequent characters in the main and test strings.

```
*   THIS PROGRAM USES A SUCCESSIVE APPROXIMATION ALGORITHM TO
*   CALCULATE THE SQUARE ROOT OF THE NUMBER CONTAINED IN LOCA-
*   TION $400.  THE SQUARE ROOT IS RETURNED IN LOCATION $402.
*   REGISTERS USED:  A0, D0, D1 AND D2
*
SQRT    CLR.L   D0              CLEAR DATA REGISTER D0
        LEA     $402,A0         A0 POINTS TO RESULT LOCATION
        MOVE    $400,D0         LOAD DATA VALUE INTO D0
        MOVE.L  D0,D2            AND D2
        DIVU    #200,D0         DIVIDE IT BY 200,
        ADD     #2,D0            THEN ADD 2
NEXT    MOVE.L  D2,D1           LOAD DATA VALUE INTO D1
        DIVU    D0,D1           DIVIDE IT BY LAST APPROX
        MOVE    D1,(A0)         STORE QUOTIENT AT $402,
        MULU    D1,D1            THEN SQUARE IT
        CMP     D1,D2           RESULT = ORIGINAL VALUE?
        BEQ.S   DONE            YES.  EXIT
        ADD     (A0),D0         NO.  SUM LAST TWO APPROXS
        LSR     #1,D0            AND DIVIDE BY 2
        BRA.S   NEXT            RETURN FOR NEXT APPROX
DONE    .
        .
        .
```

Fig. 6-19. 68000 square root benchmark.

Beginning at label MAYBE the program compares each character in the test string to its corresponding character in the main string. If all the characters in the test string match a portion of the main string, the compare instruction CMPI.B #'*',(A0) checks whether the main string character is an asterisk corresponding to the test string's asterisk. If the strings have corresponding asterisks, the search is finished, with success. If, however, the main string matches all test string characters *except* the asterisk terminator, program execution branches to label MADDR to continue the search process; this prevents a test string such as MICRO* being identified with a main string word such as MICROCOMPUTER*.

One interesting aspect of the SEARCH program is found at the three instructions that form the NOCMP loop. If a nonmatch is encountered during the search, this loop causes the remaining characters in that main string word to be skipped, and the search is resumed at the next main string word. The SEARCH program occupies 21 words in memory and takes 3392 cycles, or 424 μs, to execute for our example strings. This includes the time to execute the ISERCH initialization routine.

Square Root

This benchmark calculates the square root of a 16-bit binary integer, using a successive approximation algorithm. Fig. 6-19 shows the 68000 program for this benchmark. The program is relatively straightforward; you should have no problem following it if you understand the benchmark flowchart in Appendix A. Note that the program uses data register D2 to save the data value and employs address register A0 to access result location $402. This was done to take advantage of the fact that data register direct addressing and address register indirect addressing execute much faster than absolute addressing. The SQRT program occupies 18 words in memory. It takes 708 cycles, or 88.5 μs, to calculate the square root of the integer 58,081 or 16,384. Further, it takes 969 cycles, or 121 μs, to calculate the square root of the integer 10,000.

Lookup Table

This final benchmark finds the sine of an angle, to the nearest degree, from a lookup table in memory. The benchmark is required to accept angles from 0 degrees to 360 degrees, and to return the sine as an 8-bit sign-and-magnitude number.

Fig. 6-20 shows the 68000 benchmark program (SINANG) and its lookup table (SINTAB). This program takes its angle from the low-order word of data register D0, and returns the signed sine in the low-order byte of data register D1. After clearing the low-order byte of D1 (the sign is in bit 7 of D1), the 68000 checks whether the angle is less than 180. If it is, program execution branches to label SINPOS; otherwise, the 68000 sets the sign bit (sines above 180 degrees are negative) and subtracts 180 from the angle. With the sign bit now properly configured in D1, the CMPI instruction at label SINPOS compares the angle in D0 to 91 degrees. If the angle is greater than or equal to 91 degrees, its value must be subtracted

```
*    THIS PROGRAM CALCULATES THE SINE OF THE BINARY ANGLE
*    CONTAINED IN DATA REGISTER D0 (0 TO 360 DEGREES), USING
*    A LOOK-UP TABLE.  THE SIGNED SINE IS RETURNED IN THE
*    LOW-ORDER BYTE OF DATA REGISTER D1.
*    REGISTERS USED: A0, D0 AND D1.
*
SINANG    CLR.B     D1              INTIALIZE SIGN BIT TO 0
          CMPI      #180,D0         ANGLE LESS THAN 180 DEGS?
          BLS.S     SINPOS          YES.  CONTINUE WITH SIGN = 0
          TAS       D1              NO.  SET SIGN BIT = 1
          SUBI      #180,D0         SUBTRACT 180 DEGS FROM ANGLE
SINPOS    CMPI      #91,D0          ANGLE LESS THAN 91 DEGS?
          BMI.S     GETSIN          YES.  GO LOOK UP SINE
          NEG       D0              NO.  SUBTRACT ANGLE FROM 180
          ADDI      #180,D0
GETSIN    LEA       SINTAB,A0       LOAD TABLE ADDRESS INTO A0
          OR.B      0(A0,D0),D1     LOOK UP SINE, ADD SIGN BIT
*
*    THE SINE LOOK-UP TABLE FOLLOWS
SINTAB    DC.B      0               0 DEGREES
          DC.B      2               1 DEGREE
          DC.B      4               2 DEGREES
             •
             •                      (Remainder of the look-up
             •                       table is stored here)
          DC.B      127             90 DEGREES
```

Fig. 6-20. 68000 lookup table benchmark.

from 180. The simplest way to perform this subtraction would be with the instruction SUBI D0,#180, but the 68000 does not support this form of the SUBI instruction (only the form SUBI #data,Dn is legal), so we make the subtraction by twos complementing D0, then adding 180 to the result. The last two instructions load the table address into A0, and then look up the sine, using address register indirect with index addressing, and combine it with the sign bit, the latter operation with a single OR instruction!

The SINANG program occupies 18 words in memory. Its execution time will vary, depending on the quadrant of the lookup angle:

- For angles between 0 and 90 degrees, SINANG will execute in 62 cycles, or 7.75 μs.
- For angles between 91 and 270 degrees, SINANG will execute in 72 cycles, or 9.00 μs.
- For angles between 271 and 360 degrees, SINANG will execute in 82 cycles, or 10.25 μs.

INTERFACING

Previous portions of this chapter have described the signal lines with which external devices can be connected to the 68000 integrated circuit to form a microcomputer system. We studied the timing relationships between these signals, and observed how the 68000 can communicate with 16-bit asynchronous devices and 8-bit synchronous devices via separate control signals on the microprocessor's integrated circuit. Until now, however, the chapter has contained no information on the devices that can be physically connected, or *interfaced,* to the 68000.

For the sake of simplicity, the discussion will be limited to one of the most commonly used (and simplest) circuits in the 6800 family (Table 6-16), the 6821 peripheral interface adapter (PIA). This circuit will be interfaced to the 68000 using the synchronous bus.

The 6821 Peripheral Interface Adapter (PIA)

The 6821 PIA provides all of the necessary circuitry to interface the 6800 or the 68000, to a printer, display, keyboard, bank of switches, or a variety of other peripheral devices. The PIA communicates with the microprocessor on the system buses (data, address, and control), and it communicates with attached peripherals via two 8-bit ports, called port A and port B. Each of the 16 lines that comprise the two ports can be independently programmed, at system initialization time, to function as either an input line or an output line.

Within the PIA, each bidirectional port (port A and port B) is supported by:

Table 6-16. Available 6800 Peripheral Circuits

Part No.	Description
MC6821	Peripheral interface adapter (PIA)
MC6840	Programmable timer module (PTM)
MC6843	Floppy disk controller (FDC)
MC6845	Crt controller (CRTC)
MC6847	Video display generator (VDG)
MC6850	Asynchronous communications interface adapter (ACIA)
MC6852	Synchronous serial data adapter (SSDA)
MC6854	Advanced data link controller (ADLC)
MC6859	Data security device
MC6860	0- to 600-bps digital modem
MC6862	2400-bps modulator
MC68488	IEEE-488 Bus interface adapter (GPIA)

- A *data direction register.* Each bit of the data direction register determines whether its corresponding port line shall function as an input (0) or an output (1).
- A *control register* that holds the interrupt status flags of the port, and selects internal logic connections within the PIA.
- A *peripheral data register* that holds data being transferred between the microprocessor and an attached peripheral.
- Two *interrupt control lines* that are configured by the contents of the control register.

Six registers within the PIA are addressable: two peripheral registers, two data direction registers, and two control registers. Each peripheral register "shares" a byte location in memory with a data direction register, however, so a PIA will respond to four, rather than six, memory addresses. Readers unfamiliar with this or other characteristics of the 6821 PIA are referred to the PIA data sheet in *The Complete Motorola Microcomputer Data Library* (Reference No. 5).

Like all 8-bit devices the 6821 PIA is designed to transfer information 8 bits at a time. Transferring more than 8 bits will require additional transfer operations, if you have only one PIA. Since the 68000 has a 16-bit data bus, this microprocessor is designed to transfer information 16 bits at a time. *We can employ the PIA for 16-bit transfers by simply connecting two of these devices in parallel,* one to transfer the high-order 8 bits and the other to transfer the low-order 8 bits.

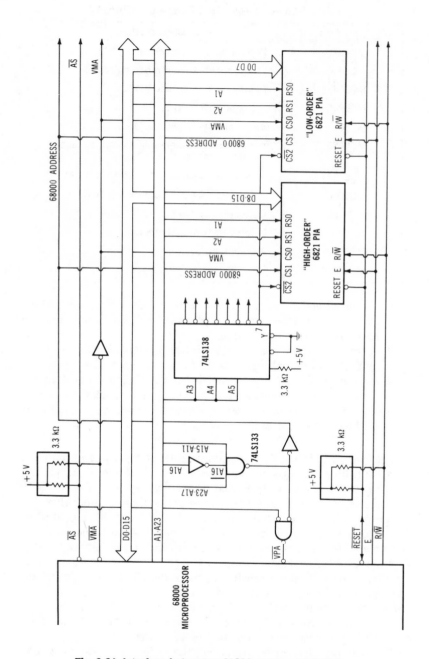

Fig. 6-21. Interface between a 68000 and two 6821 PIAs.

Fig. 6-22. PIA registers in memory.

	HIGH-ORDER PIA	LOW-ORDER PIA	
$FEFF00	PRA/DDRA	PRA/DDRA	$FEFF01
$FEFF02	CRA	CRA	$FEFF03
$FEFF04	PRB/DDRB	PRB/DDRB	$FEFF05
$FEFF06	CRB	CRB	$FEFF07

An Interface to Transfer 16-Bit Data

Fig. 6-21 shows how two 6821 PIAs can be interfaced to the 68000's synchronous control lines, to transfer 16 bits of data at a time. Note that in this particular system, 6800 peripheral devices are assumed to reside within the addressing range $FEF800 through $FEFFFF, because valid peripheral address ($\overline{VPA}$) will be asserted only if address strobe ($\overline{AS}$) and the output of the 13-input NAND gate (74LS133) are asserted. Furthermore, observe that the PIAs shown in Fig. 6-21 are selected when address lines A3, A4, and A5 are all asserted. Therefore these particular devices will respond to addresses in the range $FEF838 to $FEFFFF. Two other address lines, A1 and A2, are also connected to these PIAs. They are used to select the internal registers, as in Table 6-17.

Since each PIA occupies 4 bytes in memory, the two PIAs in Fig. 6-21 will occupy 8 bytes (four words), 4 even-numbered bytes for the "high-order" PIA and 4 odd-numbered bytes for the "low-order" PIA. Let us assume that our PIAs occupy addresses $FEFF00 through $FEFF07, as shown in Fig. 6-22.

Some Simple 16-Bit Transfers Using PIAs

For illustration purposes, assume that the PIAs in Fig. 6-21 are connected to two 16-bit peripherals. The peripheral connected to port A of both PIAs is an input-only device (perhaps a bank of switches, see Fig. 6-23). When this device has placed a word of input data on the ports' data lines (PA0–PA7), it notifies the 68000 by asserting the *data ready* signal (pin CA1) of the high-order PIA. After reading the word into memory, the 68000 informs the peripheral that the word has been read by asserting the *data taken* signal on pin CA2 of the high-order PIA.

The peripheral connected to port B of both PIAs is an output-only device (perhaps a group of LEDs, see Fig. 6-23). When the peripheral is prepared to accept a word of data, it notifies the 68000 by asserting the *peripheral ready* signal (pin CB1) of the high-order PIA. The 68000 then outputs a data word to the ports' data lines (PB0–PB7), and notifies the peripheral that it has done so by asserting the *output ready* signal (pin CB2) of the high-order PIA.

Table 6-17. Use of A1 and A2 to Select PIA Registers

A2	A1	Register Selected
0	0	PRA/DDRA
0	1	CRA
1	0	PRB/DDRB
1	1	CRB

In order for a PIA to communicate with its attached peripheral devices, it must be *programmed* to do so. PIAs will be configured at system initialization time as part of the power-up reset sequence. Fig. 6-24 is an initialization routine for the two PIAs that are under discussion. This routine assigns port A of both devices as input ports, and port B of both devices as output ports. It also sets up the hand-shaking signals on the high-order PIA. Note that Fig. 6-24 employs assembler equate directives (EQU) to assign the symbols PIAD, PIAC, PIBD, and PIBC to the high-order PIA's four byte locations in memory.

Once the PIAs have been configured, transferring information to and from their attached peripherals is relatively simple. To transfer a single 16-bit word to the output peripheral, for example, involves

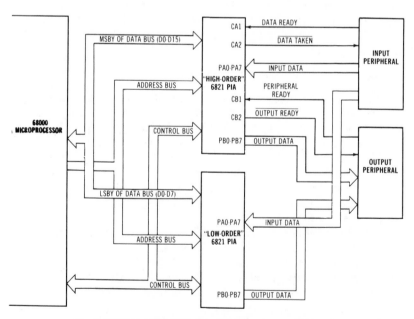

Fig. 6-23. Two 6821 PIAs interfaced to two peripherals.

```
PIAD    EQU     $FEFF00             ADDRESS OF PRA/DDRA.
PIAC    EQU     $FEFF02             ADDRESS OF CRA.
PIBD    EQU     $FEFF04             ADDRESS OF PRB/DDRB.
PIBC    EQU     $FEFF06             ADDRESS OF CRB.
* CONFIGURE THE HIGH-ORDER PIA
        CLR.B   PIAD                MAKE PORT A INPUTS,
        MOVE.B  #%00100110,PIAC     AND ENABLE HANDSHAKING.
        MOVE.B  #$FF,PIBD           MAKE PORT B OUTPUTS,
        MOVE.B  #%00100110,PIBC     AND ENABLE HANDSHAKING.
* CONFIGURE THE LOW-ORDER PIA
        CLR.B   PIAD+1              MAKE PORT A INPUTS,
        MOVE.B  #%00000100,PIAC+1   AND SELECT PRA.
        MOVE.B  #$FF,PIBD+1         MAKE PORT B OUTPUTS,
        MOVE.B  #%00000100,PIBC+1   AND SELECT PRB.
```
Fig. 6-24. Initialization routine for two PIAs.

```
* OUTPUT THE WORD CONTAINED IN DATA REGISTER D0
OUTW    TST.B   PIBC                PERIPHERAL READY?
        BPL.S   OUTW                WAIT UNTIL IT IS,
        MOVE    D0,PIBD             THEN OUTPUT THE WORD
        MOVE    PIBD,PIBD           CLEAR PERIPHERAL READY
```

Fig. 6-25. Writing a 16-bit word to a peripheral.

```
* OUTPUT THE WORD CONTAINED IN DATA REGISTER D0 CONTINUOUSLY,
* INCREMENTING IT AFTER EACH TRANSFER OPERATION
OUTD0   TST.B   PIBC                PERIPHERAL READY?
        BPL.S   OUTD0               WAIT UNTIL IT IS,
        MOVE    D0,PIBD             THEN OUTPUT ONE WORD.
        ADDQ    #1,D0               INCREMENT D0.
        MOVE    PIBD,PIBD           CLEAR PERIPHERAL READY
        BRA.S   OUTD0               AND START AGAIN.
```

Fig. 6-26. Incrementing a 16-bit word and writing it to a peripheral continuously.

waiting for the peripheral ready line to be asserted, then moving the data word to the PIAs' peripheral register B. This sequence is shown in Fig. 6-25, in which the output word is contained in the low-order 16 bits of data register D0. The instruction MOVE, PIBD,PIBD at the end of the program simply performs the read operation needed to clear the "peripheral ready" flag in bit 7 of the control register.

Transferring multiple words to the output peripheral is nearly as easy as transferring just one word, as you can see by examining Fig. 6-26. This program writes the contents of D0 out to the output peripheral continuously, incrementing the word in D0 after each transfer operation.

The program in Fig. 6-27 contains a typical input transfer operation, in which 35 words are read into consecutive memory locations. Address register indirect with postincrement addressing is used in the transfer instruction, so that the address is automatically updated to point to the next location in memory. Note that counter D0 is initialized with a value of 34, rather than 35, because the terminating instruction (DBF D0,IN35) will allow program control to "fall through" the loop when D0 has been decremented to −1, rather than 0.

```
* READ 35 WORDS INTO MEMORY, STARTING AT THE LOCATION BEING
* POINTED TO BY ADDRESS REGISTER A0.
        MOVE.L    #34,D0          SET UP COUNTER D0.
IN35    TST.B     PIAC            DATA READY?
        BPL.S     IN35            WAIT UNTIL IT IS AND
        MOVE      PIAD,(A0)+        THEN INPUT WORD.
        DBF       D0,IN35         LOOP UNTIL DONE.
```

Fig. 6-27. Reading data from an input peripheral and storing it in memory.

PROCESSING STATES

The 68000 microprocessor is always in one of three processing states: normal, halted, or exception. In the normal state the microprocessor fetches instructions from memory and executes them. In order to enter the halted state, hardware errors or problems have to occur. In the exception state the processor performs special tasks in order to service interrupts, traps, and other exceptional conditions.

Exception Processing

A number of internal and external events will cause the 68000 to enter the exception processing state. The *internal* events which will initiate exception processing are these: (1) executing a TRAP instruction; (2) executing a TRAPV instruction with the overflow (V) condition code flag set to 1; (3) executing a CHK instruction with registers out of bounds; (4) attempting to divide by zero with a DIVS or DIVU instruction; (5) addressing error; (6) attempting to execute an illegal instruction; (7) executing an unimplemented instruction; (8) executing a privileged instruction, such as STOP or RESET, from the user state; or (9) operating the 68000 in the trace mode. Note that an unimplemented instruction (condition 7) is not necessarily an illegal instruction (condition 6). An illegal instruction is one in which the bit pattern of the op word is not one of the legal (implemented) combinations. Word patterns with bits 15 through 12 equaling 1010 or 1111 are distinguished as unimplemented instructions. Use these word patterns at your own risk. They are reserved by Motorola for future instructions.

Three types of *external* events can also initiate exception processing. They are: (1) interrupts, (2) bus error, and (3) reset.

How Exception Processing Works

Regardless of the cause of the exception, the 68000 goes through five identifiable steps. In the first step the 68000 saves the contents of the status register in a nonaddressable internal register. Then the system byte's S bit is set to 1, placing the 68000 in the supervisor state, and the trace (T) bit is turned off (reset to 0). If the exception is caused by an interrupt, the interrupt mask in the system byte is updated to the incoming interrupt priority level, to "lock out" same- and lower-priority interrupts until this interrupt is serviced.

In the third step the 68000 determines the *vector number* of the exception, and multiplies this number by 4 to convert it to a *vector address*. The 68000 can recognize 256 separate vector numbers. Table 6-18 summarizes the vector assignments in terms of the vector numbers, their addresses, what privilege space they occupy (supervisor program or supervisor data), and which condition they represent. For interrupts the vector number is obtained from the peripheral generating the interrupt. For all other exceptions the 68000's microcode provides the vector number.

In the next step the current program counter value and the saved copy of the status register are pushed onto the supervisor stack. With this return information saved, the 68000 then loads the pro-

Table 6-18. Exception Vector Assignments

| Vector Number(s) | Address | | | Assignment |
	Dec	Hex	Space	
0	0	000	SP	Reset: initial SSP
	4	004	SP	Reset: initial PC
2	8	008	SD	Bus error
3	12	00C	SD	Address error
4	16	010	SD	Illegal instruction
5	20	014	SD	Zero divide
6	24	018	SD	CHK instruction
7	28	01C	SD	TRAPV instruction
8	32	020	SD	Privilege violation
9	36	024	SD	Trace
10	40	028	SD	Line 1010 emulator
11	44	02C	SD	Line 1111 emulator
12*	48	030	SD	(Unassigned, reserved)
13*	52	034	SD	(Unassigned, reserved)
14*	56	038	SD	(Unassigned, reserved)
15*	60	03C	SD	(Unassigned, reserved)
16–23*	64	040	SD	(Unassigned, reserved)
	95	05F		—
24	96	060	SD	Spurious interrupt
25	100	064	SD	Level 1 interrupt auto-vector
26	104	068	SD	Level 2 interrupt auto-vector
27	108	06C	SD	Level 3 interrupt auto-vector
28	112	070	SD	Level 4 interrupt auto-vector
29	116	074	SD	Level 5 interrupt auto-vector
30	120	078	SD	Level 6 interrupt auto-vector
31	124	07C	SD	Level 7 interrupt auto-vector
32–47	128	080	SD	TRAP instruction vectors
	191	0BF		—
48–63*	192	0C0	SD	(Unassigned, reserved)
	255	0FF		—
64–255	256	100	SD	User interrupt vectors
	1023	3FF		—

*Vector numbers 12 through 23 and 48 through 63 are reserved for future enhancements by Motorola. No user peripheral devices should be assigned these numbers.

Courtesy Motorola Semiconductor Products, Inc.

gram counter from the vector address, and begins executing the exception's service routine.

A detailed description of all of the various exceptions is beyond the scope of this book, but it is instructive to take a closer look at the 68000's interrupt structure.

Interrupt Structure

As we learned early in the chapter, interrupts in a 68000 system are assigned one of seven priority levels. Priorities range from level 0 (no interrupt) to level 7 (highest priority). The system byte of the status register contains a 3-bit *interrupt mask* that is used to specify the priority interrupt levels that the 68000 will acknowledge at any given time. If an incoming interrupt has a priority level equal to or less than the mask value, the 68000 will simply ignore that interrupt; otherwise, the microprocessor will initiate interrupt processing following the current instruction. Level 7 interrupts are always accepted. That is, they are "nonmaskable." For this reason, only the most critical interrupt conditions, such as power failure, are assigned to level 7.

Table 6-19. 68000 Peripheral Circuits

Part No.	Description
68120	Intelligent peripheral controller (IPC)
68122	Cluster terminal controller (CTC)
68540	Error detection and correction circuit (EDCC)
68451	Memory-management unit (MMU)
68450	Direct memory access controller (DMAC)
68230	Parallel interface/timer (PI/T)
68561	Multiprotocol communications controller (MPCC)
68341	Floating-point read-only memory
68340	Dual-port RAM (DPR)
68453	Bubble memory controller
68560	Serial direct memory access processor (SDMA)

Interrupts in a 68000 system may be vectored or nonvectored. That is why you saw two separate sets of interrupt vector assignments in Table 6-18. Vector numbers 25 through 31 contain the vector addresses for seven different nonvectored interrupts; the manufacturers' literature calls them "interrupt auto-vectors." Vector numbers 64 through 255 contain the vector addresses for 192 different vectored interrupts; the manufacturers' literature calls these "user interrupt vectors." Upon receiving a sufficiently high priority interrupt (greater than the mask value) the 68000 issues an interrupt acknowledge on its function control lines (see Table 6-14). The interrupting device must, in turn, identify itself as either a vectored interrupt device or a nonvectored interrupt device, by responding in one of two ways.

Vectored interrupt devices respond to the interrupt acknowledge by placing a vector number between 64 and 255 on the low byte of the data bus (lines D0 through D7) and asserting DTACK. *Nonvectored* interrupt devices are incapable of supplying a vector number during an interrupt sequence, so these devices respond to the 68000's interrupt acknowledge by asserting VPA; the interrupt control lines (IPL0 through IPL2) are used as an "auto-vector" in this case. Recall that we saw DTACK and VPA used earlier in this chapter to distinguish an asynchronous device from a synchronous device. Here, during interrupt processing, these same lines are used to distinguish a vectored interrupt device from a nonvectored interrupt device.

If several nonvectored devices in a system are assigned to a certain interrupt priority level, the service routine for that level must "poll" the attached devices, to find out *which* device generated the interrupt. This requirement causes the software for nonvectored devices to be potentially more complex than the software for vectored devices, because each vectored device transmits a unique vector number to the 68000, and need not be polled unless there are more than 192 vectored devices in the system.

SPECIAL-FUNCTION CHIPS

Table 6-19 lists support chips for the 68000.

The 68120 intelligent peripheral controller (IPC) is a general-purpose, user-programmable input/output controller. Based on an 8-bit 6801 one-chip microcomputer, the IPC is configurable as an i/o preprocessor or as a "slave" processing unit for distributed processing. In addition to the 6801 CPU, the IPC contains a system interface, a serial communications interface, 21 parallel i/o lines, a 16-bit timer, a dual-ported 128-byte read/write memory, 2048 bytes of ROM, and six semaphore registers. The 68122 cluster terminal controller (CTC) is a version of the IPC that is programmed like a serial i/o subsystem. It is used to connect up to 32 terminals to a system.

The 68540 error detection and correction circuit (EDCC) corrects single-bit errors, and detects double-bit errors, in both 8-bit and 16-bit data bus systems. The EDCC is directly expandable to 32 bits for future systems.

The 68451 memory-management unit (MMU) provides address translation and memory protection for the 68000's 16-megabyte address space. An MMU can be used to define multiple segments, as small as 256 bytes, within the address space. For each segment the MMU defines the logical address space—the program and data space for the supervisor or user state. It also specifies an offset to the physical address and the segment's memory protection characteristics. The MMU will generate a bus error exception on any unauthorized access of a segment.

The 68450 direct memory access controller (DMAC) provides four independent DMA channels which can be used to transfer data in words or blocks at up to 4 megabytes per second. This circuit will be produced by Hitachi Ltd.

The 68230 parallel interface/timer (PI/T) is a general-purpose "housekeeping" device used to handle i/o, interrupt, and timing needs. It has three 8-bit i/o ports, a multimode 24-bit programmable timer, and logic circuitry for generating prioritized interrupt vectors.

The 68561 multiprotocol communications controller (MPCC), designed by Rockwell International, is a sophisticated data communications device that will handle asynchronous, bit-oriented synchronous (X.25, SDLC, HDLC), and byte-oriented synchronous (BISYNC) and DDCMP) line protocols.

The 68341 floating-point read-only memory is a prepackaged firmware routine, programmed with position-independent, reentrant 68000 code. The software in this ROM performs the normal arithmetic operations (add, subtract, multiply, and divide) and some related operations (square root, compare, absolute value, and others) in floating-point format.

CONCLUSION

Readers of this chapter will realize by now that the 68000 is much more than a traditional microprocessor. Clearly, it is more like a *minicomputer on a chip!* Programmers will appreciate the high-level-languagelike qualities of the 68000's instruction set, the versatility of its 14 addressing modes, and the ability to process byte, word, or long word information with equal ease. Similarly, system designers will be impressed with the multiuser and multiprocessing capabilities that are built into the microprocessor, as well as its flexible "exception" structure and the ability to communicate directly with both established 8-bit synchronous devices and newer 16-bit asynchronous devices.

The 68000 is not a panacea for all of the computing world's problems, but the design features of this microprocessor represent an important inroad into areas that have heretofore been the exclusive domain of main frame and minicomputers.

REFERENCES

1. Motorola Semiconductor Products, Inc., *MC68000 Advance Information (ADI-814-1), 1980*. Austin, TX, 1980.

2. Motorola Semiconductor Products, Inc., *MC68000 16-Bit Microprocessor User's Manual, January, 1980*. Austin, TX, 1980.

3. Motorola Semiconductor Products, Inc., *MC68000 Cross Macro Assembler Reference Manual, September, 1979*. Phoenix, AZ, 1979.

4. Motorola Semiconductor Products, Inc., *MC68000 Design Module User's Guide, January, 1980*. Phoenix, AZ, 1980.

5. Motorola Semiconductor Products, Inc., *The Complete Motorola Microcomputer Data Library*. Phoenix, AZ, 1978.

6. Scanlon, L. J. *The 68000: Principles and Programming*. Indianapolis: Howard W. Sams & Co., Inc., 1981.

BIBLIOGRAPHY

Balph, T., and Kister, J. "μP Bus Gears Up to a 32-Bit Future," *Electronic Design*, July 5, 1980, pp. 97–103.

Bryce, H. "Microprogramming Makes the MC68000 a Processor Ready for the Future," *Electronic Design*, October 25, 1979, pp. 98–99.

Grappel, R., and Hemenway, J. "The MC68000—A 32-Bit μP Masquerading as a 16-Bit Device," *EDN*, February 20, 1980, pp. 127–134.

Hartman, B. "16-Bit 68000 Microprocessor Camps on 32-Bit Frontier," *Electronics*, October 11, 1979, pp. 118–125.

Kister, J. and Naugle, R. "Develop Software for 16-Bit μC Without Making Costly Commitments," *Electronic Design*, September 13, 1979, pp. 112–116.

Kister, J., and Robinson, I. "Development System Supports Today's Processors —and Tomorrow's," *Electronics*, January 31, 1980, pp. 81–88.

Morales, J. "Interface 6800-μP Peripherals to the 68000," *EDN*, March 4, 1981, pp. 159, 162.

Starnes, T. "Compact Instructions Give the MC68000 Power While Simplifying Its Operation," *Electronic Design*, September 27, 1979, pp. 70–74.

———. "Powerful Instructions and Flexible Registers of the MC68000 Make Programming Easy," *Electronic Design*, April 26, 1980, pp. 171–176.

———. "Handling Exceptions Gracefully Enhances Software Reliability," *Electronics*, September 11, 1980, pp. 163–157.

Stockton, J., and Scherer, V. "Learn the Timing and Interfacing of MC68000 Peripheral Circuits," *Electronic Design*, November 8, 1979, pp. 58–64.

7

The NS16000 Family

The NS16000 family of microprocessors—16016 and 16032—is manufactured by National Semiconductor Corporation. Only the 16032 is currently available, and it will be second sourced by Fairchild Semiconductor. The 16032 is the more powerful of the two, and it will give all of the other processors in this book a real run for the money. In many respects the 16032 incorporates many of the best features of the processors that have already been discussed.

The pin configuration of the 16032 is shown in Fig. 7-1, along with the microprocessor's internal organization. As you can see, the 16032 is a 48-pin package that contains a number of 24- and 32-bit registers. Included in its 16 registers are eight 32-bit registers, which can be used to store addresses or data values. The program counter is 24 bits wide, so the microprocessor can directly address 16M bytes of memory without the overhead and hassles of "segmentation." When reset, the microprocessor fetches the starting address of the program from the lowest memory locations, which are the only dedicated memory locations in a system. The pointers for the interrupt service subroutines are accessed with the interrupt base register, so they can be located anywhere in memory.

It is also possible for the microprocessor to operate in either the system (supervisor) or user mode, thus the need for two stack pointers. The static base, frame pointer, and module address registers are used when the microprocessor accesses memory, using many of its very sophisticated addressing modes.

This microprocessor has 81 basic instructions, which, when combined with its nine addressing modes, means that there are thousands of meaningful instructions that this processor can execute. Of course, it can perform a number of operations, including add, subtract, mul-

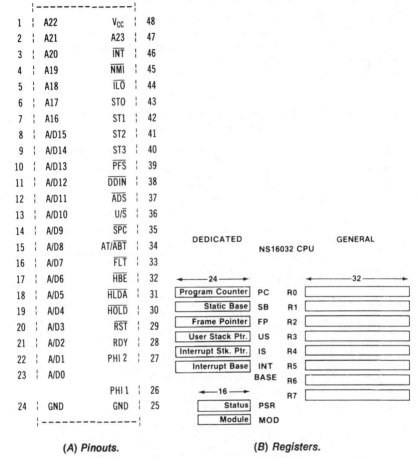

1	A22		V$_{CC}$	48
2	A21		A23	47
3	A20		$\overline{INT}$	46
4	A19		$\overline{NMI}$	45
5	A18		$\overline{ILO}$	44
6	A17		ST0	43
7	A16		ST1	42
8	A/D15		ST2	41
9	A/D14		ST3	40
10	A/D13		$\overline{PFS}$	39
11	A/D12		$\overline{DDIN}$	38
12	A/D11		$\overline{ADS}$	37
13	A/D10		U/$\overline{S}$	36
14	A/D9		$\overline{SPC}$	35
15	A/D8		AT/$\overline{ABT}$	34
16	A/D7		$\overline{FLT}$	33
17	A/D6		$\overline{HBE}$	32
18	A/D5		$\overline{HLDA}$	31
19	A/D4		$\overline{HOLD}$	30
20	A/D3		$\overline{RST}$	29
21	A/D2		RDY	28
22	A/D1		PHI 2	27
23	A/D0			
			PHI 1	26
24	GND		GND	25

(A) Pinouts.   (B) Registers.

Fig. 7-1. The pin configuration and internal registers of the NS16032.

tiply, divide, bit set, reset and test, data transfer, string, processor control, Boolean, *array* and block move, and compare. Most of the instructions can operate on bytes, words, and double words, with some instructions operating on bits and others operating on quadruple words.

The basic clock speed of the NS16032 is 10 MHz, so it has a cycle time of just 100 ns. Because of this, it is probably the fastest processor discussed in this book. Typical instruction execution times are shown in Table 7-1. What is particularly impressive about these execution times is the time required to execute a double-word multiply instruction.

Of course, Intel, Zilog, Motorola, and TI to a lesser extent have announced a number of special-function chips to go along with their high-performance CPUs, and National Semiconductor is no different from them. National Semiconductor currently has a memory-management unit, interrupt controller, clock generator, and floating-point slave processor planned for future introduction. In addition, NS also plans to manufacture the NS16016, which has 16-bit data and ad-

Table 7-1. A Comparison of Instruction Execution Times for the 8086, Z8001/2, 68000, and 16032

Operation	Data Type*	Typical Execution Time (μsec)			
		8086	Z8000	MC68000	NS16032
MOV R,R (Register to Register)	B, W	0.40	0.75	0.50	0.30
	D	0.80	1.25	0.50	0.30
MOV M,R (Memory to Register)	B,W	3.40	3.50	1.50	1.00
	D	6.80	4.25	2.00	1.40
MOV M,M (Memory to Memory)	B,W	7.00	7.00	2.50	1.60
	D	14.00	8.50	3.75	2.40
ADD M,R (Memory to Register)	B,W	3.60	3.75	1.50	1.10
	D	7.20	5.25	2.25	1.50
CMP M,M (Memory to Memory)	B,W	7.00	7.25	3.00	1.80
	D	14.00	9.50	4.00	2.60
MULT R,R (Register to Register)	B	13.00	20.25	N/A	2.80
	W	23.60	16.00	8.75	4.40
	D	115.20	85.75	43.00	7.60
BCC (Conditional branch)	(Branch Taken)	1.60	1.50	1.25	1.40
	(Branch Not Taken)	0.80	1.50	1.00	0.70
ACBI (Modify index, branch if zero)	(Branch Taken)	2.20	2.75	1.25	1.30
BSR (Branch to subroutine)		3.80	3.75	2.25	2.50
		5MHz	4MHz	8MHz	10MHz

*B = Byte
W = Word
D = Double Word

Courtesy National Semiconductor Corp.

dress registers. One interesting feature of this processor is the fact that it can execute either programs written in its own machine or assembly language or programs that have been written in 8080/8085 machine or assembly language. This dual "personality" at this programming level is unique in the semiconductor world.

National Semiconductor currently manufactures a number of Multibus-compatible peripheral and CPU boards, so it is safe to assume that they will also manufacture a 16032-based CPU board for the Multibus. This will mean that a number of the peripheral and memory boards will have to be redesigned, as Intel had to do, because of the larger address space of the 16032, compared to the 8080.

16032 GENERAL-PURPOSE REGISTERS

The eight 32-bit general-purpose registers are labeled R0 through R7 (Fig. 7-1B) and they can be used to store bytes, words, double words, and quadruple words. Unlike the 8086 and the Z8001/2, when a byte instruction is executed, only the 8 least significant bits (lsb's) in the 32-bit register are used. The other 24 bits in the register can be used for storage, but these other bytes of information cannot be addressed directly. As you will remember, in the Z8001/2 a single 16-bit register, for example, R0, contained both the RH0 and RL0 "byte registers." For 16-bit operations of the NS processors, only the 16 lsb's of a register are used, and for 32-bit operations all 32 bits of the register are used. For 64-bit operations (multiply and divide only), two of the 32-bit general-purpose registers must be used. In this case the 32 lsb's will be stored in an even-numbered register (R0, R2, R4, or R6), and *the 32 msb's of the result will be stored in the next higher odd-numbered register,* or R1, R3, R5, or R7, respectively.

16032 DEDICATED REGISTERS

The simplest of the 24-bit dedicated registers is the program counter (PC). This register addresses instructions as they are fetched from memory and are executed. Like the 68000, the PC is really a 32-bit register, but only the 24 lsb's are wired to pins on the chip. Thus the microprocessor has been designed to address 8092M bytes! The other dedicated registers are also 32 bits, but only 24 bits have been used.

The two stack pointers, SP0 and SP1, are primarily used by supervisor/interrupt/trap programs (SP0) and user programs (SP1). Thus the 16032 and the 16016 have separate supervisor and user stacks. The interrupt base (INT BASE) register contains the starting address of the "dispatch table" that points to the different interrupt service subroutines and trap software. Since this register is 24 bits, the dispatch table can be located anywhere in memory, just as was the case with the Z8001/2. Speaking of interrupts, the 16032 can easily handle 256 of them (like the 8086 and Z8001/2).

The processor status register (PSR) is just the flag word or flag register and contains 10 bits of information that can be set, cleared, and tested under software control. The structure of the PSR is shown in Fig. 7-2. As you can see, 4 of the PSR bits are privileged and can be changed only when the microprocessor is in the supervisor state. One interesting question that may come up is: how can the micro-

| 15 | | | | | | | | | | | | | 0 |

| | | | | I* | P* | S* | U* | N | Z | F | | | | L | T | C |

*ACCESSIBLE ONLY IN THE SUPERVISOR STATE

I = INTERRUPT ENABLE/DISABLE

P = PENDING FLAG (USED TO EXECUTE A SINGLE INSTRUCTION)

S = STACK CODE. SELECTS EITHER SP0 OR SP1

U = USER FLAG. SELECTS EITHER THE SUPERVISOR OR USER MODE

N = NEGATIVE FLAG

Z = ZERO FLAG

F = FLAG CODE

L = LESS THAN FLAG

T = TRACE FLAG (USED TO EXECUTE A SINGLE INSTRUCTION)

C = CARRY FLAG

Fig. 7-2. The 16032 processor status (flag) register.

processor get back into the supervisor state, if, in the user state, the U (USER) bit in the PSR cannot be changed? There are a number of ways in which the microprocessor can return to the supervisor state. One way to do this is to include a supervisor call (SVC) instruction in a program. This will cause the microprocessor to be "trapped," and as a result of this the P, S, U, and T bits of the PSR are cleared. Thus the microprocessor enters the supervisor state. If the processor attempts to execute a privileged instruction in the user state, the processor will also be "trapped" and enter the supervisor state.

The frame pointer register (FP, Fig. 7-1B) is used by some instructions to access (provide the address for) data stored on the stack. In many processors the stack pointer provides a memory address only when subroutines are called or are returned from or when data values are pushed onto or are popped off of the stack. It is often difficult or inconvenient to use the stack pointer to access data values that are stored on the stack. Hence the frame pointer is used and makes this type of addressing very easy.

The static base register (SB) and module register (MOD) are used when the processor executes a software "module." A module is simply a sequence of instructions where there are no absolute addresses. *Thus, if the microprocessor has to access a data value stored in memory, a table provides the address of this memory location.* This table is called the *link table,* and any external data value (from the module) or program that must be used by the module must be referenced in this link table. So, the link table is used to access external variables and procedures. Each entry in the link table is a double word (32 bits).

The module table is a collection of pointers and addresses that "describe" all of the modules in a program. Each module "description" consists of four double words, where one of the double words is reserved for future expansion. The remaining three double words (a) point to the variables that are external to or global to the module, (b) address the first entry in the link table for the module, and (c) point to the instructions in the module.

The MOD register is only 16 bits wide, so 65,536 bytes can be addressed. However, each module descriptor requires four double words (16 bytes), so a maximum of 4096 modules can be addressed in one 16M-byte address space. Using the 16082 memory-management unit chip, the 16032 can have two 16M-byte address spaces, so you can have two module tables, one in each address space.

ADDRESSING MEMORY AND I/O DEVICES

Since the program counter is 24 bits long, all 16M bytes of memory can be directly addressed without using segmented addresses. Of course, one advantage of this feature is the fact that you don't have to worry about the program counter wrapping around. To address i/o devices, memory-reference instructions must be used. There are no special i/o instructions, and the processor does not have a separate i/o address space. A disadvantage of this feature (as is also the case with the 68000) is that i/o "instructions" can be executed by both system/supervisor and user programs unless the operating system program prevents this. At least on the Z8001/2 the i/o instructions can only be executed in the supervisor state.

ADDRESSING MODES

The 16032 and 16016 microprocessors have nine addressing modes, and, as you would expect, some of them are the same as those for other processors. *In particular, the 16032 has register, immediate, and absolute addressing* (Fig. 7-3). *One nice feature of the 16032 is the symmetry of its instruction set. This means that all of the two-operand instructions can use all of the addressing modes.* The microprocessor can also perform memory-to-memory operations, which are not very prevalent on the other microprocessors, except the LSI-11. Most of the other processors have to have at least one of the operands or arguments in a register, in order for the microprocessor to operate on it. Thus, with a memory-to-memory architecture, the general-

REGISTER – AN OPERAND STORED IN ONE OF THE GENERAL-PURPOSE REGISTERS (R0-R7) IS ACCESSED WHEN THE REGISTER ADDRESSING MODE IS USED

IMMEDIATE – THE OPERAND IS CONTAINED WITHIN THE INSTRUCTION. THE IMMEDIATE DATA VALUE IS STORED IN MEMORY, IMMEDIATELY AFTER THE INSTRUCTION, FROM MOST SIGNIFICANT BYTE TO LEAST SIGNIFICANT BYTE

INSTRUCTION
OPERAND

ABSOLUTE – THE ABSOLUTE MEMORY ADDRESS OF THE OPERAND IS STORED IN MEMORY IMMEDIATELY AFTER THE INSTRUCTION

Fig. 7-3. The register, immediate, and absolute addressing modes.

purpose registers really do not have to be used for the temporary storage of data very often.

As an example of this power, the stack pointers can be loaded with the contents of the general-purpose registers or an immediate data byte. They, however, can also be loaded with the contents of memory, addressed by any of the other addressing modes. What are these addressing modes?

In *register relative addressing,* the content of one of the registers (R0 through R7) is added to one of the other dedicated registers (Fig. 7-4). Hence the offset in the general-purpose register can be added to either the program counter (PC), frame pointer (FP), the current stack pointer (either SP0 or SP1), or the static base register (SB). In many respects this is similar to the *indexed* addressing modes of the other processors. In the other processors, however, true relative addressing (where the content of the PC is used in the address calculations) was often limited to jump, branch, or other transfer-of-control instructions.

If *memory relative addressing* is used, *two memory addresses are actually generated by the microprocessor* (Fig. 7-5). The instruction contains two offsets, where the first offset is added to either the FP, SP, or SB. This memory address is used to read the contents of mem-

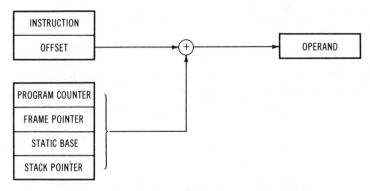

Fig. 7-4. The relative register addressing mode.

ory into the processor. This memory location, however, does not contain the operand. Instead, this value is added to the second offset specified in the instruction, and the resulting address addresses the operand stored in memory. Note that this addressing mode cannot use the PC.

Most of the previous processors have also been capable of *top-of-stack (TOS) addressing* (Fig. 7-6), but only in a very primitive manner. For instance, top-of-stack addressing is used when values are pushed onto or are popped off of the stack. The stack is also used when subroutines are called. Thus, in other processors, top-of-stack addressing is extremely limited to a very small number of instructions. In the 16032 the TOS addressing mode can be used just like any other addressing mode. This means that you can add the TOS value (the last value on the stack) to the contents of some memory loca-

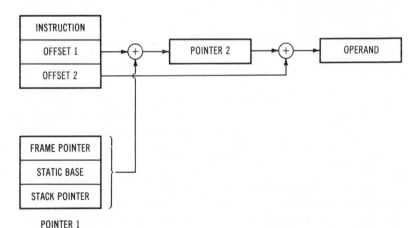

Fig. 7-5. Using the memory relative addressing mode to access data.

```
STACK POINTER ──────────────────▶ OPERAND
```

Fig. 7-6. The top-of-stack (TOS) addressing mode.

tion (addressed by any of the other addressing modes) and save the result on the stack! It is also possible to add the TOS to itself, and save the result on the TOS. From this you can see that the other processors really *don't* have TOS addressing.

Why is this addressing mode important? In many high-level languages TOS addressing is used to store data values in the order in which they must be processed. These values are then popped off of the stack as they are required. In the other processors many instructions have to be executed in order to "simulate" this TOS addressing. This not only makes the software more complex, but it also increases the program's execution time. With the 16032 and its TOS addressing modes, the program is being executed at its fastest possible speed.

The *external addressing mode* makes use of the link table that was discussed previously (Fig. 7-7). In this addressing mode the instruction contains an index and an offset. The index is added to the start-

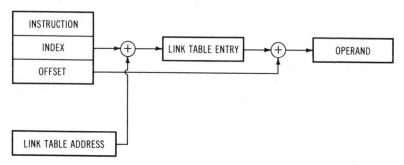

Fig. 7-7. Using a link table with software modules for external addressing.

ing address of the link table for that software module. The resulting address points to an entry in the link table. The offset in the instruction is added to this entry (address) and the result is used to address the operand in memory. *Thus, in external addressing, everything is relative to the link table;* no absolute memory addresses are required in the software module, but they are required in the link table.

The *scaled indexed addressing mode* (Fig. 7-8) is particularly useful for processing lists and arrays. When an instruction uses this addressing mode one additional byte of information must be added to the instruction. *This byte specifies the register that will provide the scaled index (entry number) into the array, and the addressing mode specified in this additional byte will be used to read the starting ad-*

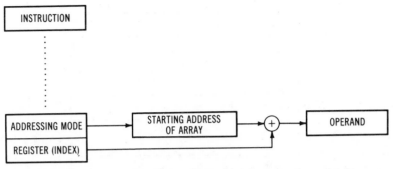

Fig. 7-8. Using scaled indexed addressing to access elements of a data structure.

dress of the array from memory. This means that two addressing modes can be used by both operands in an instruction. The first addressing mode is used to read the starting address of the array from memory, and the second addressing mode, scaled indexed, is used to access an entry in the array. Therefore, if a data value is being moved from one array to another, absolute addressing and scaled indexed addressing could be used to read a value from an array, and top-of-stack and scaled indexed addressing could be used to write the data value back into an array.

Note that the register that contains the index into the array (the entry number) will be *scaled* by 1, 2, 4, or 8, depending on the size (byte, word, double word, or quadruple word) of the entries in the array. Finally, all of the other addressing modes can be used with scaled indexed addressing, except immediate and scaled indexed addressing.

ADDRESSES IN INSTRUCTIONS

Many of the addressing modes that have been discussed require that an absolute address or relative address be "contained in" the instruction. These addresses may be either 1, 2, or 4 bytes long. One unique feature of these address bytes is the fact that they specify their own length. As an example, a byte address is a signed 6-bit number. The remaining, and most significant bit, is a logic zero, which indicates to the microprocessor that the address is a byte address (Fig. 7-9).

If the msb is a logic one, then either a word or double-word address is being specified. If this is the case, then the next less significant bit specifies whether the address is a word or double word. A zero in this bit position represents a word, and a logic one represents a double-word address. Thus there are three combinations of ones

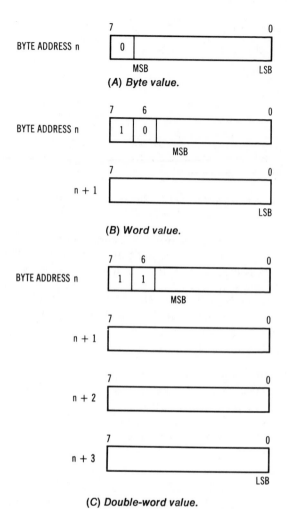

(A) Byte value.

(B) Word value.

(C) Double-word value.

Fig. 7-9. The structure of addresses (displacements) used in instructions.

and zeros that are of interest to us: 0 (byte), 10 (word), and 11 (double word) in an address.

INTEGER FORMATS

As was mentioned previously, the 16032 and its related processors can operate on bytes, words, and double words. *However, the arrangement of these values in memory is exactly opposite to the format used to store addresses* (Fig. 7-10). From Fig. 7-10 you can see that the least significant bytes are stored in lower memory loca-

SIZE	MEMORY ADDRESS	FORMAT	
BYTE	ADDRESS n	7	0
WORD	ADDRESS n	7	0
	ADDRESS n + 1	15	8
DOUBLE WORD	ADDRESS n	7	0
	ADDRESS n + 1	15	8
	ADDRESS n + 2	23	16
	ADDRESS n + 3	31	24

Fig. 7-10. The formats for bytes, words, and double words stored in memory.

tions. Also note that none of the bits within the byte, word, and double-word integer values are used to indicate the size of the integer. Thus, in the 16032 (and all of the other processors that we have discussed) the instruction's op code actually determines whether a byte, word, or double word is being operated on.

16032 INSTRUCTION SET

Because the 16032 has some very powerful addressing modes its instructions can be between 1 and 25 bytes in length! Some of the 1-byte instructions include return from subroutine, no operation, breakpoint trap, and wait. Most of the op codes for the remaining assembly language instructions are either 16 or 24 bits in length. The remaining bytes, in a 25-byte instruction, for example, are used to store memory addresses and data values.

As an example, an instruction might be composed of a 3-byte op code that is used to address two values stored in memory. If both operands are addressed using scaled index addressing, 2 additional bytes (a total of 5) are used to specify the addressing mode that is to be used to locate the first entry in an array, and also to specify the register that contains the index into the array. Assuming that the scaled index addressing mode is used in conjunction with memory relative or external addressing for the two operands, 16 additional bytes may be required. Both the memory relative and external addressing modes can have either two 4-byte offsets or a 4-byte index and a 4-byte offset. Therefore 21 bytes (5 + 16) have been used so far. In addition, if the array consists of data values that are accessed with field instructions, then up to an additional 4 bytes (25 total) are used to specify the length of the fields in the array.

As you can see, the addressing modes of the 16032 can generate long and complex (powerful) instructions. Unless you need to access complex arrangements of data in your programs, however, you probably won't have such long and complex instructions. On the other hand, if you are writing operating system programs, high-level language interpreters or compilers, or large data base management programs, you will probably use these complex instructions and will be able to appreciate their power.

Since the 16032 does have instructions that have a 1-byte op code, instructions can be stored in memory, starting at either an even or odd byte. *Therefore instructions do not have to be word aligned in memory.* Like the 8086, data values in memory also do not have to be word aligned. However, the processor will be able to access data faster if it is word aligned. In fact, National Semiconductor recommends that double words be aligned on the proper even word, so that these values can be accessed as fast as possible, if memory is ever organized as double words (32 bits wide).

Not surprisingly, the 16032 has a number of instructions that are very similar to the instructions that have been discussed previously. The 16032 has data transfer, math and logic, bit, string, block, and program control instructions. This processor, however, also has field and array instructions.

Data Transfer Instructions

Within the category of data transfer instructions the 16032 has move (MOV), save and restore (SAVE and RESTORE), which are equivalent to push and pop instructions, along with load and store processor registers (LPR and SPR). These instructions are summarized in Table 7-2. Note that the 16032 does not have any input/ output (i/o) or register exchange instructions. Since the 16032 uses memory-mapped i/o to communicate with peripherals, no separate i/o instructions are required. *Any* memory reference instruction can be used to communicate with i/o devices. Also, although the exchange instructions are nice, the equivalent operation can be performed with a few assembly instructions.

The symbols and abbreviations used in Table 7-2 and subsequent tables which show the format of the instructions are shown in Table 7-3.

As you can see, the move instruction shown in Table 7-2 can use any of the addressing modes of the 16032. Thus data values can be moved from memory to memory, register to memory, memory to

Table 7-2. Data Transfer Instructions

Mnemonic	Instruction Format	Op-Code Format
		15 0
MOV	MOV(B,W,D) operand 1, operand 2	Operand 1 | Operand 2 | 0 1 0 1 | B,W,D
MOVQ	MOVQ(B,W,D) quick, operand	Operand | Quick | 1 0 1 1 1 | B,W,D
SAVE	SAVE < R0,R1,R2,R3,R4,R5,R6,R7 >	R7 R6 R5 R4 R3 R2 R1 R0 | 0 1 1 0 0 0 1 0
RESTORE	RESTORE < R0,R1,R2,R3,R4,R5,R6,R7 >	R7 R6 R5 R4 R3 R2 R1 R0 | 0 1 1 1 0 0 1 0
LPR	LPR(B,W,D) proc. reg., operand	Operand | Proc. Reg. | 1 1 0 1 1 | B,W,D
SPR	SPR(B,W,D) proc. reg., operand	Operand | Proc. Reg. | 0 1 0 1 1 | B,W,D
ADDR	ADDR operand 1, operand 2	Operand 1 | Operand 2 | 1 0 0 1 1 0

Table 7-3. Abbreviations Used In Instruction Formats

Abbreviation	Meaning
Operand 1	5 bits defining register of addressing mode
Operand 2	5 bits defining register or addressing mode
BWD	2 bits defining a byte, word, or double word operation (00 = byte, 01 = word, 11 = double word)
BW	2 bits defining a byte or word operation
B	2 bits defining a byte operation
Quick	4-bit constant sign extended to the length of the integer specified in the instruction (byte, word, or double word)
REG.	3-bit value specifying the register (R0–R7) involved in the operation
CONS1	3- and 5-bit constants used by
CONS2	FIELD instructions
B	Bit used by string instructions to either increment (B = 0) or decrement (B = 1) pointers
T	Bit used by string instructions to translate byte integers (T = 0, no translation, T = 1, translation)
UW	String instruction is executed until match (UW = 00, while match 01 or none of the above 11)
Operand	See Operand 1 above
Condition	Branch condition codes
Proc. Reg.	PSR, FP, SP, SB, MOD, INT
C,M,F and I	Peripheral chip enable/disable bits

register, and immediate to either register or memory. Typical MOV instructions in a program might be MOVB R0,TOS (store the low byte of R0 on the stack) and MOVD 100,EXT(6) (a double-word constant (100) is stored in a double-word external variable, using external addressing of course).

The move quick (MOVQ) instruction is an interesting variation of the MOV instruction. The MOVQ instruction permits us to save a sign extended 4-bit value, as either a byte, word, or double word, in either a register or memory location. Typical MOVQ instructions in a program could be MOVQ 15,TOS and MOVQ 1,@29505.

The save and restore instructions are used to push information on to the stack, and to pop information off of the stack. Even though the 16032 has eight general-purpose 32-bit registers (R0 through R7), there is only one save and one restore instruction. How, then, can all eight or any combination of the eight registers be pushed onto or popped off of the stack? Within the op codes for these two instructions the user can specify, using a 0 or 1, which of the eight registers is to be "used" by the instruction. *Thus, with a single instruction all eight, or any combination of the eight, registers can be pushed onto or be popped off of the stack.* Typical instructions might be SAVE R0,R3,R4,R7 and RESTORE R0,R1,R2,R3. One nice feature of these two instructions is the fact that the user does not have to worry about the *order* in which information is saved on the stack. Since the other processors use a single instruction to save one register on the stack, the user has to ensure that the registers are popped in the reverse order that they were pushed. With the 16032 the user does not have to worry about the order in which information is stored on the stack.

Finally, the dedicated registers within the 16032 (the stack pointers, frame pointer, static base, module, interrupt base, processor status register, or just the unprivileged half of the PSR) can be loaded with the contents of a register, memory location, or an immediate data value. The contents of these registers can also be saved in memory or a register. The two instructions that are used to perform these operations are load processor register (LPR) and save processor register (SPR).

The 16032, like the other 16-bit microprocessors, can also manipulate the addresses of operands. Thus, to save the address of an operand in a register or memory locations, the address (ADDR) instruction would be used. Of course, this instruction operates on the 24-bit absolute address of the operand, so there are no byte, word, or double-word bits in this instruction's op code. *Likewise, if operand 1 is accessed with register addressing, the contents of the register are used as the address.* As an example, the instruction ADDR R4,@2340, would store the contents of R4 (that we assume is an address) in the double word in memory, starting at address 2340. An ADDR EXT(6),TOS instruction saves the *address* of entry 6 in the link table on the stack.

The Arithmetic Instructions

The numerous arithmetic instructions that the 16032 can execute are summarized in Table 7-4. As you can see, the 16032 can add, subtract, multiply, and divide, in addition to being able to sign extend word and double words. Like the 8086 and the Z8001/2, the 16032 has both add and add-with-carry instructions. Because of the power of the 16032, both of these instructions can operate on bytes, words, and double words. Of course, the ADDC instruction is only used with numbers larger than 32 bits. In this case the numbers would be divided into 32-bit "chunks" and then the first chunk (the 32 least significant bits) would be added with an ADDD instruction and the remaining chunks would be added with ADDCD (add-with-carry double-word) instruction. In a program typical addition instructions might include ADDB R0,R4, ADDW 4(FP),R7, and ADDD 10(2 (SB)),TOS. Of course, the ADDB R0,R4 instruction adds the byte in bits D7 through D0 of R0 to the byte in R4, and the result is stored in bits D7 through D0 of R4. The ADDW 4(FP),R7 instruction adds the fourth word relative to the frame pointer (which is usually equal to the stack pointer) to register R7. The result is placed back in R7. The last addition instruction adds a double word, which is the tenth double word from the second address relative to the static base register, to the double word at the top of the stack. The result writes over this value, when it is written back onto the stack.

A typical addition instruction sequence might be ADDD R0,R2 and ADDCD R1,R3. By executing these two instructions, the 64-bit numbers stored in R1R0 and R3R2 are added. Note that the ADDC instruction is the *second* addition instruction.

The subtract instructions that can be executed are SUB and SUBC. These instructions can operate on bytes, words, and double words, where the SUBC instruction is used to subtract 32-bit chunks of larger numbers. To subtract the least significant 32 bits of a large number, the SUB instruction would be used.

With some of the processors it is possible to process bcd numbers, but only 2 digits (8 bits) per 16-bit register. With the 16032 it is possible to store an 8-digit bcd number in a register or in memory, and add or subtract all 8 digits directly. The bcd math instructions are ADDP and SUBP (the P represents packed decimal).

The multiply and divide instructions are also very powerful, because they can be used to operate on bytes, words, and double words. The multiply instructions are MUL and MEI. *The MUL instruction is used to multiply bytes, words, and double words, and the result is the same size as the operands.* As an example, if two bytes are multiplied, the result is a word. With the MUL instruction, however, only the least significant byte of the result is saved. With the MEI instruc-

Table 7-4. The 16032 Arithmetic Instructions

Mnemonic	Instruction Format	Op-Code Format
ADD	ADD(B,W,D) operand 1, operand 2	Operand 1 | Operand 2 | 0 0 0 0 | B,W,D
ADDC	ADC(B,W,D) operand 1, operand 2	Operand 1 | Operand 2 | 0 1 0 0 | B,W,D
SUB	SUB(B,W,D) operand 1, operand 2	Operand 1 | Operand 2 | 1 0 0 0 | B,W,D
SUBC	SUBC(B,W,D) operand 1, operand 2	Operand 1 | Operand 2 | 1 1 0 0 | B,W,D
ADDP	ADDP(B,W,D) operand 1, operand 2	Operand 1 | Operand 2 | 1 1 1 1 | B,W,D | 0 1 0 0 1 1 1 0
SUBP	SUBP(B,W,D) operand 1, operand 2	Operand 1 | Operand 2 | 1 0 1 1 | B,W,D | 0 1 0 0 1 1 1 0
MUL	MUL(B,W,D) operand 1, operand 2	Operand 1 | Operand 2 | 1 0 0 0 | B,W,D | 1 1 0 0 1 1 1 0
MEI	MEI(B,W,D) operand 1, operand 2	Operand 1 | Operand 2 | 1 0 0 1 | B,W,D | 1 1 0 0 1 1 1 0
DIV	DIV(B,W,D) operand 1, operand 2	Operand 1 | Operand 2 | 1 1 1 1 | B,W,D | 1 1 0 0 1 1 1 0
DIVZ	DIVZ(B,W,D) operand 1, operand 2	Operand 1 | Operand 2 | 1 1 0 0 | B,W,D | 1 1 0 0 1 1 1 0
DEI	DEI(B,W,D) operand 1, operand 2	Operand 1 | Operand 2 | 1 0 1 1 | B,W,D | 1 1 0 0 1 1 1 0
REM	REM(B,W,D) operand 1, operand 2	Operand 1 | Operand 2 | 1 1 1 0 | B,W,D | 1 1 0 0 1 1 1 0
REMZ	REMZ(B,W,D) operand 1, operand 2	Operand 1 | Operand 2 | 1 1 0 1 | B,W,D | 1 1 0 0 1 1 1 0
NEG	NEG(B,W,D) operand 1, operand 2	Operand 1 | Operand 2 | 1 0 0 0 | B,W,D | 0 1 0 0 1 1 1 0
ABS	ABS(B,W,D) operand 1, operand 2	Operand 1 | Operand 2 | 1 1 0 0 | B,W,D | 0 1 0 0 1 1 1 0
SEW	SEW(B) operand 1, operand 2	Operand 1 | Operand 2 | 0 1 0 0 | B | 1 1 0 0 1 1 1 0
SED	SED(B,W) operand 1, operand 2	Operand 1 | Operand 2 | 0 1 1 1 | B,W | 1 1 0 0 1 1 1 0
ZEW	ZEW(B) operand 1, operand 2	Operand 1 | Operand 2 | 0 1 0 1 | B | 1 1 0 0 1 1 1 0
ZED	ZED(B,W,D) operand 1, operand 2	Operand 1 | Operand 2 | 0 1 1 0 | B,W,D | 1 1 0 0 1 1 1 0
ADDQ	ADDQ(B,W,D) quick, operand	Operand | Quick | 0 0 0 1 1 | B,W,D

tion, the double sized result (a word for byte multiplication) is saved. *Thus, with the MEI instruction, two double words (32 bits) can be multiplied and the 64-bit result is saved.* The MUL instruction generates a signed result, while the MEI instruction generates an unsigned result.

The division instructions (DIV, DIVZ, and DEI) are a little more complex. The DIV instruction divides bytes, words, and double words, with the quotient being the same size as both operands. However, the result is truncated (all computer division is truncated one way or another, because the result must be an integer) to negative infinity. Thus if −125 is divided by 60, the DIV instruction would return a result of −3. The DIVZ instruction truncates towards zero (this is the type of truncation normally encountered on computers); hence the result of −125 divided by 60 is −2. Quite often in computer division the remainder of the division is sent to "bit heaven." With the 16032, however, the remainder can actually be recovered with the REM (for the DIV instruction) and REMZ (for the DIVZ instruction) instructions.

The DEI instruction is used to divide a "double-length" operand (W, D, or QW) by another operand (B, W, or D). In this instruction the double-length operand is operand 2, so the quotient is saved in the upper half of operand 2, and the remainder is saved in the lower half of operand 2. Since the remainder is automatically stored in a register or memory location, there is no remainder instruction for the DEI instruction. Typical multiplication, division, and remainder instructions are listed in Table 7-5.

Table 7-5. Examples of Multiply and Divide Instructions

Instruction	Description
MULD R0,R1	Multiply R0 by R1 (32 × 32) and save the 32 lsb's of the result in R1
MEID R0, @3245	Multiply R0 (32 bits) by the lower 32 bits of quadruple-word memory location 3245 and save the 64-bit result in memory location 3245
DIVZW 60,R0	The signed 16-bit content of R0 is divided by the immediate value 60, and the result, which is truncated towards zero, is saved in R0
DEIB T0S,3(23(SB))	Divide the word in memory addressed by the 3 plus the content of the memory location addressed by the static base pointer plus 23, by a byte on the top of the stack. The result is stored back in memory (not the stack)
REMD R0,R1	Register R1 is loaded with the remainder (32 bits) from dividing R1 by R0 with a DIV instruction
REMZW R0,@3245	Store the remainder (16 bits) from dividing the content of memory location 3245 by R0, in memory location 3245

The last group of arithmetic instructions are fairly simple, since they are used to negate, sign extend, zero extend, and determine the absolute value of a data value. From Table 7-4 you can see that the 16032 does not have any increment or decrement instructions. However, the processor does have an add quick (ADDQ) instruction that is very similar to the move quick instruction discussed previously. In fact, this instruction can be used to increment or decrement a value by -16 to $+15$.

As always, it is extremely important that the programmer know exactly how the flags are affected when any of the arithmetic instructions are executed. Therefore you should refer to the manufacturer's literature[1] when doing assembly language programming. From this literature you will observe that *the multiply and divide instructions do not change any of the status codes or flags. However, if division by zero is attempted with any of the three divide instructions (DIV, DIVZ, or DEI), a DVZ trap will occur.* Traps are discussed in detail in another section of this chapter.

Logic Instructions

The 16032 can perform the standard logic functions, that is, AND, OR, exclusive OR, compare, complement, rotate, and shift, along with a number of bit instructions. The logic instructions and their format are summarized in Table 7-6.

As you can see from this table, the 16032 can perform these logic operations on bytes, words, and double words. One unusual feature of the AND (AND), OR (OR), and exclusive-OR (XOR) instructions is that they do not affect the state of the status codes (flags). Therefore, if you need to know whether the result of a logic operation is less than, equal to, or greater than zero (to name just a few possibilities), you would first have to perform the logic operation, followed by a compare (CMP or CMPQ) instruction. These two instructions set or clear the status code bits, which can be tested with the conditional transfer-of-control instructions. Of course, the compare quick (CMPQ) instruction lets us compare two operands, where one of them is a 4-bit value sign extended to either 8, 16, or 32 bits. *The compare instructions do not alter either operand.*

The bit clear (BIC) instruction is interesting because it performs

Table 7-6. A Summary of the 16032 Logic Instructions

Mnemonic	Instruction Format	Op-Code Format
AND	AND(B,W,D) operand 1, operand 2	Operand 1 | Operand 2 | 1 0 1 0 | B,W,D
OR	OR(B,W,D) operand 1, operand 2	Operand 1 | Operand 2 | 0 1 1 0 | B,W,D
XOR	XOR(B,W,D) operand 1, operand 2	Operand 1 | Operand 2 | 1 1 1 0 | B,W,D
CMP	CMP(B,W,D) operand 1, operand 2	Operand 1 | Operand 2 | 0 0 0 1 | B,W,D
CMPQ	CMPQ(B,W,D) quick, operand	Operand | Quick | 0 0 1 1 | B,W,D
BIC	BIC(B,W,D) operand 1, operand 2	Operand 1 | Operand 2 | 0 0 1 0 | B,W,D
COM	COM(B,W,D) operand 1, operand 2	Operand 1 | Operand 2 | 1 1 0 1 | B,W,D | 0 1 0 0 1 1 1 0
ASH	ASH(B,W,D) operand 1, operand 2	Operand 1 | Operand 2 | 0 0 0 1 | B,W,D | 0 1 0 0 1 1 1 0
LSH	LSH(B,W,D) operand 1, operand 2	Operand 1 | Operand 2 | 0 1 0 1 | B,W,D | 0 1 0 0 1 1 1 0
ROT	ROT(B,W,D) operand 1, operand 2	Operand 1 | Operand 2 | 0 0 0 0 | B,W,D | 0 1 0 0 1 1 1 0

The op-code format columns span bit positions from 15 (left) to 0 (right); the three-byte instructions (COM, ASH, LSH, ROT) span bit position 23 to 0.

the AND operation between the ones complement of operand 1 with operand 2, and saves the result in operand 2. The complement (COM) instruction is used to generate the ones complement of a number. In previous examples we have seen that operand 1 is different from operand 2. Thus the COM instruction can determine the complement of a number and store it in another register or memory location. Of course, it is always possible to determine the complement of a number and store it in the same register or memory location. Therefore, instructions such as COMW R0,R0 and COMD @1259,@1259 are possible.

The shift (ASH and LSH) and rotate (ROT) instructions can be used to operate on the content of either a register or memory location. Even though these are two-operand instructions, operand 1 is not the "source" of information and operand 2 is not the "destination" of the altered information. *Instead, operand 1 specifies the number of bits that operand 2 is to be shifted or rotated by.* As always, any of the addressing modes can be used with these instructions. Because of this, the number of bit "positions" that operand 2 is to be shifted or rotated by can be specified by an immediate data value, the contents of a register, or the contents of a memory location. Thus the 16032 has the most powerful shift and rotate instructions of the 16-bit processors that are discussed in this book. Typical instructions include ASHB 3,@7890, LSHW R0, 3(2(SB)) and ROT @12999,R5. The ASHB 3,@7890 instruction shifts the byte contents of memory location 7890 to the left by 3 bits. *The bits vacated by this left shift (D0, D1, and D2) are set to zero.* If the instruction ASHB −3,@7890 is included in a program, the content of memory location 7890 is shifted to the right by 3 bit positions, *and the sign bit is duplicated in the vacated bit positions.*

With the LSHW R0, 3(2(SB)) and ROT @12999,R5 instructions there is no way of knowing whether the shift or rotate will be to the left or right. The LSHW R0, 3(2(SB)) instruction logically shifts the word stored in the memory location addressed by 3 plus the content of the memory location addressed by the SB register plus 2. *With the LSH instruction the vacated bits are set to zero, regardless of whether the shift is to the left or right.* The rotate (ROT) instruction simply rotates the data value, such that the msb is rotated into the lsb for a rotate left, and the lsb is rotated into the msb with a rotate right. *With all of the shift and rotate instructions a positive number (operand 1) causes the data value to "move to" the left, and a negative value causes the data value to "move to" the right.*

What is unusual about the instructions ROTB 4,R0, ROTW 8,@ 1648, and ROTD 16,TOS? All of these instructions cause low and high halves of the specified data value to be "swapped" or exchanged. Therefore the ROTB 4,R0 instruction causes the two 4-bit quantities in the eight lsb's of register R0 to be swapped. This could be for processing bcd values. Any ROTW 8 instruction causes 2 bytes in a word to be swapped and any ROTD 16 instruction swaps both words in a double word.

Processor Control (Control Transfer) Instructions

The processor control instructions that the 16032 can execute are summarized in Table 7-7. The first instruction, jump (JUMP), simply loads the program counter (PC) with a 24-bit operand. This value can be an immediate data value or it may be stored in a register or memory location, where it can be accessed using all of the addressing modes of the microprocessor. Since it can use all of the addressing modes it is a very powerful instruction, giving us the ability to create "jump tables" very easily. There are no conditional jump instructions.

Table 7-7. A Summary of the 16032 Program Control Instructions

Mnemonic	Instruction Format	Op-Code Format
JUMP	JUMP operand	Operand 0 1 0 0 1 1 1 1 0 0
B	B (condition) constant	Condition 1 0 1 0
CASE	CASE(B,W,D) operand	Operand 1 1 1 0 1 1 1 1 1 B,W,D
ACB	ACB(B,W,D) quick, operand, constant	Operand Quick 1 0 0 1 1 B,W,D
JSR	JSR operand	Operand 1 1 0 0 1 1 1 1 1 B,W,D
BSR	BSR constant	0 0 0 0 0 0 0 1 0
RET	RET constant	0 0 0 1 0 0 1 0
RETI	RETI	0 1 0 1 0 0 1 0
RETT	RETT constant	0 1 0 0 0 0 1 0
CXP	CXP constant	0 0 1 0 0 0 1 0
CXPD	CXPD operand	Operand 0 0 1 0 1 1 1 1 1 1 1 1
RXP	RXP constant	0 0 1 1 0 0 1 0

The branch (B) instruction can be either conditional or unconditional, where 14 different states of the status codes can be tested (Table 7-8). This is a single-byte instruction that can be followed by a signed byte, word, or double-word address constant (Fig. 7-9). This constant is added to the PC if the branch is taken. *With these signed values the 16032 can branch to any memory location.* Remember, the address constant can be up to a 29-bit signed value, yet the PC is only 24 bits long!

Table 7-8. The Condition Codes That Can Be Tested With the Branch Instruction

Condition Code	Condition
FC	Flag code bit is clear
FS	Flag code is set
CC	Carry code clear (no carry)
CS	Carry code set (carry)
NE	Zero code clear (not equal)
EQ	Zero code set (equal)
LT	Negative code set (less than)
GT	Zero and negative code clear (greater than)
LE	Zero or negatve code set (less than or equal to)
GE	Negative code clear (greater than or equal to)
LO	Low code set (unsigned less than)
HI	Zero and low code clear (unsigned greater than)
LS	Zero or low code set (unsigned less than or equal to)
HS	Low code clear (unsigned greater than or equal to)

The case (CASE) instruction actually causes an operand to be added to the PC. The difference between the branch and case instructions is that the address in a branch instruction is fixed when the program is assembled, but the address for the case instruction can actually be altered as the program is executed. The add, compare, and branch (ACB) instruction is very similar to the 8086 LOOP and Z8001/2 DJNZ (DBJNZ) instructions. However, a "quick" value is included in the instruction, so up to a signed 29-bit address can be used, and the "quick" value can be added to a value stored in either a register or a memory location.

The 16032 can also use subroutines that can be accessed with either a JSR (jump) or BSR (branch) instruction. Of course, regardless of the instruction used to "call" the subroutine, a 24-bit return address (the PC) is always saved on the stack. The return instructions that the 16032 can execute include RET (return from subroutine), RETI (return from interrupt) and RETT (return from trap). The RETI instruction, of course, is only used at the end of interrupt service subroutines, and the RETT instruction is only executed so that the microprocessor can return from a trap instruction sequence.

An interesting feature of the return (RET) and return from trap (RETT) instructions is the fact that these instructions have an address constant appended to them. Therefore the shortest RET instruction will always be 2 bytes long, where the first byte is the op code and the second byte is a single-byte address constant. If you need the 16032 to return to the instruction immediately after the JSR or BSR instruction, a byte of 00000000 would be used. By using nonzero values for the byte, word, or double-word constant, the 16032 can skip over a number memory locations. *This is important if parameters are passed to a subroutine by means of the stack.*

When the subroutine is jumped to or branched to, the PC points to the first memory location after the JSR or BSR instruction. Using TOS addressing, any number of parameters stored in memory immediately after the JSR or BSR can be accessed. Once the 16032 has executed all of the instructions in the subroutine, however, *it must not return to and execute this data.* Instead, it must skip over this information and execute some instruction stored in memory after it. Therefore, if four words are stored in memory after the JSR or BSR instruction, a byte of 00001000 would be used after the RET instruction, so that the 16032 skips over the 8 bytes of memory used to store this data.

The CXP (call external procedure), CXPD (call external procedure with descriptor), and RXP (return from external procedure) are instructions that *are used to access sequences of instructions that are not in the program currently being executed.* With external addressing (previously described) the microprocessor is able to access data that is not included in the program currently being executed. The procedure being accessed is specified by a constant (CXP) or an operand (CXPD). This constant actually points to an entry in the link table that is addressed by the MOD register. Therefore there is basically no limit to the number of different external procedures that can be addressed. A CXP 4 instruction causes the microprocessor to execute the instructions pointed to by the fourth entry in the link table. A CXPD R0 instruction causes the microprocessor to execute the procedure addressed by the R0th entry in the link table, where R0 contains the entry number.

When external procedures are executed, the PC and MOD registers are saved on the stack, and this information has to be popped off when the processor returns from the procedure. Consequently, the 16032 has a special return-from-procedure (RXP) instruction.

Why are procedures important? Quite often in high-level languages, such as FORTRAN and Pascal, user libraries are built up that contain useful subroutines for plotting, matrix calculations, and data base management. Without the ability to call external procedures the user would either have to duplicate all of the required user subroutines in

Table 7-9. Typical Program Control Instructions

Instruction	Description
JUMP WAIT	Jump to the address that has been assigned to the character string WAIT
BNE LOOP	Branch if the Z code is clear (not equal)
CASEB @1000	Add the byte in memory location 1000 to the program counter
ACBW −1,R3,−50	The content of R3 is decremented (−1 is added to it) and the 16032 branches back 50 memory locations if the result is not zero
JSR @1571	The subroutine at memory location 1571 is called
RET 7	Return from the subroutine and skip 7 bytes after the JSR or BSR instruction
CXP 4	Call the fourth external procedure in the link table

his or her program (a long and tedious task) or the execution of the user's program would have to be simulated so that the user subroutines could be "inserted" into the user's program where required, by the operating system program.

Typical program control instructions and their operands or constants are shown in Table 7-9.

String Instructions

Like the 8086, the 16032 has three simple, yet powerful, string instructions. Like the 8086, but unlike the Z8001/2, some of the general-purpose registers (R0 through R4) are assigned specific tasks. The string instructions are summarized in Table 7-10, and the functions of the general-purpose registers are shown in Table 7-11. These instructions can operate on strings of any length, and they are interruptible.

The string instructions give the user the ability to move strings, compare them, and skip over them. The B, W, and D bits in the instructions give the 16032 the ability to operate on byte, word, and double-word strings. The addresses in registers R1 and R2 can be either incremented or decremented, as determined by the state of the B bit (0=increment, 1=decrement). As the microprocessor is operating with byte strings, they also can be translated. Finally, the microprocessor will operate on the strings with these three instructions, until either they match, they no longer match, or a count in register R0 is decremented to zero.

Table 7-10. The 16032 String Instructions

Mnemonic	Instruction Format	Op-Code Format
MOVS	MOVS(B,W,D,T)(B)(U,W)	23 `0 0 0 0 0` | `U,W` | `B` | `T` | `0 0 0 0 0` | `B,W,D` | `0 0 0 0 1 1 1 0` 0
CMPS	CMPS(B,W,D,T)(B)(U,W)	`0 0 0 0 0` | `U,W` | `B` | `T` | `0 0 0 0 1` | `B,W,D` | `0 0 0 0 1 1 1 0`
SKPS	SKPS(B,W,D,T)(B)(U,W)	`0 0 0 0 0` | `U,W` | `B` | `T` | `0 0 0 1 1` | `B,W,D` | `0 0 0 0 1 1 1 0`

Table 7-11. Register Assignments for the String Instructions

Register	Contents
R0	Number of bytes, words, or double words in the list or array
R1	Starting address of "string 1"
R2	Starting address of "string 2"
R3	Starting address (address of the first entry) in the translation table. If no translation is to occur, R3 will not be used by the string instruction
R4	String termination character

The MOVS string instruction moves a string from one section of memory to another. Of course, with the appropriate memory-mapped i/o devices, these instructions could also be used to read strings from peripherals or to output strings to peripherals. String 1 can also be translated as it is moved into string 2 if the string is a byte string and the "T bit" of the instruction is a logic one.

The compare string (CMPS) instruction can compare strings as long as they are equal, or it can compare them until they are equal. Of course, the comparison process will be terminated if R0 is decremented to zero. If string 1 is a byte string, it can also be translated before it is compared to string 2.

The skip string (SKPS) instruction, along with MOVS, uses register R4 for the match/no-match condition. In order to skip over strings the 16032 has to know either (a) where one strings ends and the next one begins or (b) the string termination character, that is, the character at the end of the string. In order to skip over a string, register R4 is loaded with the string termination character. If string 1 is a byte string, it can also be translated as the 16032 skips over it. Some examples of string instructions are shown in Table 7-12.

Block Instructions

The 16032 has two block instructions, MOVM and CMPM, which are used to either *move or compare blocks of integers of fixed length.*

Table 7-12. Typical String Instructions

Instruction	Description
MOVSTBU	The translated bytes in string 1 are moved to another section of memory. The string addresses are decremented and the string is moved until a character match occurs or the count is decremented to zero
CMPSW	The words in string 1 are compared to the words in string 2 until the strings are no longer equal or the word count is decremented to zero
SKPSBBW	A string of bytes is skipped until a character not equal to the termination character is read or the byte count is decremented to zero

These instructions can be used to operate on either bytes, words, or double words. *The maximum number of bytes that can be moved is 16,* the blocks must not overlap, and immediate addressing must not be used. The block instructions are shown in Table 7-13.

Table 7-13. The Instructions That Move and Compare Blocks of Integers

Mnemonic	Instruction Format						Op-Code Format
MOVM	MOVM(B,W,D) operand 1, operand 2, constant	Operand 1	Operand 2	0 0 0 0	B,W,D	1 1 0 0 1 1 1 0	
CMPM	CMPM(B,W,D) operand 1, operand 2, constant	Operand 1	Operand 2	0 0 0 1	B,W,D	1 1 0 0 1 1 1 0	

In a program an instruction such as **MOVMW 30(R3),TOS,7** would cause four words (eight bytes) to be moved from memory using register relative addressing, to the top of the stack. *Note that the constant (7) is one less than the number of bytes that we wish to move.*

The CMPM instruction compares blocks of data values until either the numbers are no longer equal or the constant is decremented to zero. Again, *the constant represents the number of bytes minus 1 to be compared,* immediate addressing must not be used, and the blocks must not overlap. A CMPMB 32(3(FP)),@3240,9 instruction would compare 10 bytes of information, with one block of numbers being addressed with memory relative addressing and the other block being addressed with absolute addressing.

Bit Instructions

The NS16000 processors have a number of powerful bit instructions, which are summarized in Table 7-14. These instructions are

Table 7-14. The 16000 Bit Instructions

Mnemonic	Instruction Format	Op-Code Format
		23 0
SBIT	SBIT(B,W,D) operand 1, operand 2	Operand 1 | Operand 2 | 0 1 1 0 | B,W,D | 0 1 0 0 1 1 1 0
CBIT	CBIT(B,W,D) operand 1, operand 2	Operand 1 | Operand 2 | 0 0 1 0 | B,W,D | 0 1 0 0 1 1 1 0
TBIT	TBIT(B,W,D) operand 1, operand 2	Operand 1 | Operand 2 | 1 1 0 1 | B,W,D
SBITI	SBITI(B,W,D) operand 1, operand 2	Operand 1 | Operand 2 | 0 1 1 1 | B,W,D | 0 1 0 0 1 1 0 0
CBITI	CBITI(B,W,D) operand 1, operand 2	Operand 1 | Operand 2 | 0 0 1 1 | B,W,D | 0 1 0 0 1 1 1 0
IBIT	IBIT(B,W,D) operand 1, operand 2	Operand 1 | Operand 2 | 1 1 1 0 | B,W,D | 0 1 0 0 1 1 1 0
BISPSR	BISPSR(B,W) operand	Operand | 0 1 1 0 1 1 1 1 | B,W,D
BICPSR	BICPSR(B,W) operand	Operand | 0 0 1 0 1 1 1 1 | B,W,D
FFS	FFS(B,W,D) operand 1, operand 2	Operand 1 | Operand 2 | 0 0 0 1 | B,W,D | 0 1 1 0 1 1 1 0
CVTP	CVTP reg., operand 1, operand 2	Operand 1 | Operand 2 | Reg | 0 1 1 0 1 1 1 0 1 1 1 0

used to operate on a single bit that is stored in either a register or memory. When the bit is stored in memory, *any* of the memory addressing modes can be used to locate the bit. In these instructions the user must specify a displacement. The displacement specifies either the bit in a register, starting from bit D0, or a bit in memory, starting from the address specified in the instruction.

If a bit in a register is being accessed, then the displacement must be between 0 and 31. If a bit in memory is being accessed, the displacement can be a signed byte, word, or double word.

The set bit (SBIT), clear bit (CBIT), and test bit (TBIT) instructions are the same as in other processors, except that they are two-operand instructions (like most of the previous instructions). The set bit with memory interlock (SBITI) and clear bit with memory interlock (CBITI) instructions are used to set or clear a bit in memory. However, during the time that this operation is taking place, this memory location cannot be accessed by another device, such as a direct memory access (DMA) device, if it is wired to the interlock signal generated by the CPU chip. These instructions prevent devices from accessing these bits as they are being changed.

The 16000 microprocessors can also invert a bit (IBIT) and set and clear a bit in the processor status register (BISPSR and BICPSR). The last two bit instructions are find first set bit (FFS) and convert bit pointer. The find first set (FFS) instruction searches for the first set bit in operand 1, using the displacement specified as operand 2. If no set bit is found, operand 2 is cleared to zero, and if a set bit is found, its displacement is stored in operand 2. The convert bit pointer (CVTP) instruction actually causes a displacement to be calculated. The address of the bit is operand 1 plus the displacement in a general-purpose register. The displacement of the bit, from bit zero in memory location zero to this address, is stored in operand 2. This instruction is useful in high-level languages, such as Pascal, because a field address cannot be passed to a procedure or function. If this address is converted to an integer, however, the integer can be passed to the procedure or function.

Boolean Instructions

There are two Boolean instructions that the 16000 microprocessors can execute, and they are shown in Table 7-15. The NOT instruction simply inverts the least significant bit of operand 1 and stores the result in operand 2. The S (SET) instruction tests the condition codes in processor status register (PSR) and, based on the state of the code bits, sets or clears a bit in the operand. The codes that can be tested are summarized in Table 7-8.

Table 7-15. The 16000 Boolean Instructions

Mnemonic	Instruction Format	Op-Code Format
		23 0
NOT	NOT(B,W,D) operand 1, operand 2	Operand 1 | Operand 2 | 1 0 0 1 | B,W,D | 0 1 0 0 1 1 1 0
S	S(condition)(B,W,D) operand	Operand | Condition | 0 1 1 1 | B,W,D

Field Instructions

Quite often the size of data values being operated on does not correspond to the width of memory or to a multiple of that width. For instance, a 7-bit number can be stored in a byte memory location, but 1 bit of storage is wasted. Two 7-bit numbers could be stored in a word, using a packed format, but 2 bits of storage would be wasted. Thus the *field instructions* give the programmer the ability to address a value that is composed of any number of bits, up to 32. The microprocessor keeps track of where the fields are stored, and a field can actually cross byte, word, or double-word boundaries. Therefore no memory is wasted when this information is stored in memory. Seven-bit fields are shown in Fig. 7-11 for a 16-bit-wide memory.

In order to insert a field into an array we must have a source and destination for the data. For an insertion into an array the source and destination can be either a register or memory. Thus field instructions are two-operand instructions, which can use any of the memory addressing modes (there are some limitations when immediate addressing is used). When the 16000 microprocessor actually reads a value from memory during the execution of an instruction, it cannot just read a field, but must read either a byte, word, or dou-

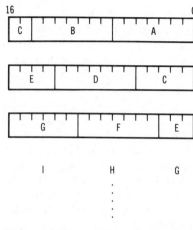

Fig. 7-11. Storing 7-bit fields in 16-bit memory words.

ble word, depending on how large the field actually is. Finally, when the field is actually inserted into the array, there has to be an *index* into the array, so the field inserted might be the fifth or 132nd element in the array. This *displacement* may be in a register or embedded in the instruction. The extract and insert field (EXT and INS) instructions require that the displacement is stored in a register, while the extract and insert field short (EXTS and INSS) instructions use a 3-bit displacement constant that is embedded in the instruction. The field instructions are summarized in Table 7-16.

Table 7-16. The Field Instructions for Accessing Arrays

Mnemonic	Instruction Format	Op-Code Format
		23 0
EXT	EXT(B,W,D) reg., oper. 1, oper. 2, constant	Operand 1 | Operand 2 | Reg | 0 | B,W,D | 0 0 1 0 1 1 1 0
INS	INS(B,W,D) reg., oper. 1, oper. 2, constant	Operand 1 | Operand 2 | Reg | 0 | B,W,D | 1 0 1 0 1 1 1 0
EXTS	EXTS(B,W,D) oper. 1, oper. 2, const. 1, const. 2	Operand 1 | Operand 2 | 0 0 1 1 | B,W,D | 1 1 0 0 1 1 1 0
INSS	INSS(B,W,D) oper. 1, oper. 2, const. 1, const. 2	Operand 1 | Operand 2 | 0 0 1 0 | B,W,D | 1 1 0 0 1 1 1 0

The insert field instruction, INS (B,W,D) reg., operand 1, operand 2, constant instruction causes a byte, word, or double word to be read from memory, using operand 1, and the field read is inserted into the array using a register for a displacement or index, from operand 2. The constant is the length of the field (1 to 32 bits). The extract field short instruction, EXTS (B,W,D) operand 1, operand 2, constant 1, constant 2, causes the 16000 to read a field of length constant 2 from the array, using constant 1 as a displacement from operand 1. The field is converted to either a byte, word, or double word, as determined by the length of the field (constant 2). This value is then written back into memory, using operand 2. *As in all of the previous instructions, the source of data is determined by the operand 1 addressing mode, and the destination of data is determined by the operand 2 addressing mode.*

Array Instructions

The two array instructions that the 16000 microprocessors can execute are summarized in Table 7-17. The INDEX instruction is used to calculate the index into a multidimensional array. The CHECK instruction is used to check that the index into an array is within bounds. Thus this instruction checks to make sure that the index is equal to or greater than one bound and less than or equal to another bound. Of course, a flag is set (F) if the index is out of bounds. This instruction also subtracts the index from the lowest index of the array and stores the result in the register specified in the instruction.

Table 7-17. Array Instructions

Mnemonic	Instruction Format		Op-Code Format
INDEX	INDEX(B,W,D) reg., operand 1, operand 2	23	Operand 1 | Operand 2 | Reg | 1 | B,W,D | 0 0 1 0 1 1 1 0 | 0
CHECK	CHECK(B,W,D) reg., operand 1, operand 2		Operand 1 | Operand 2 | Reg | 0 | B,W,D | 1 1 1 0 1 1 1 0

Processor Service Instructions

Some of the instructions that have already been described have been grouped together and are called "processor service instructions" by National Semiconductor. The instructions in this group that have already been described have dealt with processor registers. Thus the save and restore instructions, along with the load and save processor register and bit set/clear processor status register instructions, can be considered to be in this group. It really doesn't matter how you classify these instructions, as long as you have an appreciation of what they do.

Two instructions in this group that have not been discussed are ENTER and EXIT, which are used to allocate space on the stack for temporary storage. The ENTER instruction simply pushes the frame pointer (FP) on the stack and then transfers the stack pointer to the frame pointer. At this point the frame pointer and stack pointer contain the same memory address. A constant (up to 29 bits) is then subtracted from the stack pointer, and then any combination of the general-purpose registers is saved on the stack. The stack can now be used for the temporary storage of data. Once the stack has been used, the registers can be popped off of the stack with the EXIT instruction, and the stack pointer will be loaded with the content of the frame pointer, restoring the stack pointer to its previous value.

The 16000 processors also have an adjust stack pointer (ADJSP) instruction which causes an operand (up to 29 bits) to be subtracted from the stack pointer. The result is stored back into the stack pointer.

There is also a set configuration (SETCFG) instruction, which is used to set the C, M, F, and I codes in a write-only (!) configuration register. These bits are used to enable and disable external peripheral devices, such as an interrupt controller, floating-point unit, memory-management unit, and a customer-defined slave processor. These additional processor service instructions are summarized in Table 7-18.

Table 7-18. The Processor Service Instructions

Mnemonic	Instruction Format	Op-Code Format
ENTER	ENTER R0,R1,R2,R3,R4,R5,R6,R7, constant	R7 R6 R5 R4 R3 R2 R1 R0 1 0 0 0 0 0 1 0
EXIT	EXIT R0,R1,R2,R3,R4,R5,R6,R7	R7 R6 R5 R4 R3 R2 R1 R0 1 0 0 1 0 0 1 0
ADJSP	ADJSP operand	Operand 1 0 1 0 1 1 1 1 B,W,D
SETCFG	SETCFG C,M,F,I	0 0 0 0 0 C M F I 0 0 0 0 0 0 0 0 0 0 0 1 1 1 0

Miscellaneous Instructions

The simplest miscellaneous instruction is NOP, or no operation, which causes the microprocessor to waste a small amount of time, while it is being executed. The WAIT instruction puts the microprocessor into an "idle" state, where the microprocessor continues to execute the WAIT instruction until an interrupt occurs.

The trap instructions that this family of microprocessors have are FLAG, BPT, and SVC. The FLAG trap instruction will cause the FLG trap to be executed if the F code (a general-purpose flag bit used by many instructions) is set. The breakpoint trap instruction, or BPT, will cause a BPT trap to occur. The SVC, or supervisor, call trap instruction will cause a supervisor trap to occur. All of these traps are discussed, along with interrupts, in another section of this chapter. The miscellaneous instructions are listed in Table 7-19.

Expanding the Instruction Set

Because of the architecture of the 16000 family of microprocessors, the instruction set can be "expanded," depending on the type of additional control and slave devices that are in the system. As an example, both the memory-management unit and the floating-point unit have their own instructions. These instructions are used in programs just like the instructions that we have discussed. Of course, when the 16032 or one of the other processors in the family fetches one of these instructions from memory, it really cannot execute it and, for example, perform a floating-point addition. Instead, when one of these instructions is fetched from memory the 16032 tells the slave or peripheral device to execute the instruction. Once this device

Table 7-19. The Miscellaneous Instructions of the 16000 Processors

Mnemonic	Instruction Format	Op-Code Format
		7 0
NOP	NOP	`1 0 1 0 0 0 1 0`
WAIT	WAIT	`1 0 1 1 0 0 1 0`
FLAG	FLAG	`1 1 0 1 0 0 1 0`
BPT	BPT	`1 1 1 1 0 0 1 0`
SVC	SVC	`1 1 1 0 0 0 1 0`

has executed the instruction, it notifies the CPU so that the next instruction can be fetched from memory and be executed.

The instructions for the floating-point and memory-management units are *transparent* to the CPU chip. Since the CPU chip cannot execute these instructions, it directs these peripheral chips to execute them. *Of course, if the microprocessor tries to execute one of these instructions and the appropriate peripheral chip is not in the system, a trap will occur.* In fact, a trap will occur, based on the configuration of the system as determined by the SETCFG (set configuration) instruction. This is the only way that the user can inform the CPU as to which of the peripheral chips is in the system. The instruction sets for the memory-management unit and the floating-point unit are listed in Tables 7-20 and 7-21.

Instruction Set Conclusion

As you can see, the 16032 and the other microprocessor chip in this family, the 16016, are extremely powerful devices. In fact, they can probably execute the benchmarks faster than any of the other processors in this book. Unfortunately, because this device (16032) is so new, the authors have not been able to test the benchmark programs on it. With all of their powerful addressing modes, both of these devices will certainly give the other 16-bit processors real competition.

MICROPROCESSOR CHIP HARDWARE

Currently, two different CPU chips are planned: the 16032 and the 16016. The first device to appear will be the 16032, because it is the most complex. The 16032 is housed in a 48-pin package, while the 16016 processor will be available in a 40-pin package.

Table 7-20. The Memory-Management Unit Instruction Set

Instruction	Format	Description
LMR	mreg.,gen.*	Load memory-management register
SMR	mreg.,gen.	Store memory-management register
RDVAL	gen.	Validate address for reading
WRVAL	gen.	Validate address for writing
MOVF1i	gen.,gen.	Move a value from space 1 to space 2
MOVF2i	gen.,gen.	Move a value from space 2 to space 1

*"gen." is equivalent to operand 1 or operand 2, the addressing modes of the microprocessors.

Even though the processors differ greatly in the amount of memory that they can address and the instructions that they execute (the 16016 can execute 8080 programs directly), they still generate a number of the same signals.

All of the processors use a multiplexed address/data bus. Both the 16032 and 16016 multiplex the 16-bit data bus with all 16 (16016) or 16 of 24 (16032) address lines. Since the 16016 has 16 address lines, it can address 65K bytes of memory.

In order to address memory the processor has to indicate when an address is present on this multiplexed address/data lines and this signal is $\overline{ADS}$, or address strobe. There is also a high-byte enable ($\overline{HBE}$) signal, along with interrupt ($\overline{NMI}$, $\overline{INT}$), reset ($\overline{RST}$), and ready (RDY) inputs.

Surprisingly enough, none of the three microprocessors generates read or write control signals! Instead, these two signals are generated by the NS16201 clock generator chip.

As we have seen, the 16032 and the other processor in this family can read bytes, words, or double words from memory. Since memory is 16 bits wide, however, any memory operation will be either a byte or word transfer. In order to transfer double words, two words must be either written or read if the double word is aligned. If it is not aligned, up to four transfers may be required. In order to control the byte or word transfer the memory control logic must use high-byte enable ($\overline{HBE}$) and A0, which can be called low-byte enable. If both of these signals are logic zeros, then a word is being transferred, and if only one is a logic zero, then the upper or lower byte of a word is being transferred.

CPU TIMING

Typical memory-read and memory-write operations are shown in Figs. 7-12 and 7-13. As you can see from Fig. 7-12, all timing is related to the 10-MHz clock signal generated by the clock generator

Table 7-21. The Instruction Set of the NS16081 Floating-Point Unit

Instruction	Format	Description
MOVf	gen.,gen.	Move a floating-point value
MOVLF	gen.,gen	Move and shorten a long value to standard
MOVFL	gen.,gen.	Move and lengthen a standard value to long
MOVif	gen.,gen.	Convert any integer to standard or long floating
ROUNDfi	gen.,gen.	Convert to integer by rounding
TRUNCfi	gen.,gen.	Convert to integer by truncating toward zero
FLOORfi	gen.,gen.	Convert to largest integer less than or equal to value
ADDf	gen.,gen.	Add
SUBf	gen.,gen.	Subtract
MULf	gen.,gen.	Multiply
DIVf	gen.,gen.	Divide
CMPf	gen.,gen.	Compare
NEGf	gen.,gen.	Negate
MAGf	gen.,gen.	Take absolute value
FRACf	gen.,gen.	Take remainder from TRUNC
INTf	gen.,gen.	Take integer portion without converting to integer format
LFSR	gen.	Load FSR
SFSR	gen.	Store FSR
SVFREG	[freg. list]	Save floating-point registers FSR may be included in freg. list.
RSFREG	[freg. list]	Restore floating-point registers FSR may be included in freg. list.

Note:
gen. = addressing mode,
freg. = floating-point register (F0–F7),
freg. list = list of floating-point registers.

chip (CLOCK or PHI1). Note that as in previous processors, when an address is present on the address/data lines, the address strobe signal ($\overline{ADS}$) has to be generated. The data direction in ($\overline{DDIN}$) signal is also generated, so that any bidirectional buffers that are on the data bus can be "turned around" for a read operation. At some later time the read signal ($\overline{RD}$) is generated, followed by the data bus enable signal ($\overline{DBE}$). These signals would normally be gated together and would be used to gate data from memory onto the data bus. The ready (RDY) input, if it is used, can "stretch out" this read cycle, so that memories with long access times can be used with the microprocessors.

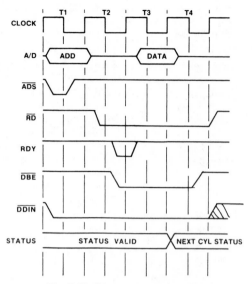

Fig. 7-12. A memory-read cycle.

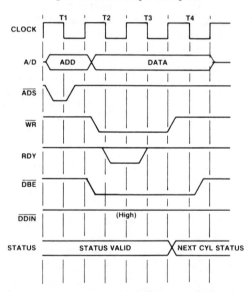

Fig. 7-13. A 16000-series CPU memory-write timing diagram.

The write cycle (Fig. 7-13) is very similar to the read cycle. As you would expect, the write ($\overline{WR}$) signal is generated instead of the $\overline{RD}$ signal, and the data direction in signal stays in the logic one state so that information from the CPU can flow through any data bus buffers out to memory. Depending on the access times of the memories used in the microcomputer system, the **RDY** input may or may not be used.

BENCHMARKS

At this time no 16032 CPU chips exist that the authors could use in order to benchmark the processor. Thus the syntax and program flow of each benchmark has not been verified. Since the first benchmark involves the sorting of 600 data values stored in memory, the first example (Fig. 7-14) contains the instructions that are used to initialize memory prior to sorting.

```
INIT:      MOVW 600,R0        ;Load R0 with decimal 600.
           MOVD LIST,R1       ;Load the starting address of LIST into R1.
LOOP:      MOVW R0,(R1)       ;Store R0 in memory addressed by R1.
           ADDQW 2,R1         :Increment the R1 address by two.
           ACBB -1,R0,LOOP    ;Decrement R0 by 1, goto LOOP if not zero.
               .              ;Continue with remainder of program.
               .

LIST EQU 4000                 :The starting address of the list is
                              :defined as decimal 4000.
```

Fig. 7-14. Initializing memory for the bubble sort program.

In Fig. 7-14 a decimal 600 (a word) is moved as an immediate data value to the R0 register. The R1 register is then loaded with the first memory address to be used by the list. Thus R1 is loaded with decimal 4000. At LOOP the content of R0 (initially 600) is stored in the memory location addressed by an offset and the content of R1. The offset is zero, so the first value is stored in memory location 4000. The content of the R1 register is then incremented by 2 by means of the ADDQW instruction and then the content of R0 is decremented by 1. If the content of R0 is not zero, the 16032 jumps back to the instruction at LOOP.

Bubble Sort

Once memory has been initialized it can be sorted by the bubble sort instructions in Fig. 7-15. At the beginning of this benchmark, R1 is loaded with the memory address stored in memory location 400 and R0 is loaded with the word count (600) that was previously stored in memory location 404. The address in R1 is then moved to R2. The exchange indicator will be a bit in R3, so the lsb of R3 is cleared by means of the BICB instruction.

Starting at UP, 2 is added to the address in R2. Thus R1 addresses the first word in the list and R2 addresses the second word. The two values addressed by these registers are then compared by the CMPW

```
BSORT:      MOVD @400,R1        ;Move an address stored in memory, into R1.
            MOVW @404,R0        ;Move the word count from memory to R0.
            MOVD R1,R2          ;Move the address to R2 also.
            BICB 0,R3           ;Clear the LSB of R3.
UP:         ADDQW 2,R2          ;Increment address in R2 by 2 (for words).
            CMPW (R2),(R1)      ;Compare the two words in memory.
            BLT OK              ;Branch if (R2) > (R1),the correct order.
            MOVW (R1),R4        ;Move larger number to R4.
            MOVW (R2),(R1)      ;Move smaller number to a lower memory location.
            MOVW R4,(R2)        ;Save the larger value back in memory.
            SBITB 0,R3          ;Set the exchange indicator.
OK:         MOVD R2,R1          ;Move the higher address to R1
            ACBW -1,R0,UP       ;If not done, update content of R2 and repeat.
            TBIT 0,R3           ;Done all 600, any exchanges take place?
            BFS BSORT           ;Yes, check the entire list again.
                .               ;When sorted, continue with the
                .               ;remainder of the program.
                .


400         Starting address of the list, 4000, is stored here
404         Number of words to be sorted, 600, is stored here.
```

Fig. 7-15. Bubble sorting 600 data values stored in memory.

instruction. If the content of memory addressed by R1 is less than the content of memory addressed by R2, the 16032 branches to OK because the data values are in the proper order. If they need to be exchanged, the larger value is moved to R4, the smaller value is moved from the higher memory location to the lower memory location, and then the larger value is moved from R4 back into memory. The exchange indicator is then set (SBITB).

At OK the higher address in R2 is moved to R1, and then the word count in R0 is decremented by 1. If the entire list has not been examined yet, the 16032 will jump back to UP. At UP the address in R2 will be incremented by 2 so that the next two values can be compared. If all 600 data values in the list have been examined, the 16032 will not branch back to UP, but instead will test the exchange indicator. If this is a logic one, the 16032 will jump back to BSORT so that the addresses and word count can be reinitialized prior to examining the entire list again. Once the list has been sorted, the exchange indicator will be zero.

ASCII String Search

The third benchmark involves finding the string MICRO* in a sequence of strings stored in memory. At the beginning of Fig. 7-16 the address of the MAIN string is loaded from memory location 406 into R1. The ASCII equivalent of the string termination character, an asterisk, is then loaded into R4. At NEXT, R2 is loaded with the address of the TEST string, which was previously stored in memory location 410. Before any comparisons can be performed the 16032 has to be programmed with the number of characters in the

```
SEARCH:    MOVD  @406,R1      ;Move MAIN address from memory to R1.
           MOVB  '*',R4       ;Load R4 with ASCII value for an asterisk.
NEXT:      MOVD  @410,R2      ;Move TEST address from memory to R2.
           MOVB  6,R0         ;Load R0 with number of characters in MICRO*.
           CMPB  '?',(R1)     ;At end of MAIN string?
           BEQ DONE           ;Yes, then didn't find the MICRO* string.
           CMPSB              ;Compare strings until no longer equal
           BFC DONE           ;They matched, R0 (count) is zero, we're done.
           MOVB  255,R0       ;Didn't match, load R0 with large count.
           CMPSU              ;Compare (R1;MAIN) until an * is found.
           JUMP NEXT          ;Then try for a match again.
DONE:        .               ;They matched, so execute the remainder
             .               ;of the program.
             .



406        The address of the MAIN string is stored here, 1000.
410        The address of the TEST string is stored here, 2000.


1000       DB    'NANO*'
1005       DB    'PICO*'
1010       DB    'MICROCOMPUTER*'
1024       DB    'MICROPROCESSOR*'
1039       DB    'MICROSYSTEM*'
1051       DB    'MICRO*'
1057       DB    '?'


2000       DB    'MICRO*'
```

Fig. 7-16. Using the 16032 to search for the MICRO* string.

MICRO* string, so R0 is loaded with 6. *The R0, R1, R2, and R4 registers must be loaded with specific types of information before any of the 16032 string instructions can be executed.* Depending on the string instructions used, R3 may also have to be used.

Once these four registers have been initialized, the 16032 compares a MAIN string character to a question mark. If the characters are the same, then the 16032 has reached the end of the MAIN string without finding the MICRO* string. Therefore it has to abandon the search. The processor does this by branching to DONE. If no question mark is found, the CMPSB instruction is executed. This instruction compares the strings addressed by R1 and R2, on a byte-by-byte basis (as specified in the instruction). The comparison process continues until either a difference between the strings is found or the count in R0 is decremented to zero.

The F code will be cleared if the R0 register has been decremented to zero, which means that the strings matched. Therefore, if a match occurs, the 16032 branches to DONE. If the strings do not match, the 16032 loads R0 with a count larger than the maximum number of characters in a string, and then compares string 1, the MAIN string, to the content of R4, an asterisk, *until* a match occurs. Once the 16032 stops executing this instruction, R1 is addressing the first character in the next string in the MAIN string, or it might possibly be pointing to the ? at the end of the MAIN string. Therefore the processor jumps back to NEXT.

As you can see, we have assumed that the TEST string is stored in memory, starting at memory address 2000, and that the MAIN string is stored in memory, starting at memory address 1000. We have also assumed that the starting addresses of the strings (1000 and 2000) are stored in memory locations 406 and 410.

Square Root Determination

The square root approximation instructions are listed in Fig. 7-17. In order to clear all 32 bits of R0 to zero, R0 is exclusive-ORed with itself. The number whose root is to be determined is then loaded from memory into R0, and this same number is then stored in R2. The content of R2 is then divided by decimal 200 and 2 is added to the result. This is the first approximation, which is stored in R2. At

```
SROOT:   XORD  RO,RO       ;Clear the 32-bit RO register to zero.
         MOVW  @4250,RO    ;Get number whose root is to be found.
         MOVW  RO,R2       ;Save the number in R2.
         DIVD  200,R2      ;Divide the number in R2 by 200.
         ADDOW 2,R2        ;Add two.  R2 is the 1st approximation.
RLOOP:   MOVW  RO,R1       ;Move the original number to R1.
         DIVD  R2,R1       ;Divide # in R1 by approx. in R2, R2=result.
         MOVW  R1,R3       ;Move division result to R3.
         MULW  R1,R1       ;Square division result in R1.
         CMPD  R1,RO       ;Squared result = original number?
         BEQ   DONE        ;Yes, approximation is in R3.
         ADDW  R3,R2       ;No, add the approximations.
         LSHW  1,R2        ;Divide R2 by 2.  This is the new approx.
         JUMP  RLOOP       ;Try R2 as the approximation.
DONE:    MOVW  R3,@4252    ;Save the approximation.
           .              ;Remainder of the program.
           .
           .
```

Fig. 7-17. 16032 instructions for approximating a square root.

RLOOP, the "original" number in R0 is moved to R1, and then this number is divided by the approximation in R2. The division result, which is a new approximation, is stored in R1, and is then moved to R3. The division result is then multiplied by itself and is compared to the "original" number stored in R0. If the two numbers are equal, the approximation stored in R3 is the square root of the number, so the 16032 branches to DONE, where this number is stored in memory location 4252. If the squared result of the approximation is not equal to the original number, the two approximations, one in R3 and one in R2, are added together and the result is divided by 2. This new approximation is stored in R2 when the processor jumps back to RLOOP.

Lookup Table

The sine "calculations" in Fig. 7-18 should look similar to some of the previous sine benchmarks. The angle is in R0 when these instructions are first executed. The first instruction causes the most significant bit in the 16-bit word of register R2 to be cleared. This bit will be used to store the sign of the sine. The angle in R0 is then compared to 180, and if the content of R0 is less than or equal to

```
SINE:       CBITW 15,R2     ;Clear bit D15 in R2 (sign bit).
            CMPW 180,R0     ;Subtract 180 from angle in R0.
            BLE LT180       ;Branch if R0 is less than or = to 180.
            SBITW 15,R2     ;More than 180, so set the sign bit.
            SUBW 180,R0     ;Subtract 180 from the large angle.
LT180:      CMPW 90,R0      ;Angle in R0 less than or = to 90?
            BLE OKASIS      ;Yes, use it as an index or offset.
            NEG RO,RO       ;Convert the angle to a negative angle.
            ADDB 90,R0      ;Add 90 to this value.
OKASIS:     MOVW 4000(R0),R0  :Register relative; 4000 offset.
            ADDW R2,R0
              .
              .             ;Then continue with the remainder
              .             ;of the program.
              .


4000        Sine of 0°
4002        Sine of 1°
4004        Sine of 2°
              .
              .
4180        Sine of 90°
```

Fig. 7-18. Determining the sine of an angle.

this number, the 16032 branches to LT180. If the angle is 181 or greater, bit 15 of R2 is set and 180 is subtracted from the angle. By the time that the microprocessor gets to LT180, all angles have been "reduced" to a value between 0 and 180. By comparing this value to 90, the processor determines if any additional operations have to be performed on the angle. If the angle in R0 is less than or equal to 90, the processor branches to OKASIS. Otherwise, the twos complement of the angle in R0 is determined and 90 is added to this value.

At OKASIS the content of R0, the reduced angle, is used as the offset in a register relative instruction. The offset of 4000 is really the starting address of the lookup table. The sine of the angle is read into register R0, and then the sign of the sine is added to the sine. As in the previous benchmark discussions the numbers used in the listings are decimal and not hexadecimal.

MICROCOMPUTER BOARDS

Currently National Semiconductor makes a number of Multibus-compatible boards. Therefore the 16032 will be available on a single Multibus-compatible board. This product will be known as the DB-16000 and will contain the 16032 CPU chip, along with sockets for optional memory-management and floating-point chips. The board can also have up to 32K of read/write memory and 8K of ROM. For communicating with peripherals, the board also has 24 parallel i/o lines and two RS-232C ports.

The RS-232C ports, when used with the software provided by National Semiconductor, can be used with a terminal and main frame computer. If just a terminal is used with the DB16000, the user can use the system monitor and debugger to program the 16032. If a larger system is available, programs can be prepared on this larger system and can then be downline loaded into the DB16000.

Of course, one of the main frames that can be used in conjunction with the DB16000 is the Starplex development system that National Semiconductor makes. With this system the user has access to USCD Pascal and the USCD operating system, along with symbolic debuggers, editors, assemblers, linking loaders, librarians (for libraries of programs and subroutines), and a simulator. Of course, with this capability, software could be prepared on any main frame computer (with the proper cross assembler) and the resulting software could be downline loaded into the DB16000.

INTERFACING

Like the LSI-11 and 68000, the 16032 does not have any special i/o instructions. Therefore all peripherals must be interfaced to the 16032 using memory-mapped i/o techniques. The timing for input and output operations is shown in Figs. 7-19 and 7-20.

In these diagrams note that the address is shown as being latched off of the address/data bus. Thus the address is present throughout the read or write cycle. *The memory timing diagrams that were just discussed could have been drawn in exactly the same manner.*

The only real difference is that the signal $\overline{PER}$ is present. This signal can be generated by *slow* peripherals, and it is wired to the clock generator chip. *By taking this input to a logic zero before the T2 timing state, five wait states are automatically inserted into the timing of the read and write operations.* This signal would only be used by slow, MOS LSI interface chips. If TTL chips are used in an interface, they are more than fast enough to be used directly with the 16000 series of CPUs. Consequently this signal would not be used.

A 16-bit output port design is shown in Fig. 7-21. In this design,

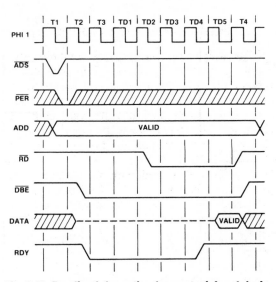

Fig. 7-19. Reading information from a peripheral device.

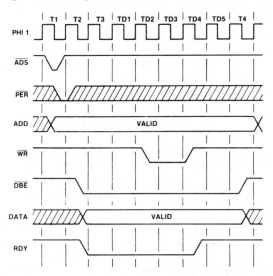

Fig. 7-20. The timing for peripheral-write operation.

decoders are wired to both address and control signals. Only when the address 110000 is present on the upper SN74LS154 will the lower decoder be enabled. With this decoder the $\overline{WR}$, $\overline{HBE}$, and address inputs A0–A2 have to be zero in order for the zero output (pin 1) to be a logic zero. This output is inverted, and the logic one is used to clock the SN74LS373 8-bit latches. Note that in order to transfer

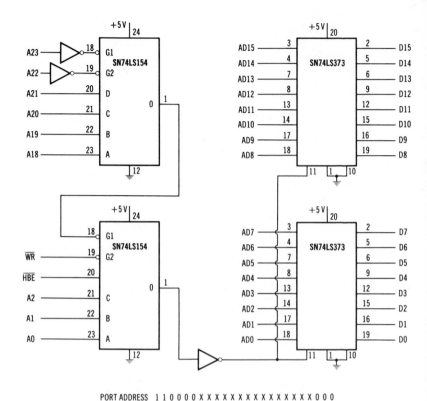

PORT ADDRESS 1 1 0 0 0 0 X X X X X X X X X X X X X X X X 0 0 0

Fig. 7-21. A typical 16-bit memory-mapped output port.

a 16-bit word, both $\overline{\text{HBE}}$ and A0 must be logic zeros. This requirement is met in the interface design. Also, since this is an output port, the $\overline{\text{WR}}$ control signal must be used somewhere in the address decoder design. This signal has actually been used to enable the lower SN-74LS154 decoder.

The address decoder in this output port design is a nonabsolute memory address decoder because not all of the address signals between A0 and A23 have been used. Therefore the output port will latch the data present on the data bus, when the address 110000XXXXXXXX-XXXXXXXX000 is present on the address bus where X can be a 0 or 1. There are 2^{15}, or 32,768, different memory addresses that can be used to communicate with this interface, because 15 of the address signals have not been used in the decoder design.

A simple 8-bit input port is shown in Fig. 7-22. In this design a slightly different decoder has been used. A NAND gate is used to gate A23 through A16 together, and only when all of these address lines are logic ones will the output of the SN74LS30 NAND gate be a logic

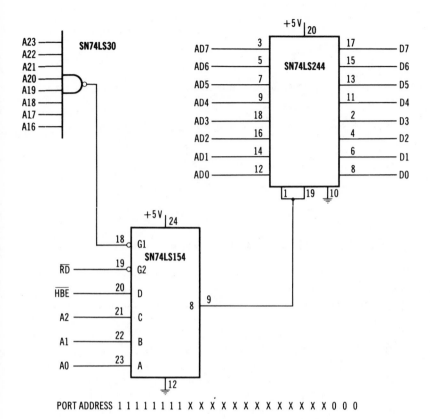

PORT ADDRESS 1 1 1 1 1 1 1 1 X X X X X X X X X X X X X 0 0 0

Fig. 7-22. An 8-bit input port (even byte address).

zero. This logic zero, along with a logic zero $\overline{RD}$ signal, is used to enable the SN74LS154 decoder. Since an 8-bit input port is being interfaced to the microcomputer, we have to decide which half of the data bus to use in the interface. In this design the input port is wired to AD0 through AD7. This means that, in order to communicate with this *byte port, A0 must be a logic zero and $\overline{HBE}$ must be a logic one.* Therefore the output 8 (pin 9) is used to enable the three-state buffers.

I/O SOFTWARE

Since all interfaces must use memory-mapped i/o, the software that is used to communicate with these ports "looks like" it is communicating with memory. Therefore any of the 16032 instructions that reference memory can be used to communicate with a properly designed interface.

```
OUTDATA:     MOVW 392,@45968        ;Move the decimal constant
                                    ;392 to "memory location"
                                    ;45968.
```

Fig. 7-23. Writing a 16-bit word stored in memory to an output port.

```
LOOP:        MOVW R3,@45968         ;Write R3 out to address 45968.
             ADDQB 1,R3             ;Add 1 to content of R3.
             JMP LOOP               ;Jump, relative to PC, to LOOP.
```

Fig. 7-24. Incrementing a register and writing it out to an output port.

```
GETPUT:      MOVB 024H,R0           ;Load R0 with decimal 35.
             MOVD 0,R1              ;Load R1 with zero.
WAIT:        TBITW 0,@45970         ;Test the flag in the interface.
             BFC WAIT               ;Branch to WAIT if zero.
             MOVW @45968,@3000(R1:W) ;Read value and save it.
             ADDQ 2,R1              ;Add 2 to the offset in R1.
             ACBB -1,R0,WAIT        ;Decrement R0, goto WAIT if not zero.
                 .                  ;Execute the remainder of the program.
                 .
```

Fig. 7-25. Reading data from an input port and storing it in memory.

In Fig. 7-23 the decimal word 392 is written out to the output port that has an absolute address of 45968. Of course, as far as the microprocessor is concerned, it is simply writing a value out to memory.

In Fig. 7-24 the contents of register R3 are output to the same output port, but then a sign extended "quick" byte of 1 is added to the content of R3. This has the effect of incrementing the content of R3 by 1. The 16032 then jumps back to the memory location assigned the "identifier" of LOOP. This is the memory location that contains the MOVW instruction. *Symbolic addresses* of this kind are very common. Of course, this jump instruction uses register relative addressing, where the offset is added to the program counter (PC).

The program of Fig. 7-25 is used to input 35 words of data from a peripheral and store them in memory. At GETPUT, register R0 is loaded with hexadecimal 23 (decimal 35). Register R1 is then loaded with zero because it will be used in a scaled indexed instruction. At WAIT, bit D0 of "memory location" 45970 (part of the interface) is tested. The F code is then tested with the BFC instruction. If the F code is cleared as a result of the TBITW instruction, the 16032 branches back to WAIT. Only when the tested bit is a logic one will the 16032 get out of the WAIT loop. At that time the word at memory location 45968 is read and is written back into memory using scaled indexed addressing.

The starting address of this array is 3000, and R1 provides the array index. Therefore the first word will be written into memory location 3000. The index in R1 is then incremented by 2 (ADDQ) and the content of R0 is decremented by 1 (ACBB). If the result of this instruction is nonzero, the 16032 branches back to WAIT.

Once this loop has been executed 35 times, we will have stored an array of words in memory, starting at decimal memory address 3000, up to address 3070. The first data value will be stored in 3000 and the last data value will be stored in 3070.

INTERRUPTS

In many instances interrupts are used with peripheral devices so that the peripheral can notify the CPU instantly if it has data, needs data, or, therefore, needs *servicing*. Quite often the term "interrupt" is used to describe external events and trap is used to describe an internal event. Regardless of whether a trap or interrupt has occurred, they are serviced in much the same manner.

The traps that the 16000 series of CPU chips will recognize are summarized in Table 7-22. The traps that we are familiar with include the illegal instruction trap, supervisor call trap, divide-by-zero trap, and trace trap. As you can see, the floating-point math chip and the memory-management chip can also generate traps. The FLG trap will occur if the FLAG instruction is executed when the F code is set and the BPT (breakpoint) trap will occur if the breakpoint instruction (BPT) is executed.

From Table 7-22 you can see that there can be up to 256 interrupts and traps. Each one of these interrupts or traps is identified with a vector (number) within the range of 0 to 255. When an interrupt or trap occurs, this vector is added to the content of the interrupt (INT) register to provide an address into a dispatch table. This table contains double-word entries, hence the interrupt and trap service instructions can reside anywhere in memory.

Of course, if a trap occurs, internal CPU logic provides the vector

Table 7-22. Trap and Interrupt Vector Values

Vector	Mnemonic	Description
0	NVI	Nonvectored interrupt
1	NMI	Nonmaskable interrupt
2	ABT	Address translation or bus error trap
3	FPU	Floating-point-unit error trap
4	ILL	Illegal instruction trap
5	SVC	Supervisor call trap
6	DVZ	Divide by zero trap
7	FLG	Flag trap
8	BPT	Breakpoint trap
9	TRC	Trace trap
10	UND	Undefined instruction trap
11–15		Reserved
16–255		Vector interrupts

for the trap. If an external interrupt occurs, the interrupt control logic contained in the interface must provide the vector. For this reason, interrupt control chips are often used in systems to provide these vectors.

When a trap or interrupt occurs the MOD and PSR registers are pushed onto the stack (either the supervisor or user). The P, S, U, and T codes in the PSR are then cleared. The PC is also pushed onto the stack, but its value depends on the trap or interrupt that occurred. For all but the trace (TRC) trap, any trap will cause the content of the PC that is addressing the *current instruction* to be pushed onto the stack. For the trace (TRC) trap and all interrupts, the PC content that addresses the *next instruction* that would have been executed, had the TRC trap or interrupt not occurred, is pushed onto the stack.

The fact that most of the traps do not update the PC before it is pushed on to the stack is very important. This means that if some action of a peripheral device, such as the floating-point and memory-management chips, causes the execution of an instruction to be *aborted,* the processor can try to execute the same instruction again, when the problem in the peripheral chips is removed. Once the trap or interrupt has been serviced, the RETI and RETT instructions are used at the end of the interrupt or trap service subroutines so that the microprocessor returns to the proper point in the task that was being executed.

If an interrupt must be used by a peripheral device, two inputs to the chip, $\overline{\text{INT}}$ and $\overline{\text{NMI}}$, can be used. The $\overline{\text{INT}}$ interrupt input is usually used with the NS16202 interrupt controller. More than one of these devices can be used with a system, so many of the vectors between 16 and 255 could be assigned to these devices. If the NS-16202 is not used in the system, then the device wired to the $\overline{\text{INT}}$ input will be the nonvectored interrupt device, so the internal logic in the CPU chip will always generate a vector of zero. The $\overline{\text{NMI}}$ is an interrupt input that can never be disabled, so it could be wired to some power-fail circuitry.

How does the CPU chip know that if no interrupt controller is in the system the $\overline{\text{INT}}$ pin will generate a vector of zero, and if a controller chip is in the system it will provide vectors between 16 and 255? The only way that the system knows in which mode to operate is by the interrupt (I) code of the configuration register and the set configuration (SETCFG) instruction. Note that there are no instructions that can be used to read the contents of the configuration register.

As with all of the previous processors, the interrupts and traps have different priorities. This means that if two interrupts or traps occur at the same time, one of them (the one with the higher priority) will be serviced first. *The abort (ABT) trap has the highest priority of all traps and interrupts.* This trap is usually generated by the memory-management chip. All of the remaining traps, except the trace (TRC) trap, have the next highest priority. The nonmaskable interrupt input (NMI) is next, followed by the device that is wired to the INT interrupt input. Regardless of what is wired to the INT input, the device or devices will always have a priority that is less than that of the NMI input. If the 16202 interrupt controller is wired to this input, then the controller will assign vectors and priority to each of the peripheral devices that is wired to it. If no controller chip is used in the system, then the nonvectored interrupt will be used, and it will have a priority less than the nonmaskable interrupt.

TRAPS

As we have seen, the traps and interrupts use the same dispatch table that is addressed by the interrupt (INT) register. Of course, before traps and interrupts are used, this register must be loaded with the starting address of the table.

A number of the traps that the 16032 has are similar to the traps of other processors. The ABT trap is usually generated by the memory-management chip if you try to access information that is not currently stored in memory (we will discuss more on this later). The illegal instruction trap (ILL) is generated if a user program (as opposed to a supervisor program) tries to execute a privileged instruction. Privileged instructions are instructions that try to modify the privileged half of the PSR.

The supervisor call trap (SVC) occurs if a SVC instruction is executed in a program. Unlike many of the other 16-bit processors, there is no identifier associated with the SVC trap. Therefore there is only one SVC trap, rather than the 16 to 256 associated with some of the other processors. Of course, the SVC trap software could "decode" a byte or word stored on the stack prior to the SVC instruction being executed. Thus the ability to have a number of different supervisor calls does exist, but it will require a bit of software overhead.

The divide-by-zero trap at this point should be self-explanatory, and the breakpoint and flag traps occur only if the appropriate 1-byte instructions are executed in a program. The trace (TRC) trap is the trap used to single-step the 16032 through a program, one instruction at a time. The 16000 series of processors are similar to the 8086 and 68000 in this regard. Finally, the undefined instruction trap (UND) will occur if the processor tries to execute an instruction that is not in its instruction set. This means that if the user tries to execute a floating-point or memory-management instruction without these chips being in the system, a UND trap will occur. As these chips are added, the instructions for these chips are "added" to the instruction set of the CPU chip by means of the set configuration (SETCFG) instruction.

SPECIAL-FUNCTION CHIPS

The special-function chips that will be available for the 16032 and 16016 are summarized below in Table 7-23. The 16201 clock generator chip is a necessary part of an 16000-based microcomputer, because it provides the basic clock for the CPU chip and also the $\overline{RD}$ and $\overline{WR}$ control signals. This device also has the $\overline{PER}$ peripheral wait input, which inserts five wait states into a peripheral-read or -write cycle, if slow peripheral devices are involved in the data transfer. This device also has four programmable, binary, wait state inputs, which can be used by memory or peripheral devices. As memories with different access times are accessed, the memory control logic can program the clock generator to insert a different number of wait states into the memory-read and -write cycles. As an example, a different number of wait states would be required if slow EPROMs are accessed and then fast read/write (R/W) memory is accessed.

Table 7-23. Support Chips for the 16032/16016/16008

Name	Function
16201 Clock generator	System clock, read/write control signals
16202 Interrupt controller	Eight external interrupts, two counters
16203 DMA controller	Direct memory acess controller
16204 Bus arbitor	Arbitrates bus usage among many processors
16081 Floating-point unit	High-speed floating-point calculations
16082 Memory-management unit	Virtual memory, debug, and trace facilities

The 16202 interrupt controller chip can generate up to 16 vectored, prioritized interrupts, with up to eight of these interrupts coming from external peripheral devices. This chip also contains two 16-bit, 10-MHz counters, which can also be used to generate interrupts. The two counters can also be cascaded into one 32-bit counter. Additional 16202s can be used in a system, along with a "master" 16202.

For very high-speed peripheral devices, such as fixed disks, the

16203 DMA controller would be used in the interface between the disk and the microcomputer. This device can transfer up to 5M bytes per second, and can also be used to pack two 8-bit bytes into a 16-bit word, in order to reduce the number of memory accesses it must make.

The 16204 bus arbitor is used to determine which of two or more CPUs can access the buses in a microcomputer system. This device is used only when there are two or more CPUs in a single computer system.

The 16081 floating-point unit is designed to relieve the CPU from complex floating-point calculations. This device can be operated as either a slave processor or as a peripheral, and it meets the IEEE proposed standard for floating-point number formats. This device has its own instruction set (Table 7-21) and its own general-purpose registers.

MEMORY MANAGEMENT

The 16082 memory-management unit is a very complex chip (as is the 16081 FPU) but it gives the user the feature of *virtual memory*. In most cases, virtual memory is associated with multimillion-dollar main frames. With the availability of 65K-bit R/W memory chips, however, it is easy to foresee that a small microcomputer could have 1M or 2M bytes of memory, at which point it would probably need virtual memory.

What is virtual memory? As an example, let us assume we have a microcomputer with 1000 words of memory. If we take a very simplistic approach, this means that we must limit our programs to no more than 1000 16-bit instructions. Of course, this assumes that no data will be stored in memory (there won't be any room for it) and also that all instructions are 16 bits in length, which they are not. However, even with these simplifications, the point is that we simply cannot have programs that are larger than the amount of memory that is present in the system. If the program grows to 2000 or 3000 instructions, we have a real problem.

One solution to this problem would be to buy more memory for the system. With very large programs, however, we are talking about ½M or 1M bytes of memory, which is still relatively expensive. On the other hand, suppose that we have a mass storage device, such as a floppy or fixed-head disk. With some complex (but writable) software (the operating system) we could store portions of our 3000-instruction program on one of these devices. A small portion of the program could then be read into memory and be executed. If it needs to access a portion of the program that is stored on the *mass storage* or *secondary storage* device, the operating system software would read it into memory so that the first portion of the program can access it. As you can imagine, this operating system program is very complex, and fortunately most of us don't have to write one.

When the 3000-instruction program is actually written, it is written as if there is enough money in the system to store the entire program all at once (even though there isn't). One of the addressing modes that the 16032 has is absolute addressing, so it is conceivable that there might be a reference to absolute address 2093 or 1854. All of the addresses in this program are called *virtual addresses*.

When a portion of the program is loaded into memory, it might actually reference one of these memory locations, but the instruction or data being referenced might actually be loaded into memory location 539. Remember, the operating system loads portions of the program into memory wherever it can fit them (Fig. 7-26). Therefore the operating system has to convert all of these absolute addresses and all of the other addresses used in the program to the addresses of the memory locations where the instructions or data are *actually* stored. Again, this is a complex and time consuming task.

In essence, the 16082 MMU chip takes care of a lot of these *housekeeping* tasks. When the 3000-instruction program is first executed, the beginning of the program, along with possibly some subroutines and data values are loaded into memory. Based on this the operating system software builds a *page table,* where a page is a 512-byte portion of the program being executed. The contents of the page table

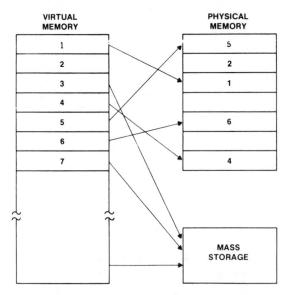

Fig. 7-26. Loading portions of a virtual memory program into memory.

indicate which portions of the program are actually stored in memory. The starting address of the page table is stored in a *page table register* in the MMU chip. Thus, when portions of the 3000-instruction program are executed, the 16032 actually places a 24-bit virtual address on the address bus. The MMU chip, using this address, decides if the appropriate page is stored in memory, by means of accessing the page table. If the page is stored in memory, the MMU converts or translates the virtual address to the physical or actual memory address. If the page is not in memory or it is protected (a user program should not be able to access supervisor data, no writes into read-only storage, etc.), an *abort* signal will be issued by the MMU, causing an ABT trap to be generated. When this occurs, the PC pointing to the instruction that caused the abort to occur is saved. Thus once the abort situation is corrected, the same instruction can be reexecuted and, it is hoped, an abort will not recur.

Once the abort occurs, the 16032 has to determine why it occurred, and then perform the appropriate actions to correct the situation. This might consist of printing an error message (UNAUTHORIZED ACCESS TO A SUPERVISOR FILE) or a page on the secondary storage device (disk, magnetic tape) could be swapped with a page in main memory. If pages are swapped, the page table would be updated so that the instruction can be executed successfully.

As you can imagine, the MMU chip is very complex. It has a number of error codes and status flags that are used to indicate the type of page (user, supervisor, read-only, read/write) and whether the page has ever been referenced, to name just a few. The actual translation of the virtual addresses to physical addresses is extremely complex, and fortunately, since most of us don't write operating systems, it is really not necessary to understand how it is done.

Not only does the MMU give us virtual memory, but it also has a number of features that makes it fairly easy to debug programs. Included on the MMU chip are four 32-bit breakpoint registers and a breakpoint counter. The breakpoint registers can be loaded with 24-bit physical addresses which, when present on the address bus, will cause a BPT trap to occur. Associated with the first breakpoint register is a counter. A breakpoint trap can be programmed by the user to occur when an address matches the address in one of the breakpoint registers, or when the counter has counted to zero, with the count being decremented by 1 each time the address on the bus matches the address in the first breakpoint register. There are also four 32-bit program flow registers and four 16-bit sequential count registers. These registers are used to store the flow or "history" of a program, based on the nonsequential instructions such as jumps or branches.

As a final note, we must observe that National Semiconductor recommends that *no* absolute addresses be used in a program. In many of the instruction examples in this chapter, at least one of the operands was addressed using absolute addressing. This was done to keep the example simple. If both operands were accessed with memory relative or scaled indexed addressing, it might be difficult to see exactly what the instruction is doing and which memory locations are affected. The reason that National Semiconductor suggests that no absolute addresses be used is so that all programs and subroutines can be relocated. This is particularly important when the memory-management chip is used along with virtual memory. In fact, National Semiconductor even recommends that references to i/o devices use external addressing. By doing this a single address in the link table can be changed so that the program references a completely new set or configuration of peripheral devices.

CONCLUSION

There is little doubt that the 16032 and its associated peripheral chips can be used to make an extremely powerful and versatile microcomputer system. With the large nonsegmented address space of the 16032, the user does not have to worry about segmentation. For very large programs, virtual memory may have to be implemented, but this is transparent to the programmer. With its instruction set the 16032 can operate on more different kinds of data types (bit, packed bcd, double-word) and data structures (bit fields) than any of the other processors in this book.

REFERENCES

1. National Semiconductor Corp. *The NS16000 Family Programmer's Manual.* Santa Clara, CA 95051, 1980.

BIBLIOGRAPHY

Bal, S.; Chao, G.; and Soha, Z. "Bilingual, 16-Bit μP Summons Large-Scale Computer Power," *Electronic Design,* January 18, 1980, pp. 66–70.

Bal, S., *et al.* "System Capabilities Get a Boost From a High-Powered Dedicated Slave," *Electronic Design*, March 1, 1980.

Lavi, Y., *et al.* "16-bit Microprocessor Enters Virtual Memory Domain," *Electronics,* April 24, 1980, pp. 123–129.

O'Dowd, D.; Kohn, L.; and Soha, Z. "Architecture of 16-Bit Micro Underpins VLSI Computing," *Electronic Design,* June 7, 1980.

Benchmarks

This appendix gives additional information on the four benchmarks used in the text: bubble sort, ASCII string search, multiply/divide, and lookup table benchmarks.

BUBBLE SORT BENCHMARK

Although the bubble sort algorithm (Fig. A-1) is one of the slowest sorting algorithms, it is also one of the easiest to write. This benchmark involves sorting 600_{10} sixteen-bit data values (words) that are stored in memory. The number of values to be sorted, along with the starting address of the list to be sorted, is also stored in memory. The starting address of the list and the "word count" must be stored in a section of memory *away* from the section of memory used to store the list. This prevents the programmer from simply reading the starting address and count from memory and then incrementing a pointer once or twice to get to the beginning of the list. As an example, for the 8086 the starting address and word count might be stored in memory as follows:

Memory Address	Content
0200	address (low 16 bits)
0202	address (high 16 bits)
0204	word count (16 bits)

If the microprocessor being benchmarked can only address 65K bytes or less, you can store the word count in the memory location immediately following the address. The address(es) and word count stored in these memory locations must not be altered by the benchmark program. Also, memory locations 0200 through 0202 (0204) do not have to be used to store the memory address(es) and word count.

The list to be sorted must be stored in another section of memory, possibly only 10 or 20 memory locations away from the starting address and word count. The starting address of the list (use any one that is compatible with your system) will be considered to be X. The last address used by the list will therefore be X+599. When the list has been sorted, the smallest value will be stored in memory location X and the largest value will be stored in memory location X+599.

To ensure that the benchmarks are valid, all processors will sort the same values. Memory location X should contain 599_{10}, location X+1 should contain 598_{10}, and so on, up to location X+599, which would contain zero. As you can see, the values to be sorted are in the *reverse order* that they will be in when they are sorted. This is the worst-case situation for the bubble sort algorithm, and it will generate the longest sorting times.

Although the flowchart shown in Fig. A-1 is very specific, if the processor being benchmarked has instructions that are more sophisticated than the ones shown, such as exchange, load and autoincrement, bit set, reset, and test, then they can be used. Readers familiar with sorting and bubble sorting in particular will realize that as the list is sorted, the microprocessor should not use the same word count of 600_{10}. Instead, as a data value is put back into a list at the proper position, the count being used should be decremented. Thus once all but 10_{10} data values are sorted, a count of 10 should be used, rather than a count of 600.

ASCII STRING SEARCH BENCHMARK

In this benchmark the processor compares a short string of ASCII characters (to be called the *test string*) to a large string of ASCII characters (to be called the *main string*). The test string will be MICRO and the main string will contain a number of strings that contain MICRO.

As in the bubble sort benchmark the starting addresses of both the main and test strings must be stored in memory. When the string search benchmark is executed (Fig. A-2), these addresses should either be read into registers or be moved to other memory locations so that the original addresses are not altered. These addresses should not be stored in memory just before either the test or main string (see the bubble sort comments).

The words to be stored in the main string consist of NANO, PICO, MICROCOMPUTER, MICROPROCESSOR, MICROSYSTEM, and, finally, MICRO. Of course, the test string MICRO should only

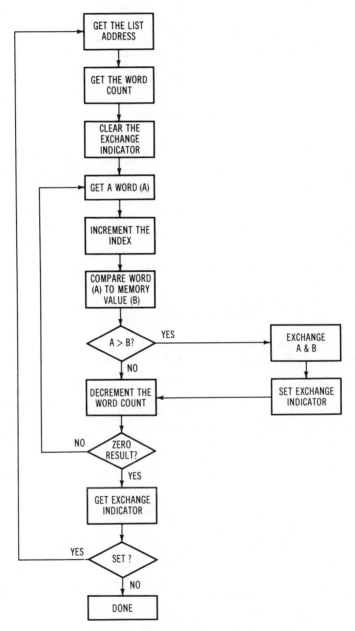

Fig. A-1. The bubble sort algorithm.

337

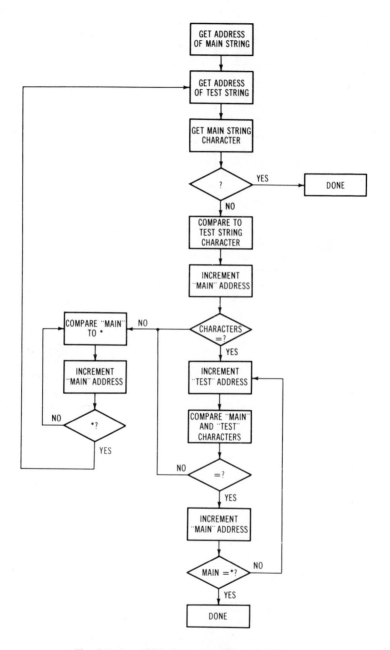

Fig. A-2. Searching for a matching ASCII string.

338

"match" with the MICRO string in the main string and not with the strings MICROCOMPUTER, MICROPROCESSOR, or MICRO-SYSTEM. To separate the strings in the main string, asterisks will be used. Therefore the ASCII characters in the main string will actually be stored in memory as follows:

NANO*PICO*MICROCOMPUTER*MICROPROCESSOR*MICROSYSTEM*
MICRO*?

The question mark at the end of the main string indicates the end-of-string condition. The test string, which can be stored in memory just before or just after the main string, consists of the characters MICRO*.

MULTIPLICATION/DIVISION

In this benchmark the microprocessor has to perform a number of multiplications and divisions. Therefore, in order to make it do these operations, it must be programmed to calculate the square root of a number (Fig. A-3) using one of the "classical" approximation techniques.

The number whose square root is to be determined will be considered to be N. As an example, assume that N = 10,000. The first approximation for the square root is calculated using the formula 2 + (N/200). The value for N is then divided by this first approximation. The result of this division is then added to the first approximation, and the sum is divided by 2. This result is the new approximation. As a check to see if the approximation is actually the square root of the number, the approximation is multiplied by itself, and only when the result equals the original number does the microprocessor stop the approximation process.

For the square root of 10,000:

N = 10,000; the first approximation is 2 + (10,000/200), or 52
52 × 52 = 2704, not equal to 10,000 so continue.
10,000/52 = 192; (192 + 52)/2 = 122
122 × 122 = 14,884, not equal to 10,000 so continue.
10,000/122 = 81; (122 + 81)/2 = 101
101 × 101 = 10,201, not equal to 10,000 so continue.
10,000/101 = 99; (101 + 99)/2 = 100
100 × 100 = 10,000, result equals 10,000 so the square root has been determined.

As you can see, only integer values have been used; no fractions are permitted. There are also a number of different methods that can be used to terminate the approximation process. For example, if the approximations converge to within 0.5 percent of each other or if at

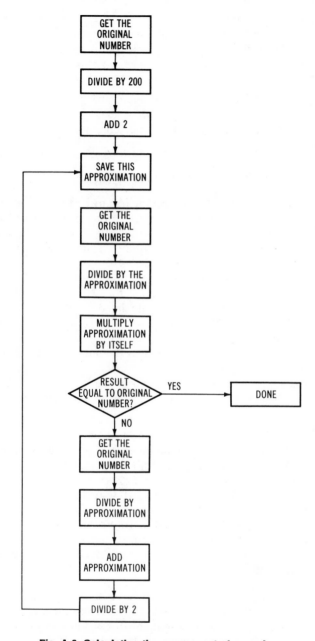

Fig. A-3. Calculating the square root of a number.

least 10 approximations have been made, the approximation process is terminated.

In the technique that we have chosen, the approximation is actually multiplied by itself, and only when the result is equal to the original number does the microprocessor stop approximating. The danger here is that some square roots can never be evaluated if only integer values are used. This means that we must be very careful about picking the numbers whose square roots are to be determined.

Using the benchmark program or instructions, the square roots of 58,081, 10,000, and 16,384 should be determined. The number whose square root is to be determined should be stored in memory, along with the calculated square root. This benchmark should really be executed three times and each time with one of the numbers listed above. Do not try to store all three numbers in memory and then have the microprocessor loop through the square root calculations three times. If this is done, timing the benchmark will be extremely difficult.

LOOKUP TABLES

The sine of an angle can be determined by an approximation (series) method or it can be "calculated" by using a lookup table. To use a lookup table the angle (expressed in either degrees or radians) is added to the base or starting address of the lookup table. The resulting address points to the memory location(s) within the table that contain the sine of the angle (Fig. A-4).

Lookup tables can be used not only to calculate the sine of an angle but also the cosine or tangent. In general, lookup tables are used to convert information from one data domain to another data domain. They can be used to convert ASCII characters to EBCDIC, binary numbers to bcd, bcd numbers to a seven-segment code, or to linearize some type of analog sensor contained in the microcomputer system (thermocouple, strain gage, etc.).

To make this benchmark a little more interesting, the microprocessor must determine the sine of any angle between 0 and 360 degrees, expressed in degrees, to the nearest degree, using a lookup table that contains only the sines of angles between 0 and 90 degrees. This means that all angles between 0 and 360 degrees have to be "reduced" to angles between 0 and 90 degrees. Of course, the microprocessor must also keep track of the sign of the sine. A 16-bit value for the sine should be determined, with one bit, bit D15, the msb, being dedicated to the sign of the sine. The sine of the angle will be represented by a sign and magnitude value, not the twos complement. It is not necessary to include the actual lookup table in the benchmark listing.

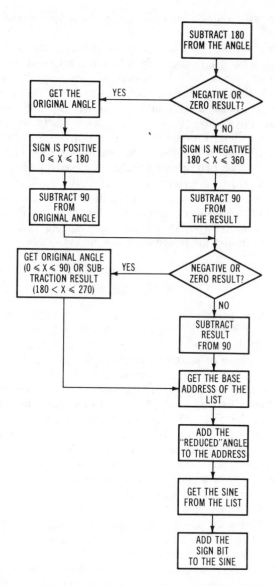

Fig. A-4. Using a lookup table to calculate the sine of an angle.

To reduce all angles between 0 and 360 degrees to angles between 0 and 90 degrees, the following equations can be used:

If $0 \leqslant X \leqslant 90$ degrees, then add X to the base address.
If $90 < X \leqslant 180$ degrees, then add $90-(X-90)$ to the base address.

If $180 < X \leqslant 270$ degrees, then add $X-180$ to the base address.

If $270 < X \leqslant 360$ degrees, then add $90-(X-270)$ to the base address.

The flowchart for this benchmark is shown in Fig. A-4.

Index

READER SERVICE CARD

To better serve you, the reader, please take a moment to fill out this card, or a copy of it, for us. Not only will you be kept up to date on the Blacksburg Series books, but as an extra bonus, **we will randomly select five cards every month, from all of the cards sent to us during the previous month. The names that are drawn will win, absolutely free, a book from the Blacksburg Continuing Education Series.** Therefore, make sure to indicate your choice in the space provided below. For a complete listing of all the books to choose from, refer to the inside front cover of this book. Please, one card per person. Give everyone a chance.

In order to find out who has won a book in your area, call (703) 953-1861 anytime during the night or weekend. When you do call, an answering machine will let you know the monthly winners. Too good to be true? Just give us a call. Good luck.

If I win, please send me a copy of:

_____

I understand that this book will be sent to me absolutely free, if my card is selected.

For our information, how about telling us a little about yourself. We are interested in your occupation, how and where you normally purchase books and the books that you would like to see in the Blacksburg Series. We are also interested in finding authors for the series, so if you have a book idea, write to The Blacksburg Group, Inc., P.O. Box 242, Blacksburg, VA 24060 and ask for an Author Packet. We are also interested in TRS-80, APPLE, OSI and PET BASIC programs.

My occupation is _____

I buy books through/from _____

Would you buy books through the mail? _____

I'd like to see a book about _____

Name _____

Address _____

City _____

State _____ Zip _____

MAIL TO: BOOKS, BOX 715, BLACKSBURG, VA 24060
!!!!!PLEASE PRINT!!!!!

21805